Major Henry Court, Sardha Ram

History of the Sikhs

Major Henry Court, Sardha Ram
History of the Sikhs
ISBN/EAN: 9783744669474

Printed in Europe, USA, Canada, Australia, Japan

Cover: Foto ©ninafisch / pixelio.de

More available books at **www.hansebooks.com**

HISTORY OF THE SIKHS;

OR,

TRANSLATION

OF THE

SIKKHÁN DE RÁJ DÍ VIKHIÁ,

AS LAID DOWN FOR THE EXAMINATION IN PANJABI.

AND CONTAINING

Narratives of the ten Gurús, history of the Sikhs from the rise of Mahárája Ranjít Singh to the occupation of the Panjáb by the English, a short resumé of the customs, rites, songs, and proverbs of the Sikhs, and twenty discourses regarding events in the life of Gurú Nának, taken from the Janam Sakhi, or Life of Nának.

TOGETHER WITH

A SHORT GURMUKHI GRAMMAR,

AND

An Appendix containing some useful technical words in Roman Character.

TRANSLATED AND EDITED

BY

MAJOR HENRY COURT

Lieut.-Colonel, 15th Bengal Cavalry,

Translator of the Aráish-i-Mahfil, Nasr-i-Be Nazir, and Selections from the Kullíyát-i-Saudá.

AND

Editor of Malcolm's History of Persia, Vol. II, adapted to the Persian Translation of Mirzá Hairat.

[COPYRIGHT RESERVED.]

Lahore:

PRINTED AT THE "CIVIL AND MILITARY GAZETTE" PRESS.

1888.

Dedicated

(BY PERMISSION)

TO THE

Hon'ble Sir JAMES BROADWOOD LYALL, K.C.S.I.,

Lieutenant-Governor of the Punjab,

As a mark of personal respect and esteem.

By

His humble servant,

THE TRANSLATOR
AND EDITOR.

TRANSLATOR'S PREFACE.

The translation of this work has been by no means an easy task, as the sentences in the original, and in the last part more particularly, are so disjointed, that it was very difficult to render them into English. I have, therefore, made the translation as nearly literal as possible adding words, in brackets, to connect the meaning.

Wherever I have been able to find a translation of the verses in Dr. Trumpp's Ādi Granth, I have given his translation as well as my own; for although I believe in many instances, he has lost the point of the verses, still I do not consider myself a sufficiently competent authority to pronounce that he is wrong, and I leave it to others to decide on this point, and they will, at all events, have both versions before them, and can select which they prefer. All I would add on the subject is that Pandat Nihāl Chand, of Lahore, by whom I have been most materially aided in this work, and with whom I read it most carefully through, considered mine to be the more correct.

I am certain there are many errors, or if not errors, at least differences of opinion, in the way of rendering a number of the passages; I hope that these may be fully pointed out, and, in bringing out the second edition, every consideration shall be paid to all suggestions made in the way of criticism. I do not ask to be spared, for my object is to present a really useful and correct translation to the public, and this I can only hope to arrive at, by others, better acquainted with the language than myself, kindly pointing out any errors which they may notice.

The grammar I have added, as I believed it to be much needed, and the Roman character was, I considered, the best form in which to present it. I do not lay claim to any originality in this, for it is epitomized, and slightly changed, from an old grammar published some years ago at the American Presbyterian Mission Press, Ludhiána. I have often tried, but in vain, to get a grammar, and my aim in inserting one has been simply to supply this want.

The appendix of technical words and terms has been chiefly taken from the Panjábí Dictionary published at the Mission Press, Ludhiána, but I have arranged it, for general utility and easy reference, in its present alphabetical form, and have added a reverse index in English to enable a word to be easily found, if required, in translating English into Gurmukhí.

At the commencement of the grammar, I have given the alphabet in the Gurmukhí character, adding its name, pronunciation, and equivalent in English. In transcribing names, I have kept to the Gurmukhí way of spelling, as this, whilst giving the student a good view of the names as pronounced by the Sikhs, at the same time enabled me to adhere to an uniform system of transliteration.

I have been asked to bring this work out as soon as possible, as it was much required, and I have, therefore, done so as quickly as I could. I have priced the work at six rupees to subscribers, and eight rupees to non-subscribers, so as to put it within reach of all.

Should the demand for it be such as I have been led to expect, I hope to bring out a second, and, with the aid of kind criticisms, a better, edition of the work.

I must not conclude without publicly acknowledging my best and warmest thanks to Pandat Nihál Chand, of Lahore, with whom I carefully read through, and corrected, the translation. He is well known to many officers, who have already passed in Panjábí, and to those, who have not yet made his acquaintance, but wish for a really good instructor in Panjábí, I would say, secure his services, and success in passing is certain.

M. H. COURT, LIEUT.-COL.,
15th Bengal Cavalry.

MUSSOORIE ;

The 30th May 1888.

TABLE OF CONTENTS.

Translator's Preface iii
Table of Contents vi
Gurmukhí Grammar viii
Appendix of Technical Words and Terms (Gurmukhí) ... xlix
   Do.   do.   do.   (English) ... lxxvii
Author's Preface lxxxiii

PART I.—NARRATIVES OF THE TEN GURÚS.

Chapter	I.	Account of Bába Nának ...	...	1
Do.	II.	„ Gurú Angad ...		11
Do.	III.	„ „ Amardás ...	...	15
Do.	IV.	„ „ Rám Dás ...	...	19
Do.	V.	„ „ Arjan ...	...	21
Do.	VI.	„ „ Hargovind	...	24
Do.	VII.	„ „ Harrái ...		26
Do. VIII.		„ „ Har Kisan		32
Do.	IX.	„ „ Teg Bahádur		35
Do.	X.	„ „ Govind Singh	...	40

Code of the Sikhs 41
Jafar náma, or letter of victory 47

PART II.—HISTORY OF THE SIKHS.

Chapter	I.	The names of the twelve Misals ...	... 60
Do.	II.	Account of the Misals	... 63
Do.	III.	Rise of Mahárája Ranjít Singh	... 66
Do.	IV.	Character of Ranjít Singh ...	... 75
Do.	V.	Account of Mahárája Kharak Singh	... 77
Do.	VI.	„ „ Nau Nihál Singh	... 79
Do.	VII.	The Láhaur Campaign	... 82

PART III.—CASTES, RITES, SONGS AND PROVERBS.

Chapter I. Castes and rites 100
Do. II. Music and songs 116
Do. III. Proverbs 136

PART IV.—TWENTY DISCOURSES ON EVENTS IN THE LIFE OF BÁBA NÁNAK.

Chapter I. Discourse with Gupál Pándhá 142
Do. II. ,, regarding the putting on the Brahminical thread 146
Do. III. Discourse with the physician .. 150
Do. IV. ,, regarding the store 152
Do. V. ,, ,, the betrothal of Nának 157
Do. VI. ,, ,, the marriage of Nának 163
Do. VII. ,, with Sámá Pandat 170
Do. VIII. ,, ,, Nabáb Daulát Khán ... 172
Do. IX. ,, ,, Rái Bulhár 178
Do. X. ,, regarding the (idol) Sálig Rám 184
Do. XI. ,, ,, ,, Árti Sohilá ... 187
Do. XII. ,, in Sanglá (Ceylon) with Rája Sív Náth 190
Do. XIII. Discourse with Mián Mitthá 193
Do. XIV. ,, ,, the Siddhs 201
Do. XV. ,, ,, worshippers of Govind ... 206
Do. XVI. ,, ,, the demon Kaundá ... 214
Do. XVII. ,, ,, Sultán Hamíd Kárún ... 217
Do. XVIII. ,, ,, Chattardás Pandat ... 225
Do. XIX. ,, .. Kálú 228
Do. XX. ,, ,, the Pandats of Kánsí (Banáras) 237

PANJÁBÍ GRAMMAR.

1. The Panjábí, or Gurmukhí, alphabet consists of thirty-five letters, and is hence called Paintí (thirty-five) as under :—

	Form.	English equivalent.	Name.	Pronounced as
1	ਅ	a	áirá	a in *woman*.
2	ੲ	i	írí	i in *this*.
3	ੳ	u	úrá	u in *thus*.
4	ਸ	s	sassá	s in *son*.
5	ਹ	h	hahá	h in *him*.
6	ਕ	k	kakká	k in *kind*.
7	ਖ	kh	khakhá	kh in *khán*.
8	ਗ	g	gaggá	g in *good*.
9	ਘ	gh	ghaggá	gh in *ghost*.
10	ਙ	ng	ngungá	ng in *sing*.
11	ਚ	ch	chachchá	ch in *church*.
12	ਛ	chh	chhachchha	ch aspirated.
13	ਜ	j	jajjá	j in *jug*.
14	ਝ	jh	jhajjhá	j aspirated.
15	ਞ	ny	nyanya	ny (y being hardly audible).
16	ਟ	t	tainká	t hard.
17	ਠ	th	thatthá	t hard aspirated.
18	ਡ	d	daddá	d hard.
19	ਢ	dh	dhaddhú	d hard aspirated.
20	ਣ	n	náná	n hard.
21	ਤ	t	tattá	t soft.
22	ਥ	th	thathá	t soft aspirated.

PANJÁBÍ GRAMMAR.

	Form.	English equivalent.	Name.	Pronounced as
23	ਟ	d	daddá	d soft.
24	ਢ	dh	dhaddhá	d soft aspirated.
25	ਣ	n	nanná	n soft as in *nigh*.
26	ਪ	p	pappá	p in *pull*.
27	ਫ	ph	phapphá	ph in *physic*.
28	ਬ	b	babbá	b in *ball*.
29	ਭ	bh	bhabbhá	b aspirated.
30	ਮ	m	mammá	m in *may*.
31	ਯ	y	yayyá	y in *youth*.
32	ਰ	r	rárá	r soft.
33	ਲ	l	lallá	l in *lord*.
34	ਵ	w	wawwá	w in *wine*.
35	ੜ	r	rárá	r hard.

2. The vowels are—

Initial form.	Medial or final form.	Equivalent.	Pronounced as
ਅ		a	a in *woman*.
ਆ	ਾ	á	a in *far*.
ਇ	ਿ	i	i in *this*.
ਈ	ੀ	í	ee in *thee*.
ਉ	ੁ	u	u in *thus*.
ਊ	ੂ	ú	u in *rule*.
ਏ	ੇ	e	e in *they*.
ਐ	ੈ	ai	ai in *aisle*.
ਓ	ੋ	o	o in *hole*.
ਔ	ੌ	au	ow in *owl*.

3. The following marks are also used ̊ bindí tippí,
• adhak.

Bindí and tippí are abbreviated forms of letters,
and have the same power as, and are substituted for, *ng*, *ny*,

n, ṅ, or m : after a vowel they simply stand for a nasal n. Adhak is placed between two letters, to double the latter.

4. The following consonants are compounded :—

ਗ੍ਯ gy, ਨ੍ਹ nh, ਮ੍ਹ mh, ਰ੍ਹ rh, ਲ੍ਹ lh, ੜ੍ਹ ṛh, ਸ੍ਰ sr, ਕ੍ਰ kr, ਖ੍ਰ khr, ਗ੍ਰ gr, ਘ੍ਰ ghr, ਤ੍ਰ tr, ਦ੍ਰ dr, ਪ੍ਰ pr, ਬ੍ਰ br, ਭ੍ਰ bhr.

5. The numerical figures are—

੧ 1, ੨ 2, ੩ 3, ੪ 4, ੫ 5, ੬ 6, ੭ 7, ੮ 8, ੯ 9, ੦ 0.

6. *N.B.*—If the two letters in the following, kh, gh, *ng, jh, ny, th, dh*, th, dh, ph, bh, are separate letters, they will be shewn with a hyphen between them, *e.g.*, k-h, &c. It must be remembered that ái and áu are two distinct letters, and not the same as ai and au.

7. There are eight parts of speech : Noun, Adjective, Pronoun, Verb, Adverb, Conjunction, Preposition, and Interjection.

8. Nouns, Adjectives, Pronouns and Verb are all liable to inflexions for gender, number, and case.

9. There are two genders, Masculine and Feminine, and two numbers, Singular and Plural; and seven cases, Nominative, Instrumental, Genitive, Dative, Accusative, Vocative, and Ablative.

10. The cases are distinguished from each other, partly by inflexions, partly by the use of prepositions and other particles, and partly by connection.

11. The Instrumental answers to the Agent in Hindústání and is governed by the same rules. The ne is, however, sometimes omitted altogether, and, at others, its place supplied by the terminations ਨ and ਈਂ

12. The Genitive takes dá, dí, de, after it, which are governed by the same rules as the ká, kí, ke in Hindústání, and is inflected as under, by the word which governs it. The governing word is the following word, not the preceding one:—

If the governing word is—	Masculine.	Feminine.
Nominative, Singular, it is	dá	dí
Vocative, Singular, it is	de, diá	dí, díe
Other cases, Singular, it is	de	dí
Nominative, Plural, it is	de	dián
Vocative, Plural, it is	de, dio	dío
Other cases, Plural, it is	de, diáṅ	diáṅ

The terminations rá, dá, and ná of pronouns are governed by the same rules of inflexion.

13. The Dative and Accusative are followed by nún.
14. The Ablative takes a preposition.
15. The Vocative has 'he' or 'e' prefixed.

NOUNS.

16. There are three declensions with two or more variations in each.

Declension I.

17. The first declension is distinguished by inflecting the oblique cases, and the nominative plural, and comprehends all masculines ending in á or án, except Khudá, *God*, pitá, *father*, and a few others. The latter, pitá, is indeclinable, and Khudá conforms to the second declension, first variety.

18. The first variation, first declension, embraces those nouns, in which the final á is preceded by a consonant as mundá, *a boy*, rájá, *a king*, and is declined as follows :—

	SINGULAR.	PLURAL.
N	mundá	munde,
I	munde nai	mundián nai
G	munde dá, &c,	mundián dá, &c.
D	munde nún	mundián nún
Ac	munde nún	mundián nún
Ab	munde te	mundián te
V	e mundiá	e mundio

19. The second variation embraces those nouns, in which the final á or án is preceded by a vowel, *e.g.*, parkháná, *a tempter*, bánián, *a shop-keeper*, uskaliá, *a calumniator*, and is declined as under :—

	SINGULAR.	PLURAL.	SINGULAR.	PLURAL.
N	parkháná	parkháne	bánián	bánien
I	parkháne nai	parkhánán nai, or parkhánián nai	banien nái	bánián nai
G	parkháne dá, &c.	parkhánán dá, &c. or parkhánián dá, &c.	bánien dá &c.	banián dá &c.
D	parkháne nún	parkhánán nún, or parkhánián nún	bánien nun	bánián nún
Ac	parkháne nún	parkhánán nún or parkhánián nún	bánien nún	bánián nún
Ab	parkháne te	parkhánán te or parkhánián te.	bánien te	bániáu te
V	e parkháne or parkhániá	o parkháno or parkhánio	e bánien or bánián	e bánio

Declension II.

20. The second declension is distinguished by not inflecting the oblique cases (singular,) vocative excepted, or the nominative plural. It includes only masculine nouns, and has two variations.

21. The first variation embraces all masculines ending with a consonant as putt, *a son*, manukkh *a man*, and such as end with the long vowels í and ú, as bháí, *a brother;* páli, *a herdsman*, kháú, *a glutton*, and anyjhú *a tear*, and is declined as under:—

	Singular.	Plural.	Singular.	Plural.
N	manukkh	manukkh	páli	páli
I	manukkh nai	manukkhán nai	páli nai	pálián nai
G	manukkh dá, &c.	manukkhán dá, &c.	páli dá &c.	pálián dá, &c.
D	manukkh nún	manukkhán nún	páli nún	pálián nún
Ab	manukkh nún	manukkhán nún	páli nún	pálián nún
Ac	manukkh te	manukkhán te	páli te	pálián te
V	e manukkh or manukkhá	e manukkho	e páli or páliá	e pálio

22. The second variation embraces masculines ending in u and un, as piu or peu, *a father*, bharáu or bhiráu *a brother*, káun, *a crow*, and is declined as under:—

	Singular.	Plural.	Singular.	Plural.
N	piu or peo	piu, pio, or peu	káun	káun
I	piu nai	pewán nai	káun nai	káwán nai
G	piu da, &c.	pewán da &c.	káun dá, &c.	káwán da, &c.
D or Ac	piu nún	pewán nún	káun nún	káwán nún
Ab	piu te	pewán te	káun te	káwán te
V	e piu or pewá	e pewo or peo	e káwán	e káwon or káon.

Declension III.

23. The third declension is distinguished by inflecting the nominative plural, but not the oblique cases, singular, (vocative excepted). All nouns of this declension are feminine. The variations are three.

24. The first variation embraces all feminines ending in á, as balá, *calamity*, duá *a blessing*, and is declined as under:—

	Singular.	Plural.
N	balá	baláíu or baláián
I	balá nai	baláián nai
G	balá dá &c.	baláián dá, &c.
D or Ac	balá nún	baláián nún
Ab	balá te	baláián te
V	e baláo	e baláio, or baláo

To this form there are some exceptions, *e.g.*, jágá, *place*, makes in the plural jágán.

25. The second variation embraces feminines ending in n or un, as máu, or mánn, *a mother*, and is declined as under :—

	SINGULAR.	PLURAL.
N	máun	máwán
I	máun nai	máwán nai
G	máun dá &c.,	máwan dá &c.,
D or Ac	máun nún	máwan nún
Ab	máun te	máwan te
V	e máun, or máwen	e maun or mawou

26. The third variation includes all other nouns feminine of any other termination, as dhí, *a daughter*, gall, *a word*, gáín, *a cow*, bánh or báhan, *an arm*, and is declined as under :—

	SINGULAR.	PLURAL.
N	dhí	dhíán
I	dhí nai	dhíán nai
G	dhí dá, &c.	dhíán dá, &c.
D or Ac	dhí nún	dhíán nún
Ab	dhí te	dhíán te
V	e dhíe	e dhío

27. When the final vowel of a noun is followed by a tippí or bindí, these are always thrown forward, if, in declension, a syllable is added, so as still to occupy the final place, *e.g.*, gáín, *a cow*, plural, gáíán.

28. Some nouns are indeclinable as jokhon, *danger*, tarán, *manner*, málá, *a rosary*, and mátá, *a mother*.

29. Nouns derived from foreign sources are sometimes declined irregularly, as basat, *a thing*, plural basatún.

30. The ablative is often subjected to a change in the final letter, by which the governing preposition is dispensed with, *e.g.*, gharon for ghar te, *from the house*; gharín for gharán wichch, *in the houses*; us de hatthín for us de hatthán nál (or te) *by his hands*, i.e., *by his means*; us de dargáhe for us dí dargáh wichch, *in his court or his presence*; us pásion for us páse te, *from that side.*

31. There are no definite rules for determining genders of nouns; practice alone can teach this.

32. Compounds follow the gender of the last of the component parts.

33. Derivatives are formed in a variety of ways, and follow the usages of Hindí, *e.g.*

(*i*) by changing termination of infinitive into hat, as chiláuná *to scream*, chiláhat, *screaming*;

(*ii*) by changing the final vowel á of the adjective into í, as utáula, *hasty*, utáulí, *haste*;

(iii) by adding áí, áít, or át, to the adjective as chatur, *clever*, chaturáí, *cleverness* ; bahut, *many*, bahutáít, or bahutát, *abundance*.

(iv) by changing final á of adjective into iáí, or án, as wadá, *great*, wadiáí, *greatness* ; uchchá *high*, uchcbán *height*.

(v.) By changing final á of noun into puná, as uchakká, *a pickpocket*, uchakkpuná *pickpocketing*.

34. Feminines are formed from masculines by changing the terminations as under :—

(i) á into í as ghorá, *a horse*, ghorí, *a mare* ; í, iá, iá, iyá into n, as uskalí, or uskaliyá, a *calumniator*, uskalan, *a female calumniator*.

(ii) í into ání, as Khattrí—Khattrání.

(iii) by adding ní or ání to the masculine as únt, *a camel*, úntní *a she camel* ; mugal, *Moghul*, mugalání, *a female Moghul*.

35. Feminines in í, derived from masculines in á, when denoting things without life, have a diminutive sense as ghará, *an earthen jar*, gharí, *a small earthen pot*.

ADJECTIVES.

36. Adjectives are formed as follows :—

(i.) Derived from nouns, by adding í, as asmán, *heaven*, asmání, *heavenly*.

(ii.) Derived from nouns, by adding á, as bhár, *a load*, bhárá, *heavy*.

(iii.) Derived from verbs, as anján, *ignorant*, from jánná, *to know*, auparhiá *unread*, from parhná *to read*.

(iv.) By adding wálá to a noun, as kapprá, *clothes*, kapprewálá saudúk, *clothes box*, but kapprewálá is also used as a substantive for *a clothman*.

37. A class of words, used both as nouns and adjectives, are derived from verbs by adding ú to the root as kháú, *glutton* or *gluttonous*, from khá, *eat*.

38. Adjectives ending in á are inflected like nouns, *e.g.* chittá, *white*.

	SINGULAR		PLURAL	
	Masculine	Feminine	Masculine	Feminine
N	chittá	chittí	chitte	chittíán
Objective cases	chitte	chittí	chittián	chittíán
V	chitte, chittiá	chittí, chittíe,	chitte, chittio, chittío	

39. Masculines ending in í are declined like páli (see. 21).

40. Adjectives ending in a consonant are not inflected, except the numerals, which are declined as under, e.g., das, ten :—

	Masculine.	Feminine.
N	das	dasán
Objective cases	dasún	dasán

N.B.—*Do, two*, when inflected becomes douán or dohán.

41. Degrees of comparison are expressed as in Urdú, by the help of prepositions, and an adjective pronoun denoting "all," thus—

Positive.—*This is a good word*, ih changi gall hai.

Comparative.—*This is a better word*, us de nal, or uste, ih changí gall hai.

Superlative.—*This is the best word*, ih sáríán gallán te changí hai, or sabhnán wichchon changí gall tá ih hai, or sabhnán nálon ih changí gall hai.

PRONOUNS.

42. Pronouns are personal or adjective.

43. The simple personal pronouns are main, *I* ; tún, *thou* ; uh, *he, she, it* ; which are declined thus—

	Singular.	Plural.	Singular.	Plural.	Singular.	Plural.
N	main	asín	tun	tusín	uh, oh	uh, oh
I	main nai	asín nai	tain nai	tusín nai	un nai, on nai	unhín, hai unhon nai
G	merú, &c.	asáda, &c.	terá, &c.	tusáda, &c. tuháda, &c.	usdá, &c. uldá, &c.	unhán da, &c.
D or Ac	main nún	asá nún	tai nún	tusá nún tuhá nún	us nún uh nún	unhán nún
Ab	mai te, or mai thon	asá te	tai te, thon	taí tusá te tuhá te	us te uh te	unhán te
V	...	...	...	...	...	...

44. The simple adjective pronouns are divided into two classes ; definite and indefinite.

45. The definite pronouns are ih, ah, *this* ; uh, *that* ; har, *every one;* sabh, sárá, sarbatt, *all, the whole.*

46. Ih, is declined like uh (*see* 43) ; har is indeclinable ; sárá is declined like chittá (see 38), sabh is used throughout the singular, and in the nominative plural : in the oblique cases plural sabhnán ; it becomes in the instrumental plural, sabhnín, and sabhnán nai.

47. The indefinite adjective pronouns are koí or káí, *any* ; kuch, kujh, kuhun, *some* ; kaí kitne, *several* ; bájá, *some* ; thuhurá, *little, few* ; bahut, bahutá, batherá, *much, many* : bass, *enough* ; hor, horas, *more*. Koí and kuchh are often used personally, meaning *some one* and *some thing*.

48. Koí is declined thus—

	Singular.	Plural.
N	koí	koí
I	kise nai, kisí nai	kise nai, kisí nai; kinhán nai
G	kise dá, &c., kisí dá &c.,	kise dá, &c., kisí dá &c., kinhán dá, &c.
D or Ac	kise nún, kisí nún	kise nún, kisí nún, kinhán nún
Ab	kise te, kisí te	kise te, kisí te, kinhán te

The plural, however, is very seldom used; káí is declined like koí.

49. Kuchh, kujh, kuhun, bahut, bass, and horas are indeclinable; horas is only used in the singular.

50. Bájá, bahutá, thuhurá and batherá are declined like chittá (see 38).

51. Hor is indeclinable in the singular; in the oblique cases plural, it becomes horán and hornán; instrumental, horín and hornín, or horán nai, hornán nai.

52. Kaí and kitne are used only in the plural, and are declined like nouns of similar termination, thus—

	Masculine.	Feminine.
N	kaí	kitne kitníán
I	kaíán nai or kitne nai or kitnián nai, &c. kitníán nai, &c.	

RELATIVE PRONOUNS.

53. The Relative Pronouns are jo, *who, which, that, what*; jihrá or johrá, *whosoever, whichsoever, who, which, that*; jitná; *as much as, as many as*; jihá or jehá, *of what sort*; jed, jaid, jedá, *as large as, as long as*.

54. Jo, *who, &c.*, is declined as under—

	Singular.	Plural.
N	jo	jo
I	jin nai	jinín nai, jinhín nai
G	jis dá, &c., jih dá, &c.	jinán dá, &c., jinhán da, &c.
D or Ac	jis nún, jih nún	jinán nún, jinhán nún
Ab	jis te, jih te	jinán te, jinhán te

55. Jihrá, jitna, jihá, and jedá are declined like chittá (see 38).

56. Jed and jaid are indeclinable.

CORRELATIVE PRONOUNS.

57. The Correlative Pronouns are so, *this, that, he, she, it*; itná, *this much*; utná, titná, *that much*; aisá, ajihá, ajehá, *of such a sort*; ihá, ehá *of this sort*, tihá, tehá, *of that sort*; aid, aidá, *so large, so long*.

58. So is declined like jo (see 54); itná, utná, titná, aisá, ajihá, ihá, tihá, and aidá are declined like chittá, (see 38). Aid is indeclinable.

INTERROGATIVE PRONOUNS.

59. The Interrogative Pronouns are kaun, *who? which?*; kihṛá or kehṛá, *which one?*; kí or kia, *what?*; kitná, *how much? how many?*; kai, *how many?*; kihá, kehá, *of what sort?*; kaid, kedá or kaidá, *how large? how long?*

60. Kaun is declined like jo (see 54.)

61. Kihṛá, kitná, kihá, and kaidá are declined like **chittá** (see 38). Kaid is indeclinable; kai is only used in plural, and is indeclinable.

62. Kí or kiá, *what?* is used only in singular and is declined thus—

N	kí, kiá
I	kás nai
G	kás dá, &c., káh dá, &c.
D or Ac	kás nún, káh nún
Ab	kás te káh te

REFLECTIVE PRONOUNS.

63. The reflective pronouns are áp, *myself, thyself*, &c., and ápas, *each other*.

64. Áp is sometimes used respectfully as in Urdú, and is then treated as a plural.

65. Áp is declined as under—

	Singular.	Plural.
N	áp, ápne áp	áp, ápne áp
I	áp nai.	ápnián nai, ápnín
G	ápná, &c.	ápná, &c.
D or Ac	áp nún, ápne nún, ápne áp nún	áp nún, ápnián nún,
Ab	áp te, ápne te, ápne áp te	áp te, ápnián te
V	ápniá, ápne	ápnio

66. Ápas is used only in genitive, dative, accusative, and ablative cases plural.

COMPOUND PRONOUNS.

67. The following are the compound pronouns used: jo koí, *whoever*; jo kuchh, *whatever*; jiharó kuchh, *whichever*; koí ná koí, *one or another*; kuchh ná kuchh, *something or other*; kuchh dá kuchh, *something else*; hor koí, *another*; hor kuchh, *something else*; ihá jihá, ahá jahá, *of this sort*: uhá jihá, *of that sort*; jihá kihá, *of what sort soever*; hor kí, *what else*; sabb koí, *all*; sabh dá sabh, *all*; sabh kuchh, *everything*; harek every one, *all*; koí ikk, *any one*; har koí, *every one*.

68. Jo koí, koí ná koí, ihá jihá, ahá jahá, uhá jihá, and jihá kihá are declined in both their component parts thus—

	Masculine.		Feminine.
N	jo koí	ihá jihá	ihí jihí
I	jis kisí nai	iho jiho nai	ihí jihí nai
&c.,	&c.	&c.	&c.

69. Hor koí, hor kí, sabh koí, sabh dá sabh, har koí, only change in the latter component, thus—

	Singular.		Plural.
N	hor koí	sabh dá sabh	sabh de sabh
I	hor kisí nai	sabh de sabh nai	sabh de sabhnán nai
&c.	&c.	&c.	&c.

70. In koí ikk, the first component only is inflected.

71. The rest are all indeclinable.

72. Í, e, and o are sometimes added to pronouns to make them emphatic as uho, iho, uhí, soí, *this or that very one, the same* : sabhe, sabho, *the whole* ; ápo, *one's very self*. In other cases, the particle hí gives the same emphasis.

73. Sárá and jihá are also used as adjuncts of emphasis, as bahut sárá, *a great deal* ; thuhurá jihá, *very little* ; and are also attached to adjectives of size and quantity, as well as to adjective pronouns, *e.g.*, wadá sárá, *very large* ; chhotá jihá, *very small*.

74. Pronouns in the Instrumental generally follow the usage of nouns, by taking nai ; as asá nai, tusá nái ; us nai, unhán nai, kis nai, kinán nai, jis ne, jinhán nai, &c., but nai is often omitted.

75. In the ablative, more te, tere te, are often substituted for mai te and tai te.

76. In the oblique cases of uh, ih, jo, so, kaun, koí, the termination s is sometimes changed into t ; as nt, it, jit, tit kit, kite for us, is, &c.

77. Pronouns, like nouns and adjectives, by being repeated, express the idea of emphasis or distribution ; thus—

(i) uh ápne ápne ghar nún gae, *they went each to his own home*.

(ii) jo jo chíján tuháde karm áungián, so so le jáo, *take the particular things that will be of use to you*.

(iii) kuch kuch, *very little*, and koí koí, *very few*.

78. Pronouns sometimes undergo elision in the final letter, or even in several letters, by being joined to nouns *e.g.*, jiddin for jisdin, *on what day* ; jichchar for jitná chir, *as long a time as* ; in such cases the first consonant of the noun takes an adhak,

but such words are really adverbs, and should be treated as such.

79. Contractions and transpositions are sometimes used; as koík for koí ikk, and ikas for kisí ikk.

VERBS.

80. Verbs are active and neuter, transitive and intransitive.

81. Voices are two; active and passive.

82. There are five moods; Indicative, Potential, Subjunctive, Imperative, Infinitive. The Subjunctive is formed by prefixing je or jekar, *if*, to the Indicative or Potential.

83. Tenses are twelve, viz., (*i*) Present, (*ii*) Definite Present, (*iii*) Habitual Present, (*iv*) Imperfect, (*v*) Imperfect Habitual, (*vi*) Future Probable, (*vii*) Future Habitual, (*viii*) Past, (*ix*) Perfect, (*x*) Pluperfect, (*xi*) Future Past, (*xii*) Future.

84. Every verb has four Participles and a Gerund. The participles are Present, Past, Indefinite, and Substantive.

85. The second person singular imperative is the root; all the tenses are formed, with the help of auxiliaries, either from the root, or from the present and past participles, and the future tense potential.

86. If the root ends in u, present participle is formed by placing a bindí over it, and adding dá, e.g., áu, *come*; áundá, *coming*; seu, *serve*; seundá, *serving*; the past participle, by changing u into iá or wiá, e.g., áiá, *being come*; sewiá, *being served*; the future potential, by changing u into wán, as áwán, *I may come*.

87. In regular verbs, if the root ends with a consonant, the present participle is formed by adding dá, the past, by adding iá; and the future potential, by adding án, c.g., ghalldá, *sending*; ghalliá, *being sent*; ghallán, *I may send*.

88. The indefinite participle is formed by adding ke to the root; as ghall, ghall ke, *having sent*; except in roots ending in u, when u is dropped, and ke affixed to preceding vowel, e.g., ghalláu, *cause to be sent*, ghalláke, *having caused to be sent*, but i is sometimes substituted for u, eg., áu, áike, *having come*. Sometimes the ke is omitted altogether.

89. The substantive participle is so called, because, while it retains the power of the verb, from which it is derived, it often assumes the attributes of a substantive. It is formed by adding wálá, hár, or hárá to the oblique form of the infinitive, e.g., ghallnewálá, *a sender*.

90. The infinitive is formed by adding *ná* or *ná* to the root.

91. The gerund has generally the same form as the past participle.

92. The auxiliaries used are the defective verb hán, *am*, and honá, *to be*, and jáná *to go*.

93. The defective substantive verb, hán, *I am*, is declined as follows:—

INDICATIVE MOOD.

PRESENT.—*I am*

Singular		Plural	
Masculine.	*Feminine.*	*Masculine.*	*Feminine.*
1. hán, hangá	hán, hangí	hán, hánge	hán, hángián
2. hain, haingá	hain, haingí	ho, hoge	ho, hogián
3. hai, haigá	hai haigí	han, hange, hain	hán, hangián

N.B.—The pronouns will not be given, but, 1, 2, 3 will be inserted throughout the conjugation of Verbs, to show first, second, and third person.

PAST.—*I was.*

MASCULINE.

Singular.

1. sá, súgá, sí, sigá, sán, sángá, thá, haisán
2. sá, súgá, sí, sigá, thá, haisí
3. sá, súgá, sí, sigá, thá, haisí

FEMININE.

Singular.

sí, sigí, sán, sángí, thí, haisan
sí, sigí, thí, haisí
sí, sigí, thí, haisí

Plural.

1. se, sege, sí, sige, sán, sánge, the, haise
2. se, sege, sí, sige, the, haise,
3. se, sege, sí, sige, sán, súnge, sain, the, haisan

Plural.

sían, sigían, sán, sángián, thían
sían, sigían, thían, haisían
sían, sigían, san, sangián, sain

94. Honá, *to be*, neuter and auxiliary verb, is declined as follows:—

Root, ho, *be, exist, become.*

Principal parts. Present participle, hundá; past participle, hoiá; future tense, howán.

IMPERATIVE MOOD.

PRESENT.—*Be thou.*

SINGULAR.	PLURAL.
2. ho	howe.

FUTURE.—*Be thou (hereafter)*

2. hoín   hoio.

Present participle, Hundá, hundá hoiń, *being, becoming,* declined like *chitta* (*see* 38).

Past participle, Hoiú hoiá, *having become.* Declined like *chittá* (*see* 38).

N.B.—In the last number of the reduplicated form, the ho is often changed into o, as hoiá oiá for hoiá hoiá.

Indefinite participle. (Indeclinable.)

Ho, hoke, hoike, *being, having become.*

PANJÁBÍ GRAMMAR.   xxi

Substantive participle, *being, one that is, or is to be, becoming,*
Honewálá, honwálá, honehár, honhár, honehárá, honhárá. Forms
1, 2, 5 and 6 are declined like *chittá* (see 38); forms 3 and 4 like
manukkh (see 21) in the masculine, and like *gall* (see 26) in the
feminine.

GERUND.—*Being.*

	SINGULAR		PLURAL	
	Masculine.	*Feminine.*	*Masculine.*	*Feminine.*
N	hoiá	hoí	hoe	hoíán
Oblique cases	hoe	hoí	hoíán	hoíán

Infinitive, hon, honá, *to be, becoming.*

Hon is indeclinable in the singular masculine and feminine; it is not used in the feminine plural, and becomes hone in all the cases of the masculine plural. Honá is declined like *chittá* (see 38).

INDICATIVE MOOD.

PRESENT TENSE.—*I exist.*

	SINGULAR		PLURAL	
	Masculine.	*Feminine.*	*Masculine.*	*Feminine.*
1.	hundá	hundí	hunde	hundíán
2.	hundá	hundí	hunde	hundíán
3.	hundá	hundí	hunde	hundíán

DEFINITE PRESENT.—*I am existing.*

	SINGULAR		PLURAL	
	Masculine.	*Feminine.*	*Masculine.*	*Feminine.*
1.	hundá hán	hundí hán	hunde hán	hundíán hán
2.	hundá hain	hundí hain	hunde ho	hundíán ho
3.	hundá hai	hundí hai	hunde han	hundíán han

IMPERFECT.—*I was existing.*

	SINGULAR		PLURAL	
	Masculine.	*Feminine.*	*Masculine.*	*Feminine.*
1.	hundá sá	hundí sí	hunde se	hundíán sián
2.	hundá sá	hundí sí	hunde se	hundíán sián
3.	hundá sá	hundí sí	hunde se	hundíán sián

FUTURE PROBABLE.—*I probably am, shall be, or may have been, existing.*

	SINGULAR		PLURAL	
	Masculine.	*Feminine.*	*Masculine.*	*Feminine.*
1.	hundá howángá	hundí howángí	hunde howánge	hundíán howángián
2.	hundá howengá	hundí howengí	hunde howege	hundíán l owegián
3.	hundá howegá	hundí howegí	hunde howge	hundíán hongián

PAST.—*I became.*

	SINGULAR		PLURAL	
	Masculine.	*Feminine.*	*Masculine.*	*Feminine.*
1. 2. 3. }	hoiá	hoí	hoe	hoíán

PERFECT.—*I have become.*

	SINGULAR		PLURAL	
	Masculine.	*Feminine.*	*Masculine.*	*Feminine.*
1.	hoiá hán	hoí hán	hoe hán	hoíán hán
2.	hoiá hain	hoí hain	hoe ho	hoíán ho
3.	hoiá hai	hoí hai	hoe han	hoíán han

PLUPERFECT.—*I had become.*

	SINGULAR.		PLURAL.	
	Masculine.	*Feminine.*	*Masculine.*	*Feminine.*
1. 2. 3. } hoiá sí		hoí sí	hoo se	hoíán síán

FUTURE PAST.—*I probably have, or shall have, become.*

	SINGULAR.		PLURAL.	
	Masculine.	*Feminine.*	*Masculine.*	*Feminine.*
1.	hoiá howángá	hoí howángí	hoo howánge	hoíán howángíán
2.	hoiá howengá	hoí howengí	hoo howoge	hoíán howongíán
3.	hoiá howegá	hoí howegí	hoo honge	hoíán hongíán

FUTURE.—*I shall be.*

	SINGULAR.		PLURAL.	
	Masculine.	*Feminine.*	*Masculine.*	*Feminine.*
1.	howángá	howángí	howánge	howángíán
3.	howengá	howengí	howoge	howogíán
2.	howogá	howegí	honge	hongíán

POTENTIAL MOOD.

PRESENT.—*I would be.*

	SINGULAR.		PLURAL.	
	Masculine.	*Feminine.*	*Masculine.*	*Feminine.*
1. 2. 3. } hundá		hundí	hunde	hundíán

DEFINITE PRESENT.—*I may be existing.*

	SINGULAR.		PLURAL.	
	Masculine.	*Feminine.*	*Masculine.*	*Feminine.*
1.	hundá howán	hundí howán	hunde hoye	hundíán hoye
2.	hundá howen	hundí howen	hunde howo	hundíán howe
3.	hundá howe	hundí howe	hunde hon	hundíán hon

IMPERFECT.—*I would have become.*

	SINGULAR.		PLURAL.	
	Masculine.	*Feminine.*	*Masculine.*	*Feminine.*
1. 2. 3. } hoiá hundá		hoí hundí	hoo hunde	hoíán hundíán

FUTURE PAST.—*I shall have become.*

	SINGULAR.		PLURAL.	
	Masculine.	*Feminine.*	*Masculine.*	*Feminine.*
1.	hoiá howán	hoí howán	hoo hoye	hoíán hoye
2.	hoiá howen	hoí howen	hoo howo	hoíán howe
3.	hoiá howe	hoí howe	hoo hon	hoíán hon

FUTURE.—*I may or shall be, I may or shall become.*

	SINGULAR.	PLURAL.
1.	howán	hoye
2.	howen	howo, hoo
3.	howe	hon

95. Irregular neuter and auxiliary verb **jáná**, *to go*. Root, **jáh,** *go*.

Present participle, jándá, past participle, giá, future tense, jáwáu.

IMPERATIVE MOOD.
PRESENT.—Go thou.

Singular.	Plural.
2. jáh	jáo, jáwo

FUTURE.—Go thou (hereafter).

2. jáíu	jáio

Present participle, jándá, jándá hoiá. Declined like chittá (see 38).

Past participle, Masculine giá, giá hoiá, Feminine gaí, gaí hoí. Declined like chittá (see 38).

Indefinite participle. (Indeclinable).
Já, jáke, jáike *going, having gone*.

Substantive participle, *going, one that goes, or is to go*.

Jánewálá, jánwálá, jánchára, jánhár, jánebárá, jánhárá. Forms 1, 2, 5, and 6 are declined like chittá (see 38); forms 3 and 4 like manukkh (see 21) in the masculine, and like gall (see 26) in the feminine.

GERUND.—Going.

Singular.

	Masculine.	Feminine.
N.	... jáyú, jáiá, gaiá, giá	jáí, gaí
Oblique cases	... jáye, jáiáu, jáiáu hoiáu, gae, gaiáu, giáuhoiáu	jáí, gaí

Plural.

	Masculine.	Feminine.
N.	..., jáe, gae	jáiáu, gaiáu
Oblique cases	... jáiáu, ga-iáu, giáu	jaiáu, gaiáu

INFINITIVE MOOD.—To go, going.

	Singular.		Plural.	
	Masculine.	Feminine.	Masculine.	Feminine.
N.	.. jáná, jáu	jání	jáne	jáníáu
Oblique cases	jáne, jáu	jání, jáu	jáne, jáníáu	jáníáu

INDICATIVE MOOD.

PRESENT.—I go.

Singular.		Plural.	
Masculine.	Feminine.	Masculine.	Feminine.
1. 2. 3. } jándá	jándí	jánde	jándíáu

DEFINITE PRESENT.—I am going.

Singular.		Plural.	
Masculine.	Feminine.	Masculine.	Feminine.
1. jándá hán	jándí hán	jánde hán	jándíáu hán
2. jándá hain	jándí hain	jánde ho	jándíáu ho
3. jándá hai	jándí hai	jánde han	jándíáu han

PANJÁBÍ GRAMMAR.

PRESENT HABITUAL.—*I am in the habit of going.*

	SINGULAR		PLURAL	
	Masculine.	*Feminine.*	*Masculine.*	*Feminine.*
1.	jándá hundá hán	jándí hundí hán	jánde hunde hán	jándíán hundíán hán
2.	jándá hundá hain	jándí hundí hain	jánde hunde ho	jándíán hundíán ho
3.	jándá hundá hai	jándí hundí hai	jánde hunde han	jándíán hundíán han

IMPERFECT.—*I was going.*

	SINGULAR		PLURAL	
	Masculine.	*Feminine.*	*Masculine.*	*Feminine.*
1. 2. 3.	jándá sá	jándí sí	jánde se	jándíán síán

IMPERFECT HABITUAL.—*I was in the habit of going.*

	SINGULAR		PLURAL	
	Masculine.	*Feminine.*	*Masculine.*	*Feminine.*
1. 2. 3.	jándá hundá sá	jándí hundí sí	jánde hunde se	jándíán hundíán síán

FUTURE PROBABLE.—*I am probably, or shall be, going.*

	SINGULAR		PLURAL	
	Masculine.	*Feminine.*	*Masculine.*	*Feminine.*
1.	jándá howángá	jándí howángí	jánde howonge	jándíán howongíán
2.	jándá howengá	jándí howengí	jánde hawego	jándíán howegián
3.	jándá howegá	jándí howegí	jánde honge	jándíán hongíán

FUTURE HABITUAL.—*I am probably, or shall be, in the habit of going.*

	SINGULAR		PLURAL	
	Masculine.	*Feminine.*	*Masculine.*	*Feminine.*
1.	jándá hundá howángá	jándí hundí howángí	jánde hunde howánge	jándíán hundíán howángíán
2.	jándá hundá howengá	jándí hundí howengí	jánde hunde howoge	jándíán hundíán howogíán
3.	jándá hundá howegá	jándí hundí howegí	jánde hunde honge	jándíán hundíán hongíán

PAST.—*I went.*

	SINGULAR		PLURAL	
	Masculine.	*Feminine.*	*Masculine.*	*Feminine.*
1. 2. 3.	giá	gaí	gae	gaíán

PERFECT.—*I have gone.*

	SINGULAR		PLURAL	
	Masculine.	*Feminine.*	*Masculine.*	*Feminine.*
1.	giá hán	gaí hán	gae hán	gaíán hán
2.	giá hain	gaí hain	gae ho	gaíán ho
3.	giá hai	gaí hai	gae han	gaíán han

PLUPERFECT.—*I had gone.*

	SINGULAR		PLURAL	
	Masculine.	*Feminine.*	*Masculine.*	*Feminine.*
1. 2. 3.	giá sá	gaí sí	gae se	gaíán síán

PANJÁBÍ GRAMMAR.

FUTURE PAST.—*I probably have, or shall have, gone.*

SINGULAR.		PLURAL.	
Masculine.	Feminine.	Masculine.	Feminine.
1. giá howángá	gaí howángí	gao howángo	gaíán howángíán
2. giá howengá	gaí howengí	gao howogo	gaíán howogíán
3. giá howegá	gaí howegí	gao hongo	gaíán hongíán

FUTURE.—*I shall or will go.*

SINGULAR.		PLURAL.	
Masculine.	Feminine.	Masculine.	Feminine.
1. jáwángá	jáwángí	jáwángo	jáwángíán
2. jáwengá	jáwengí	jáoge, jawogo	jáogíán, jáwogíán
3. jáwegá	jáwegí	jángo	jángíán

POTENTIAL MOOD.—*I would go.*
PRESENT.

SINGULAR.		PLURAL.	
Masculine.	Feminine.	Masculine.	Feminine.
1. }			
2. } jáudá	jándí	jándo	jándíán
3. }			

DEFINITE PRESENT.—*I would be going.*

SINGULAR.		PLURAL.	
Masculine.	Feminine.	Masculine.	Feminine.
1. }			
2. } jándá hundá	jándí hundí	jándo hundo	jándíán hundíán
3. }			

PRESENT HABITUAL.—*I would be in the habit of going.*
is the same as definite present.

FUTURE PROBABLE.—*I may be going.*

SINGULAR.		PLURAL.	
Masculine.	Feminine.	Masculine.	Feminine.
1. jándá howán	jándí howán	jándo hoyo	jándíyán hoyo
2. jándá howen	jándí howen	jándo howo	jándíyán howo
3. jándá howe	jándí howe	jándo hon	jándíyán hon

FUTURE HABITUAL.—*I may be in the habit of going.*

SINGULAR.		PLURAL.	
Masculine.	Feminine.	Masculine.	Feminine.
1. jándá hundá howán	jándí hundí howan	jándo hundo hoyo	jándíán hundíán hoyo
2. jándá hundá howen	jándí hundí howen	jándo hundo howo	jándíán hundíán howo
3. jándá hundá howo	jándí hundí howe	jándo hundo hon	jándíán hundíán hon

PERFECT.—*I would have gone.*

SINGULAR.		PLURAL.	
Masculine.	Feminine.	Masculine.	Feminine.
1. }			
2. } giá hundá	gaí hundí	gao hundo	gaíán hundíán
3. }			

FUTURE PAST. —*I may have gone.*

Singular.		Plural.	
Masculine.	*Feminine.*	*Masculine.*	*Feminine.*
1. giá howán	gaí howán	gae hoye	gaíán hoyo
2. giá howen	gaí howen	gae howo	gaíán howo
3. giá howe	gaí howo	gae hon	gaíán hon

FUTURE.—*I may, or shall, go.*

Singular.	Plural.
Masculine and Feminine.	*Masculine and Feminine.*
1. jáwán	jáye
2. jáwou	jáo, jáwo
3. jáwe	ján

96. Regular verb, ghallná, *to send.*
Root, ghall, *send.*
Principal parts. Present participle, ghalldá. Past participle, ghalliá. Future tense, ghallán.

ACTIVE VOICE.

IMPERATIVE MOOD.

PRESENT TENSE.—*Send.*

Singular.	Plural.
2. ghall	ghallo

FUTURE.— *Send (hereafter).*

Singular.	Plural.
2. ghallín	ghallio

PARTICIPLES.

PRESENT. *Sending.*

	Singular.		Plural.	
	Masculine.	*Feminine.*	*Masculine.*	*Feminine.*
N.	ghalldá, ghalldá hoiá	ghalldí, ghalldí hoí	ghallde, ghalldo hoe	ghalldíán, ghalldíán hoíán
Obl. cases.	ghallde, ghallde hoe	ghalldí, ghalldí hoí	ghalldíán ghalldíán hoíán	ghalldíán, ghalldíán hoíán
V.	ghallde, ghalldiá, ghalldiá hoiá	ghalldíe, ghalldíe hoíe	ghalldío, ghallde hoio	ghalldío, ghalldío hoio ghalldíán hoío

PAST.—*Having sent.*

	Singular.		Plural.	
	Masculine.	*Feminine.*	*Masculine.*	*Feminine.*
N.	ghalliá hoiá	ghallí hoí	ghallo hoe	ghallíán hoíán
Obq. cases.	ghalle hoe	ghalli hoí	ghallíán hoiou	ghallíán hoíán.
V.	ghalle hoe, ghalliá hoiá	ghalliá hoíe, ghalliá hoíe	ghallio hoie	ghallío hoío, ghallíán hoío.

INDEFINITE.—*Having sent.*

Ghall, ghall ke (Indeclinable).

SUBSTANTIVE.—*Sending, one that sends, or is to send.*

Ghallanwálá, ghallnewálá, ghallanhár, ghallnehár, ghallanhárá, ghallnehárá.

PANJÁBÍ GRAMMAR. xxvii

Forms 1, 2, 5 and 6 are declined like *chittá* (see 38); forms 3 and 4 like *manukkh* (see 21) in the masculine, and like *ghall* (see 26) in the feminine.

GERUND.—*Sending.*

SINGULAR.   PLURAL.

Masculine.   *Feminine.*   *Masculine.*   *Feminine.*
N.   ghalliá   ghallí   ghallo   ghallíán
Oblique cases ghallo   ghallí   ghalliáu   ghallíán

INFINITIVE MOOD.—*To send, sending.*

SINGULAR.   PLURAL.

Masculine.   *Feminine.*   *Masculine.*   *Feminine.*
N.   ghallná, ghallan   ghallní   ghallno   ghallníán
Obl. ghallne, ghallan   ghallní, ghallan ghallne, ghallnián   ghallníán
cases.

INDICATIVE MOOD.

PRESENT.—*I send.*

SINGULAR.   PLURAL.

Masculine.   *Feminine.*   *Masculine.*   *Feminine.*
1.
2. ghalldá   -   ghalldí   ghallde   ghalldíán
3.

DEFINITE PRESENT.—*I am sending.*

SINGULAR.   PLURAL.

Masculine.   *Feminine.*   *Masculine.*   *Feminine.*
1. ghalldá hán   ghalldí hán   ghallde hán   ghalldíán hán
2. ghalldá hain   ghalldí hain   ghallde ho   ghalldíán ho
3. ghalldá hai   ghalldí hai   ghallde han   ghalldíán han

PRESENT HABITUAL.—*I am in the habit of sending.*

SINGULAR.   PLURAL.

Masculine.   *Feminine.*   *Masculine.*   *Feminine.*
1. ghalldá hundá hán   ghalldí hundí hán.   ghallde hunde hán   ghalldíán hundíán hán
2. ghalldá hundá hain ghalldí hundí hain. ghallde hunde ho   ghalldíán hundíán ho
3. ghalldá hundá hai   ghalldí hundí hai.   ghallde hunde han   ghalldíán hundíán han

IMPERFECT.—*I was sending.*

SINGULAR.   PLURAL.

Masculine.   *Feminine.*   *Masculine.*   *Feminine.*
1.
2. ghalldá sá   ghalldí sí   ghallde se   ghalldíán síán
3

IMPERFECT HABITUAL.—*I was in the habit of sending.*

SINGULAR.   PLURAL.

Masculine.   *Feminine.*   *Masculine.*   *Feminine.*
1.
2. ghalldá hundá sá   ghalldí hundí sí   ghallde hunde se   ghalldíán hundíán síán.
3

FUTURE PROBABLE.—*I am probably, or shall be, sending.*

Singular.		Plural.	
Masculine.	Feminine.	Masculine.	Feminine.
1. ghalldá howángá	ghalldí howángí	ghalldo howángo	ghalldíán howángíán
2. ghalldá howengá	ghalldí howengí	ghalldo howogo	ghalldíáu howogíán
3. ghalldá howegá	ghalldí howegí	ghalldo hongo	ghalldíán hongíán

FUTURE HABITUAL.—*I am probably, or shall be, in the habit of sending.*

Singular.		Plural.	
Masculine.	Feminine.	Masculine.	Feminine.
1. ghalldá hundá howángá	ghalldí hundí howángí	ghalldo hundo howángo	ghalldíáu hundíáu howángíáu
2. ghalldá hundá howengá	ghalldí hundí howengí	ghalldo hundo howogo	ghalldíán hundíáu howogíán
3. ghalldá hundá howegá	ghalldí hundí howegí	ghalldo hundo hongo	ghalldíán hundíáu hongíán

PAST.—*I sent.*

Singular and Plural.

Masculine.	Feminine.
1. 2. 3. } ghalliá, ghallo	ghallí, ghallíán

PERFECT.—*I have sent.*

Singular and Plural.

Masculine.	Feminine.
1. 2. 3. } ghalliá hai, ghallo ha*n*	ghallí hai, ghallíán ha*n*

PLUPERFECT.—*I had sent.*

Singular and Plural.

Masculine.	Feminine.
1. 2. 3. } ghalliá sá, ghallo so	ghallí sí, ghallíán síán

FUTURE PAST.—*I probably have, or shall have, sent.*

Singular and Plural.

Masculine.	Feminine.
1. 2. 3. } ghalliá howegá, ghalle hongo	ghallí howegí, ghallíán hongíán

N.B.—In these past tenses, the noun or pronoun would be in the instrumental case.

FUTURE.—*I shall send.*

Singular.		Plural.	
Masculine.	Feminine.	Masculine.	Feminine.
1. ghallángá	ghallángí	ghallángo	ghallángíán
2. ghallengá	ghalleugí	ghallogo	ghallogíán
3. ghallegá	ghallegí	ghallango	ghallangíán

POTENTIAL MOOD.
PRESENT.—*I would send.*

	SINGULAR.		PLURAL.	
	Masculine.	*Feminine.*	*Masculine.*	*Feminine.*
1. 2. 3.	ghalldá	ghalldí	ghallde	ghalldíán

DEFINITE PRESENT.—*I would be sending.*

	SINGULAR.		PLURAL.	
	Masculine.	*Feminine.*	*Masculine.*	*Feminine.*
1. 2. 3.	ghalldá hundá	ghalldí hundí	ghallde hunde,	ghalldíán hundíán

PRESENT HABITUAL.—*I would be in the habit of sending.*

Is the same as the definite present.

FUTURE PROBABLE.—*I may be sending.*

	SINGULAR.		PLURAL.	
	Masculine.	*Feminine.*	*Masculine.*	*Feminine.*
1.	ghalldá howán	ghalldí howán	ghallde hoye	ghalldíán hoge
2.	ghalldá howen	ghalldí howen	ghallde howo	ghalldíán howo
3.	ghalldá howe	ghalldí howe	ghallde hon	ghalldíán hon

FUTURE HABITUAL. *I may be in the habit of sending.*

	SINGULAR.		PLURAL.	
	Masculine.	*Feminine.*	*Masculine.*	*Feminine.*
1.	ghalldá hundá howán	ghalldí hundí howán	ghallde hunde hoye	ghalldíán hundíán hoye
2.	ghalldá hundá howen	ghalldí hundí howen	ghallde hunde howo	ghalldíán hundíán howo
3.	ghalldá hundá howe	ghalldí hundí howe	ghallde hunde hon	ghalldíán hundíán hon

PERFECT.—*I would have sent.*

	SINGULAR AND PLURAL.	
	Masculine.	*Feminine.*
1. 2. 3.	ghalliá hundá, ghalle hunde	ghallí hundí, ghallián hundíán

FUTURE PAST.—*I may have sent.*

	SINGULAR AND PLURAL.	
	Masculine.	*Feminine.*
1. 2. 3.	ghalliá howe, ghalle hon	ghallí howo, ghallíán hon

N.B.—The noun or pronoun in these two past tenses would be in the instrumental case.

FUTURE.—*I may or would send.*

	SINGULAR AND PLURAL.	SINGULAR AND PLURAL.
	Masculine and Feminine.	*Masculine and Feminine.*
1.	ghallán	ghallaye
2.	ghallen	ghalio
3.	ghalle	ghallan

Passive.

97. The passive voice has neither an imperative mood nor a gerund, and the past participle active is used with a passive meaning.

INFINITIVE MOOD.—*To be sent, having been sent.*

	Singular.		Plural.	
	Masculine.	Feminine.	Masculine.	Feminine.
N.	... ghalliá jáná, ghalliá jáń	ghallí jání	ghalle jáno	ghallí jáníán
Obq. cases	ghallé jáne, ghalle jáne	ghalle ján, ghalliá jáne	ghalle jáníán janíán	ghalle ghallián jáníán

This form is however seldom used.

INDICATIVE MOOD.

PRESENT.—*I am sent.*

	Singular.		Plural.	
	Masculine.	Feminine.	Masculine.	Feminine.
1. 2. 3.	ghalliá jándá	ghallí jándí	ghalle jánde	ghallián jándíán

DEFINITE PRESENT.—*I am being sent.*

	Singular.		Plural.	
	Masculine.	Feminine.	Masculine.	Feminine.
1.	ghalliá jándá hán	ghallí jándí hán	ghalle jánde hán	ghallián jándíán hán
2.	ghalliá jándá hain	ghallí jándí hain	ghalle jánde ho	ghallián jándíán ho
3.	ghalliá jándá hai	ghallí jándí hai	ghalle jánde han	ghallián jándíán han

PRESENT HABITUAL.—*I am in the habit of being sent.*

	Singular.		Plural.	
	Masculine.	Feminine.	Masculine.	Feminine.
1.	ghalliá jándá hundá hán	ghallí jándí hundí hán	ghalle jánde hunde hán	ghallián jándíán hundíán hán
2.	ghalliá jándá hundá hain	ghallí jándí hundí hain	ghalle jánde hunde ho	ghallián jándíán hundíán ho
3.	ghalliá jándá hundá hai	ghallí jándí hundí hai	ghalle jánde hunde han	ghallián jándíán hundíán han

IMPERFECT.—*I was being sent.*

	Singular.		Plural.	
	Masculine.	Feminine.	Masculine.	Feminine.
1. 2. 3.	ghalliá jándá sá	ghallí jándí sí	ghalle jánde se	ghallián jándíán sián

IMPERFECT HABITUAL.—*I was in the habit of being sent.*

	Singular.		Plural.	
	Masculine.	Feminine.	Masculine.	Feminine.
1. 2. 3.	ghalliá jándá hundá sá	ghallí jándi hundí sí	ghalle jánde hunde se	ghallián jándíán hundíán sían

PANJÁBÍ GRAMMAR.

FUTURE PROBABLE.—*I will be, or probably am being, sent.*

SINGULAR.

Masculine.	Feminine.
1. ghalliá jándá howángá	ghallí jándí howángí
2. ghalliá jándá howeugá	ghallí jándí howengí
3. ghalliá jándá howegá	ghallí jándí howegí

PLURAL

Masculine.	Feminine.
1. ghalle jánde howánge	ghallíán jándíán howángíán
2. ghalle jánde howoge	ghallíán jándíán howogíán
3. ghalle jánde honge	ghallíán jándíán hongíán

PAST.—*I was sent.*

SINGULAR

Masculine.	Feminine.
1. 2. 3. } ghalliá giá	ghallí gaí

PLURAL.

Masculine.	Feminine.
ghalle gae	ghallíán gaíán

PERFECT.—*I have been sent*

SINGULAR.

Masculine.	Feminine.
1. ghalliá giá hán	ghallí gaí hán
2. ghalliá giá hain	ghallí gaí hain
3. ghalliá giá hai	ghallí gaí hai

PLURAL.

Masculine.	Feminine.
ghalle gae hán	ghallíán gaíán hán
ghalle gae ho	ghallíán gaíán ho
ghalle gae han	ghallíán gaíán han

PLUPERFECT.—*I had been sent.*

SINGULAR.

Masculine.	Feminine.
1. 2. 3. } ghalliá giá sá	ghallí gaí sí

PLURAL.

Masculine.	Feminine.
ghalle gae se	ghallíán gaíán síán

FUTURE PAST.—*I shall have been, or probably was, sent.*

SINGULAR.

Masculine	Feminine.
1. ghalliá giá, or ghalliá hoiá, howángá	ghallí gaí, or ghallí hoí, howángí
2. ghalliá giá, or ghalliá hoiá, howeugá	ghallí gaí, or ghallí hoí, howengí
3. ghalliá giá, or ghalliá hoiá, howegá	ghallí gaí, or ghallí hoí, howegí

PLURAL.

1. ghalle gae, or ghalle hoe, howánge	ghallíán gaíán, or ghallíán hoíán, howángíán
2. ghalle gae, or ghalle hoe, howoge	ghallíán gaíán, or ghallíán hoíán, howogíán
3. ghalle gae, or ghalle hoe, honge	ghallíán gaíán, or ghallíán hoíán, hongíán

FUTURE.—*I shall be sent.*

SINGULAR.

Masculine.	Feminine.
1. ghalliá jáwángá	ghallí jáwángí
2. ghalliá jáwengá	ghallí jáwengí
3. ghalliá jáwegá	ghallí jáwegí

PLURAL.

Masculine.	Feminine.
ghalle jáwánge	ghallíán jáwángíán
ghalle jáwoge	ghallíán jáwogíán
ghalle jánge	ghallíán jángíán

POTENTIAL MOOD.

PRESENT.—*I would be sent.*

SINGULAR.

Masculine.	Feminine.
1. 2. 3. } ghalliá jándá	ghallí jándí

PLURAL.

Masculine.	Feminine.
ghalle jánde	ghallíán jándíán

PANJÁBÍ GRAMMAR.

DEFINITE PRESENT.—*I am to be sent.*

	SINGULAR.		PLURAL.	
	Masculine.	*Feminine.*	*Masculine.*	*Feminine.*
1. 2. 3.	ghalliá jándá hundá	ghallí jándí hundí	ghalle jánde hunde	ghallíán jándíán hundíán

FUTURE PROBABLE.—*I may be sent.*

SINGULAR. PLURAL.
Masculine. *Feminine.* *Masculine.* *Feminine.*

1. ghalliá jándá howán   ghallí jándí howán   ghalle jánde hoye   ghallíán jándíán hoye
2. ghalliá jándá howen   ghallí jándí howen   ghalle jánde howo   ghallíán jándíán howo
3. ghalliá jándá howe   ghallí jándí howe   ghalle jánde hon   ghallíán jándíán hon

FUTURE HABITUAL.—*I may be in the habit of being sent.*

SINGULAR. PLURAL.
Masculine. *Feminine.* *Masculine.* *Feminine.*

1. ghalliá jándá hundá howán   ghallí jándí hundí howán   ghalle jánde hunde hoye   ghallíán jándíán hundíán hoye
2. ghalliá jándá hundá howen   ghallí jándí hundí howen   ghalle jánde hunde howo   ghallíán jándíán hundíán howo
3. ghalliá jándá hundá howe   ghallí jándí hundí howe   ghalle jánde hon   ghallíán jándíán hundíán hon

PERFECT.—*I would have been sent.*

SINGULAR. PLURAL.
Masculine. *Feminine.* *Masculine.* *Feminine.*

1. 2. 3. } ghalliá giá hundá   ghallí gaí hundí   ghalle gae hunde   ghallíán gaíán hundíán

FUTURE PAST.—*I may, or shall have been, sent.*

SINGULAR.
Masculine.   *Feminine.*

1. ghalliá giá, or ghalliá hoiá, howán   ghallí gaí, or ghallí hoí, howán
2. ghalliá giá, or ghalliá hoiá, howen   ghallí gaí, or ghallí hoí, howen
3. ghalliá giá, or ghalliá hoiá, howe   ghallí gaí, or ghallí hoí, howe

PLURAL.

1. ghalle gae, or ghalle hoe, hoye   ghallíán gaíán or ghallíán hoíán hoye
2. ghalle gae, or ghalle hoe, howo   ghallíán gaíán or ghallíán hoíán howo
3. ghalle gae, or ghalle hoe, hon   ghallíán gaíán or ghallíán hoíán hon

FUTURE.—*I may, or shall, be sent.*

SINGULAR. PLURAL.
Masculine. *Feminine.* *Masculine.* *Feminine.*

1. ghalliá júwán   ghallí jáwán   ghalle jáye   ghallíán jáye
2. ghalliá jáwen   ghallí jáwen   ghalle jáwo   ghallíán jáwo
3. ghalliá jáwe   ghallí jáwe   ghalle ján   ghallíán ján

98. The following is another form of the passive voice; active, *márná, to beat.*—Root, már.

Principal parts; present participle, *márdá*, past participle, *máriá*; future tense, *márán*.

PANJÁBÍ GRAMMAR. xxxiii

PASSIVE VOICE.
INFINITIVE MOOD.—*To be beaten.*

SINGULAR. PLURAL.

Masculine.	Feminine.	Masculine.	Feminine.
N. máridá ján, máridá jáná	máridí jání	máride jáne	máridíán jánián
Obq. case máride ján, máride jáne	máridí jání, máridí ján	máride jánián, máride ján	máridíán jánián

INDICATIVE MOOD.
PRESENT.—*I am beaten.*

SINGULAR. PLURAL.

Masculine.	Feminine.	Masculine.	Feminine.
1. 2. 3. } máridá	máridí	máride	máridián

DEFINITE PRESENT.—*I am being beaten.*

SINGULAR. PLURAL.

Masculine.	Feminine.	Masculine.	Feminine.
1. máridá hún	máridí hán	máride hán	máridíán hán
2. máridá hain	máridí hain	máride ho	máridíán ho
3. máridá hai	máridí hai	máride han	máridíán han

PRESENT HABITUAL.—*I am in the habit of being beaten.*

SINGULAR. PLURAL.

Masculine.	Feminine.	Masculine.	Feminine.
1. máridá hundá hún	máridí hundí háu	máride hunde hún	máridíán hundíán háu
2. máridá hundá hain	máridí hundí hain	máride hunde ho	máridíán hundíán ho
3. máridá hundá hai	máridí hundí hai	máride hunde han	máridíán hundíán han

IMPERFECT.—*I was being beaten.*

SINGULAR. PLURAL.

Masculine.	Feminine.	Masculine.	Feminine.
1. 2. 3. } máridá sá	máridí sí	máride se	máridíán síán

IMPERFECT HABITUAL.—*I was in the habit of being beaten.*

SINGULAR. PLURAL.

Masculine.	Feminine.	Masculine.	Feminine.
1. 2. 3. } máridá hundá sá	máridí hundí sí	máride hunde se	máridíán hundíán síán

FUTURE PROBABLE.—*I shall be, or probably am being, beaten.*

SINGULAR. PLURAL.

Masculine.	Feminine.	Masculine.	Feminine.
1. máridá howángá	máridí howángí	máride howánge	máridíán howángián
2. máridá howengá	máridí howengí	máride howoge	máridíán howogián
3. máridá howegá	máridí howegí	máride honge	máridíán hongián

FUTURE.—I shall be beaten.

SINGULAR.		PLURAL.	
Masculine.	Feminine.	Masculine.	Feminine.
1. máríángá	máríángí	máríánge	máríángián
2. máríengá	máríengí	máríoge	máríogián
3. máríegá	máríegí	máríange	máríangián

This form is however seldom used.

POTENTIAL MOOD.
PRESENT.—I would be beaten.

SINGULAR.		PLURAL.	
Masculine.	Feminine.	Masculine.	Feminine.
1. }			
2. } márídá	márídí	máríde	márídián
3. }			

DEFINITE PRESENT.—I am to be, or could be, beaten.

SINGULAR.		PLURAL.	
Masculine.	Feminine.	Masculine.	Feminine.
1. }			
2. } márídá hundá	márídí hundí	máríde hunde	márídián hundián
3. }			

FUTURE PROBABLE.—I may be beaten.

SINGULAR.		PLURAL.	
Masculine.	Feminine.	Masculine.	Feminine.
1. márídá howán	márídí howán	máríde hoye	márídián hoye
2. márídá howen	márídí howen	máríde howo	márídián howo
3. márídá howe	márídí howe	máríde hon	márídián hon

FUTURE HABITUAL.—I may be habitually beaten.

SINGULAR.		PLURAL.	
Masculine.	Feminine.	Masculine.	Feminine.
1. márídá howán	hundá	márídí howán	hundí	máríde hoye	hunde	márídián hoye	hundián
2. márídá howen	hundá	márídí howen	hundí	máríde howo	hunde	márídián howo	hundián
3. márídá howe	hundá	márídí howe	hundí	máríde hon	hunde	márídián hon	hundián

FUTURE.—I shall, or will, be beaten.

SINGULAR.	PLURAL.
Masculine and Feminine.	Masculine and Feminine.
1. máríán	máríye
2. máríen	mário
3. márie	máríán

This tense is seldom used.

99. The other forms of hán are also often used as auxiliaries, although not given above. Sí, instead of só, is often used in the masculine of past tenses.

Irregular Verbs.

100. The following are some of the most common irregular verbs; in the parts not referred to, the conjugation is regular :—

Infinitive.	Present participle.	Past participle.	Future tense.	Gerund.	Remarks.
siuná, to sew	...	síta, siá	...	siá.	
honá, to be	hundá	...	...	...	
karní, to do	...	kítá	...	...	also regular
kháná, to eat	...	khándá, khádhá	...	kháiá, khádhá	also regular
jauná, to bear (young)	...	jáiá	...	...	also regular
jáuná, to know	...	játá	...	...	Imper. jáh
jáná, to go	...	giá gáiá	...	jáyá giá	
dhauná, } to fall down	...	dhatthá	...	...	also regular
dhainá, }	...		...		also regular
dekhná, to see	dinda	ditthá, dithá	...	diá	Imper. dih, plur dio, dewo
dená, to give	...	dictá	dián, dewán		also regular
nahauná, to bathe	...	...	...	nahátiá	also regular
pahunchná, to arrive	...	pahuntá, panjiá	pahután	...	
paíná, } to fall	...	piá	pawán		
parná, }	...				
barasná, to rain	...	battáá	...	...	also regular
bandhná, to bind	...	baddhá	...	...	also regular
rahná, to stay	...	ríhá	...	...	Imper. rahu; also regular
lená, to take	...	liá, laiá, litá	lawán	liá.	
pachhánná, to recognise	...	pachhátá	...		alsoregular

Casual Verbs.

101. Casual verbs are used to express what is done by the instrumentality of another person, and are formed either from active or neuter verbs, (i) by adding an, wán, lán, ál to the root; e.g.,

kar, do, karán or karwán, cause to do.

dekh, see, dikhlán or dekhál, cause to see, show.

(ii) by changing the last short vowel of the root into a long one, e.g.,

bal, burn, bál, cause to burn, kindle,

ukhar, be rooted up, ukher, root up,

tur, depart, tor, send away.

Moods, Tenses, &c.

102. The syllable "we" in the third person singular, future, both indicative and potential, of such verbs as terminate their roots in n, is often changed into e as jáegá for jáwegá.

103. The syllable "ye" of the indefinite future potential, is often changed into iye and íe, as kariye, chalíe; and the third person future, potential and indicative admits of "wa" being inserted before final n, as howan for hon.

104. The past tenses are sometimes used for the future, e.g., Je tain agge pair dhárá, tán main terí ján laí, *If you put a foot forward, I will take your life.*

105. The past and imperfect are often used interchangeably; so are the present and the definite present.

106. The future potential is sometimes used for the future indicative, e.g., Je hukam howe tán main jáwán, *If there is an order, I will go.*

107. The infinitive, governed by an active verb, sometimes drops the termination ná, ná, &c. e.g., Tusín achchhián chíján de jánde ho, *You know how to give good things;* Tún parh jándá hain, *Do you know how to read?*

108. The "nai" of the instrumental case being originally a preposition meaning, "by," the infinitive is often construed with this case, to express certainty or obligation, the verb hán or honá being at the same time either expressed or understood; thus, main áuná, I will certainly come; us ne áuná sá, he was to have come; tusín áuná, you must come.

109. In the passive voice, honá is sometimes substituted for jáná, as Bahut máyá kharchí hoí hai, *Much wealth has been expended;* Mihnat kítí hundí hai. *Labour is being performed.*

110. Neuter verbs can, in some cases, be used in the passive form, but without a passive meaning, e.g., prápat hoídá *acquires* ; jáídá *goes*.

111. In some parts of the Panjáb, the following peculiarities prevail ; instead of the instrumental pronoun " us ne," the verb takes the suffix " os ", and at the same time drops its own final letter, as Kitos, *he did*, for Us ne kítá ; Pínde asán, *we are drinking*, is used for Asín pínde hánge ; Main kardá ahá, *I was doing*, for main kardá sá ; uh karsí, *he will do*, for uh karegá ; nase, *was not*, for nahín sá.

COMPOUND VERBS.

112. Compound verbs are formed :—

(i). by uniting a verb with a noun ; as Mull lená, *to buy* ; kabúl karná, *to accept*, bián honá, *to be explained*.

(ii). by repeating a verb with some slight variation, to give greater emphasis, as Ukharná pukharná, *to be plucked up root and branch*. Both parts are conjugated throughout.

(iii). by prefixing, to verbal roots, certain other verbs, which enable them to express possibility, inception, transition, completion, &c., e.g., Wách akná *to be able to read* ; turpainá, *to set out* ; bahí jáná, *to sit down* ; khá hatná, *to finish eating*.

(iv). by prefixing a gerund to the verb karná, thus denoting habit, as Uh parhiá kardá, *he is in the habit of reading*.

(v). by prefixing a participle, either past or present, to a verb denoting action or rest, to signify the idea of continuance, as Uh mai nún márí hí giá, *he went on beating me* ; gajní unhán de hathon jándí laggí, *Ghazní began to go gradually out of their hands* ; uh kamm kardá jándá hai, *he goes on doing the work*. If the participle is repeated, the meaning is different, as Uh kamm kardá kardá jándá hai, *he does the work as he goes*.

ADVERBS.

113. Many adverbs were originally nouns, or a combination of nouns with other parts of speech, as " uthe," there, from " as tháun," that place ; " kichchar," *how long*, from " kitná," *how much*, " chir," *time* ; they are therefore often construed with prepositions, as if they were nouns still, as " uthe te " or " uthon," *from there, thence* ; also with adjectives, as " har kite," *every where*.

Conjunctions.

114. The following are some of the conjunctions in most frequent use ;

ake, ke, *or*.
ate, te, *and*.
apar ; aipar *except, but*.
athwá, *or*.
ar *and*.
magwán, magon, *but, but even*.
je, jekar, *if*.

tán, *then*.
tán bhí, *nevertheless, still*.
nálo, *also, both and*.
par, *but*.
balak, *but, but even*.
bháwen, *although*.
yá, *or*.

115. Some of these are used as correlatives to each other as, je *if*—tán, *then* ; bháwen, *although*—tán bhí, *still* ; nálo, *both*—nálo, *and*. Of those that naturally go together, the former is sometimes understood, as Hukm howe, tán maín jáwán, *if I have permission, I will go* ; je being understood.

Prepositions.

116. What has been said of the origin of adverbs (113), likewise applies to prepositions, and they, therefore, have the same power to control the gender of words depending on them, that nouns have; *e.g.*, chaphere, *on all sides*, derived from chár, *four*, and pherá, *a circuit*, requires the genitive particle of the word, which it governs, to be in the masculine gender, as Us makán de chaphere, *all around that place*.

117. Two prepositions are often used together as wichch te, or wichchon, *out of, from the midst of* ; wichdon, *through the midst of*.

118. "Don" is never used, except in composition with other prepositions or with adverbs.

119. "On" is an inseparable preposition, and is written as part of the word which it governs as gharon, *from home*.

120. The following prepositions govern the genitive case:—

agge, *before*.
aggion, *from before*.
annsár, *according to*.
ang sang, *accompanying*.
andar, *within*.
andaron, *from within*.
andardon,   } *by the way of*
andardion, } *the inside of*.
rde girde, *about*.
ute *above, on*.
npar *over, on*.
nparon, *from above*.
upardon,   } *by the way of the*
upardion, } *upper side of*.

sane   } *together with*.
samet, }
sáhmne, *before*.
sáhmnion, *from before*.
sáth,   } *with*.
sang,   }
sababh, *on account of*.
heth, *below*.
hethon, *from below*.
hethdon, *by the way of the underside of*.
hakk wichch, *respecting*.
kol, *by*.
kolo, *from*.

koldou, ⎱ *along by.*
koldiou, ⎰
kárau, ⎱ *on account of.*
káran, ⎰
girde, *around.*
gabhbhe, *in the midst of.*
gel, *with.*
chhutt, *without.*
táíu, *to.*
nál, *with.*
nálon, *from, in comparison with.*
nere ⎱ *near.*
nere, tere ⎰
nerion, *from the vicinity of.*
nerdon, *through the vicinity of.*
níche, *below.*
níchon, *from beneath.*
niáín, *like.*
páh, ⎱ *by.*
pás, ⎰
páhon, ⎱ *from.*
páson, ⎰
pichchhe, *after.*
pichchhon, *after, from behind.*
barabbar, ⎱
barúbar, ⎬ *even with, equal to.*
barobar, ⎰
bábat, *concerning.*
báhar, *outside of.*
báharon, *from without.*

báhardou, ⎱ *by the way of the*
báhardiou, ⎰ *outside of.*
bagal, *on the side of.*
bagalon, *from the side of.*
bagaldou, *by the side of.*
bájh, *besides.*
bájhon, *besides.*
magar, *behind.*
magaron, *from behind, after*
magardon, *by the rear of.*
muhre, *before.*
muhron, *from before.*
lág, *adjacent to.*
lágon, *from contact with.*
lagbhag, *about.*
lai, *for.*
lánbh, *by the side of.*
lánbh cháubh, *about, in the vicinity of.*
wal, *towards.*
walon, *from the direction of.*
wichch, *in, among.*
wichchon, *from within, from amongst.*
wichdon, *by the way of the inside of, through.*
wichchín, *through.*
wichále, ⎱
wichkáhe, ⎬ *between, in the midst of.*
wichkár, ⎰
wikhe, *in, respecting.*
wáste, *for, on account of.*
wánjhú, *like.*

121. The prepositions governing the dative case are Nún, táín, torí, tíkka, and tíkur, and they all mean *to* or *for*.

122. The following prepositions are used with the ablative:—

Sir, *on the head of exactly at or on, on with*
pnr ⎱
utte ⎬ *on, upon.*
te ⎰
puron, ⎱ *from on, off.*
porte, ⎰
utton, ⎰

te, ⎱
thín, ⎬ *by, of, out of.*
thon. ⎰
on, ⎱
karke, *by, by means of, by the means of.*

NUMBERS AND NUMERALS.

123. The names of the figures are:—

Eká, *one,* dúá, *two,* tíá, *three,* chauká, *four,* pánjá, *five,* chhakká, *six,* sátá, *seven,* áthá, *eight,* náiá, náián, or na-uká *nine,* bindi, *cipher,*

124. The figures are also sometimes called, ikánk or ikáng, dúánk or dúáng, &c.

125. The cardinal and ordinal numbers are as follows:—

Cardinals.	Ordinals.	
1 ikk.	pahilá,	1st
2 do.	dujá, dúá,	2nd
3 tinn, trai.	tíjá, tíá,	3rd
4 chár.	chauthá,	4th
5 panj.	panjwán,	5th
6 chhe.	chhewán,	6th
7 satt.	sattwán,	7th
8 a*tth*.	a*tth*wán,	8th
9 nau, na-uu.	naowán, na-nwán	9th
10 das.	daswán,	10th
11 giárán, yárán.	giárnwán, yárwán	11th
12 bárán.	bárawán,	12th
13 terán.	terawán,	13th
14 chaudán	chaudhwán,	14th
15 pandrán.	pandharwán,	15th
16 soláh.	solawán,	16th
17 satárán.	satárawán,	17th
18 a*th*árán.	a*th*árawán,	18th
19 unní.	unníhwán,	19th
20 bíh, wíh.	bíhwán,	20th
21 ikkí.	ikkíhwán,	21st
22 báí.	báíswán,	22nd
23 teí, treí.	teiswán, treiswán,	23rd
24 chauwí, chawwí, chaubí, chabbí.	chaubiswán, chawíhwán,	24th
25 panjí, pachchí.	pachiswán, panjíhwán,	25th
26 chhabbí.	chhabbiswán,	26th
27 satáí.	satáíswán,	27th
28 atháí.	atháíswán,	28th
29 unattí, unattrí.	unnatíswán,	29th
30 tíh, tríh.	tíswán, tíhwán, tríbwán,	30th
31 ikattí, akattí, akattrí.	iktíswán, akattíswán,	31st
32 battí, battrí.	battíswán,	32nd
33 tetí, tetrí.	tetíswán,	33rd
34 chantí, chautrí.	chautíswán,	34th
35 paintí, paintrí.	paintíswán,	35th
36 chhattí, chhattrí.	chhattíswán,	36th
37 saintí, saintrí.	saintíswán,	37th
38 a*th*attí, a*th*attrí.	a*th*attíswán,	38th
39 nntálí.	nntálíswán,	39th
40 chálí.	chálíwán, chálíswán,	40th
41 iktálí.	iktáhalwán,	41st
42 baitálí, batálí.	biaháhwán,	42nd
43 titálí, taitálí, tirtálí.	titáhalwán,	43rd
44 chautálí.	chutáhalwán,	44th
45 paintálí, pautálí.	paintáhalwán,	45th
46 chhitálí, chhatalí.	chhitáhalwán,	46th
47 saintálí, santálí.	saintáhalwán,	47th
48 a*th*tálí.	a*th*táhalwán,	48th
49 unanjá, unwaujá.	unanjhwán,	49th
50 panjáh.	panjáhwán,	50th
51 ikwanjá.	ikwanjhwán,	51st
52 bawanjá.	bawanjhwán,	52nd
53 tiwanjá, tirwanjá.	tiwanjhwán,	53rd
54 chuhanjá, chuuranjá.	churaujhwán,	54th
55 pachwanjá.	pachwanjhwán,	55th
56 chhiwanjá, chhipanjá.	chhiwanjhwán, chhipanjhwán,	56th
57 satwanjá.	satwaujhwán,	57th

Cardinals.		Ordinals.	
58 a*th*wanjá.		a*th*wanjhwán,	58th
59 unáhat.		unúha*t*wán,	59th
60 sa*tth*.		sa*tth*wán,	60th
61 ikáha*t*.		ikáha*t*wán,	61st
62 báha*t*.		báha*t*wán,	62nd
63 treba*t*, *t*eha*t*.		treha*t*wán,	63rd
64 chauha*t*.		chauha*t*wán,	64th
65 painha*t*.		painha*t*wán,	65th
66 chhiáhá*t*.		chhiáha*t*wán,	66th
67 satáhat.		satáhatwán,	67th
68 a*th*áhat.		a*th*áha*t*wán,	68th
69 u*n*hattar.		unhattarwán,	69th
70 sattar.		sattarwán,	70th
71 ikhattar, akhattar.		ikhattarwán,	71st
72 bahattar.		bahattarwán,	72nd
73 tihattar.		tihattarwán,	73rd
74 chuhattar, chauhattar.		chuhattarwán,	74th
75 panjhattar.		panjhattarwán,	75th
76 chhihattar.		chhihattarwán,	76th
77 satattar.		sutattarwán,	77th
78 a*th*attar.		a*th*attarwán,	78th
79 unásí.		unásíwán,	79th
80 assí.		assíhwán,	80th
81 ikásí.		ikáhásíwán, ikásíwán,	81st
82 biásí.		biáhásíwán, biásíwan,	82nd
83 tírásí, tíásí.		tirásíwán,	83rd
84 chnrásí, chaurásí.		churúsíwán,	84th
85 pachásí.		pachásíwán,	85th
86 chhiásí.		chhiásíwán,	86th
87 satásí.		satásíwán,	87th
88 a*th*ásí.		a*th*ásíwán,	88th
89 unáuwen.		unáhauwán,	89th
90 nuwwe, nabbe.		nabhbhán, nabhbhwán,	90th
91 kánwen, ikánmen.		ikáhanwán,	91st
92 bánwen, bánmen.		báhanwán,	92nd
93 tiránwen, tiránmen.		tiránwán, tiránhwán, triánhwán,	93rd
94 churánwen, churánmen.		chnráhanwán, churáuhwán,	94th
95 pacháuwen, pacháumen.		pacháhanwán, pachánhwán,	95th
96 chhiánwen, chhiánme.		chiáhanwán, chhiánhwán,	96th
97 satánwen, satánmen.		satáhanwán, satánhwán,	97th
98 a*th*ánwen, a*th*ánmen.		a*th*áhanwán, a*th*ánhwán,	98th
99 niraunwen, niraunmen.		nirannwán,	99th
100 sai, saikrá, sau.		sa-iá, saiá, sauwán,	100th

N.B.—In the ordinals, the terminal "wáu" is liable to be changed into "mán."

126. The aggregate numbers are :—

1 káu or kaun, 1½ dudhá, 2 dúní, 2½ dháiá, 3 tiáun or tiáún, 3½ úta, úntá, or úthá, 4 chauká, 4½ dhaunchá, dhaunchá, 5 pánjá, 6 chhakká, 7 sátá, 8 á*th*á, 9 náián, 10 dáhá, daháká, dahákká, 20 korí, bihrá, wíhá, 50 panjáh, 100 sai, saikrá, sau, 1,000 hajár, sah sar, sahansar, 1,00,000 lakkh, 10,000,000 karor, 1,000,000,000 arab, 100,000,000,000 kharab, 10,000.000,000,000 níl, 1,000,000,000,000,000 padam, 100,000,000,000,000,000 dhajam. 10,000,000,000,000,000,000 sankh.

127. The following words denote proportions :
Dudhí 1½ to 1 ; panj duwanji 2 to 3 ; panjotrí or pachotrí 5 to 100; dasotrí 10 to 100 ; adhdharí 1 to 1.

128. The fractional numbers are :—

¼ addh páu ; ⅓ páu, chuthái, ½ tihái, ¾ dúdh páu, ½ addh, addhú, ⅔ do tihái, ¾ paun, tinn páu, 1¼ sawá, sawái, sawáiá, 1½ dudh, dedh, deudhá, 1¾ paune do, 2¼ sawá do, 2½ dhái, 2¾ páune tín, 3¼ sawá tinn, 3½ sádho tinn, 3¾ paune chár, 4¼ sawá chár, 4½ sádho chár, &c.

129. The following words, expressing aggregate numbers, have special applications :—

Jor or *jorú, a pair* ; *takká, two pice* ; *gandá, four cowries, four pice* or *four rupees;* *dháiá* or *dháyá, two and a half seers* ; *paser,* or *battí, five seers* ; *dharí, ten seers* ; *dhauun, twenty seers* ; *man, forty seers* ; *mání* 12 *mans* ; *nokará, nine pieces of cloth.*

130. Words denoting "fold" are :—

Dúná, dúní, *two fold* ; tiuná, tiguná., *three fold;* chauná, chauguná *four fold*; pachauná, panjauná, *five fold*; chhiauná chhiguná *six fold*; satauná, satguná, *seven fold*; athauná, athguná, *eight fold* ; nauná, nauguná, *nine fold* ; dasaunú, dasguná *ten fold.*

131. *One and three quarter fold* is expressed paundúne ; *two and a half fold,* dhaguná, dháguná ; *two and three quarter fold,* paune tiúne, &c.

132. Single, double, &c., are expressed as follows :—

Single, ikahrá, or kahirá ; *double,* dohará or doharas ; *triple* tiharíá or tiharas ; *quadruple* chaudará, cha-uhará, cha-uharas ; *quintuple,* panjauhará or paja-uharas; *sextuple,* chhcaurá ; *septuple,* &c., sataurá, &c.

133. Adverbs of time are :—

To-day ajj ; *yesterday or to-morrow* kall ; *to-morrow,* bhalak, bhalke ; *day before yesterday, day after to-morrow,* parason ; *fourth day (inclusive) before or after,* chauth ; *fifth day (inclusive) before or after;* panjauth ; *sixth day (inclusive) before or after* chhiauth ; *seventh day (inclusive) before or after,* satauth ; *eighth day (inclusive) before or after,* athauth.

134. The days of the week are :—

Sunday áitwár ; *Monday,* somwár or pír ; *Tuesday,* mangal ; *Wednesday,* budh ; *Thursday,* bír, wír, jumerát ; *Friday,* sukkar, jumá ; *Saturday* bár, saníchhar, haftá.

135. The months are:—

Chet	from middle of	March to middle of	April.
Baisákh	,,	April ,,	May.
Jeth	,,	May ,,	June.
Hár, Hárh	,,	June ,,	July.
Sáun	,,	July ,,	August.
Bhádon, Bhádron	,,	August ,,	September.
Assu	,,	September ,,	October.
Kattak	,,	October ,,	November.
Maghghar	,,	November ,,	December.
Poh	,,	December ,,	January.
Mágh	,,	January ,,	February.
Phaggan	,,	February ,,	March.

136. The civil year begins with Chet; the astronomical, with Baisákh.

137. Each lunar month is divided into two parts of fifteen days each; the first, from new to full moon, is called sudí, or *the light half*, and the second, from full moon to new, badí, or *the dark half*. The dates, "tith, or thith," are as follows:—

1st ekam.
2nd dúj.
3rd tij.
4th chanth.
5th panchmí.
6th chhuth chath, khastí.
7th satain, satmí.
8th athain, athmí, astmí, athon.
9th nanmí, na-umí.
10th dasmí.
11th ikádsí, kádsí.
12th duádsí.
13th tirádsí.
14th chaude.
15th (sudí) punniá, puranmásí.
15th (badí) maus, amassiá.

138. The principal points of the compass are:—

N. utar.
S. dakkhan.
E. párab.
W. pachchham.
N. E. isan kaun.
S. E. agan kaun.
S. W. nairit kaun.
N. W. baib kaun.

SYNTAX.

Nouns and Personal Pronouns.

139. Two or more nouns coming together, and meaning the same thing, have a common government, e.g., Ih tá sáde piu dharam singh dá mál hai, *This is the property of our father, Dharm Singh.*

Nominative.

140. The subject of a verb, except with the past tenses of active verbs, is required to be in the Nominative, e.g., Ghorá achchhá tarán nál chaldá hai, *The horse goes well.*

Instrumental.

141. The instrumental case is used to express the subject of any of the past tenses of active verbs, except kúná *to say*; bolná *to speak*, liáuná *to bring*, and all verbs compounded with chukkná *to finish.*

142. In some parts, the sign "nai" is commonly omitted.

Genitive.

143. The genitive case is construed with several parts of speech :—

(i.) With nouns, as Sarkár dá mál, *The property of the state;*

(ii.) With substantive participles, used as nouns, as Bálakan dá bharáunwálá, *The teacher of the boys;*

(iii.) With adjectives, as Is kamm de laik, *Fit for this business,*

(iv.) With gerunds, as Uh phal de kháhadián rogí hogiá, *He became ill by eating fruit;*

(v.) With verbs in the infinitive mood, as Uh mere áun te akk giá, *He was offended at my coming;*

(VI.) With prepositions (*see* 120), as Guáchí hoí pothí mere bharáw de kaul haí, *The lost book is with my brother;*

(VII.) With a participle, as Uh mere áunde hí margiá, *He died at the moment of my coming.*

144. The noun, which governs the genitive, is sometimes omitted, as Rája de (ghar) ikk putt janmiá, *A son was born to the king*; usdí (gall) sun, *hear him*; ghar diân (lokán de) wánjhú, *like the people of the house.*

145. The preposition is not always expressed, as Main usí jágá rahángá, *I will stay in this very place.*

146. The sign of the genitive is very often omitted, as Is laí for Is dá la-i, *on this account;* ikk Nának pádrí áiá, *a priest of Nának came.*

147. The genitive is usually, though not always, placed before the noun that governs it.

148. The genitive with táin is sometimes substituted for the dative or accusative, as Un mere táin káchú dittá, *He gave me a knife;* uh mere táin ápne nál le giá, *he took me with him.*

Dative.

149. The dative preposition nún is often omitted, as Uh ghar giá, *He went home.*

Accusative.

150. The accusative is used after an active verb, as Uh manukkh ápne ghore nún márdá hai, *the man is beating his horse.*

151. The nominative form of the noun is frequently used for the accusative, especially after verbs denoting giving, asking, or receiving, as Uh pothí mai nún dio, *Give me that book;* un ikk sawwál mai nún puchhiá, *he asked me one question.*

Ablative.

152. Instead of taking a preposition, the ablative sometimes adds *i* or *e* to the final syllable, e.g., Merí jabání, for Merí jabán te, *By my tongue*; phajre, *in the morning* (see also 30).

153. Nouns of time and place are often repeated, and used in the ablative without a preposition, to express the idea of continued succession; as Uh gharí gharí áiá, *He came continually*; nagar de phúk jándí khabar ghar ghar khind rahí sí, *the news of the burning of the city spread from house to house*; but they are more properly adverbs.

Vocative.

154. The vocative is construed with an interjection, either expressed or understood, as He mundiá, *O boy!* marukkhá *O man!*

Adjectives, adjective pronouns, and participles.

155. Such must agree in gender, number, and case with the nouns, pronouns or infinitives, which they qualify, e.g., Uh oprián gaián nún rakkhdá sá, *He was keeping other people's cows*; asín ihián jihián gallán nahin suniún sián, *we had not heard such words as these*; ih kurí wadí hassanwálí haí, *this girl is a great laugher*.

156. When used to qualify several nouns of different genders, connected with each other by a conjunction, they must either agree in gender and number with the nearest, or be put in the masculine, generally the masculine plural, in reference to them all.

Verbs.

157. A Verb must agree in gender, number, and person, with its subject, whenever that subject is in the nominative case, e.g., Jimídár lok bhaun nún báhan de se, *The farmers were ploughing the ground*; sárián trimatán milke kamm karangián, *all the women united will do the work*.

158. When a verb has two or more nominatives in the singular number, united by a conjunction, it may be made plural, so as to agree with all of them; but if they are of different genders, the verb must be in the masculine form, e.g., Pitá ar dhí katthe jámde se, *The father and daughter were going together.*

159. If all the nominatives are plural, or even the one adjacent to the verb, their persons being the same, the verb refers directly to the last only, and agrees with it in gender, and number, e.g., Pitá ar uh dián dhián katthián jándían sián, *The father and his daughters were going together.*

160. When the nominatives are of different persons, the verb conforms to the first, rather than to the second, and to the

second rather than to the third, *e.g.*, Main ar tún jáwángé, *I and you will go*, tún ar tere bháí jáoge, *you and your brothers will go*; but the third person, if plural, and nearest the verb, may prevail over both the other persons, if singular, *e.g.*, Main ar tún ar tere bháí kat́t́he jánge, *I, and you, and your brothers, will go together.*

161. An active verb, in the past tenses, when the instrumental is used, agrees with its object, if used in the nominative form of the accusative, in gender and number, *e.g.*, Ráj nai uchchí kandh usárí, *The mason built a high wall*; but if the object is in the accusative form, the verb must be in the third person, masculine, singular, *e.g.*, Ráj nai uchhí kandh nún usáríá, *The mason built a high wall.*

162. When there is more than one object in the nominative form, the verb should agree in gender and number with the nearest.

Infinitive and gerund.

163. Verbs in the infinitive, and gerunds, are subject to the same general rules as nouns.

164. The infinitive of an active verb, which has a noun in the nominative form for its object, must agree with that noun in gender and number, *e.g.*, Kachíchíán láiníán hon gián, *There will be gnashing of teeth.*

165. Gerunds also sometimes conform their gender to that of the nouns they govern, *e.g.*, Merá bharáu merí jamín atte haweli páí cháhandá hai, *My brother wishes to build a house on my ground*; but not always, *e.g.*, Asín pothíán parhíá karde hán, *We are in the habit of reading books.*

INDEX TO GRAMMAR.

A

Ablative case, 14, 30.
  ,,   ,, prepositions governing, 122.
  ,,   ,, rules regarding, 152, 153.
Accusative case, 13.
  ,,   ,, rules regarding, 150, 151.
Adjective pronouns, agreement of, 155, 156.
Adjectives, agreement of, 155, 156.
  ,, declension of, 38, 39, 40.
  ,, formation of, 36, 37.
Adverbs, 113.
  ,, of time, 133.
Aggregate numbers, 126, 129.
Alphabet, Gurmukhi, 1.
Áp, pronoun, used respectfully, 64.
Astronomical year commences, 136.
Auxiliaries used in forming tenses, 92.
  ,, hán, &c., other forms of, also used, 99.

B

Bindí, rules regarding position of, in declension of nouns, 27.

C

Cardinal numbers, 125
Case inflexions, 8.
Cases, how many, 9.
  ,, distinction of, 10.
Casual verbs, how formed, 101.
Changes allowed in moods and tenses, 102–106.
Civil year commences, 136.
Comparison, degrees of, 41.
Compass, principal points of, 138.
Compound nouns, &c., gender of, 32.
  ,, verbs, how formed, 112.
Conjunctions, 114, 115.
Consonants, compound, 4.

D

Dative case, 13.
  ,, prepositions governing, 121.
  ,, rules regarding, 149.
Days of week, 134.
Declensions how many, 16.
  ,, first, how distinguished, 17.
  ,, ,, first variation, 18.

D.—concld.

Declensions second variation, 19.
  ,, second, how distinguished, 20.
  ,, first variation, 21.
  ,, second ,, 22.
  ,, third, how distinguished, 23.
  ,, ,, first variation, 24.
  ,, ,, second ,, 25.
  ,, ,, third ,, 26.
Derivatives, how formed, 33.

F

Feminines ending in í, meaning of, 35.
  ,, how formed from masculines, 34.
Figures, names of, 123, 124.
  ,, numerical, 5.
"Fold," words denoting, 130, 131.
Foreign nouns, declension of, 29.
Fractional numbers, 128.
Future potential, how formed, 86, 87.

G

Genders, 9.
  ,, inflexion of, 8.
  ,, rules for determining, 31.
Genitive case, prepositions governing, 120.
Genitive case, rules regarding, 12, 143–147.
Genitive case, substituted for dative or accusative, 148.
Gerunds, 184.
  ,, formation of, 91.

H

Honá substituted for jáná in passive, 109.

I

Indeclinable nouns, 28.
Infinitive, how formed, 90.
Instrumental case, rules regarding, 11, 141, 142, 161, 162.
Instrumental case with infinitive, expresses certainty, &c., 108.
Irregular verbs, table of, 100.

xlviii INDEX TO GRAMMAR.

K

Koí, declension of, 48.

L

Letters, distinction of, 6.
Lunar months, divisions and dates of, 137.

M

Marks used in writing, 3.
Months, names of, 135.
Moods of verbs, 82.

N

Neuter verbs in passive, 110.
Nominative case, rules regarding, 110.
Nouns, syntax of, 139.
Numbers, 9.
,, inflexions of, 8.
Numerals, declension of, 40.

O

Ordinal numbers, 125.

P

Participles, agreement of, with nouns, &c., 155, 156.
Participles, indefinite how formed, 88.
,, of verbs, 84.
,, past how formed, 86, 87.
,, present, how formed, 86, 87.
,, substantive, how formed, 89.
Parts of speech, 7.
Peculiarities in parts of Panjáb, 111.
Prepositions, 116, 118, 119.
,, used together, 117.
,, governing ablative, 122.
,, ,, dative, 121.
,, ,, genitive, 120.
Pronouns, ablative of personal, I and thou, 75.
Pronouns, compound, 67.
,, ,, declension of, 68—71.
Pronouns, contractions in, 79.
,, correlative, 57.
,, ,, declension of, 58.
,, definite, 45.

P—concld.

Pronouns definite declension of, 46.
,, elision in, 78.
,, government of, in syntax, 139.
,, how made emphatic, 72, 73, 77.
,, indefinite 47.
,, ,, declension of, 49—52.
Pronouns, instrumental case, rules regarding, 74.
Pronouns, interrogative, 59.
,, ,, declension of 60 62.
Pronouns, kinds of, 42.
,, oblique cases of, change in, 76.
,, reflective, 63, 64.
,, ,, declension of, 65,66.
,, relative, 53.
,, ,, declension, 54—56.
,, simple adjective, 44.
,, ,, personal, 43.
Proportion, words denoting, 127.

R

Root of verbs, 85.

S

Single, double, &c., how expressed, 132.

T

Tenses of verbs, 83.
,, ,, how formed, 85.
Tippí, rules regarding, in declension of nouns, 27.

V

Verb gballna (active of) declined, 96.
,, (passive of) ,, 97.
hán ,, 93.
honá ,, 94.
jáná ,, 95.
márná (passive of) ,, 98.
Verbs, kinds of, 80.
,, rules regarding syntax of, 157—165.
Vocative case, 15, 154.
Voices of verbs, 81.
Vowels, 2.

GLOSSARY

OF

TECHNICAL TERMS AND WORDS.

Gurumukhí.   English.

A

Á	The sound with which singers begin their music.
ABDHÚT	... A kind of Hindú devotee who worships Shiv, neglects the ceremonies of religion, and goes naked, having the body besmeared with ashes.
ADDIÁU	... Fees or presents, given to priests, musicians, &c.
ADES	... A salutation of Jogís.
ADHARWANJÁ	... Tying one end of a sheet round the naked waist, and throwing the other end over he shoulder, a common preliminary to cooking among Hindú women.
ADHIÁRÁ	An arrangement, by which the profits of cultivation or cattle-rearing are devoted equally between the pe son who furnishes the land or stock and the labour.
AGAST	... A thing formed of paper, somewhat like an umbrella, and turned constantly over the head of a bridegroom, as part of the marriage ceremony.
AKÁSBIRT	... Living on what Providence may send from day to day.
AKÁSDÍP	... A lamp, which Hindús hang aloft on a bamboo, in the month Kattak; also a beacon.
AKÁSPAUN	... Inhaling and holding the breath, a Jogí ceremony.
AKHÁRÁ	A place for wrestling or fencing or other sports.
AKK	... A plant, containing a milky juice, which grows abundantly in sandy jungles.
ÁLÁP	... Tuning the voice for singing, taking the pitch.
ALLÍ	... A gold or silver ornament, worn on the forehead, commonly consisting of several pieces.
AMBÁRÍ	... A litter or seat, with a canopy, to ride in placed on an elephant or camel.

GLOSSARY OF TECHNICAL TERMS.

A—*continued.*

AMBCHÚR	Parings of the mango, dried in the sun.
AMBÍR	The coloured powder, thrown by Hindús on each other during the Holí.
AMRAT	The food of the gods, ambrosia, nectar, immortality.
ANWLÁ	The name of an acid fruit, which is used for medicinal, dyeing, and other purposes.
ARGJÁ	The name of a perfume of a yellow colour and composed of several scented ingredients.
ÁRSÍ	A gold or silver ring, with a mirror set in it, worn on the thumb.
ÁRTÍ	A ceremony, performed in adoration of the gods, by moving burning lamps circularly round the head of the image, or before it, accompanied with boisterous music and ringing of bells.
ASÁURÍ	A kind of song or musical mode.
AST	The ashes of the dead, the bones, &c., which remain unconsumed by the fire of a funeral pile.
ASTAK	A song in honour of a tutelary saint or deity.
AUGHAR	A kind of Hindú fakír, whose habits are very filthy, and who wears brass rings in his ears.
AUNSÍ	A kind of figure drawn on the ground, in the form of the head of a rake, by which a superstitious ceremony is performed, by way of prognosticating the visits of friends.
AUTÁR	Birth, incarnation.

B

BÁBAL	A father, a term used by daughters, and especially in the songs, which are sung at weddings.
BABÁN	A bier for an aged person, prepared with special expense, as a mark of respect.
BABRÁNÁ	The long, loose, dishevelled hair of a fakír.
BÁBRÍÁN	Hair too short to be tied into a knot.
BÁCH	An assessment, or exaction of labour and produce, made by Government, in addition to the regular taxes.
BÁCHBIGÁR	Exaction of labour without compensation.
BADÁNÁ	The name of a sweetmeat, resembling the mulberry, made of gram, clarified butter and sugar.
BADDH	The stubble of wheat, &c., still standing in the field.

GLOSSARY OF TECHNICAL TERMS. li

B—continued.

BÁDLÁ ...	... A certificate, given to a Government servant, stating the terms of service, &c.
BÁGHÍ PÁUNÍ ...	To flap the arms against the sides, at the same time making a loud tremulous sound with the voice, done by beggars to excite in the spectators an almsgiving humour.
BÁGPHARÁÍ	... That which is given to a groom by the buyer, after a horse is sold.
BÁGPHARÁÍ	... That which is given to the sister of a bridegroom when she leaves him, after having led or attended him a short distance on the wedding journey.
BÁH	... Flowing in of sand and water from the bottom of a well.
BAHÍ	... A ridged cylinder of gold or silver, worn on the arm by women as an ornament.
BAHIK	... A common, or open ground, near a village where cattle assemble.
BAHINDÁ	... The stripping and robbing by native women of any one whom they may meet on the 1st of Magh.
BÁHIRÁ ...	... Eating stale bread and drinking water drawn the previous day, practised as a religious rite by Hindús, on the Tuesdays of the month Chet, in worship of the goddess of small-pox.
BAHORÁ ...	... Gifts to the bridegroom's mother, at a wedding, by the bride's father.
BAHORE DÁ TEUR ...	... The petticoat, sheet and breast piece, given to a bridegroom's mother, at a wedding, by the bride's father.
BAHUTTÁ	... An ornament worn on the upper part of the arm.
BAINCHHAR ...	... A man remarkable for corpulence and strength, but not for wits.
BÁISÍ ...	... A kingdom of twenty-two states, spoken of a hill sovereignty.
BAITHAK ...	A place where people meet to sit and converse.
BAJNÍ ...	... A percentage of the produce of a field set apart for the benefit of the poorer classes, as barbers, blacksmiths, bards, &c.
BAKÁIN ...	... The name of a tree, having a thick umbrella-shaped top.
BAKHÚKÁ	... A place prepared by Hindús to the memory and for the worship, of ancestors, consisting of a pit, and a pillar formed of the earth taken out of the pit; there are generally three or four together.
BAKHALÍÁN ...	... Wheat, gram, maize, &c., boiled whole and eaten with condiments, such as salt pepper, oil, &c.

B—continued.

BALÁJ	That which is given to carpenters and other artisans, also to Bráhmans, on the first or second days after the Diwálí.
BALBAKKARÁ	A goat that has been offered to a deity.
BALBALJÁNÁ	To go round and round a person, in token of devotion to his interests.
BALBHAKKU	One who eats what has been offered to a deity, it being supposed that he does so at his peril.
BÁLBHOG	An offering to Krishna, presented early in the morning.
BALGUN	The wall, hedge, or fence, surrounding a piece of ground.
BALL	The leather thong used in driving a suhága or drag over ploughed ground.
BAM	A medium musical mode.
BAM	A mumbling sound, made by the worshippers of Shiv, and supposed to be pleasing to him as "Bam, Mahádew, bam, bam."
BÁN	A well, or reservoir, with steps leading down to the water.
BANBAJÍR	A person who has charge of a forest district.
BAND	A mixed feed given to cows and buffaloes to increase their milk.
BÁNDH	Embargo laid on an article.
BÁNDHÁ	An article set apart as a pledge for the payment of a sum of money.
BÁNDHÁ	Property devoted to religious or charitable purposes, to procure the recovery of a person from sickness.
BÁNDHÁ	Any thing forbidden to be sold publicly.
BANDHÁ	A string put about the neck in connection with a vow.
BANDHEJ	A sum, given by stipulation to certain fakírs at weddings, to prevent them from giving trouble.
BANDÍ	The name of an ornament, worn by women on the forehead.
BANDNÁ	The Hindú ceremony of swinging a young child over a heap of mud on the 12th of the first pakkh of Bhádon.
BANG	An ornament, worn on the wrists, made of glass, &c.
BÁNGAR	Land, watered neither from well nor river, but dependent on the rain.
BANGNÁ	An ornament, worn by women on the forehead.
BANGRÍ	A kind of bracelet worn by women on the wrist.
BÁNÍ	The devotional service of the Sikhs.

B—continued.

BÁNK	An ankle ornament, worn by women, usually made of silver.
BÁNK	A wooden dagger used in fencing.
BÁNK	A large oil or ghí vessel made of skin.
BÁNKPATÁ	Single-stick, dagger-exercise.
BANNÁ CHANNÁ	Earth thrown up into a ridge to form a boundary.
BÁNSTOR	The name of a caste who work in bamboos.
BÁNYÁN	A Hindú shopkeeper.
BÁR	A dirge sung for those slain in battle.
BÁRÁ	A leather well-bucket.
BÁRÁ	A sheep fold or enclosure.
BÁRÁ	Ground on which melons, etc., are planted.
BARÁGÍ	A class of fakírs, who are under a vow to abstain from flesh and wine.
BARAN	A caste, one of the four primary Hindú castes.
BARAR	The name of a low caste, much given to begging.
BARÁ SÚHÍ	The clothing, &c., given to a bride by the bridegroom's father on the day of the wedding.
BARÁT	A bridegroom's party at a wedding.
BARÁTH	The material manifestation of the Deity, viz., the universe viewed as constituting his bodily parts.
BARÍÁN	Dál soaked, ground, and made up into balls with condiments, and dried in the sun.
BÁRNÁ	To devote an article, usually money, by passing it round the head of a friend in token of attachment and devotion to him, after which it is given away to the poor.
BARNÁ	A present of clothing, jewels, etc., sent to a bride before marriage, by the family of the bridegroom.
BARNÍ	Performing religious rites for a family; the office of a household priest.
BÁSAKNÁG	The name of the fabled snake, which is said to be coiled round the earth, to keep it from bursting.
BASANT	The spring of the year (from middle of March to middle of May) according to the Shástras, but among the common people, from middle of February to middle of April.
BASANT-PANCHMÍN	The fifth day of Magh, distinguished among the Sikhs as the anniversary of Gurú Govind Singh's decease.
BATÁÍ	The share of produce which belongs to Government.

B—continued.

BATARNÍ	The river, over which Hindús suppose the souls of the departed pass, in entering the invisible world; also a cow offered to Bráhmans, when one is near dying, with a view to his safe passage over.
BATÁSÁ	... A sweetmeat.
BATEHRÍ	... Food sent by the family of a bride, of the higher class of Hindús to the lodgings of the groom and his family, on the first day of the wedding ceremonies, it being contrary to rule to receive them under the bridal roof on the first day.
BATLOH	... A large brass vessel, containing one or two maunds, in which Hindús cook their food when large quantities are required.
BATNÁ	... A mixture of meal, oil, and some fragrant material, which is used as a substitute for soap, having the property of making the skin soft and delicate.
BATT	... A boundary line between fields.
BÁTTÍ	... Extra allowance of food to sepoys.
BÁULÍ	... A well, in which there are steps leading down to the water.
BÁURYÁ	... A low caste, who inhabit the jungles, and live partly by the game they catch, and partly by thieving.
BED	... A wooden canopy or pavilion, underneath which Hindú marriages are performed.
BEDÁNT	... The name of a Hindú system of philosophy.
BEDÍ	... A division of the Khattrí caste, to which Gurú Nának belonged.
BEGÁRÍ	... One who works under compulsion, whether paid or not.
BEHÍ	... The food placed before a wedding party at the bride's house.
BEÍN	... An irregular stream with a clay bottom, having the appearance of a canal, of which there are two in the Jalandhar Doáb.
BEL	... Money given to dancing girls and others at a wedding.
BELNÁ	... The stick, with which the hand of a bridegroom is struck, as a part of the marriage ceremony.
BER	... A coarse rope made of grass, straw, etc.
BET	... The low land bordering on a river.
BHÁBRÁ	... A caste of the Jainí persuasion, chiefly employed in traffic.
BHABÚTIÁ	... A fakír who rubs himself with ashes.
BHADDAN	... The first shaving of a child's hair.
BHÁÍ	... An honorary title amongst Sikhs.

GLOSSARY OF TECHNICAL TERMS.

B—*continued.*

BHÁJÍ	A present of fruits, sweetmeats, etc., sent by the parents of a bride and bridegroom to their friends, when inviting them to the wedding.
BHAJWÁN	Salmon-coloured, reddish-yellow, coloured with gerú (fakír's clothes).
BHÁN	The mark made through a green field by turning down the stalks on both sides, in dividing it between two parties.
BHAND	One who sings or recites verses in abuse of another, and with a view to injure his character.
BHANDÁR	A fakír's cooking-place.
BHARBHARÍ	A sudden rise in the price of grain, etc.
BHARO	A watering-place for travellers, etc., being furnished with vessels ready filled.
BHARWÁÍ	Wages given to a teacher.
BHATHIÁRÁ	One who prepares victuals for travellers at an inn.
BHÁTÍ	Land bestowed on a Bráhman or fakír by a ruler, as an act of religious almsgiving.
BHÁTRÁ	A low caste of Bráhmans, that subsist by begging.
BHATT	A division of the Bráhman caste, generally employed in singing the praises of persons in the hope of remuneration.
BHATTÁ	Food taken to farmers and their workmen in the field.
BHATTÍ	Food prepared for the family of a deceased person by a relative or friend.
BHATTÍ	Grain given by a zamíndár to a blacksmith, on having a new hoe or ploughshare made.
BHÁULÍ	Paying a share of grain, etc., as rent or revenue, the cutting and gathering being done under the inspection of a servant of the government or landlord.
BHA-UNÍ	The wheel on which the rope of a well-bucket turns.
BHAUR	The sound made with the beating of shoes, "as the shoes went bhaur, bhaur," spoken of one cast in a suit.
BHET	A sacrifice, offering, or song of praise, in honour of a goddess.
BHITTÁ	The white earth, which, when ground and mixed with water, is used by boys in learning to write.
BHOJKÍ	A Bráhman, who officiates and receives the offerings at certain shrines.
BHONDÁN	Money given to the presiding Bráhmans at the close of a wedding.

B—continued.

BHUÁRÁ	Prevalence of an epidemic or other sickness in a particular locality.
BHUÁRÁ	A place, enclosed with a thorn hedge, outside of a village, where cattle are kept, each zamíndár having his own.
BIÁHNÚ	A suit of clothes, given to the bride by the bridegroom's father, two days after marriage.
BIÁR	A vegetable or fruit left for seed.
BICHHÚÁ	A ring, worn by women on the toes, the upper side of which is broad.
BICHKANUÁ	An ornament worn on the central part of the ear.
BIDÁIGÍ	A present given to a person on dismissing him.
BIDDH	The timbers, set obliquely at the edge of a well, to support the wheel on which the rope runs.
BÍJAK	Invoice, or price ticket.
BÍN	A name applied to two kinds of musical instruments, the one a stringed, the other, a wind, instrument.
BIND	A coarse rope of grass or withs, coiled within a kachchá well, as a support to keep the sides from falling in.
BINDÍ	The name of an ornament worn by women on the forehead.
BINNÚ	A pad or mat placed on the head to support a burden.
BÍR	Meadow or woodland reserved for the Government.
BÍR	A boundary line between fields.
BIRÁGÍ	A religious ascetic, who abandons terrestial objects, thoughts, passions, etc.
BISARJAN	A mantar, repeated by Bráhmans, etc., at the close of pújá for the purpose of giving the God his dismission.
BODDÍ	The small tuft of hair that a Hindú retains on the crown of his head.
BOHUL	A heap of grain on a threshing floor, winnowed and ready for storing away.
BOK	A he-goat, especially one kept for breeding purposes.
BOKKÁ	A leather-bucket used in drawing water from a well.
BOR	A kind of silver or gold ornament, worn on the feet, loins, arms, &c., made so as to tinkle.
BRÁÍ	Grain given to carpenters, etc., at sowing time.
BUDHKÁ	A boy's pigment-stand, used by school boys in writing on their wooden tablets.

B—continued.

BUHUNÍ	... The first sale in the morning, for which the cash is paid down.
BUNJÁHÍ	... A division of the Khattrí caste, comprising fifty-two gots, the members of which intermarry among themselves, but remain separate from other Khattrís.
BURDO BURDÍ	.. Fighting cocks, &c., on the condition that the owner of the winner takes both.
BYÁNÁ	A pledge or earnest money, a rupee generally being placed as a deposit, after a bargain is made, and before the full price is paid up, to prevent either party retracting.

C

CHABÚTARÁ	... An elevated place to sit on, made of bricks or earth.
CHÁDARÁ	... The ceremony, among Sikhs, of marrying a widow to a brother, or other relative, of the deceased husband, which consists in having a single sheet spread over the contracting parties by the officiating Granthí.
CHAKAR	... A sharp-edged iron, or steel, discus, carried on the head by Akális, and used as a weapon.
CHAKK	... A frame on which the wall of a well is built.
CHANDÁL	.. A low mean person, one of low caste, an outcast.
CHANDAÚÁ	A coloured awning, stretched with the Granth over a bride or bridegroom, in the ceremony of Máyán at weddings.
CHAUDHARÍ	... The headman of a village or of a trade.
CHARH	... A trench dug in the ground and used as a fireplace, when large dinners are to be cooked, and several pots are to be set on at one time.
CHÁT	... A mess for cattle, made of átá, salt and water.
CHATTH	... The ceremony of feeding Bráhmans and others on special occasions, as on the consecration of a well or tank to expiate the guilt supposed to have been acquired by killing insects in digging it.
CHÁU	... The colter of a plough.
CHAU BACHCHÁ	... A reservoir of masonry, usually adjacent to a well.
CHAUKÁ	A place besmeared with a mixture of cow-dung and mud where Hindús eat.
CHAUNK	... A square place prepared on the ground, over which átá is spread at weddings, dedications, &c.; on the átá, marks are made by a Bráhman or barber to obtain favourable omens from the planets, and these marks are worshipped by the bride and bridegroom, or other parties concerned.

C—continued.

CHAUNKÍ BHARNÍ	... To sleep on the ground, instead of on a bed, from religious motives; to fulfil a pilgrimage without sleeping on a bedstead, *i.e.*, when a company of pilgrims stop at a place on their way, those, who intend joining them there from the surrounding villages, come in, and with them many of their friends, who keep watch through the night, and return home the next morning.
CHAUNPKALÍ ...	... A kind of necklace worn by women.
CHAUNTRÁ ...	... See Chabútará.
CHAUPAR ...	... A game played with long oblong dice.
CHET	... The name of the first month in the civil year.
CHHÁBBÁ ...	... A small basket used for keeping bread in.
CHHAKK ...	... Presents given to a bride by her maternal grand-parents.
CHHATTÍ	... A piece of red silk sent to announce the death of a person to his relatives.
CHHEDNÍ	... A shoemaker's awl, but used in the Panjáb only to cut leather, not to bore holes, and its blade is always flat.
CHHÍMBÁ	... A washerman.
CHHÚCHHÍ	... The part of a gun-stock, in which the ramrod is inserted.
CHIKÁ	... A funeral pile, a bier.
CHIPPÍ	... An oval-shaped dish usually made of wood, used by fakirs.
CHITTHÁ	... A memorandum of money paid, or wages of servants.
CHOLÍ	... A short gown, worn by women, reaching only to the waist.
CHOTÍ	.. A large lock of hair on the top of the head.
CHUÁRÍ	... A bamboo, used for raising a load to be deposited on the back of a beast of burden.
CHUHARHTHÁ...	... A well with four Persian wheels.
CHÚHRÁ... ...	... The name of a very low caste, whose business is sweeping.
CHUKÁWÁ	... The rent of a village or district.
CHUKANTÍ	The sum agreed upon as the price of any thing.
CHUNGÍ	... Tax levied on merchants by weighmen, being a handful of whatever is weighed.
CHÚR	... A set of bracelets, extending from the wrist up the fore-arm.
CHÚRMÁ...	... A dish consisting of bread broken and mixed with ghí and sugar.
CHUTKÁ...	... A large handful, as much as can be taken up with the hand and fingers extended.
CHUTKÍ	... A small handful, as much as can be taken up with the thumb and fingers.

GLOSSARY OF TECHNICAL TERMS. lix

D

DACHCHNÁ	... A present to Bráhmans on solemn or sacrificial occasions.
DAHÁ	... A stick fastened to the neck of cattle, to keep them from running away.
DÁÍ	... The bride's attendant, who instructs her in the performance of the ceremonies.
DÁLÁ	The bridegroom's attendant, who instructs him in the performance of the ceremonies.
DAKAUT	... A caste of Bráhmans, who consider themselves able to bear the calamity of the jabhardán, and therefore do not hesitate to receive it.
DÁKHULÁ	... The entrance of a wedding party into a city or village.
DAMDAMA	... A monument raised in commemoration of great Gurús among the Sikhs.
DAMMÁNSÍHÍ ...	... A proportionate distribution of a bankrupt's property among his creditors.
DAND	... An ornament worn round the arm above the elbow.
DANDÁ ...	... A fakír whose head and feet are naked.
DANDAUT ...	... A Hindú salutation.
DÁNPATTAR	... A deed of conveyance for a gift.
DARAÍN ...	... An inflated buffalo-skin used as a buoy in ferrying a stream (common in the hills.)
DARBÁR ...	... The common appellation of the great Sikh temple at Anmritsar.
DARMADÁRÍ	... Adjustment of a dispute.
DARSANÍ ...	... A draft payable at sight to one bearing certain marks, which it describes.
DASAUNDH	A tithe or votive offering of one-tenth of the estimated value of a person or animal, given to a god.
DASOGIÁHRÍ	... A method of sharing, by which one takes ten, and the other eleven parts.
DASOTRÁ	... Ten per cent. of revenue given to the headman of the village.
DASTAK ...	Demurrage or fine imposed and renewed daily for delay in obeying orders.
DAUNDAUNKARNÁ ...	To publish by beat of drum.
DEHRÁ ..	... A sacred sepulchral monument or Gurú's seat.
DHÁB	An unwalled tank or pond.
DHÁHÁ	.. The high ground which has not been overflown by the current of a river.
DHAÍDENÍ	.. To sit before anyone, and obstinately refuse to leave, by way of extorting compliance with some demand.
DHANÁSARÍ	... The name of a musical mode, which is only performed after three in the afternoon.

GLOSSARY OF TECHNICAL TERMS.

D—*continued.*

DHARÁ	Something thrown into the opposite scale, to balance a vessel in which a liquid is to be weighed.
DHARÁÍ ...	... Hire for taking care of articles.
DHARAB ..	... A heap of grain, or quantity of other merchandise, collected to be weighed.
DHARMSÁLÁ	... An inn, where poor travellers are supplied gratuitously.
DHÍNGULÍ	... A well-bucket attached to a pole, which works on the lever principle.
DHOK	... An appointment for two litigants to meet at a certain place to have their cause adjudicated.
DHÚÁN ...	An ignited pile of chaff and rubbish, around which people warm themselves in cold weather.
DIBBH	... A species of spear grass used in several ceremonies.
DOÁBÁ ...	.. A country between two rivers.
DOHAR ...	... Ploughing a field both ways, length and cross.
DORÁ ...	... An ornament worn by the bride at weddings.
DONNÁ ...	... The country between two small streams.
DŬM ...	... The name of a caste of Muhammadan musicians and bards.
DŬN	... A tract of country lying between two mountain ridges.
DUNGWÁÍ	... Collecting grain, harvesting.

E

ENDWÍ	... A hoop-shaped mat or cushion, made of cord or cloth, and placed on the crown of the head by those who carry burdens, especially by those who carry vessels of water.

G

GAHÁ	.. Seizing and holding under restraint persons or property belonging to a debtor, in order to compel payment.
GAHÁÍ	Threshing or treading out corn with oxen.
GÁITRÍ	... The name of a mantar, a prayer repeated by Bráhmans with the rosary.
GANDÁ ...	... A string with knots, worn on the neck, &c., as a charm.
GANDHÍLÁ	... The name of a very low caste, a sort of gipsies.
GANGAUTÍ	... A kind of earth obtained from the Ganges and used for marking the forehead.
GARASNÁ	... To get one into trouble by pressing a claim which cannot easily be met.
GARIST ...	... The married state or condition of a secular (not a monk.)

G—continued.

GAUNÍMÁR	A caste of people whose women, wandering away from home, pretend to be widows, and having induced persons of wealth to marry them, watch their opportunity to seize and carry off valuable property.
GA-UR	The name of a musical mode, sung at midday.
GAUR	The name of a caste of Bráhmans that had their origin in the country of Gaur.
GA-URÍ	The name of a musical mode, sung towards evening.
GHEULÍ	A cow that gives rich milk.
GHUNGANÍ	Grain of any kind, boiled whole.
GIRDÁ	The circle of hair round the head, when the crown is shaven.
GIRÍ	A title of a class of Hindú fakírs.
GOKHRÚ	An ornament worn on the wrist, being a ring with a ridged back.
GOT KUNÁLÁ	The eating together of persons of the same family on the bringing home of a bride.
GRANTHÍ	One whose business it is to read and expound the Granth,—very few, however are able to do the latter.
GUHÁ	A dried cake of cow-dung.
GUHARÁ	A stack of dried cow-dung.
GUJJAR	A caste of people who sell milk.
GÚN	A hair-cloth, or hemp, sack used for loading asses, oxen, and mules.
GURBHÁÍ	A fellow-disciple of the same Gurú.
GURWÁR	The day on which one is initiated as a disciple.
GUTÁWÁ	A mess for cattle, made of cut straw, oil cake, meal, water, &c.
GUTT	A women's hair, plaited and hanging down the back.

H

HÁL	A state of ecstacy into which fakírs work themselves.
HÁR	A string of beads.
HÁR	A long succession of fields with luxuriant crops.
HARH	A mountain torrent.
HARHAT	A Persian wheel.
HARÍ	A portion of land-tax levied while the corn is standing, before it is ripe, practised by the Sikh government.
HÁRNÁ	To guess at the weight of a thing by lifting it.

GLOSSARY OF TECHNICAL TERMS.

H—*continued.*

HASLÍ	... A gold or silver collar worn by women and children as an ornament.
HATTÁL ...	... Shutting up all the shops in a market.
HÍLÁ WASÍLÁ ...	... One by whose aid employment is obtained.
HINDAKÍ	... The character and writing in which accounts are kept.
HOKÁ	... A public proclamation.
HUNDÁBHARÁ...	... Contract for transportation of goods, including the payment of duties, without extra expenses.
HÚN KÚN...	... The ups and downs of life.

I

INÁMÍ	... Land, &c, free from toll, &c.
INDRÍ	... An organ of sense, a name given to the different organs of action and perception; those of action being the hand, the foot, the voice, the organ of generation and the organ of excretion. Those of perception being the brain or mind, the eye, the ear, the nose, the tongue and the skin.
IST	... A favourite, or patron, deity.

J

JABHEDÁR	... A man of rank and spirit.
JAGG	... A great feast given to Bráhmans and the poor from religious motives.
JÁGÍR	... Land given by Government as a reward for service.
JAJMÁN ...	... A person, on whose custom Bráhmans, barbers, and others have a legal claim. The hereditary Bráhman or barber, &c., of a village must be paid his fees, whether he be employed, or another.
JAKHMÁNÁ	... Compensation to a soldier for a wound or the loss of a limb in battle.
JAKKH ...	... A very holy man and most devoted worshipper.
JÁMAN TÁHAD	... Bail or security.
JÁNAMPATRÍ ...	... A horoscope in which the birth of a child, year, lunar date and configuration of the planets at time of birth, are detailed.
JANEÚ	... A string worn round the neck by Bráhmans and Khattrís.
JANGAM...	... A class of Hindú fakírs, who wear matted hair, and ring a bell.
JANNY	... The company, which attends a bridegroom at a wedding.
JAP	... Silent repetition of the Name of God.

J—continued.

JÁP	A devotion which consists in silent repetition of the Name of God, and counting the beads on a rosary.
JAT	Matted hair as worn by fakírs.
JATT	A caste of farmers.
JHARÁL	An excavation by the side of a river, from which water is drawn up for irrigation.
JHARÍ	Long continued rain.
JHÍWAR	The name of a caste who catch fish and birds, and carry pálkís.
JHUSMUSÁ	The morning or evening twilight.
JÍUN BÚTÍ	A favourite source of gratification, a besetting sin.
JOG	Austere devotion and intense meditation, practised by Jogís.
JUHÁR	A Hindú salutation.
JÚN	One of the eighty-four lakhs of births or transmigrations, to which bad men are subject.

K

KACHCHH	Measuring land or estimating the produce.
KACHKOL	A dish used by devotees to collect their offerings in, being half the shell of a cocoa-nut.
KADHÁÍ	Weeds, &c., cleaned out of a field.
KAHÁNÍ	A marriage engagement.
KAJJAL	Lampblack, with which the eye-lids are painted.
KALANDAR	A kind of monk, who deserts home and friends, and travels about with shaven head and beard.
KALS	An earthen water-vessel, used in Hindú worship.
KÁMAN	The jugglery performed by women at the time of marriage, by which it is supposed the bridegroom is affected, and ensnared in the bride's love.
KAMARKOT	An exterior city wall built for defence.
KANGAN	An ornament worn on the wrists by men and women.
KÁNGANÁ	A parti-coloured thread, tied round the right wrist of a bridegroom or bride.
KANGHÁ	A large comb used by Sikhs.
KÁNGRE	The name of a game, in which boys draw lines with charcoal on stones in two different places.
KANJAR	A class of people, who wander about manufacturing and selling surki mats, baskets, &c.

GLOSSARY OF TECHNICAL TERMS.

K—continued.

KANOÍ	An officer appointed by Government to value a crop.
KANTHÁ ...	A rosary, made of large beads of gold, silver, crystal or onyx.
KÁNÚNGO	An officer, who keeps an account of the tenures by which lands are held.
KAPÁL KIRYÁ ...	A ceremony among Hindús, by which, when a corpse is burnt, the nearest relative breaks the skull, in order to allow the tenth sáns to escape, nine being supposed to have departed at the time of death.
KARÁH ...	A board used for levelling ground drawn by men or oxen.
KARÁH PARSÁD	A kind of sweetmeat, made of flour, sugar and ghí.
KARBATT	Self sacrifice, with a view to obtain salvation.
KATH	A marriage engagement.
KES	Hair of the head.
KHABCHÚ	A left-handed man.
KHÁDAR...	The lowland on the margin of a river, which is occasionally overflowed.
KHADDA...	Stream running through a ravine.
KHANDÁ ...	A two-edged dagger, worn on the head by Akális.
KHANNÍ ...	An ordeal of fire taken into the hands, to prove one's innocence.
KHAPPAR	The alms-cup of fakírs.
KHARAR ...	A blanket, placed on the top of a cart, for carrying food for the bullocks.
KHARÁUN	A wooden sandal, fastened on with thongs.
KHÁRÍ	A creek, inlet or deep water-course.
KHARJ ...	The bass in music.
KHASRÁ	Appraisement of a crop, and the book in which recorded.
KHATT ...	A lot of presents, given to a bride by her parents.
KHÁTTÁ ...	Daily account, or waste-book.
KHEP	A trip; the goods carried in a single trip.
KHIDÁÍ ...	Compensation for amusing a child.
KHING	A stringed instrument, played with the fingers.
KHINTHÁ	A patched quilt, worn by ascetics.
KHOBHÁ	Marshy ground, a bog.
KHOJJÍ ...	A detective or tracker of thieves.
KHOSSA...	One who has no hair except on the chin.
KHUCHCH	A thorough investigation.
KHÚD ...	Green barley or wheat, cut for horse feed.

GLOSSARY OF TECHNICAL TERMS.

K—continued.

KINNÁ	To rain moderately, to sprinkle.
KÍRNE	Artificial mourning and weeping at funerals.
KOH	A large leather vessel for drawing water from a well.
KULPAT	Family reputation.
KULTÁRAK	A youth, who is a credit to his family.
KUNDAL	An iron ring on an ox's neck, by which he is secured against thieves.
KUNGÚ	The name of a very fine composition of red colour, made of ánulá, used by women to ornament their foreheads.
KUPP	A stack of chaff.
KURAM KARÁHÍ	A dish prepared to be eaten on the occasion of the first meeting of the parents of a bride and bridegroom, and in which other persons are not allowed to participate.

L

LADDÁ	A load or burden for a hired animal.
LADDÁ BÁHUNÁ	To carry on hire (on mules, horses, &c.)
LÁG	The fees given to various functionaries at weddings, &c.
LAGAN	A present, sent by a bride's father to the house of the bridegroom, with the summons to the wedding.
LÁGMÁR	Withholding fees from Bráhmans and others at weddings, &c.
LAIPÁLAK	An adopted child.
LAJJU	A well-rope drawn by the hand.
LALER	A cocoanut.
LALERÁ	An empty cocoanut shell.
LAMBARDÁR	The headman of a village.
LÁMBÚ	A wisp of grass, &c., used in lighting a funeral pile.
LÁNÁ	A farmer's estate, with all its appurtenances, oxen, ploughs, &c.
LANGHÁÍ	Ferriage, or hire of a boat, or toll at a bridge.
LANGHÁNÍ	A rude stile in a hedge, consisting of a forked stick.
LAT	The current of a river.
LA-U	A crop or cutting of grain or grass, &c., that is cut more than once in the same season.
LÁU	A slanderous charge.
LÁULASHKAR	An army including baggage, followers, &c.
LÁUN	A well-rope drawn by oxen.
LÁUN	A ceremony at Hindú weddings, in which the bride and bridegroom make four circuits round a fire.

L—continued.

LÁUPÁU	Something given instead of cash to discharge an obligation.
LAUS	Extra pay to servants, &c., on a journey.
LÁVIHÁR	A hired reaper.

M

MÁHAL	The framework of rope to which the earthen pots of a Persian wheel are attached.
MAHÁPARSÁD	Meat, or food presented as an offering to an idol.
MAHANT	A headman among Hindú fakírs.
MAHASSUL	One appointed by Government or a landlord to superintend the harvesting of grain, etc., that is raised on shares.
MAHITÁ	A title of respect applied to Bráhmans and others.
MAHÚRAT	The time supposed favourable for engaging in any enterprise or entering upon any business, as determined by divination.
MAJABÍ	A Chúrha who has become a Sikh.
MALWÁ	That which is spent on account of a village, by the headman for the benefit of fakirs etc., settled by a tax levied half-yearly.
MANAUTÍ	Agreeing to meet pecuniary obligations for another.
MAND	Low moist ground on the bank of a river.
MANG	A betrothed female.
MANGETAR	A betrothed boy or man.
MANHÁ	An elevated platform in a cornfield, on which one sits to watch.
MÁNJHÁ	The central portion of the Bárí Doáb.
MANSÁT	A man's height, used in speaking of the depth of water in a well or tank.
MANTRA	An incantation or chant.
MARH	A monument erected in memory of a deceased Hindú.
MÁRÍ	A small room, erected on the roof of a house.
MASÁN	A place where corpses are burnt; also the bones that remain after a burning.
MASANDA	A Gurú's priest, who receives offerings and presents them to the Gurú.
MAT	A monument erected in memory of a deceased Hindú.
MAT	An abbey or cloister of Sanniásí fakírs.
MA-ULÍ	A wreath of thread of various colours, chiefly saffron and white, worn by women on the head at weddings.
MA-UN	The masonry work of a well that remains above ground.

GLOSSARY OF TECHNICAL TERMS. lxvii

M—continued.

MEDNÍ	A body of pilgrims going to visit the tomb of a saint.
MELAN	A female guest at a wedding.
MELÍ	A male guest at a wedding.
MILKU	A family estate or patrimony.
MIRÁSÍ	A caste of Musalmáns, employed as musicians, and bards.
MISAL	A petty dependency subservient to the authority of a Rája.
MISSAR	A title of respect for Bráhmans.
MITÍ	Day from which interest is reckoned.
MODHÍ	The man, who stands on the edge of a well, and handles the charas, in drawing water.
MODÍ	A storekeeper.
MUCHALLAKÁ	A fine, imposed in certain cases of arbitration, upon the party refusing to abide by the decision.
MUKAT	Deliverance of the soul from the body and exemption from further transmigration.
MUKHÁLÚ	A passage by which mountains are entered.
MUKLÁWÁ	Bringing home a wife after marriage.
MULHO	A bait-bird, set near a trap, to entice others of the same species.
MUNIÁR	A manufacturer of glass armlets.
MUSADDÍ	A headman in a Rája's, or Sardár's household.
MUSALLÁ	A kind of staff, T shaped, carried by fakírs, to place the head on in prayer.

N

NAKHÁS	An open market where horses cattle, &c., are sold.
NAMONARÁIN	A form of salutation among Sunniásís.
NÁNKÁR	An allowance in land or money, to husbandmen and others.
NANT	A gold ear-ring worn by Hindús.
NAT	The name of a tribe of jugglers and rope dancers.
NECHÍ	Food given to Bráhmans daily for one year, for the benefit of a deceased person.
NEUNDÁ	An invitation to a feast.

P

PÁHÍ	A farmer who rents and cultivates land belonging to another.
PAHILÚN	A cow, or buffalo, that has given, or is about to give, her first calf.

GLOSSARY OF TECHNICAL TERMS.

P—continued.

PÁHUL	The Sikh baptism, or rite of initiation, which consists in sprinkling, on the face of the candidate, a kind of sherbee, previously consecrated, and passing round what remains, to be drunk by all the initiated, who are present, out of the same cup.
PAINTH	An open market, or market place.
PAIRÍ	The walk for bullocks in drawing water from a well.
PAKKHULÍ	The large canvas sheet, spread at the bottom of a cart.
PALÁCH	Ground left for a time, untilled and fallow.
PALÍTÁ	A roll of candle-wick used in exorcising evil spirits.
PAMMÁ	A name given in ridicule to Bráhmans in the Panjáb.
PANCH or PANCHÁIT	A Committee of arbitration.
PÁNDHÁ	A school-master, or Bráhman who directs the weddings and other ceremonies of a family.
PANJOTRÁ	Five per cent. of the revenue, given to the headman of a village.
PANJRATNÁ	Five things put into the mouth of a deceased Hindú, viz., gold, silver, copper, pearl and coral.
PARAMHANS	An ascetic, who professes to have subdued all his passions by meditation.
PARB	A sacred day, or season of religious, idolatrous festivity.
PARITÁ	One of the Bráhmans, that officiates at a wedding, holding a secondary place, and attending to anything that may require his services.
PARSÁD	Food, or sweetmeats, offered to the gods.
PÁSANG	A make-weight to balance the scales.
PÁTH	Reading the sacred books as an act of devotion.
PATTAN	A landing-place, or ferry, where the shore is smooth and hard, and the water fordable.
PATTH	A young goat, that has not yet begun to give milk.
PATWÁRÍ	One who keeps the land accounts of a village.
PÁULÍ	A four anna piece.
PAWITTRÁ	A ring, made of dabbh grass, and worn on the fourth finger, on occasions of presenting certain offerings.
PETLÁ	A bathing place, where there is little or no descent to the water.
PEURÍ	A wafer, pasted by Hindús on the forehead.
PHÁHURÁ	A wooden scraper for removing manure from a stable.

GLOSSARY OF TECHNICAL TERMS. lxix

P—continued.

PHAKK	A gentle shower of rain, a drizzle.
PHÁLÁ	The cotter of a plough.
PHALKÁ	A square wooden frame, slightly loaded, drawn by oxen in treading out corn.
PHÁLÚ	A plough-share.
PHÁNT	The arm of a river.
PHARÁKÁ	The shining-out of the sun on a rainy day.
PHATKÁ	A winnowing of grain.
PINGAL	A treatise on prosody or versification.
PÍR	A threshing floor, or place where grain is stacked up.
POR	A hollow bamboo, attached to a plough perpendicularly, with the lower end behind the share, and the upper having a hopper to contain the seed, which is thus drilled into the furrow in passing along.
PUJJAT	That which has been paid on a sum due.
PUNN	Charity given to obtain merit.
PURÁN	The name of one of the eighteen Hindú Sástras.

R

RABÁB	A kind of violin with three strings.
RÁG	A musical mode of which there are six, named after six Deotás.
RÁGNÍ	A tune of a class distinct from the rágs; there are thirty, named after different goddesses or devís.
RAHÁU	A pause, or repeat, in music.
RÁHIT NÁMA	The name of the Sikh Code.
RAHURÁS	A form of worship, used by Sikhs in the evening.
RAKKH	Land reserved by Government, the wood, grass, &c., on which, is not to be cut.
RÁKKHÍ	Wages for keeping watch.
RANBÁS	The apartments occupied by Ránís.
RANGÍSAUDÁ	Merchandise bespoken at a certain rate, irrespective of what the market rate may turn out to be.
RAPTÍ	A village chaukidár, who reports to Government.
RAR	A level piece of ground.
RASÓI	The place where Hindús cook and eat their food.
RÁTAB	Daily allowance of food for horses, cattle, etc.
RATH	A four-wheeled native carriage.
RA-U	The course, or dry bed of a river.

R—continued.

RÁUL	A wandering class, who practise begging, quackery, *thagi*, etc.
RAUN	A marshy spot in a field, or on the border of a stream.
RAUNÍ	Watering a field previous to ploughing.
RAUR	Level ground, bare of verdure.
REJ	The soaking of the ground, produced by the over-flowing of a river.
REURÍ	A preparation of sugar, etc., in small cakes covered with til-seed.
RIND	A man who is inattentive to religious duties.
ROJANDAR	A day-labourer.
ROKAR	Cash, ready money.
ROKARYÁ	One who pays cash; a cash-keeper.
ROLÁ	The red powder, used by Hindús at weddings and at the Holi.
ROPNÁ	That which is sent by a girl's father to the bridegroom elect in the ceremony of magní, consisting of seven dried dates, and various other things.
RUHAR	The course, or dry bed, of a river.
RULD	A sponge, one who lives on others.
RUNGÁ	Something additional asked for by a purchaser, after a bargain is concluded.
RURH	A torrent formed by rain.

S

SÁDH	A religious person or saint.
SADHWÁÍ	The stick put under the hinder part of a cart, to prevent it from tilting.
SAGAN	Presents, or alms, given on contracting a marriage.
SÁHÁ	The day appointed for a wedding, and fixed by astrologers.
SAHÚKÁR	A money-dealer or capitalist.
SÁÍ	A small sum given to seal a bargain.
SALHÁBÍ	Damp, applied to land subject to inundations, or that is well watered by the proximity of a stream.
SAMÁDH	A Hindú, or Sikh, tomb.
SÁMÍ	A defendant in a law suit; also, a cultivator of the soil.
SAMRAN	Mentioning the Name of God.
SANDHÍ	A child or animal, etc., dedicated to the gods, and to be redeemed at one-eleventh of the value set upon it.
SANDHIÁ	Repeating mantras, and sipping water, at sunrise, sunset, and midday, a ceremony performed by Bráhmans, Chattrís and Vaisas.

S—*continued.*

SANDHÚ	The name of a family among the Jatts.
SANHSÍ	The name of a class among the Jatts.
SANÍ	Cut straw, mixed with grain, oil-cake and water, as food for cattle.
SANKALAP	A vow, or consecrating a thing, to God.
SANKH	A shell blown by Hindús at worship.
SANNIÁSÍ	A devotee, who professes to have abandoned the world.
SAPARDÁ	A musician, attending on singing women.
SAPARDÁÍ	Musicians, attending dancing girls.
SARÁDH	A Hindú ceremony, in which they worship and feed Bráhmans on some day during the month Assú, in commemoration of their deceased ancestors, and for their special benefit.
SÁRANG	The name of a musical mode.
SÁRANGÍ	A musical instrument like a violin.
SAREWARÁ	A Jain devotee, who wears a slip of cloth over his mouth, to avoid the inhalation of animalculæ.
SARGAM	The seven sounds of an octave; the gamut.
SARGAST	A thing, formed of paper, somewhat like an umbrella, and turned over the head of a bridegroom in the marriage ceremony.
SÁRÍNÁ	The grain given by farmers to the Chámars, inhabiting their villages, in compensation for the menial services occasionally exacted of them.
SARNÁÍ	An inflated skin used to carry passengers across a river.
SASTAR BASTAR	Arms and accoutrements.
SATÁBÁ	A match for firing a gun.
SATÍ	A woman who immolates herself on the funeral pile of her husband.
SATTÍ	A market where dry goods are bartered, the price being fixed by a go-between.
SAURH SALÍTÁ	Tent, bags, bedding, &c., loaded on a camel in travelling.
SÁWADHÁN	A form of benediction, used by Bráhmans to inferiors.
SAWAYYA	The name of a measure in poetry, and a mode in music.
SIÁPÁ	The ceremony of weeping, or making lamentation, for the dead performed by women.
SIDDH	A fakír of great attainments, a wonder-worker, eighty-four of whom are generally stated to exist.
SIHRÁ	A chaplet of flowers, or a piece of gold or silver fringe, worn round the forehead by a bridegroom at the time of marriage.

S—*continued.*

SIKKH	A disciple, or follower, of Nának.
SINGH	A Sikkh, who is a follower of Govind Singh, and has been formally initiated by receiving the páhul.
SIRBÁLÁ	The attendant of a bridegroom, who rides behind him on horseback in the marriage procession.
SIRHÍ	A bier, shaped like a ladder, used by Hindús.
SIRÍRÁG	The name of a musical mode, appropriated to the afternoon in winter.
SIRNÍ	Sweetmeats offered to saints.
SITTUNÍ	Obscene or abusive songs, sung by women at weddings.
SODHÍ	A title of the Gurú, who resides at Kartárpur, and of his followers.
SÚDRA	The name of the lowest of the four great Hindú castes.
SUKKH	A vow made to obtain some temporal blessing.
SUNDKA	A pack-saddle.
SÚTAK	Ceremonial uncleanness from child-birth, lasting forty days, and extending to every thing in the house.

T

TAKÁ	A copper coin equal to two pice.
TAKNÁ	A small hatchet, carried by Sikhs to cut toothbrushes for themselves.
TAKYA	The dwelling place of a fakír.
TALLÁ	Low ground, contiguous to a mountain.
TANGAR	A net, in which cut straw is carried.
TAP	A kind of austere devotion.
TARÁÍ	A marsh, or meadow land.
TEUR BEUR	A full suit of woman's clothes the teur consisting of three pieces, the petticoat, short gown and shawl; the beur, of two bodice and veil.
TEWÁ	The record of one's birth, from which one's fortune is to be calculated.
THADDÁ	A land-mark, or boundary pillar.
THÁPÍ	Dried cakes of cow-dung.
THOKÁ SIKKH	The carpenter caste among Sikhs.
THOSSÁ	The thumb presented turned down, in token of denial.
TIKKÁ	A mark, made by Hindús, on the forehead, &c., as a sectarian distinction.
TIKTIKÍ	A prop, shaped like a T, on which fakírs lean to rest or pray.

GLOSSARY OF TECHNICAL TERMS. lxxiii

T—*continued.*

TIRLOK	The three worlds; heaven, earth, and hell.
TULSÍ	The name of a plant, (basil), which Hindús deem sacred, and worship.

U

UDHÁL	A woman, who leaves her husband, and takes up with another man.
ÚJ	Accusation of an innocent person.

V

VÁCH	A tax levied by the lambardár of a village on those who are not zamíndárs.
VACHOLÁ	One who mediates between two parties, a mediator.
VADDH	Ground from which the crop has been removed.
VADHÁWÁ	A song, sung on the birth of a child.
VAHN	The surface of a roughly ploughed field.
VAJNÍ	See bajní.
VANG	An ornament, worn on the wrists, made of glass, lac, etc.
VÁRÁ	A sheep-fold, or enclosure, with a hedge round it.
VÁRNÁ	See búrná.
VATAHERÍ	See Ba*t*ehri.
VATNÁ	See Ba*t*ná.
VATT	See Ba*t*t.
VATT	Moisture of ground, making it fit to plough; also the proper time for sowing.
VED	See Bed.
VERARÁ	Wheat and gram sown mixed together.
VIÁHTÁ	A lawfully married wife.
VIHRÁ	A yard, surrounded by buildings.
VIRÁGÍ	A kind of wandering fakír, who practises certain austerities.
VIRT	The clientship (jajmání) of a Bráhman, Náí, etc.

GLOSSARY
OF
TECHNICAL TERMS AND WORDS.

English.   Gurumukhi.

A

ACCOUNTS (*Terms with reference to*) ... ... Chitthá; hindakí; khasrá.
APARTMENTS (*Queens'*) ... Ranbás.
ARBITRATORS (*Terms for*) ... Panch; pancháit.

B

BARDS (*Terms for*) ... ... Bhand.
BASKETS (*Kinds of*) ... ... Chhabbá.
BATHING PLACES (*Term for*) Petlá.
BEACON ... ... Akás díp.
BIRTHS (*Terms referring to*) ... Janampatrí; sútak; tewá; vadháwá.
BOOKS (*Names of*) ... ... Pingal; purán.
BURDENS (*Pad for carrying*) ... Binnú; Endwí.
  (*Terms used with reference to*) Chuárí; gún; kharar; khep; laddá; laddá; bahuná; pakkhulí; sadhwáí; taugar.
BURYING PLACES (*Terms for*) Masán, samádh.

C

CARRIAGES (*Kinds of*) ... Rath.
CASTES (*Different*) ... ... Bániyán; baran; barar; bánryá; báustor; bunjáhí; bedí; bhatt; bhábrá; bhátrá; chandá; chahrá; dakaut; dúm; garist; giristi; gujjar; gannímár; gaur; jatt; jhíwar; kanjar; majabí; mirásí; nat; rául; sandhú; sanníásí; sánhsí; súdra.
CATTLE (*Common for*) ... Bahik.
  (*Enclosure for*) ... ... Bhuárá.
  (*Food for*) ... ... Band; bár; chát; gutáwá; khúd; rátab; sání.
  (*Instruments for*) ... ... Dahá; kundál.
CEREMONIES (*Various*) ... Babindá; bakhúká; bahirá; balbaljáná; banduá; bárná; chatth; chaunkí; bharní; sandhu; sarádh; várna.
  (*Terms with reference to*) ... Pawittrá.
CHAFF (*Stack of*) ... ... Kupp.
CHARITY (*Term for*)... ... Punn.

GLOSSARY OF TECHNICAL TERMS. lxxvii

C—*continued.*

CHARMS (*Kinds of*) ... Bandhá; bisarjan; ganda; gáitrí; gátrí; janeú; kauthá; mantra; palítá.
CHILD (*Adopted*) ... ... Laipálak.
CITIES (*Terms with reference to*) Kamarkot.
CLIENT (*Terms for*) ... Jajmán; virt.
CLOTHES (*Kinds of*) ... ... Cholí; teur benr.
COOKING (*Customs at*) ... Adhar wanyjá.
CONTEMPT (*Terms of*)... ... Bainchhar.
COW (*Terms relating to*) ... Guhá; guhúrá; ghculí; palilúu; thápí.

CULTIVATION (*Customs regarding*) ... Adhiárá; bajní; batáí; brúí; bhánlí.

(*Terms*) ... Ball; bach; biár; bohnl; bhattá; bhúttí; bhan; cha-u; dasogiárí; dohar; dungwáí; gabaí; húr; kadháí; karáh; langhání; la-u; lávihar; manhá; phahúrá; phálá; phálkí; phatká; phálú; pir; por; raun; rauní; rej; salhábí; vaddh; vahn; vatt; vatt; vcrárá.

D

DEATH (*Bones collected after*) Ast.
(*Bier used at*) ... Babán; chikká, sirhí.
(*Ceremonies at*) ... Kapál kiryá; uechí; panjratna, satí.
(*Dirges sung at*) ... Bár; kírne; siápá.
(*Food used at*) ... Bhattí.
(*Mode of announcement of*) Chhattí.
DEBTS (*Terms with reference to*) Dammán sáhí; lánpáu; manantí; mití; pnjjat.
DECOY BIRD (*Term for*) ... Mulho.
DEEDS (*Kinds of*) ... ... Dánpattar.
DEVOTEES (*Kinds of*) .. ... Abdhút; anghar; barágí; bhabútiá; biragí, dandá; giri; jakkh; jaugam; kalandar; paramhans; sarewará; sádh: siddh; virágí.

(*Practices of*) ... Akáspaun; akúsbirt; hál; jap; jáp; jog; sanıran; tap.
(*Salutations of*) ... Ades; dandaut; jubár; namonaráin; rám rám; sámadhán.
(*Terms relating to*)... Babráná; bam; bhajwán; bhandár; chippí; kachkol; khappar; khinthá; mahant; mat; musallú; saukh; tiktikí; takiya.

DEVOTION (*Kinds of*) ... ... Jap; jáp; páth; tap.
DIGNITARIES (*Various*) ... Chaudharí; jabhedár; lambardár; musaddí; patwárí.
DISTRICTS (*Names for*) ... Mánjhá.
DRAFTS (*Name for*) ... ... Darsaní.

E

EARTH (*Kind of*) ... Gaugauti.
ESTATES (*Term for*) ... Milkh.

F

FATHER (*Term used for*) ... Bábal.
FAMILY PRIEST (*Term for*) ... Pándhá.
FARM (*Terms referring to*) ... Lániá; páhí.
FEES (*Given to priests, musicians, etc.*) ... Addíán!; balój; bharwáí; bhattí; bidúigí; dachchhnú; laus.
FERRIES (*Terms applicable to*) Laughúí; pattau.
FESTIVALS (*Powder used at*) ... Ambír; rolá.
(*Apparatus used at*) Akúsdíp.
(*Various*) ... ... Basant panchmín; jagg; parb.
FIELDS (*Boundaries, etc., of*) ... Baddh; balgun; banná; balt; bír; channá;
FOODS (*Kinds of*) ... ... Bakkalíán; baríán; churmá; ghunganí; parsád.
FORESTS (*Term relating to*) ... Banbajír.
FRUITS (*Dried*) ... ... Ambchúr.
(*Kinds of*) ... ... Auwla; laler; lalerá.

G

GAME (*Kind of*) ... ... Chaupar.
GESTURES (*Terms applicable to*) ... ... Bághí pauní.
GOAT (*Sacrificial*) ... ... Balbakkará.
(*Breeding*) ... ... Bok.
(*Young*) ... ... Patth.
GODS (*Food of*) ... ... Amrat.
(*Incarnation of*) ... ... Autár; baráth.
(*Songs in honour of*) ... Ártí; astak.
(*Terms used with reference to*) Balbhakkh, ist.
GUNS (*Term with reference to*) Chhúchhí.
GRASS (*Kinds of*) ... ... Dibbh; lámbú.

H

HAIR (*Terms used with reference to*) ... ... Babríán; boddí; bhaddan; chotí; girdá; gntt; jat: kes; khossá.
HANDFUL (*Terms for*) ... Chutká; chutkí.
HIRE (*Kinds of*) ... ... Dharáí; khidáí; rakkhí.
HOUSE (*Room above*) ... ... Márí.

I

INN (*Terms with reference to*) ... Bharo; bhathiárá; dharmsálá.
INVITATION (*To a feast*) ... Neundá.
IRRIGATION (*Term*) ... ... Jharál.

GLOSSARY OF TECHNICAL TERMS. lxxix

L

LABOUR (*Terms applicable to*)	..	Bách; báchbigár; bigárí; rojandar.
LAND (*Terms applicable to*)	...	Bángar; bará; bet; bhátí; bír; dhábá; doábá; donna; dún; inámí; jágír; khádar; khobhá; mand; palách; rakkh; rar; raur; tarái; thaddá; tallá.
LAW (*Terms*)	...	Darmadárí; dastak; dhoh; gahá; jáman táhad khanní; khojjí; khuchchh; láu; missal; muchallaká; raptí; sámí; új; vacholá.
LAMPBLACK (*Term for*)	...	Kajjal.

M

MARKET (*Terms*)	...	Nakhás; painth; sattí.
MARKS (*Terms for*)	...	Pourí; tikká.
MILITARY (*Terms*)	...	Báttí; jakhmáuá; lau laskar; sastar bastar; satábá.
MISCELLANEOUS (*Terms*)	...	Daun daun karná; dhai doní; garasná; hattál; hún; kún híla wasíla; hoká; jíun bútí; khabchú; misal; páulí; rind; ruld; thossá.
MONEY (*Terms with reference to*)	...	Rokar; rokaryá; sahúkár; taká.
MONUMENTS (*Kinds of*)	...	Dehrá: marh; mat; samádh.
MOUNTAIN PASS (*Term for*)		Mukhálú.
MUSIC (*Notes*)	...	Á; sargam.
(*Kinds of*)	...	Asáurí; dhanúsarí; ga-ur; ga-urí; rág; rágní; sárang; sawayya; sirí rág.
(*Terms of*)	...	Álúp; bam; kharj; raháu.
(*Instruments*)	...	Bín; khing; rabáb; sárangí.
(*Attendants*)	...	Sapardá; sapardáí.

O

OFFERINGS (*Kinds of*)	...	Balbhog; bhet; dasaundh; karáhparsád; karbatt; mahú parsád.
OMENS (*Ways of taking*)	...	Annsí; chaunk; kángro; mahúrat.
ORGANS (*The*)	...	Indrí.
ORNAMENTS (*Kinds of*)	...	Allí; ársí; bahí; bahuttá; bandí; bang; bangrá; bangrí; bánk; bichkanná; bicbhúá; bindí; bor; chaukar; chaunpkalí; chur; dand; dorá; gokhrú; hár; haslí; kangan; nant; vang.

P

PERFUMES (*Kinds of*)	...	Argjá; batná; kungír; vatná.
PHILOSOPHY (*Hindú*)	...	Vedánt.
PIGMENT (*Used for writing with*)	...	Budhká; bhittá.
PILGRIMS (*Term for*)	...	Mední.

P—continued.

PLACES (*For meeting, etc.*) ... Baithak; chabútará; chauntrá; dhúán.
PLANTS (*Kinds of*) ... ... Akk; tulsí.
PLEDGES (*Term used with reference to*) ... . Bándhá.
PRIESTS (*Terms relating to*) ... Baruí; bhojkí.
PROPERTY (*Term used with reference to*) ... ... Bándhá.
PURCHASES (*Terms relating to*) Bágpharáí; byáná.

R

RAINS (*Storm at end of*) ... Agatth.
    (*Kinds of*) ... ... Jharí; kinna; phakk.
    (*Sun shining after*) ... Pharáká.
REPUTATION (*Man of*) ... Kaltárak.
    (*Family*) ... Kalpat.
REVENUE (*Terms*) ... ... Chukáná; dasotrá; barí; inámí; kachchh; kanoí; kánúgo; mahassul; malwá; nánkár; panjotrá; patwárí; sámí; saríná; vách; vajní.
RIVER (*Sacred*) ... ... Batarní.
    (*Kinds of*) ... ... Boín; barh; khaddá; kbárí; pháut; rurh.
    (*Skins for swimming*) ... Darain; sarnáí.
    (*Current of*) ... ... Lat.
    (*Course of*) ... ... Ra-u; ruhar.
ROPE (*Kind of*) ... Bor.

S

SALES (*Terms used with reference to*) ... ... Bándh; bándhá; bharbharí; bíjak; buhuní; dharat; hárná; rangí; saudá; rokar; rokaryá; ruugá; súí.
SALVATION (*Term for*) ... Mukat.
SANDALS (*Kind of*) ... ... Kharáun.
SERVICE (*Certificate of*) ... Bádlá.
SHEEP (*Enclosure for*) ... ... Bárá; várá.
SHOEMAKERS (*Instruments*)... Chbední.
SICKNESS (*Term relating to*) ... Bhnárá.
SIKHS (*Special terms relating to*) Bání; bháí; chádará; darbár; granthí; gurbháí; gurwár; kánghá; khandá; masanda; majabí; páhul; rábatnóma; rahurás; sikkh; singh; sodhí; takuá; thoká sikkh.
SINGLESTICK (*Terms used at*) Bank; bánkpatá.
SNAKE (*Kind of*) ... Básaknág.
SPORTS (*Place for*) ... ... Akhárá.
    (*Term applicable to*) ... Burdo burdí.
SPRING (*Name for*) ... ... Basant.

GLOSSARY OF TECHNICAL TERMS. lxxxi

S—continued.

STATES (*Hill, term for*)	Báisí.
STOREKEEPER (*Term for*)	Modí.
SUITS (*Term used with reference to*)	Bhaur.
SWEETMEATS (*Kinds of*)	Batásá; badáuá; reurí; sirní.

T

TANKS (*Kind of*)	Dhab.
TITLES (*Of respect*)	Mahant, mahitá, missar.
(*Of ridicule*)	Pammá.
TRADES (*Term for*)	Muniár.
TRANSMIGRATION (*Term with reference to*)	Jiun.
TRAVELLING (*Terms used with reference to*)	Sa-urh salítá; sundká.
TREE (*Kind of*)	Bakáin.
TWILIGHT (*Morning or evening*)	Jhusmusá.

V

VESSELS (*Various kinds of*)	Bánk; batloh; kals
VOW (*Kind of*)	Sukkh.

W

WASHERMAN	Chhimbá.
WEAPON (*Kind of*)	Khandá.
WEDDINGS (*Ceremonies at*)	Agast; chandánú; káman; láun; sargast; sutthní.
(*Gifts*)	Bahorú; bahoro de teur; barásuhí; barná; brahmíchhakk; khatt; lagan; ropná; sagan.
(*Food at*)	Batehrí; behí; bhají; got knuálá; kuram karáhí; vátaherí.
(*Fees given at*)	Bágpharáí; bandhej; bel; bhomdún; lág,
(*Different parties at, names of*).	Barát; dáí; dáiá; mel; melan; paritá; sarbálá.
(*Apparatus used at*)	Bed; bedí; belná; kanganá; ma-nlí; sihrá; ved.
(*Terms with reference to*).	Dákhalá; gatth; janny; kath; kuhúní; lágmár; maug; mangetar; mukláwá; sáhá.
WEIGHTS (*Terms with reference to*)	Dharú, pásang.
WELLS (*Kinds of*)	Bán; baulí; chuharhtá; harhat.
(*Terms regarding*)	Báh; biddh; bind; chakk; chaubachcha; mansát; ma-un; modhí; pairí.
(*Instruments*)	Bárú; bhauní; bokkú; dhíngulí; koh; lajjú; láun; máhal.

W—*continued.*

WOMEN (*Terms applicable to*)... Udhál; viáhtá.
WORLDS (*Three*) ... ... Tirlok.
WORSHIP (*Ceremonies at*) ... Ártí.

Y

YARD (*Surrounded by buildings*) Vahrá.
YEAR (*Term for*) ... ... Chot.

AUTHOR'S PREFACE.

How excellent is that Supreme Being, who, by His Power, having created the garden of the earth, adorned it with various kinds of colours and shapes, and made each flower and fruit in it so beautiful in its excellence, that, to the present day, no wise man, by his wisdom, has been able to alter the original form of even one single leaf in it, or to make and manifest anything after a new fashion. Again, how very extremely powerful is that Supreme Being, who does whatever He wills. Behold! the same man is sometimes poor, sometimes rich, now a king, and now a beggar; and how exceedingly wonderful is His Creation, for the form of one does not blend with that of another. From hearing of these factories,[1] which He has continually made and obliterated up to the present time, it is plainly manifest that the Creator has no need of any one; and this also becomes known, that He has made the world in such a wonderful way, that the making and effacing of it is His custom from old. Behold! the holy, the pious, the bad, the good, kings, and subjects, who have come into it, they have never been allowed always to remain in it. If you ask the truth, then the world is a place of halting, and those people, who come here and live long, and, forgetting their death, become oblivious of their Creator, they lose their birth[2] in play. If I were to write an account of the people of the whole world, then I would never come to an end, but in this book I will narrate somewhat of the circumstances of a very small portion of the world, namely, of the Panjáb, and the people who have come into this land during the last four centuries, and the deeds and acts which they did before they, at last, took their original road. There are three parts in this book. In the first part, there is a short account of the life and deeds of the ten Gurús (spiritual teachers) commencing with Bábá Nának, who was one of the best amongst the holy men of this country, down to Gurú Govind Singh, who laid the foundation of the Sikh religion. In the second part, there is a narration of events, commencing from the Mahárájah Ranjít Singh down to the arrival of the

---

[1] *I.e.*, persons, who are His workshops in which His doings are carried on.
[2] The expressions "birth and death" "coming and going," &c., are repeatedly used to signify life.

PREFACE.

English in the Panjáb. In the third part, there is an account of the songs and stories and rites and customs of this country, and a short enumeration of the castes, religions, and beliefs. This book I, Pandat Sardhá Rám, who live in the city of Phalour, in the district of Jálandhar, prepared agreeably to the desire of His Honor (possessed of high virtues, most merciful, the ocean of kindness) Mr. (Sir Donald) MacLeod, Lieutenant-Governor of the Panjáb, in the year 1922, Bir Bikramájít, *i.e.*, 1866 A.D.; whoever shall fix his thoughts on it, and travel through it from beginning to end, will place in his mind the full particulars of the Panjáb.

HISTORY OF THE SIKHS.

PART I.

CHAPTER I.

Account of Bábá Nának.

IN a village, called Ráibhondí Talwandí, which is now known as Nankálá, situated in the district of the Tasíl of Sarakpur, and the division of Láhaur, in the house of a Khatrí Vedí,[3] named Kálú, who, at that time, was the Patwárí (land steward), in the year 1526 B.B. *i.e.*, the year 1469 A.D., on the day of the full moon of the bright half of the month Káttak, at midnight, a son was born. When Kálú gave information to his family priest, then he, having meditated according to the customs of the Sástras, called the name of that child Nának, and said, "O Kálú! this child will be of a very good and religious nature, and many people will follow after him; he is the beloved of God, and will remove the perplexities of many people; and remember this also, that this is no child but an Incarnation of the Deity; for this reason, his name is Nának Nirangkárí (Nának, the incorporeal). He will regard the one Incorporeal Lord only as true, and will reverence no one else." On hearing this, Kálú was greatly pleased. When he had accomplished all the rites and customs observed at birth, and had dismissed the priest with much kindness, he said, "O Lord, I thank Thee, with all my heart and soul, for that Thou hast caused such a wonderful son to be born in the house of such a poor one as I." Now they relate his history thus; that when Nának was nine years old, then, agreeably to his father's command, in the hot season, he went to a jungle to graze his buffaloes, and becoming distressed from the heat, he went to sleep under a tree; people say that a black snake crawled

---

[3] The Bábá Khatrís (or the Khatrís of the line of Nának) are divided into two families, the Sodhí and Vedí, but the term Sodhí is generally applied to the disciples of, or converts to, the Sikh religion from Gurú Govind's time, and Vedí is applied to those who were converted by Nának, but they are not called Singhs, for it must be remembered that the Sikh race only took firm root and began to be so called from the time of the last Gurú, Govind Singh.

on to him, and, having spread its hood over his face, shaded him. In the meanwhile, Ráibúlár, who was the proprietor of that village, having seen this his state, said to himself, " This child is some worshipper of the Deity," and having come to his father, began to say to him : " This thy son is very holy." When Nának was fifteen years old, then his father, having given him twenty rupees, and sent with him (to attend on him) a servant, named Bhái Bálá, who from old had lived in the house, said to him, " O son! do thou go and purchase some good merchandise." Then Nának, taking him (Bálá) with himself, issued forth to buy something; after having gone a little way, he saw a company of beggars, who were destitute of food and clothes, and, having taken compassion on them, fed them with those twenty rupees. Bálá, his servant, admonished him much, saying, " Kálú sent you to buy some good merchandise, why do you throw away these rupees to no purpose?" Nának did not heed him in the least, but thus addressed him, " O Bálá, what merchandise is better than feeding the holy in the Name of God?" and having thus said, he returned home. When Kálú heard this, he beat Nának very severely, and the news of it reached Ráibúlár, who, from having seen the snake overshadowing the face of Nának, had great faith in him ; he, Ráibúlár, gave the twenty rupees from his own pocket, and thus relieved him from his beating ; but as Nának still used to take money from the house (of his father), and expend it in the name of God, at last his father sent him to the city of Sultánpur, which is in the district of Kapúrthala, to the house of his sister Nánaki, and wrote a letter to this effect to Lálá Jairám, who was Nának's brother-in-law. " Whereas Nának causes much loss here, I have, therefore, sent him to you ; do you keep him with you, and teach him some business and profession, that he may eschew the society of beggars, and become fit to associate with the good." When Nának arrived in Sultánpur, then Nánaki and Jairám, on seeing him, were much pleased ; moreover, after a few days, in the year 1540, on the 14th of the bright half of the month Maghar, they placed the lad in service as storekeeper[1] to the Nawáb Daulat Khán Lodí, and having made over to him a thousand rupees in cash, said, " O Nának! now take up this business, and do not cause any loss ! if God wills, then thou wilt obtain much profit from this occupation." Nának, having taken with him that servant, whose name was Bhái Bálá, and who, by caste, was a Sandhu Jatt, began to carry on the transaction of the business ; still his custom of giving food and drink, to and bestowing clothes on, the good and holy, which he had from old, did not depart from his heart. When, in this

---

[1] A store is kept up by all small chiefs from which supplies of flour, dál, &c., are issued to their attendants ; this is called the Modí Kháua or Commissariat godown.

manner, he had continued carrying on, for some time, the affairs of the business, and had rendered his accounts in full, then in the year 1544, on the 5th of the bright half of the month Maghar, he became betrothed, in Pakhoke Randháwa, to the daughter of Múla Khatrí, who, by family, was a Choná. When the day of his marriage drew near, then Nának's father, Kálú, together with his brotherhood, setting forth from Talwandí, came to Sultánpur, and thence, having formed the marriage assembly, in the year 1545, on the seventh of the bright half of the month Bhádon, went to Pakhoke Randháwa, and performed the marriage of Nának. Having completed the marriage, Nának went for some days to Talwandí; then, when some days had passed, having come from there to Sultánpur, he began to carry on the business of the store. Nának, who always remained engaged in the worship of his Lord and performance of service to the good and holy, did not show much affection to his wife. One day, when his sister Nánakí had admonished him much, he cohabited with his wife. After a short time, in his thirty-second year, a son was born in the house of Bába Nának, and his name was called Sirí Chand. When Sirí Chand was four-and-a-half years old, then another son was conceived. This is the occurrence of one day; Nának, from the desire of worshipping his Lord, went out and did not return home for three days; on this, it became reported in the city, and, in Nawáb Daulat's (mind) there arose this suspicion, that Nának, having embezzled the money of the store, had gone away somewhere. When the Nawáb had spoken some severe words about Nának to Nának's brother-in-law, Jairám, then Nának, having returned on the third day, rendered his accounts in full, besides a surplus of seven hundred and sixty rupees in the accounts to the Nawáb's credit; this sum he asked to be distributed to the good and holy, and from that very day, having left his family and the business, he became a free man. The Nawáb and other people admonished him much, but he would not listen to what any one said; but, from that day forth, he took up his abode in the jungles and tombs, and, seated there, commenced to give utterance to the songs, full of the sorrow of separation, which are written in the Granth-Sáhib. Then, after three months, that child, which had been conceived, was born, and his name was called Lakhmí Dás. When Sirí Chand was four and three-quarter years old, and Lakhmí Dás a baby in arms, and Bába Nának had turned devotee, then Nának's father-in-law kept Sirí Chand with himself, and left Lakhmí Dás, who was young, together with his mother, in Sultánpur, in the house of Jairám, who was Nának's brother-in-law. In the meanwhile, news reached Nának's father in Talwandí, that Nának had turned fakír. Kálú, on hearing it, became very anxious, and calling Mardána the Dúm, who was the Mirásí (family bard) of the family, said to him: "Do thou go and bring news of Nának from Sultánpur." When Mardána came to Nának, on seeing his fakír-like state, he commenced to say: "O Nának! what disguise is this thou hast assumed? and what advantage is there, in leaving thy family, and becoming a fakír?" Nának said to him: "That house is false, but this abode to which I have attained is true; but come, I have, for a long time, desired thee, do thou remain with me." Mardána at first refused to remain with him, but afterwards, of his own accord, accepting hunger and nakedness, he began to live with him. Náuak, having called that Bháí Bálá, who was his old servant, sent him to Talwandí, saying, "Do thou go in place of Mardána, and give Lála Kálú certain intelligence of Nának having become a fakír." Then Mardána and Nának both began to live together, and when Bába Nának gave utterance to songs in the worship of his Lord, Mardána, having set those songs to music, used to play them on the rebec, and sing them. Seeing his new customs and strange habits, all the neighbouring people began to call him a wanderer from the right road. When Mardána, a Mirásí by caste, who was weak at heart, heard himself called a wanderer by his brethren, he became sorrowful; on which Nának said: "O Mardána! do not thou become wavering; this is the custom of the world that those, who leave their ways, and follow the road of God, them they call mad and wanderers; but there is nothing to fear, for we have no regard for them, and have sold ourselves in the name of God, who is Lord of all." Then Nának, together with Mardána, having come to Emnáwád, to the house of Lálo the carpenter, who was a very good holy man, lived there. When he had determined to remain there a while, then Mardána went to Talwandí for some time to visit his family. At first, on the very hearing of the words of Bálá, Mahitá Kálú and his brother Lálú were much grieved about Nának; but when Mardána gave them further full news of him, they became still more distressed, and were greatly enraged at him (Mardána).[5] Mardána explained much to Kálú, "O Mahitá! Nának has not become a fakír, but a banker of bankers, and a king of kings"; but Kálú, on hearing his words, heaved many deep sighs of regret. In the meanwhile, Ráibúlár, hearing of this circumstance, that Mardána had come from Nának, called him to himself, and asked Nának's news. When Mardána had told

---

[1] In consequence of what he had told them. "Gal dá hár honá" means to become like the necklace round the neck. When a person comes and bothers any one and annoys him greatly, the common expression used is "You have become a weight on me like the necklace round my neck."

CHAP. I.—ACCOUNT OF BÁBA NÁNAK. 5

him of his holy state, then the Rái, with much entreaty, said, "If thou wilt also obtain me a sight of him, I shall ever remain under a debt of gratitude to thee." Mardána replied, "O Rái! I have no control over the fakír, but, on my own part, I will show no remissness in taking you to him." In the meanwhile, Mardána, according to his promise, set forth to return, and taking Bháí Bálá, who had arrived before him, came to the house of Lálo, the carpenter, and, rejoining Nának, told him the news of all being well at Talwandí. One day, when they saw Nának seated alone, Mardána and Bálá, joining their hands, petitioned : "O Gurú! Ráibúlár is very anxious to obtain a sight of you, and if to-day you will go to Talwandí, then his desire will be fulfilled." Nának, having agreed to their request, took his leave of Lálo, the carpenter, and, departing thence, reached Talwandí, and, having arrived at the well of Bálá, stopped there. Then Nának's household, having heard of it, came, and, immediately on seeing his fakír-like state, storming, began to say, "O Nának! what disguise is this thou hast assumed? Behold we, thy father and mother, uncle and other relations, seeing thee, are greatly distressed ; does no pity arise in thee?" Hearing this speech, Nának gave utterance to this song in the Márú Rág :

"Call patient endurance[6] my mother, and contentment my father ;

"Call truth my uncle, for with these my heart has conquered its passions.[7]

"Listen Lálú, to these good qualities, but, as all people are bound in chains,

"How can they tell what are good qualities ?

"Affection for God is my brother, and love of the True God is my son :

"Patience has become my daughter, and in such I am absorbed.

"Forbearance is my companion, and prudence is my disciple ;

"Call these my family, who always remain with me ;

"The one Supreme Being is my Lord, and He it is who created me ;

"If Nának left Him and became attached to some one else, he would be put to pain."

Hearing this, they all brought him to the Rái, and the Rái was greatly pleased to see him. The Rái entreated him

---

[6] "Khimá" also means "pardon."
[7] Viz., Kám (lust) moh (worldly fascination) krodh (anger) lobh (covetousness) and hinkár (pride).

much, "O Nának! do thou remain here. I will give thee some land free." But Nának would not agree to remain there. His household also exhorted him greatly, but Nának would not listen to what any one said, and after a few days, made preparations to return. Nának's uncle, Lálú, said to him, "If thou art determined to wander about over the country, then do thou take some money, and traffic in horses; but it is not becoming for one like thee, to wander about like a fakír." Nának, then, uttering this couplet, gave reply:

"I will listen to the Sástras, make them my merchandise, and, take about (for sale) the horses of truth;

"I will make good works my cash, and will not delay this till to-morrow:

"I will go to God's country, for, there, I shall obtain an abode of joy."

At last, when Nának began to depart, then the Rái said: "Point me out some work (to do)." Nának said nothing with his mouth, but by signs gave him to understand: "Do you cause an unwalled tank [8] to be dug here." The Rái, there and then, agreed (to do so), and Nának, together with Bháí Bálá and Mardána, again came and lived in the house of that same Lálo, the carpenter. When fifteen days had passed there, then Nának consulted with Mardána and Bálá, saying, "Come, let us traverse some distant country;" upon which, he, with those two, prepared (to do so). In short when Nának set out from there, he went to the country of Bangála, and, in that country, visited various places of pilgrimage, and cities, and it is commonly reported, that in that country, by reason of being a stranger, he underwent much fatigue in many places. Whilst he travelled over Bangála, he saw many other countries and mountains also, which were in its neighbourhood; moreover, as he formed friendships in those lands with many people, in some places he sang some of the songs, which are in the Granth; and at other places they visited, when Mardána the Mirásí, losing heart, became sad, Nának used to give him advice and show him some miracles, and thus gave him much comfort. In short, Bába Nának, always in company with those two, went also to Makka and Madína, and his discourses with the shrine attendants and priests at those places, are written in the book of the Janam Sákhi. [9] After a time Nának,

---

[8] Tobhá is an unwalled tank, a walled one being called tál.
[9] It must be borne in mind that this work contains only selections from the real Janam Sákhi, which is deposited in the Golden Temple at Amritsar, and is about five times the size of this. It has been printed and copies can be obtained for fifteen rupees from the Government Book Depôt, Lahore.

making up his mind, returned from Makka to Sultánpur to see his sister Nánakí, and, having remained there a while, departed (again) to travel in the mountains, and, wandering about there, met with many good and holy men; moreover, he there met with Gorakhnáth Jogí, who founded the sect of the Kánpátí Jogís.[10] In short, Bábá Nának went to many islands and harbours of the sea, and had a great fancy for visiting other countries, and that Mardána, the Mirásí, who always accompanied him, also died in a strange land in a city called Khurma near Kábul. Although, by caste he was a Mirásí, i.e., a Musalmán, still during his life-time he used to say, "O Gurú! do not bury me according to the Musalmán rites, but burn me as a Hindú." Nának, although in his heart he had no leaning towards either Hindú or Musalmán customs, still thought it right to burn Mardána agreeably to what he had said. Then Bábá Nának, with Bálá, went to Setband Ramesur, and there again met Gorakhnáth Jogí. When he returned from there, he came to Achal which is near to the city of Watála; after attending a fair there, he again went back to Talwandí, which is quite close to it; and, on arrival, heard that his father Kálú, and Ráíbúlár, had died, and his uncle Lálú was alive. Nának, on his arrival there, did not think it proper to see any one, but taking only a son of Mardána Mirásí, named Sajáda, with him, went to Multán. When he came to Talambha, then a Thag, who was seated disguised as a good and holy man, taking him to his house under the pretence of feeding him, imprisoned Sajáda, Mirásí, who had gone to wander about the city, and said: "Give me whatever thou hast, otherwise thou shalt be killed." Nának, having obtained information of this, sent Bháí Bálá to that deceitful one, and got Sajáda released, and, having gone to that impostor saint, shamed him much, saying: "O holy brother! what is this you practice? but although people, seeing thy disguised state, regard thee as a holy man, how will this remain hid from that Supreme Being, who knows the inward thoughts of every one." In this way, when he had admonished him much, and shamed him, that Thag, falling at the feet of Nának, petitioned, "O true Gurú! I am a great sinner, and a wretched man, but (listen to) my repentance! I will never do such a thing again." Nának, hearing this, placed his hand on his head, and saying "God forgive thy sins" departed from there. Again, wandering about, he came to that city Khurma, and left Sajáda there at the tomb of his father, (while) he himself, with Bálá, went to Kandhár. On the road, he placed his hand on a certain spot,

---

[10] This sect of Jogís can be distinguished by their split ears; hence the name kán (ear) pátí (split).

the name of which has therefore been called Panja Sáhib; in
short on his hand, he there also bore up a mountain. Reaching Kábul, he admonished many Musalmáns and Híndús in the
name of God, and, afterwards met with a Jogí, Bálgudáí, on a
mountain, which was known by his name, *i.e.*, called the hill of
Bálgudáí. Departing thence, he again came to the house of the
carpenter Lálo. There the wife of Hayát Khán, Manjh Musalmán, who formerly, seeing the goodness of Nának, had believed
in him, gave him her young daughter (in marriage), and, from
that date, her name was called Mátá Manjhot. Then Nának,
having made her his own, (married her), left her at Lálo's
house, and himself, taking Bálá with him, went to Kulchhetr for
the fair of the eclipse of the sun. There were a great many
fakirs assembled there, who, on hearing Nának's name and
description, became very angry with him; and other people
also, who were Grihasts, [11] and had gone to that fair, and
looked on Nának as a wanderer from the right road, kept
their distance from him. Moreover, a Khatrí, who was a
Munshí, having gone to King Bahirám Khán, Lodí, son of
Sikandar Khán, Lodí, reported secretly to him, "A fakír, named
Nának, who has come to the fair, regards neither the Vedás
nor the Kurán; if you will ask him what is his faith, then it
will be well." Bahirám Khán, having called Nának, asked him,
and, becoming angry at his answers, imprisoned him in his
prison-house, and caused Nának and Bálá to grind at a mill.
When seven months had passed, at the battle of Pánipat, Bábar
Chugatta[12] overcame Bahirám Khán, Lodí, and the rule of
Bábar was established over the whole country. On the seventh
day, Bábar, hearing of Bába Nának being imprisoned without
fault, let him go, and said, "Go, O Nának; go wherever thou
wilt." Nának, together with Bálá, came to Pakhoke-randháwá,
the village of his father-in-law, and blessing Jite randháwá,
who was by caste a Jatt, in the name of God, made him his
own disciple. Again, after some days, he sent Jite and Bálá
to the house of Lálo, the carpenter, saying, "Go and bring the
daughter of Hayát Khán Manjh:" and they both brought Mátá
Manjhot. When he was giving her a place to put up in at the
house of Jite, his first wife also, who was known as Máta Choní,
taking both her sons, named Sirí Chand and Lakhmí Das with
her, came and lived with Bába Nának. Whilst Nának remained
there, many persons were blessed by hearing the name of God.
One day Nának, having given advice in the name of God, to a
Jatt named Bura Randháwá, made him happy; and Málo, the

---

[11] Grihast are those who marry and have families.
[12] This is evidently Bábar Chugattai, the contemporary of Salím Sháh of Delhi, the builder of the fort called Salímgarh.

carpenter, a Musalmán, also received the blessing of (learning what true) worship is from Nának, and his friend Ubára Khán, Pathán, was also converted to the worship of God by Nának. In this same way, many persons obtained (the blessing of hearing) the Name of God, through the kindness of Nának. Mátá Manjhot lived seven years with Nának, and died leaving two daughters. Again, Bábá Nának taking Bálá with him, went to the country of Sindh, and there met with many people, and gave utterance to some of his songs. When he returned from there, he came to Pák Patan, which belongs to Sheikh Faríd, Fakír, and met a person named Bahirám, who was a very good and holy man; moreover, at his suggestion, Nának gave utterance to the song of Ásá [13], which is a very celebrated devotional song amongst the Sikhs. Then Bábá Nának came and lived in Pakhoke-randháwá, and Bhai Bálá, who from old had remained with him, having received permission from him, went to Talwandí. Now Bálá had become a very good man through the kindness of Nának, and, when he was setting off for Talwandí, he asked, "O Nának! who will be Gurú in this country after you? so that following after him, I may obtain salvation from his society." Gurú Nának said, "O Bálá, the dignity of the Guruship will be given to one Lahina Khatrí, who is a Tehun by family, and he will be quite like me, and a devotee of God; my followers from following after him will enjoy peace (of mind)." On hearing this Bálá went to Talwandí, and Bábá Nának remained there. Dwelling there, he converted many people; moreover, in that place, he also bestowed the Guruship on Gurú Angad, who is called the second king, and then, wandering about, he left this world in the year 1596 B.B., *i.e.* 1539 A.D., at a place called Kartárpur, which is now called the Dehra (shrine) of Bábá Nának. In short, on his death, the Hindús said; "This was our Gurú, we must burn his body," and the Musalmáns, calling him their spiritual guide, wished to bury him. Whilst, in this way, much disputing was going on, his body disappeared and could not be found in the clothes which had been put on his corpse. For this reason, there is no tomb of his anywhere in the world; but wherever there are any of his worshippers, there either his Kharáwán,[14] or likeness, or else some cloth or flag, is reverently put up.

This Bábá Nának was not a very learned or literate man, but, from merely associating with some holy man, the love of the service of God was aroused in him. His belief was somewhat different from the old Sástras, and books, and Muhammadan

---

[13] A translation of it is given in Trumpp's Adi-Granth, page 472.
[14] Kharáwán are wooden sandals, which are fastened on to the feet by means of leather thongs, very much resembling clogs or pattens.

prophets and Hindú incarnations, for he did not hold deities and images and places of pilgrimage in much respect; he only regarded one God, and considered all good and evil as coming from Him; and from every song and word of his, his belief is clear, viz., that no living creature has any power. God does whatever He wills—if He wishes, He can manifest good; and if He wills, He can shew forth evil.

VERSE.

There is always an incessant movement [15] in this fair.[16]
The whole fair, without the worship of God, is contemptible.

[15] Coming and going, i.e., being born and dying.
[16] i.e., the world.

CHAPTER II.

The Circumstances of Gurú Angad.

THEY narrate his circumstances (life) thus; one day a Tehun Khatrí, named Lahina, went from his own village, which was one of the villages in the jungle, together with the members of his family, to obtain a sight of the goddess of Kot Kángrá. When he arrived where Bába Nának lived, it entered his head that as, at that place, there was a certain Nának Nirangkárí, who was reported to be a very good and holy man, he should go and obtain a sight of him also, and see of what kind and of what sect he was a fakír. Having thus reflected, and found out Nának, he went to him and, approaching him, obtained a sight of him. When he had bent his head in obeisance, then Nának asked; "O brother Sikh! Who art thou? and whence art thou come! and tell me this also, what is thy name, and whither goest thou?" He replied, "O holy Sir—I am by family a Tehun Khatrí and my name is Lahina; I have come here only to obtain a sight of you, and am going with my family to Kángra." On hearing this speech, Nának answered, "Well, brother, go and obtain a sight of the goddess," but he replied, "O Gurú, my heart now does not desire to go further, for, from seeing thee, it has become satisfied; now I have no care for any god or goddess; this is now my desire, that I may always remain at thy feet, and may employ my hands and feet in thy service." Nának, on hearing this, said to him over and over again, "Do thou now go to thy home, and afterwards come back again." But he would not agree to go from there. All his relations, who were with him, seeing this his state, became much distressed, but, at last being helpless, they went away to their own homes. When Lahina, having remained there, with his whole body and soul, commenced to work and labour for Nának, then there sprang up much affection between them, for he (Lahina) began to regard Nának as equal to God, and all the other Sikhs began to speak highly of his labour and toil. Sirí Chand and Lakhmí Dás also, who were the sons of Bába Nának, could not perform as much service as Lahina commenced to do. To write here in full an account of this his obedience would be unprofitable: but I will narrate somewhat of it. One day, Bába Nának and his two sons and Lahina were going somewhere, when a metal cup fell from the hand of

Nának into some thick mud, which was very deep. Nának said to Sirí Chand, "Son! pull out the cup." He replied, "O father, my clothes are very beautiful and will get besmeared with mud; come, let us go on, and I will send back some labourer to get it out." Again, Nának addressed Lakhmí Dás to the same effect, on which he gave that same reply. Then, when he looked towards that Sikh Lahina, he, joining his hands, asked, "O holy Gurú, what are your commands"? Nának replied, "Dig out that metal cup." He, immediately on hearing it, jumped in with his clothes on, and, having dug out the metal cup from the mud, made it over to the Gurú, and from that very day he grew very dear to Bába Nának. Again, another time, when a great crowd had assembled around Nának, then he, becoming agitated, wished to separate himself from them; at that time, making himself naked from his body to his head,[17] he rubbed ashes over himself, and, assuming a very hideous disguise, began to eat (carrion) with the dogs; on this, all the people, calling him mad and a vile creature, ran away; but Lahina alone still remained with him. Nának too, also, tried greatly to drive him away, but he would not leave him. Moreover, seeing a dead body lying in a certain place, Nának, to prove his sincerity, said, " O brother Lahina! if thou wishest to remain with me, then eat that dead body." When he, at once, on hearing this order, ran towards the corpse, then Nának, knowing him to be a true lover of himself, kissed his head, and said, " O dear one! thy name is Lahina (to take), and I know that thou must take something from me also." In this way, he never turned away from any command of Nának, but, day by day, his increasing love waxed greater.

One day Mátá Choní asked Nának, "Why do you show greater love to Lahina than to Sirí Chand and Lakhmí Dás"? Then he replied, " Lahina, although he is another man's son, still never disobeys my orders; but by these, who are called my sons, my orders are never obeyed; accordingly I love him, who studies me with all his body and soul." One day, Nának pressed him to his breast before a whole assembly, and, placing five pice and a cocoanut before him, first himself bent his head in obeisance to him, and then said to all the assembly, "O brother Sikhs! from to-day I have given the Guruship to him; whoever is a Sikh (disciple) of mine, let him, regarding him as Gurú, bend his head in obedience to him. He is a truly holy man. Now there will be no change in this; God has made him His own, and he will accomplish the business (desires) of many." He said this also, " Before, his name was Lahina, but now as I have pressed him to my body and bestowed

---

[17] i.e. taking off his dhoti or waist cloth.

on him the power of the adoration of God, therefore his name is called Gurú Angad."[18] Then the disciples petitioned: "O Gurú! agreeably to your orders, we will regard him as our Gurú, but what shall we regard them as, who are your sons?" Then Nának replied, "God himself will take care of them; it is no concern of yours; do you place the worship and offerings of the Gurú before him, who has brought himself into the way of God with all his body and soul." On hearing this, all the assembly bowed to Gurú Angad, and whatever orders he used to give, those they used to place on their heads (i.e., to obey); and Angad also followed all the advice he had received from Bába Nának, and kept straight the road of religion. After Angad had remained there some time, then he came and lived at Káhirián de Khadúr, and used to earn the means and necessaries for his food and clothes by making rope. When all the Sikhs heard that Bába Nának had seated Angad on the seat of the Gurú, then they all began to come to him: moreover that Bhái Bálá also, who had remained with Nának from old, came to get a sight of him, and Angad heard from him all the particulars about Nának from his birth up; and this Bálá, after a few days, died there. Whatever exhortations Nának used to make in the name of the Wáh Gurú (God), these Angad also continued to make. The interpretation of this name, Wáh Gurú, (which is the chief incantation in the Sikh religion), is said to be this: In the incantation, Wáh Gúrú, are these four letters w, h, g, r; of these the w, refers to Wásdeo, the h, to Harí, and the third, which is g, to Gobind, and the r to Rám, and this is the adoration of the incarnations of the four Yogs.[19] And some people give another meaning, that Wáh is a word of praise, and Gurú is the name Gurdeo, therefore, from this the Gurú is praised; and others say, a great person is called Gurú, and as God is greater than all, from this name Wáh Gurú, the Supreme Being is praised.[20] Although the Sikhs made many offerings to Bába Angad, still he never spent any of them on himself, but, expending them all in the Name of God, got his own livelihood entirely by rope making. And these Gurú-mukhí letters also, which are known throughout the Panjáb, he arranged and altered from the letters of the Sástras; the thirty-five devotional songs[21] also, which the Sikhs read, were all compiled by him. He did not compose

---

[18] These two words mean "Teacher body" the title "Gurú," being given him in reference to his having bestowed on him the power of teaching others the way to God, and "body" in reference to his having been pressed to Nának's body (ang).

[19] Yog or period, viz., golden, silver, brass, and iron; the present is the Kalyog or iron age.

[20] This last is, I believe, nearest the truth, as set forth by Bába Nának.

[21] Each of these begin with one of the thirty-five letters of the Alphabet vide Trumpp's Adi-Granth, page 602.

anything else besides, but he converted many people ; and those also, who were sinners, from associating with him, eschewed their sins, and obtained inward peace and the (blessing of the) Name of God. Then, having placed before the third king, i.e., Gurú Amardás, five pice and a cocoanut, and, having bent his head in homage, he gave him the seat of Guruship and himself left this body (died) in the year 1609 B.B, i.e. the year 1552 A.D.

COUPLET.

Whom shall one regard as an enemy, and with whom make friendship ?

All the world is like a dream, and an ever shifting play.

CHAPTER III.

The Circumstances of **Gurú** *Amardás.*

Gurú Amardás, who is known as the third king, was a Bhalá Khatrí, of a village Wásarkí, which is in the district of Anmritsar, and, from his very childhood, he was of so good a disposition that, wherever a religious assembly was collected, there he used to go and, to the best of his power, perform the service of the good and holy with much affection. Although his father and mother, on seeing this his state, used even to be somewhat angry in their hearts, still he, according to his good disposition, never withdrew from the service of the holy. Once, Amardás went to Harduár to bathe in the holy Ganges, and when he arrived there, it so happened that a thirsty Pandat drank water from his hands. When his thirst had abated, the Pandat asked him, "Who mayst thou be, and whence hast thou come?" He replied, "O your Highness, I am a Bhalá Khatri, and have come from a village named Wásarkí in the country of the Panjáb." Again the Pandat asked, "Who is thy Gurú?" He replied, "O holy Sir, at present I have not adopted any Gurú." On hearing this, the Pandat was greatly distressed, and, calling out, said, "Alas! a great misfortune has befallen me, that I have drunk water at the hands of this person, who has no Gurú. Alas! I am a great sinner that, at the time of my thirst, (I did not consider); how will this my sin be forgiven?" Amardás, on hearing this, became very much ashamed in his heart; moreover, falling at the feet of that Pandat, he petitioned: "If your Highness will now forgive my fault, then I, immediately on going home, will adopt a Gurú." When Amardás came home, he began to make search for a Gurú. One day, he heard from some one that close to there, in Kábirián de Khadúr, Bába Angad, a perfect Gurú, was living, and whoever took his advice obtained salvation, and those good qualities, which became a Gurú, *viz.*, patience, contentment, forbearance, clemency, devotion, &c., were all to be found in him. Immediately on hearing this, he went to Khadúr, and, seizing the feet of Gurú Angad, said, " O holy Sir, I, having heard your name, have come to you to obtain salvation; do you have compassion on me, and give me instruction; nowhere do I see such a perfect Gurú as you: all people wish to make disciples to do them service, but I have not heard of any Gurú but yourself, who bestows salvation on his disciples." Bába

Angad, on seeing his devotion, was much pleased, and, giving him advice in the name of the Wáh Gurú, said, "O brother Sikh ! you must repeat this name with every breath with a true heart ; and in the morning, having bathed, you must meditate on the Name of God." He further said, "This body is a cage of bones and flesh, and in a very few days it will be broken and shattered to pieces : that, indeed, is a moment of profit when, with this body, one can become of service to any holy, good, hungry, or thirsty person. Do thou eschew the vain thoughts of thy mind, and always remain engaged in the worship of thy Lord, and be contented with His will : this is the sum total of my instruction and advice." Amardás, with all his body and soul, adopted this advice, and, from that day, began to act agreeably to it, and did not again return and go to his home, but began to live there, regarding the sight of his Gurú and the service of his disciples, as true gain. In short, he accepted the service of the Gurú with all his heart and soul, but he would not eat any thing, not even bread, from the Gurú's cooking square. This was his custom, that he used to carry about a bundle of salt and go to people's houses and sell it, and whatever he obtained from this, with it he used to pay for the expenses of his food and clothing, and never tasted a single grain from the Gurú, for he thought thus : "It behoves me with my body and soul and wealth to do service to my Gurú ; therefore it is not becoming for me to get my food from him." And this was the manner of his service ; that he used always to go from Khadúr to the river near Gobindwál, which was two kos from there, to bring large brass pots of water for his Gurú to bathe with ; and there was this great hardship in it, that, when he used to go from Khadúr to fill the pots, he went backwards to the river near Gobindwál ; when he had filled it, (he returned) looking to his front, for he thought that he must never turn his back towards his Gurú. Again, all who were celebrated holy disciples there, for all of them also he used to fill and bring water ; and whether any one asked for it in the day or night, still he would go to the river and bring it, and he never turned away his face from the command of his Gurú and the holy. This is the occurrence of one day; that when Amardás was bringing water at night, on the road he stumbled into a weaver's hole [22] and fell. When the weaver asked, "Who is there "? then the weaver's wife, who always saw him fetching water, gave reply, "Who else can have fallen in at this time ? It must be the stricken-by-calamity, and he who has no home, Amrú." [23] Amardás, getting up, again went to the river,

---
[22] Khaddí is the hole in the ground in which a weaver puts his feet when sitting at the loom.
[23] Amrú is the short for Amardás.

CHAP. III.—ACCOUNT OF GURÚ AMARDÁS.

and in that same way, having drawn water, came to the Gurú. When the Gurú heard from some one, that people said that he was homeless, then, having seen his sincerity and devotion, he embraced him and said, "O people! Amrú is not homeless, but, from to-day, the Supreme Being has made him the home of the homeless, and the help of the helpless; whoever becomes attached to him will attain great happiness;" and that very day he placed before him five pice and a cocoanut, and bent his head in obeisance to him, and said to all assembled : "To-day I have made over to Gurú Amardás the throne of the Gurúship ; let all people do obeisance to him, for he is a perfect Gurú ; to-day the Supreme Being has taken him for His own; then whoever follows him, will please the great Lord." After the death of Gurú Angad, the whole body of followers obeyed Gurú Amardás, and he also converted many people, and kept straight the road of religion. This Gurú Amardás was a very good holy man : they say that no one ever saw him angry in his whole life-time ; he was of a very cool-tempered disposition, the beloved of God, and merciful, and he never brought his heart to do any base action, but always remained employed in good works and religion, and always continued firm in that road, which Gurú Angad had pointed out to him. They narrate this story of his forbearance; that when, after the death of Angad, Amardás came and lived in Gobindwál, the Musalmáns, who bore enmity towards him, began to afflict him much, still he never took any notice, but made this request to God : "O Lord, do thou direct their hearts." One day, when his disciples, having filled some pots with water, were bringing it for him to cook with, then a lot of Musalmán boys, shooting at them with pellet bows, broke the pots to pieces. His disciples came and said : "O Gurú! the Turks are always breaking our pots, what remedy shall we apply for this?" The Gurú, with much forbearance, gave reply, "From to-day, do you bring water in water bags, for they cannot be broken with pellet bows." The Sikhs acted accordingly, but the Musalmáns did not alter their behaviour. When the Sikhs began to bring water in bags, they split the bags with arrows. The Sikhs again pointed this out to the Gurú ; and the Gurú again answered, "O brother Sikhs ! do you bring the water in brass pots." The Sikhs acted agreeably to this word, but again the Musalmáns, throwing bricks, began to smash the pots. In short, although the Musalmáns harassed Bába Amardás and his disciples much, still he never used any harsh words toward them, but in his heart prayed for their welfare, for he considered all grief and happiness as coming from God. When his disciples addressed him saying, "O Gurú! how long shall we bear the tyranny of the Musalmáns?" then he answered, "Bear them all your life, for to take revenge is not the religion of the good; moreover, remember that there is no penance equal to patience, and there is no happiness equal to forbearance, and no sin greater than covetousness, and no duty greater than mercy, and no weapon better than clemency." On hearing this, all his disciples became quiet. Amardás also was not very learned or literate, but was entirely taken up with the worship of the Supreme God. The Anand Báni (the song of joy), which is written in the Granth, and which all good disciples, committing to memory, continually sing, was composed by him, but except it he composed no other song. The very large baolí,[24] which is in Gobindwál, was built by him; they say, whoever sits on every one of its eighty-four steps and bathes at them, and shall, at each step, repeat in full the Japjí Sáhib, he will be freed from passing through the births and deaths of the eighty-four lakhs of living things[25] and will go to heaven.

At that baolí, every year, a large fair takes place, and many people recite the Japjí Sáhib in full in that way at its steps. Amardás, having bestowed salvation on many people, at last, in the year 1631 B.B., i.e. the year 1574 A.D., reached his full age, and after him Gurú Rám Dás began to perform the business of Gurúship.

Verses.

One stretches one's feet for two days in this world,
And at last departs silently; this world is altogether false.

---

[24] A baolí is a very large well with steps leading down to it.
[25] The total number of living spirits is said to be 84,00,000.

CHAPTER IV.

The Circumstances of Gurú Rám Dás.

Rám Dás was a *Sodhí*[26] Khatrí, an inhabitant of the village called Gurúchakk, and in his very early years came to Gobindwāl, and lived in the house of his mother's family. The members of his mother's family were very poor, and he used always to sell ghunggani,[27] and thus got the means for their and his own livelihood. This is the occurrence of one day; he was seated near the door of Bába Amardás' house selling chunggani, when suddenly Bába Amardás called his priest and said, "O holy Sir! my daughter is now grown up; do you go and search for a good family and a husband for her, and pray get her betrothed." When the priest was about to set forth, then the wife of the Gurú said, "That boy, who sells ghunggani, is a lad of equal age with her; do you get him for my daughter, for my daughter is the same age." At that time Gurú Amardás said to himself, "Now my daughter has become (the wife) of this young lad, for it is the religion of the Khatrís that the purpose, which first comes into the heart, that you ought to accomplish." Having thus reflected, he called that lad and asked him, "O dear boy! who mayst thou be?" He replied, "I am a *Sodhí* Khatrí." Amardás, on hearing this, thanked the Supreme Being, saying, "Praised art Thou, O Lord! that Thou hast had respect for my vow, for if this lad had not been a Khatrí, then my companions would have reproached me much for giving my daughter to him." Immediately, he placed the betrothal gifts in the lap of that lad, and after a few days, having married her, Rám Dás took that girl to his own home in Gurúchakk. On one occasion, that girl, together with her husband, Rám Dás, came to her father; and as all the other disciples and attendants were doing service to the Gurú, she also, regarding him as the true Gurú, began to perform his service and do attendance. One day it thus happened that, as her father was seated on a square wooden stool bathing, and this girl was pouring water over his body, a nail in the stool ran into her foot; but she, thinking that if she lifted her foot, her father, seeing the blood, would forego bathing, did not lift her foot off the nail. When the

---

[26] See note 3.
[27] Ghunggani is grain of any kind boiled whole, and then dipped in salt, pepper, oil, and other seasonings.

blood reached down to below the stool, then the Gurú said, "Daughter, whence has the blood come?" The daughter, who did not think it right to tell an untruth, on her father enquiring several times, told him the whole truth. Gurú Amardás, on hearing it, embraced his daughter, and said, "I have got nothing else with me at this time, but go, from to-day I have bestowed on you the badge of Guruship." The daughter, joining her hands, petitioned, "O true Gurú, O my father! do you give this badge to my husband." The Gurú, there and then, before all the disciples, placed the five pice and a cocoanut before her husband, Rám Dás, and, making obeisance to him, said: "To-day I bestow the badge of Guruship on Rám Dás; let those who are my disciples, look on him as their Gurú." Then, having given Rám Dás advice in the name of the Wáh Gurú, he taught him all the rites and customs, and by his kindness set him on the road of religion. After the death of Amardás, Gurú Rám Dás began to live at his home in Gurúchakk, and all the Sikhs used to come there, and all the assembly looked on Gurúchakk as the abode of the Gurú. This Rám Dás became a good holy man, and, having obtained the greatness of Guruship, still even did not become proud. His disposition was very gentle, and he used always, agreeably to the custom of Bábá Nának, to place his thoughts on the Supreme Being. Once, in a certain place, he met with Gurú Sirí Chand, who was the son of Bábá Nának; and Sirí Chand, seeing that his beard was very long, asked, "O Rám Dás! why have you let your beard grow so long?" Rám Dás gave reply, "I have let it grow, to wipe off the dust of your feet with." On hearing this, Sirí Chand said, "Brother! you people, having spoken such words of love and devotion, have obtained the badge of Guruship, and we, who are sons, by reason of pride, have been deprived of it."

In short Gurú Rám Dás was a very good person, and having obtained greatness, did not become proud. This very Bábá Rám Dás, having discovered an old tank in Gurúchakk, called its name Anmritsar, and in the centre built a place of chanting, and called its name Harmandirjí (Temple of God); then, on account of that tank, the name of Gurúchakk was changed to Sirí Anmritsar.

This Gurú Rám Dás also composed many songs; then, having given over the Guruship to his own son Arjan, he marched from the world in the year 1638 B.B. the year 1574 A.D.

COUPLET.

This world is a dream of the night, which, immediately on your
    seeing it, passes away;
Good and bad,—all will go,—none will escape.

CHAPTER V.
The Circumstances of Gurú Arjan.

Arjan, from his childhood, always obeyed the commands of his father, and fixed his thoughts on the worship of the Supreme Being. Seeing his goodness, his father bestowed on him the Gurúship, according to former rites, before all his disciples, and publicly gave him the name of Gurú Arjan Sáhib. When Arjan, after his father, began to direct the road of religion, then great assemblies began to collect. One day, all the disciples petitioned, saying, "O Gurú! from hearing the songs that Gurú Nának used to sing, one's heart obtains quiet, and the desire of worship is increased; but other Sodhí[28] (Gurús) have also composed many songs and verses, to which they have appended the name of Bábá Nának; and from reading them, in a man's heart, a haughty spirit and intellectual pride[29] are created; for this reason, it behoves that some mark should be attached to the songs of Bábá Nának, that people may be able to distinguish them from the verses of others." On hearing this, Gurú Arjan collected from various places the verses of Bábá Nának, and those of the other Gurús (Angad, &c.,) who lived after Nának, and other devotees also, which were not opposed to the songs of Bábá Nának. These he collected together and gave to the scribe Bháí Gurdás to write, so that he might transcribe them all together in the Gurmukhí character; and for this reason, that Angad and the other Gurús also had placed the name of Nának to their verses, he, therefore, thought it would be difficult for his disciples to separate the verses of Nának; he accordingly put this distinguishing mark to those verses which were Nának's, viz., " Mahala pahila, or first Mahala (or Gurú) "; and those songs that were sung by the second Gurú, those he called " The second Mahala;" and in this way calling them "The third Mahala" and "The fourth Mahala" he separated all the songs of the Gurús ; and those songs which he himself also had composed, although these also were called by Bábá Nának's name, he designated "The fifth Mahala," and separated them from the rest. And the verses of Kabír and Rámanand and Dhana Bhagat and Nám Deo and Raidás, &c., which he wrote in it, to them he affixed the names of those several devotees,

---
[28] This is the title of the Gurú who resides at Kartárpur.
[29] Instead of humility and a low opinion of one's self.

but he did not write in it the verses of those people who composed verses after the Vaidant religion and other creeds, which were opposed to their worship. In this way, he collected all their songs and made a big book; and when that book was ready, its name was called the "Granth Sahib," and he proclaimed to all the Sikhs (disciples), "O brother Sikhs! behold, whatever is in this book is fit for you to obey, and whatever songs are not in it, although any one may give them out in the name of Nának, still it behoves you not to accept them." Moreover, he left a few pages blank in it and said, "The verses of the ninth Gurú, who shall hereafter succeed me, shall be written in these pages, and the songs of no Gurú, except him (the 9th Gurú), shall be entered." A son was born in the house of the Gurú Arjan, and his name was called Hargovind. When the child grew up, then a barber and a Bráhman came and betrothed him to a daughter of Chandú Sháh, who was a servant of the Kings of Delhi. When Chandú Sháh heard from people that he, to whom his daughter was betrothed, was of the character of fakírs, and subsisted on offerings, then, becoming very angry with the Bráhman and the barber, he turned them out of his house.[30] When Arjan heard this, that the barber and the Bráhman had suffered punishment on his account, then he wrote thus to Chandú Sháh. "We have dissolved the betrothal of your daughter, do you betroth her in some other place ; we will not accept this betrothal." Chandú Sháh was much disgraced in the eyes of people, on account of the dissolution of his daughter's betrothal, and from that day became very hostile to Gurú Arjan. Having brought false accusations before the King, he had Gurú Arjan summoned several times to Láhaur, and inflicted on him much serious annoyance; but Gurú Arjan always looked on those afflictions as the decree of God, and never became depressed; and thinking thus, "If such be the will of the Supreme Being towards me (so let it be)," he always remained happy. One day, that sinner instructed the King thus, "Do you call that fakír, who is an unbeliever in the (Shará) Muhammadan law, and, tying him in a raw hide, which is an abomination to Hindús, burn him." When the hide was brought before the Gurú, then the Gurú said, "Having bathed in the Raví, I will be ready to die, but I cannot agree to die without bathing: afterwards you may do whatever you like." The king, on hearing this his speech of helplessness, cooled down a little, and commanded, "Let him bathe." On this, Arjan took a leap into the Raví, and disappeared in it; people searched much for his corpse, still it did not come to hand.

---

[30] i.e., out of his family employment.

When he had thus given up this life, then it became reported among the people that the Gurú had drowned himself in the Ravi because he was to be burned in a raw hide. He had, prior to this, bestowed the seat of Guruship on his young son, Hargovind, who was very obedient, and a worshipper of the Supreme Being. Afterwards, on account of the enmity of Chandú Sháh, he departed this life in the Ravi near Láhaur in the year 1663 B.B., i.e., the year 1606 A.D.

COUPLET.

Be one great, very holy, good, respectable, rich or poor.

Death overcomes all; therefore preserve the worship of God in your mind.

CHAPTER VI.

The Circumstances of Gurú Hargovind.

He, from his very childhood, always obeyed the command of his father, and remained doing service and homage to him. Lálla Pirthí Mal, who was his uncle, from the desire of getting the seat of Gurúship, used to bear much hatred towards him in his inmost heart. One day Gurú Arjan said to Pirthí Mal, "O brother! for about six months I have business; do thou go and remain iu Láhaur." Pirthí Mal, thinking that perhaps, after he went, the seat of Gurúship might be given to Hargovind, did not agree to go to Láhaur. He (Arjan) then said to Hargovind, "Son! do thou go and remain about six months in Láhaur." He replied, "Sir! very well"; and, having made his obeisance, went to Láhaur. When he had passed six months there, then he thus wrote to his father. "If it be your command, then I will come and see you." When that letter arrived in Anmritsar, then Pirthí Mal did not allow it to reach the Gurú, but, having read it, kept it himself. In this way, he wrote and sent five other letters, but Pirthí Mal did not shew them to his father; then, writing a seventh letter with much affection, he sent it, and in it wrote thus, "O father! what disobedience have I committed, that you do not call me to see you, or send an answer to my letters; as I greatly desire to see you, do you have compassion on me and call me." Those verses which were written in that letter are called "the Hajáre Sabd." That letter, by some means, reached his father's hands. When his father had read the affectionate words, and had discovered that, before this, six of his letters had not reached him, then he asked Pirthí Mal what was the reason of this. At first he denied much (knowing anything about it), but afterwards he admitted, "O Gurú! I did not let the letters reach you." The Gurú, taking the letters, called Hargovind from Láhaur, and although Pirthí Mal expostulated and said much, still he bestowed the seat of Gurúship, before all the people, according to former rites, on Hargovind. When all the assemblage had made their obeisance to Hargovind, then Pirthí Mal became very envious. One day he devised this plan, viz., he would go to Chandú Sháh, who was his father's enemy, and make him very angry with him (Hargovind), in the hope that he, having killed him, would take and bestow the seat on himself. Having thus devised, he went to Delhi and thus said to Chandú Sháh, "Hargovind, the son of

CHAP. VI.—ACCOUNT OF GURÚ HARGOVIND.

Gurú Arjan, intends bringing an army of his Sikh followers and attacking you, and desires to take his father's revenge; whatever you can do, devise at once, for, afterwards, you will not be able to do anything." Chandú Sháh, on hearing this, became bitter in his heart, and from that day began to devise plans for seizing him. One day, he said to the astrologers, " Do you cause doubt to arise in the king's mind, and say to him, 'There is some danger to thee, and these days are heavy for thee[31]; if Gurú Hargovind, who is of the sect of Nának, shall come and perform some homage to thee, thou shalt obtain ease." The Pandats went and said thus to the king. " For a month and a quarter, it will be anxious times for thee, but if Gurú Hargovind shall come, then all thy troubles shall be removed." The king, having sent and called the Gurú from Anmritsar, said to him, " Do you sit for forty days in the prison house, and offer up prayers for me." The Gurú, on hearing this, was much distressed, but afterwards, regarding it as the decree of the Creator, went with three Sikhs, and remained in the prison house. Some people also say thus, that he was sent to the fort of Gnáliár to offer prayers (for the king), and whatever cash and food, and clothes the king used to send, these he used to distribute to the prisoners; and whatever the three Sikhs used to bring from their labours in the city, that they used to eat. When the forty days had passed, then a Sikh, named Bidhí Chand, who used to remain with Gurú Hargovind, assuming the disguise of a physician, obtained an interview with the king, and said, " That Hargovind, whom you called from the Panjáb, and kept like a prisoner in the jail for the sake of your obtaining ease, he is a very good and holy man, and the beloved of the Supreme Being; quickly give him his discharge; those people, who delivered him over to you, are his enemies." The king, believing what he said, forthwith called Gurú Hargovind, and petitioned, saying, " A great fault has been committed by me; do you forgive me, O fakír!" Hargovind said to the king. " May God forgive you." Hargovind had by him a large, most valuable pearl; this he presented as an offering to the king. When the king saw its splendour and lustre, he was greatly pleased, and said, "O holy sir! if another like this could be found, then it would be a very good thing." The Gurú said, " There was a very valuable rosary with one hundred and eight similar pearls in it, which my father, Gurú Arjan, used to wear round his neck, and it is now in the possession of your minister, Chandú Sháh; you can take as many pearls from it as you please." The king, on hearing this, was astonished, and asked, " How did Chandú Sháh take them from your father?" The Gurú, his

---

[31] i.e., it is an anxious time for thee.

eyes being filled with the water (of his tears), and heaving a deep sigh, related all that had occurred from the day of the breaking off of the betrothal, to the time that Chandú Sháh gave affliction to Gurú Arjan in Láhaur, and added. " When my father, being afflicted at his hands, died in Láhaur, then he took the whole necklace off his neck." The king, on hearing this, became very angry, and said, "Alas! alas! my minister has committed great injustice towards these fakírs." When he began to ask other people also for a confirmation of this speech, then they all said that the information was true, and some added this also, "That, on the present occasion also, when he (Hargovind) was called from the Panjáb, and made over to you on some pretence, this also, he (Chandú Sháh) did from his old enmity." The King, on hearing this, became still more angry; moreover, there and then, sending for Chandú Sháh, he made him over to the Gurú, saying : " Take him, he is your prisoner; take whatever revenge you wish, and if you can get your necklace too, which is in his possession, take it also from him."

Gurú Hargovind, taking Chandú Sháh with him, set out from Dillí, and, when he arrived at Anmritsar, he then began to give him punishment. In short, they used to put ropes round his feet, and drag him daily round the bazaars of Anmritsar and Láhaur ; and in the same way as he used to make Gurú Arjan sit on hot iron girdles and hot sand, and give him affliction, so also did Hargovind afflict him (Chandú Sháh). At last, one day, he died as he was being dragged about the bazaars. After this, many other Musalmáns formed hatred to Gurú Hargovind, and he, being always sneered at by every one, used to wander about quarrelling and fighting with them.

This very Hargovind founded Sirí Hargovindpur, which is situated on the banks of the river Wiásá[32]; in short, at the time of founding it also, the Gurú had a great fight with a certain Pathán, but at last the Gurú, getting the victory over him, laid the foundation of that city. He always remained engaged in quarrels, and never composed any songs. He remained very firm in the business of the Gurúship, and, if any Sikhs came to him, he used to give them advice, and direct them on the road of religion ; he gave purification (from their sins) to the people of many places ; accordingly his followers and disciples lived in Guáliár, and Agra, and Oojain, and Gujrát, and in Bangál also. It appears from many of his words, that he himself visited other countries also. It is said that, in Kartárpur also, he had a great fight with a Pathán. The circumstances of that fight are thus ; a Pathán, named Paindo Khán, used to live

---

[32] The Beas.

CHAP. VI.—ACCOUNT OF GURÚ HARGOVIND.

in the tent of the Gurú. One day, a certain Sikh brought and placed a sword, a hawk, and some very handsome clothes, as an offering, before the Gurú; as Painde Khán was seated near him at the time, the Gurú gave all those things to him, and said, "When you come to me, do you come, having adorned yourself with these things." Then he, taking these things, went to his house, and gave all those articles to his son-in-law. The Gurú, on receiving this information, asked him, "Why have you given all these things to some one else?" He denied it before the Gurú, saying "I have them all, and have given them to no one." The Gurú forthwith sent a Sikh, and had all these things brought from the house of his son-in-law, and said to him, "O Painde Khán! you have told an untruth before the Gurú; now you are not fit to remain here." On hearing this, the Sikhs gave him a push, and, beating him well, turned him outside. Painde Khán went to Láhaur, and made a complaint of his having been beaten, and bringing some of the king's army with him, came and blockaded him in Kartárpur. As, at that time, there was a large assembly with the Gurú also, they commenced to fight with the king's army, and many brave men of both sides were killed there; but, at last, Gurú Hargovind, having killed Painde Khán, obtained the victory in battle. Again, in the same way, once, at Láhaur, there was a fight with the Gurú, because he seized some of the king's horses in Láhaur. In short, the Gurú, in his life-time, obtained little repose from fighting and quarrels; at last, leaving his own home, he came and stopped with his son, named Gurditta, who lived in Kiratpur, in the house of Bábá Budha, and, after some time, gave the badge of Gurúship to his grandson Harrái, and then in the year 1695, i.e., the year 1638 A.D., he there left this body.

VERSES.

Many persons have come into this world, and sounded their drums;[33]
All the world is a full boat, no one has been able to stop in it.[34]

---

[33] Of royalty, i.e., have been kings.
[34] That is to say, it is like a boat which, when filled, crosses over, and the passengers all disembark; people come into this world and live their day, and then depart out of it.

CHAPTER VII.

The Circumstances of Gurú Harrái.

Gurú Hargovind had five sons; the name of the first was Gurditta, whom people now call Bába Gurditta, and the name of the second was Atall, who is now known as Bába Atall; the name of the third was Teg Bahádur, who is reckoned as the ninth Gurú; the name of the fourth was Aní Rái; and the name of the fifth Súrat Mal. Four of these used always to live for their own comfort and pleasure, but the fifth, Teg Bahádur, from his very childhood even, was fascinated with the worship of God, and used to take no thought for the ease or comfort of his own body. When the four grew up, they always had this thought in their hearts, "Will my father give the seat of Gurúship to me?" Moreover, the four were not able to look at each other by reason of the desire for that seat. Gurú Hargovind also used continually to reflect "To whom shall I give the Gurúship?"; for the four appeared to the Gurú to be very greedy and covetous for it. All the Sikhs also, seated together, used to reflect in their hearts, "Teg Bahádur, who is the rightful possessor and worthy of the Gurúship, always sits quietly apart like a madman, and has no care for any thing; and the other four sons of the Gurú remain fighting with each other; let us see whom the Gurú will seat on the throne of the Gurúship." This is what occurred one day. Gurú Hargovind was stopping at Kíratpur, which is near Anandpur; his other sons and a number of people were also assembled there. In the meanwhile, Harrái, the son of Bába Gurditta, who was then merely a child, playing, came and sat on the lap of the Gurú Hargovind; on this the Gurú, regarding him as his grandson, began to caress him; then Harrái, taking off Hargovind's pagrí, put it on his own head. As the Gurú, who was not well pleased with his sons, used always to be thinking of the bestowal of the seat, he, on seeing this, was very much delighted, and said to himself; "This is a very good opportunity which has come to hand; well, I will give the seat to this child, and it is a very good thing for this reason also, that the mouths of the brothers will be closed; if I had given the seat to one, then the four brothers would have been enemies with that one, and, fighting together, would have been killed; but now God has shown great kindness, in that He has put an end to all quarrels, and has devised another better way." Thinking thus, the Gurú, in the presence of the assembly, placing a cocoanut shell and five pice (before him), made obeisance to Harrái, and said, "O Bhái Sikhs! as God Himself has placed the pagrí of my Gurúship on this child's head, therefore no one can raise any objection; those, who are my disciples, will all regard Harrái as Gurú, for he will be a very perfect saint." The assembly, hearing this, were very pleased, because the Gurú had effaced all quarrels, and they all made obeisance before Gurú Harrái; and the four brothers also, who, for the sake of getting the Gurúship, bore enmity to each other, seeing this decree, were silenced, and no one had sufficient power to take away the Gurúship from Harrái. This Gurú Harrái was very clever, and always directed the road of religion well; this was one very good characteristic of his, that, according as he saw a man's understanding, so he gave him advice One day, a very foolish Sikh came to him, and the Gurú, they say, thus brought him to the (road of) religion, viz., he said to him, "O Bhái Sikh! man cannot be born again, therefore, to the best of thy power, worship God and do service to the holy." He replied, "O Gurú! I am a man with a family, and obtain not repose from cherishing them, so that I might come for a time to serve God, and do service to the holy. My only thought is how to provide for them; if I should employ myself in worship, they would all die of hunger; for I am the only one in the house, who can earn anything." On hearing this, the Gurú said, "O simple one! without God we cannot provide for any one; thou, in thy folly, regardest their provision as pertaining to thyself, but if thou wert not, then He would appoint some one else to provide for them : God has created, along with every one, the means of their existence. Behold! birds neither sow nor reap grain, but God never allows them to remain hungry." That Sikh replied, "This speech is very true, but my children are very young, and, except myself, no one can keep them alive : when, having worked all day, I bring home something, then they eat it; their love to me, too, is very great, and if I were hidden from them for a while[35], they would be agitated and die." The Gurú said, "This also is your way of thinking; but if you considered justly, then you would know that without any one even (to look after them), one does not die; every one lives his appointed life." When that Sikh then even did not believe, then the Gurú, giving him a letter, said, "Do you go and give this my letter to a certain Sikh in a certain village." He went to that village, and gave that letter; when that Sikh had read the Gurú's letter, then this was what was written in it. "Do you shut and lock up the bearer of this letter in a house, and whatever he requires, give it him within (the house), and until we write and send to you, till then, allow him not to come out." In that place, it became the lot of his family that when people knew that their man (head of the house) had disappeared somewhere, each of the neighbours sent a plate of flour to the house, and when that flour was finished, they gave more in the same way. Again people, taking pity, brought and gave his young children something to do, and made over some work to his wife also; in this way, their means increased beyond what it was before, and, for some days remembering their man (father), they afterwards forgot him. After some months, the Gurú sent and let the Sikh out of the house, and said, "Go, Bháí Sikh, and see your family now." At first he said, "O Gurú! she, together with all my children, on account of separation from me, will be dead; whom shall I go and see?" but afterwards, he went to his village. On going to his house, he beheld, that their state was even better than formerly, and all his young children were happy, well, and comfortable, and had no thought for him; on seeing them so happy in every respect, he became aware of his folly, and repented saying; "Alas! I used to regard their care, as depending on myself, but this was a great error of mine: now it has become clearly shown to me, that what the Gurú said to me was true; God is the giver of all (things) and no one need have any thought for any but Him." There and then, leaving them all, he came to the Gurú and said "O Gurú! you said the truth; in the world, God is the provider of all; I have now left them all, and will do the service of the holy." The Gurú, having pointed out to him the manner of worship, again sent him to his home, and said "Go, Bháí! there is nothing wrong in living in your home, but it was very wrong of you to think that their provision lay with you." Gurú Harráí always lived at Kíratpur with his father Bába Gurditta, and his father died there also, and his tomb at Kíratpur is a very great shrine. Gurditta's brother Atall, died in Anmritsar and his place of rest also, which is known as the tomb of Bába Atall, is a very large and lofty erection in Anmritsar, and many oblations are offered there, but of all things, bread is the most offered. The following saying of that place is well known in the Panjáb, and people repeat it in every place, "O Bába Atall, give me well-cooked bread."[36] The resting places of Aní Ráí, and Súrat Mal, are not so celebrated. At

[36] This is a very common proverb in the Panjáb. When a person arrives off a journey, if his host say to him." "Cook yourself some food," the usual reply is "Bába Atall pakkiáu pakkáiáu ghall" or "give me O Bába Atall (i.e. for Bába Atall's sake) some ready cooked food." Large quantities of cooked bread are daily offered at this shrine in Anmritsar, and distributed to the poor.

last Gurú Harrái, having given this seat to his young son, Har Kisan, himself in the year 1717 B.B. *i.e.* 1660 A.D., left this body in Kíratpur.

Verses.

All the gardens and orchards, which are in this world,
Are profitable to the gardeners for two days : afterwards they dry up.[37]

---

[37]. *i.e.* life lasts but a short time.

CHAPTER VIII.

The Circumstances of Gurú Har Kisan.

Gurú Harrái had two sons; the name of the elder was **Rám Rái**, and the name of the younger Har Kisan. This younger son was a very wise and religious person, and he, commencing from his childhood, never disobeyed any order of his father, but, with his body and soul, performed service to his father, and used to occupy himself looking after the holy; and although the other, Rám Rái, used to occupy himself much in the service of God, still his father, seeing certain qualities in him, used to be displeased with him; for Rám Rái used to give himself out to people as a Sidh and Auliyá[38]; and, in every place, this was commonly reported amongst the people, that Rám Rái was a worker of miracles. He, in the pride of his intellect, used to hold his assemblies separate from the Gurú's, and entertained this proud thought, "I am very clever, and expert in making disciples and followers, therefore my father will give me the Guruship;" but the Gurú, having heard of his miracles and shrewdness, used not to be pleased at heart. This is the occurrence of one time; Rám Rái had then gone to his disciples in the country of the Mián Duáb, and the Gurú, seeing the devotion and meekness of Har Kisan, before the whole assembly, according to former rites, gave him the Guruship, and said to all the Sikhs; "Although Rám Rái, my eldest son, is very clever, and the rightful possessor of the Guruship, still I will give the badge of Guruship to my younger son, who is a true devotee and very obedient; from to-day, his name is Gurú Har Kisan; let those, who are my disciples, do obeisance to him." When Rám Rái heard that the badge of Guruship, after he left, had been bestowed on Har Kisan, then he became very sad at heart. In short, at that time, Rám Rái said before the disciples; "At present Har Kisan is very young and has not yet suffered from small-pox; if he shall escape from small-pox, then he shall obtain the Guruship." Gurú Har Kisan, in his early years even, used to give advice to his disciples. This is what occurred one day; the King of Dillí asked his attendants, "Of those, who were formerly called the fakírs of Bába Nának, who is now the chief?" The attendants respectfully replied, O your Highness! a very young lad, named Har Kisan, is said to be

---

[38] A Sidh is a Hindu, and an Auliyá, a Muhammadan, saint.

sitting on their (chiefs') seat, and it is said that, even in his childhood, he is a very good and perfect fakír." The King said, " Quickly call him to Dillí; I also wish to see him." A Khatrí, who was one of the king's ministers, and was also called a disciple of the Gurú, got up and respectfully said. "O true King! I will bring Har Kisan." Having thus said, he took a large cavalcade with him, and, having come to Kíratpur, informed the Gurú of the circumstances of the king having called him. The Gurú went with him to Dillí, seated in a pálkí, with a very large assemblage of his followers, and, on arrival there, stopped at the house of the minister, who was his disciple; when it became night, then the Gurú was there attacked with small-pox; and the small-pox came out so severely, that he had not sufficient strength left in him to visit the king. The disciples, seeing him greatly afflicted, began to say "O Gurú! the king desired much to see you, what shall we say to him?" At that time, the Gurú replied: "The king does not wish to see me, but he has sent for me to argue with me, but I have now no hopes of remaining in this body." Then the Gurú, having given some advice and words of religious counsel to the minister, said, " Tell the king these words from me ;" those said words are written in several places in the books of the Sikhs, and many Sikhs have committed them to memory also. When the Gurú became much afflicted, then his disciples asked him, "O your Highness! whom shall we regard as the Gurú after you?" The Gurú thought to himself, " My father used to be displeased with my brother Rám Ráí on account of his manifesting miracles, and I cannot see any one fit for the post, to whom shall I make over the badge of Gurúship?" He then again reflected, "Bába Teg Bahádur, who now lives in the village called Bakála, although he does not pay much heed to the affairs of the world, still I do not see any one except him who is fit for the Gurúship." Thus thinking, and placing his thoughts on Bába Teg Bahádur, he placed five pice and a cocoanut shell on the ground, and, having done obeisance to him, said to his disciples, " Go! your Gurú is in a village called Bakála near Anandpur; he will direct you all in the road of religion." Having thus said, he himself left his body in the year 1721 B.B. *i.e.* 1664 A.D.

The circumstances of his elder brother, Rám Ráí are thus:—Inasmuch as he had a great desire for visiting countries, wandering about, he came through the mountains to Dehra Dún; there a large concourse came to him to see his miracles, and he also increased their belief in himself. Remaining there, he made many persons, his disciples, and all those persons, who became his disciples, them he directed in his new road. He was living also in the time of Gurú Govind Singh, who is called the tenth Gurú; moreover, he often quarrelled with him; but Gurú Govind Singh never bore enmity towards him in his heart, although he, Rám Rái, used always to remain angry with him; he also taught his disciples thus, "You must not do obeisance to any one but myself," and also told them that no goddess or god, except himself, was fit for them to worship. To the present day his disciples, who are called Rám Ráiyás, do not worship any one else; moreover the Rám Ráiyás do not bend their heads at any of those tombs, which are regarded as (the burying place of) the incarnations of the tenth Gurú. Once, Rám Rái, for the sake of one of his disciples, sat in a very deep cave, and began to perform penance according to the rites of the Jogabhiyás. When his life had reached the tenth door,[39] then his disciples, who were near, knew that the Gurú had died; all his disciples and followers, reflecting on the circumstances of his death, burnt his body according to the rites of the Hindús, and, having erected a mausoleum there, called its name, "The (dehra) resting place of Rám Rái" and for this reason the name of the mountain is known as Dehra Dún. Here, year by year, a large fair is held, and many good and holy men are collected together.

VERSES.

Whoever has come (into this world), he will go (from it); this world is a dream:—

He is happy who worships his Creator in this world.

[39] The ten doors are the two eyes, two ears, two nostrils, mouth, the organ of generation, the organ of excretion, and the brain; the tenth alone is a closed organ; hence the sentence "his life had reached the tenth door," means, his life had gone above to his brain i.e. was closed up.

CHAPTER IX.

The Circumstances of Gurú Teg Bahádur.

As Har Kisan, at the time of his death, made over the seat of Gurúship in the name of Teg Bahádur, the assemblage came to Bakála to pay their respects to the Gurú. There, many Sodhís had given themselves out as the Gurú, but a Labána Sikh, having found out Gurú Teg Bahádur, did obeisance to him, and said. " O Gurú! Har Kisan has told us to follow you; do you show kindness, and let us see you." Teg Bahádur used to live aloof like a madman, disgusted with the world, and in wretched circumstances, wearing dirty clothes: his mother explained to him saying, "O Son! Gurú Har Kisan has appointed you Gurú; do you now dress yourself properly, for the people have come to pay you their respects." Teg Bahádur, who was disgusted with the pleasures of the world, and eschewed all bodily comforts, said, "O mother! all this world appears false to me, and all its joys and wealth seem to give pain; I do not care to have the Gurúship, for to be a Gurú is a thing which gives much trouble; knowingly to become ensnared in the net of honour and glory is not the religion of the wise; I cannot carry this load; do you appoint some one else as Gurú." His mother and all the assembly, with much entreaty, besought him, saying, "O true king! do not bewilder us, for we will now follow no one but you; it is not good for you also to subvert the order of Gurú Har Kisan." In short, at last Gurú Teg Bahádur sat on the throne, and began to perform the duties of the Gurú.

Departing from Bakála, the Gurú came and lived afterwards in Mákhowál, which is near Kíratpur, on the banks of the Satluj; at first its name was Mákhowál, but afterwards, on account of the Gurú living there, its name was called Anandpur. Although Gurú Teg Bahádur sat on the throne of Gurúship, still his asceticism did not depart from his heart, and he always remained disgusted with the world; moreover the songs and couplets, which he composed, are very full of asceticism, and whoever shall read them with true heart, he, regarding the pleasures of the world as contemptible, will undoubtedly be filled with the love of God. All those verses are written in the Granth Sáhib, in that place where Gurú Arjan, at the time of making the Granth, left some blank pages. Although the name of

Nának is to be found (affixed) to all these verses, still on account of their being the ninth Mahalá, all people know that they are the verses of Gurú Teg Bahádur.

Once Gurú Teg Bahádur, with his wife and other relatives, went to perform pilgrimage, and, in their pilgrimage, came and stopped in the city of Patna, at which time Govind Singh was born there. The Gurú remained there five or six years, and at last on account of some quarrel with the people, he left that place and came and lived in Anandpur. Gurú Teg Bahádur was always occupied with this thought, "When Govind Singh is grown up, I will make over the business of Guruship to him, and, unharassed, I will worship my Lord."

This was always his custom, viz., to go out of the city, and live wandering about the jungles. This is what occurred one day; taking two or three Sikhs with him, he went to wander about in the jungles, and went away to Hindustán; when he arrived in Agra, then he went and put up in a garden, and sent his seal ring and a shawl, by a disciple (Sikh) to the bazaar, saying, "Take them to some confectioner—and bring me some food." The confectioner, thinking, that perhaps it was stolen property, took it to the Kotwál. The Kotwál took that seal ring, and came to Teg Bahádur in the garden, and began to ask, "Who are you, and whence have you come?" Teg Bahádur, giving his name and abode, said, "I have at present come from Anandpur to wander about." The Kotwál forthwith wrote to Dillí to King Aurangzeb, saying, "The priest of the Hindús Gurú Teg Bahádur, who is of the sect of Nának, has suddenly fallen into my hands; whatever you may order, I will do." In the heart of King Aurangzeb, there was this desire, that the whole world should accept the Musalmán religion; moreover, in those days, he had imprisoned many Bráhmans, hoping that, if these people first turned Musalmáns, then the desire for it would of itself arise in other people's hearts. When the king heard this, that Gurú Teg Bahádur had been seized, then he became very pleased at heart, for he, having before heard of the sect of Nának from various people, had been very desirous to meet with it. He forthwith wrote and sent to Agra, saying, "Quickly send him to Dillí." When the Gurú came to Dillí, then the king disputed and argued with him much, and, having asked him various religious questions, at last said this, "Do you accept my religion, otherwise you shall be killed;"—Teg Bahádur, who was an artless and simple fakír, and entirely taken up with worship, gave no answer to his words, but, seeing his violence, laughed in his heart, for he was not well read in the Vedás, and did not know how to converse. The king then

CHAP. IX.—ACCOUNT OF GURÚ TEG BAHÁDUR.

asked him to show some miracles, but he still remained perfectly quiet; at last, the king sent him, with his three disciples, to prison and said, "You shall not be released, until you accept this religion." When he went to jail, the king first offered him many things to tempt him, but when he, even then, did not agree to become a Musalmán, he then began to afflict him much. The Gurú, having undergone much trouble, wrote a letter to Govind Singh at Anandpur, to this effect: "The Musalmáns have made me very helpless," and in that letter he also wrote this, " My power is broken, and I am bound in chains, and can devise no means of escape; agreeably to Nának's saying, now my help lies with God only; He will help me as He helped the elephant"[40] The meaning of this is, that his power was broken, and he was imprisoned, and there remained no means of escape; now, agreeably to Nának's saying, help was to be looked for only from God, and, as Vishnu helped the afflicted elephant, so also would He help him. Govind Singh, having read the letter, became very afflicted, and, as he could not go himself on account of his helplessness, he sent a letter in answer to it, to this effect; "You are yourself the most powerful of all, and can do whatsoever you wish, for God always is with you." The Gurú, regarding the afflictions, which he suffered at the hands of the king, as the decree of God, bore them patiently. Two of his disciples (Sikhs), seeing the afflictions of that place, ran away. but one who was a true devotee, would not separate from the Gurú, and used often to say thus, "O Gurú! my head is sold to you; whatever shall be your state, shall be my state, and I will now never separate from you." When the Musalmáns had much afflicted the Gurú in that place, then he thought, "Now it is better not to live, for the king uses much force to make me turn Musalmán." After this, the Gurú had a conversation with the king about religious matters, in which he said, "If God had wished to make all the world Musalmáns, then why did He leave other religions in the world? for whatever He wishes, that comes to pass." On hearing these words, the king became still more angry, and began to afflict him even more than before.

One day, Gurú Teg Bahádur said to his disciple (Sikh):—"Now this is my desire, that I should leave my life;

---

[40] The story is that an exceedingly powerful elephant was once attacked by a small river insect and was rendered helpless by it; many elephants came to his assistance to try and help him, but could do nothing; at last the elephant prayed to God. acknowledging its own inability to help itself, and then God delivered it out of its troubles.

so when I tell you, do you with your hand, cut off my head." He said, "O Gurú! how can this fearful thing be done by me? for I regard you as my saviour and my god. For me to cut off your head is out of the question; moreover if any one were to disturb a single hair of your head, I would, there and then, make a heap (of dust) of him." The Gurú said, "You have truly said, and I know that there is no deficiency in your devotion and love, but do you also consider this, that to disobey the order of a Gurú is not the custom of a disciple; I say this to you with much affection, that if you, according to my command, will cut off my head, and release me from this torment, then there will no blame attach to you in this." The Sikh, on hearing this, trembled, and began to say in his heart, "Alas! Alas! now what shall I do? if I disobey the order,—then I will falsify my religion, and if I cut off the Gurú's head, then I shall become a very great sinner." The Gurú, having narrated to him many proofs, at last made him agree to cut off his head. When the morning broke, then the Gurú first bathed, and, having repeated the Japjí, placed his head on the ground to do obeisance to his Lord; and then gave a sign, saying "O Sikh! fulfil the command." That Sikh gave a blow with his sword and separated his head. When the news reached Govind Singh in Anandpur of the death of the Gurú, then he became very afflicted; but afterwards, having accepted it as the decree of God, said to his sweepers, "Do you, by some means, bring the body of the Gurú here, for if we sent any men of high birth, or one of our disciples (Sikhs), then they would not be able to get into the royal prison; but you are poor people, and, under the pretence of sweeping, can go in, and accomplish this business." They at once went to Dillí, and, having hid his body in a cart of grass, brought it to Anandpur. Govind Singh was much pleased with them; moreover that very day, having blessed them, he said, "From to-day, you are the sons of the Gurú, and will be called Rangharetas."[41] They, who, in the present day, are called Majabí Sikhs in the Panjáb, are all their descendants. The body was burnt in Anandpur, and, with much joy and rejoicing, a very large huge mausoleum was erected there, and its name has become known, as the shrine of Teg Bahádur. The head of the Gurú which had remained in Dillí, that head the Sikhs burnt there, and the tomb, which was erected over it, became known by the name of Sisgang (Head Heap), and crowds go there also to visit it, and make their offerings. In the mind of Gurú Teg Bahádur, it had always been settled to give the seat of Guruship to Govind

---

[41] The Ranghars, or Musalmán Rájpúts, are considered a very brave race of men; hence rangharota implies "brave heroes."

CHAP. IX.—ACCOUNT OF GURÚ TEG BAHÁDUR

Singh, for, from his childhood, he appeard very active and clever; and as Teg Bahádur never cared for the business of the Gurúship, he wished, when Govind Singh grew up, that he should make over the business of the Gurúship to him, and himself escape from the burden. At last, taking this wish in his heart, his head was cut off in the year 1732 B.B., *i.e.* the year 1675 A.D., and the throne of the Gurúship came into the possession of Govind Singh:—

VERSES.

God alone is true, all the world is false;

Therefore do not sit in this country of dreams with your legs stretched out (*i.e.* at ease).

CHAPTER X.

The Circumstances of Gurú Govind Singh.

This Gurú Govind Singh, from his very childhood, was exceedingly expert, and, in his early years even, he learnt archery so well, that none of his companions were able to shoot arrows like him. It appears from many of his words, that he also knew Persian; and although he had no knowledge, except of Persian and Gurumukhí, still on account of his associating with Pandats and maulvis and other wise people, he could talk and discourse very nicely, and, by his arguments, he drew many people to himself. When he sat on the seat of Guráship, and crowds came to see him, then he thought thus to himself "The Musalmáns have much afflicted the Gurús and holy men and other devotees, who were before me; I must now, with the help of these assemblies, take their revenge from the Turks." And he reflected thus too: "The disposition of all these assemblies from the time of Gurú Nának has been like that of fakirs, and they do not know the ways of battle and war; it behoves me to make a new sect in my own name, and, having taught them the use of arms and the mode of government, get them to fight with the Turks." Thus thinking, he departed from Anandpur, and went to the peak of Náinadeví, situated in the mountains about five kos distance from there; then, having gone inside her temple, and joining his hands before the goddess, he petitioned; "O Durga! I, for the sake of taking revenge on the Turks, wish to make a sect, do you give me this power." Having thus said, he called the Pandats, and began to perform penance according to their directions. When he had finished his penance, the Pandats began to make him offer burnt offerings. When a hundred maunds of wheat, sugar, fruit and molasses had been placed on the fire, and the burnt offering had been completed, then the Pandats said: "O Gurú, now in this instance for a sacrifice of oblation, do you cut off the head of your son, and offer it up." Govind Singh had four sons; the name of one was Joráwar Singh, of the second Fatch Singh, of the third Jujhár Singh, and of the fourth Jít Singh. When the Gurú asked the mothers to offer up their sons as a sacrifice, then they said: "We will withdraw from forwarding your new sect; to kill your sons to create your sect is not pleasing to us." When he could not get a son, then he again asked the Pandats. "Now do you please name some other offering." The Pandats fulfilled the sacrifice, by offering up some thing else. It is reported, that the goddess appeared and said "Go! your sect will be set going in the world." Then Govind Singh, having come to Anandpur, and collected all the assembly, wished to see who were really in earnest. The Gurú, having called all the assembly, said "I require the head of one man; let him, who loves his Gurú, give his head to me." On hearing this, most of the people ran away, and the sincerity of many was shattered; but amongst them all, five disciples, getting up, said: "O true king! our heads are present; cut them off when you please." Of these five, the name of one was Dharm Singh, of the second Sukhá Singh, of the third Dayá Singh, of the fourth Himmat Singh, and of the fifth Mukhan Singh. The Gurú, having taken these five into a room, began to say: "O beloved! I have been much pleased with your faith and sincerity, for you have not refused to give your heads in the name of the Gurú; come now, I will baptize you in the true religion." Then, having caused these five to bathe, he seated them together, and then, having dissolved some sweetmeats in water, and stirred it up with a knife[12], and having read some verses composed by himself, which are written in the book called Akal Ustút (or immortal praise), he gave them some of that sharbat to drink, and put some on their heads, and what was left, he sprinkled on their bodies, and then, patting them with his own hands, called out with a loud voice and said, "Say O sect of the Wáh Gurú (God), 'Victory be to the Lord (Wáh Gurú)'." Then having baptized those five, he was himself afterwards baptized in the same way: and then said to them "Whoever is my disciple will always keep five things, the first letter (of the names) of which is K; namely kes (hair), kanghá (comb), karad (knife), kirpán (talwár or sword) and kachh[13]: and he who shall leave off wearing any of these things, he shall not be my disciple (Sikh)." Then, having written what else was to be recognized as the principles, rites, and usages of his disciples, he gave it to them; and, at the present time, the Sikhs call that writing their Rahit Námá or code. It is useless to pen the whole of that code here, but the parts of it, which it is necessary for foreigners to know, I will write here.—

The Code of the Sikhs.

Not to believe in the Vedas, Sástras, Puráns, or the Kurán.

---

[12] Khaudá is the two edged pointed weapon worn in the head-dress of the Akálís.

[13] Kachh are short breeches, reaching to the knees, worn by Sikhs.

Not to pay any heed to the word of Pandats, Pándhas, Miyáns, or Mahitas.

Not to perform any funeral obsequies (sarádh)[44] (khíáh),[45] (karam kiria) ;[46] but when performed, to do so according to the decrees of the Granthjí.

Not to wear any janeú (Brahminical thread) Bodí (tuft of hair) Málá (necklace) kan*th*i (rosary).

Not to worship at any marí (grave) or masán (burning place).

Not to perform Sandhiá Gátri,[47] Páth (reading Brahminical books), or Pújá (worship) ; only to read the japjí, jápjí, &c.

Not to give food[48] to any but disciples.

Not to regard Bráhmans and Saiads as high in rank.

Never to bare the head.

Never to touch a hukka or tobacco.

Never to apply a razor to the head or beard.

Never to covet another man's wife or another man's goods.

Never to read Mantras, according to the rites of the Vedas, at marriages, deaths, or births.

Never to be disobedient to the Gurú.

Never to mix with the following five sects, namely, Dhirmalliyas, Rámráias, Mínas, Masands, and Sirgunms, and never to consort with these five.

The Dhirmalliyas are those, who are of the offspring of Dhirmall. The Rámráias are those, who are called the disciples of Gurú Rám Ráí of Dehra Dún. The Mínas are those, who are of the family of Pirthí Mall, the uncle of Hargovind ; that Pirthí Mall hid six letters, which were sent from Láhaur. The Masands are those, who go before the Gurú and collect disciples, and eat what belongs to the offerings of the Gurús. The Sirgunms are those, who are called atheists, Sarawagís and Jains.

If any disciple, by mistake, shall have dealings with any of these, five sects, then he must present a rupee and a quarter's worth of Karáh Parsád,[49] and offer it up with his knife stuck in

---

[44] Sarádh is the commemoration of one's deceased ancestors in the month Assu.
[45] Khíáh is the yearly remembrance of the dead on the anniversary of death.
[46] Karam kiria are the obsequies performed at a funeral.
[47] Forms of Brahminical prayers.
[48] Neandá means holy food, given as alms.
[49] Karáh Parshád or halwa is a sweatmeat, made of flour, sugar and clarified butter.

CHAP. X.—ACCOUNT OF GURÚ GOVIND SINGH.

it, and, joining his hands, ask forgiveness of his fault from God. In place of Saudhiá Gátrí, to read the Rahurás, Arti Suhla[50] and the Japjí and Jápjí. On the occasion of a marriage, to read the Anand (song of joy) and, at the time of a death, meditate on the Granthjí. In short, whatever is laid down to be done in the Sástras, or is according to the customs of the country, shall be performed according to the decrees of the Granthjí; and if the bones of the dead can be thrown into the Ganges, it is well; otherwise, if they are deposited in the district of Anmritsar, this will be equal to throwing them into the Ganges. In this way he pointed out many other rules also, and, in a few days, thousands of Sikhs, having been baptized, joined him. The sharbat, which is given to drink at the time of baptism, its name they call Anmrit (nectar) or the water of life.

HISTORY OF GOVIND SINGH—continued.

One day, Govind Singh took a fancy that he would send for the book of the Granth Sáhib, and write something more in it; but as, at that time, that book was in the house of the Sodhís of Kartárpur, they would not give it to Govind Singh; moreover, they said thus: " As Govind Singh also calls himself the Gurú, let him, by his own power, make another new Granthjí." When the Gurú heard that they would not give the book, then, after a few days, the Gurú discovered that, from reading the original Granthjí, the Sikhs became very feeble hearted; he therefore determined himself to compose such a Granth, that, from reading it, his disciples, having learnt the science of government and the use of weapons, and other kinds of expertness, should become fit for fighting. Accordingly, from that very day, he commenced to make a very large Granth, and when it was finished in the year 1753 B.B. on the eighth of the light half of the month Bhádon, on a Sunday, then he called its name " The Granth Sáhib of the tenth Gurú." This Granth is very difficult, and is composed in many measures in the Hindí dialect, and in it there are many counsels from the Sástras on the manner of giving battle and making war, and about the wiles of women and their arts, and about devotion and the knowledge of God. From it, it appears that Govind Singh was very expert in making poetry. When from all sides, crowds began to come to him, then the talk of his new sect began to spread about in all places; moreover, the news was also conveyed to the king of Dilli; (it was) also (reported) that a large army always remained with Govind Singh, and the king was continually anxious about this matter. When his (Govind Singh's) Sikhs began to plunder in all quarters, and to commit robberies, then the kings

---

[50] These are the names of various Sikh hymns.

of the hills beyond Anandpur also began to consult about making war against him. This is what occurred one day; the hill kings sent a message to Govind Singh, saying " In your possession is a certain elephant, which you must send to us." As there were many good qualities in that elephant, and the Gurú was very fond of it, on this account, the Gurú did not agree to send it. The hill people, being greatly displeased at this affair, and taking very many soldiers with them, came to Anandpur. The fight lasted very severely for several days, and innumerable soldiers of both sides were killed; moreover, two of Govind Singh's sons were killed in that fight at a city called Chamkaur, and a shrine was erected there, and called Chamkaur Sáhib. They say that Govind Singh several times defeated and put to flight the hill people, but afterwards when they attacked Anandpur with the assistance of the king's army, then Govind Singh thought it better to go away from Anandpur. Govind Singh, leaving all his army there, and taking those his first five disciples, and his two sons with him, came and lived in the house of a Sikh in a city called Máchhúwára. When the armies came after him there also, then Govind Singh, dyeing his clothes in surma (antimony), got off disguised as a Musalmán through the midst of the armies. He set off with those same five Sikhs to the country of Málwa, but his two sons remained there; when those two lads fell into the hands of the army, then the army seized and sent them to a city called Sarand. The governor of that place, by name Wazír Khán, sent information to the king at Dillí, saying : " Two sons of Gurú Govind Singh, who has set going the Khálsa sect, have fallen into my hands ; whatever you shall order, that shall be done to them." As King Aurangzeb, from hearing the report of them, had already become distressed, on receiving this (news), he became glad at heart, and wrote and sent this answer " Do you take the lives of these two lads." On reading the royal command, the governor, having taken the lads, buried them under a foundation (of a building), and, having erected a wall over it, built a house there. At that time, from observing the orphan state of these children, the very walls even wept; but from seeing the crying and sobbing of these children, no pity came to that vile governor. That day, all the people in Sarand remained uttering " Alas! alas!" and heaving regrets, and no one ate their food with any appetite. At the time of their being put to death, all the attendants, who were present, from fear of the governor, said nothing, except a Pathán of Maler Kotla, who expostulated much with the governor, saying, " What have these orphan children taken belonging to you?" but that wretch heeded not in the least. When the news of the killing of his sons reached Govind Singh on the road, then those five Sikhs began to give vent to words of sorrow. Govind Singh, for the sake of removing their sorrow, having drawn two lines on the ground, effaced them, and said, "O brother Sikhs! as, from the drawing and effacing of these lines, you feel no joy or sorrow, so also should you know that God has made the whole world as lines according to His desire; and when it is His pleasure, He effaces them; therefore it behoves the wise to remain silent regarding His decrees." Then the Gurú went and stood at the gate of a fort in a village named Kotkapúra, which is in Málwa, on which a Jatt, named Kapúrá, who was the commander of that fort, came out from within; then the Gurú asked him for a place to hide himself. He gave reply, "You have come here, having killed your sons, and now you wish to have me killed also by the king." The Gurú, heaving a sigh, said, "Very well, if God wills, then you will be hanged also." In short, when the Gurú went from there and lived in a place called Mukatsar, which is in the district of Firozpur, then that Jatt named Kapúrá, who was the commander of Kotkapúrá, was hung agreeably to the orders of the king.

Afterwards, the king and the hill chiefs received information that Govind Singh had gone and taken up his residence in Mukatsar; but there was this thing to be considered, that, on account of the scarcity of water in that country, the army would suffer much hardship. Although, after reflecting over this matter, the heart of the king hesitated much at sending an army, still the hill chiefs, by urging him on, had armies despatched from Dilli and came and surrounded Mukatsar. As Gurú Govind Singh was seated there without any thought thereof, when he saw himself surrounded by the army, he became much perplexed. At last, having called his Sikhs from the surrounding country, he encouraged them to fight. In short, at that time, many thousands Sikhs, all ready to lay down their lives, joined Govind Singh; when the fight commenced on both sides, then many thousand men of the king's army were killed; and although many Sikhs of Govind Singh's (army) were also killed, still they did not leave the battle field. At last, the king's army was obliged to retreat for want of water, and Govind Singh began to live there; at the place at which the fight took place, Govind Singh caused a very large tank to be dug, and called its name Mukatsar; and, by reason of the making of that tank, the name of that place, which was before but a small village, became renowned as Mukatsar. Govind Singh explained to his disciples "Many people have obtained salvation here, so now, whoever shall perform ablution in this place with true love and devotion, he, too, will obtain salvation." Now-a-days, every year on the first of the month Magh (12th January to 12th February), a very large fair is held there. Afterwards, when all the quarrels with the king had come to an end, then Govind Singh, taking a large concourse with him, came and lived in a village of Málwa, and for sometime enjoyed quiet there. The people of Málwa are very simple and artless, and thousands of them, from associating with him, were baptized as his disciples. The Gurú made a very beautiful place there for himself to live in, and called its name the Damdama. Now-a-days, a very large fair is held there, and many people go there to learn the words of wisdom, and stop there some time; for Gurú Govind Singh, after building that place, made it known among his disciples, that whoever should come here and live, he, however, great a fool he might be, would become wise; at the present time, many disciples and holy saints, who are very good and wise, live there; and whoever, having left his family, shall go there, merely for the sake of getting wisdom, he will surely become wise; and there is this very good point also about this place, that as many writers of the Gurumukhi letters live there, and they write a very good hand, none but their pupils can write as they do; that place is now known as the Damdama Sáhib. After this, departing from there, the Gurú came to Sarand, where his two sons had been murdered by being buried under a foundation. When the Gurú arrived at that house, where his two sons were buried, then he became very sad, but, by reason of the strength of his religious understanding, he did not manifest the grief of his heart. His disciples petitioned him, saying, "O Gurú! if you command, then we will set fire to this city of Sarand, for it is not good for such a vile city as this, in which the sons of the Gurú were murdered without fault, to exist in the world!" The Gurú replied: "O Bháí Sikhs! no fault attaches to the whole city, but the fault is merely the king's, and God himself will take vengeance on him." Again also, when his disciples petitioned, saying: "O true king! we feel very angry with this city; if you will give us the command, we will raze it to the ground and efface its foundation and site." The Gurú, seeing the obstinacy of his disciples, thought thus: "If I were to give the order to burn and raze this city, then the anger of the king would be aroused against me afresh. It is therefore better that I should give them some other order." Having thus thought, calling out, he said to his disciples: "Let whoever is my disciple, when he goes from Sarand to the Ganges, take two bricks from here, and throw them into the Jamna; and when he returns, then let him take two bricks and throw them into the Satluj; whoever does not obey this my command, his bathing in the Ganges will be of no account" He said this also: "From to-day, let no one call it Sarand; its name is Gurúmárí (cursed); accordingly to the present day, people take bricks from there and throw them into the Jamna and Satluj ; and, rising in the morning, no Hindú mentions the name of it.[51] Afterwards, the disciples made a very large tomb there, and all Sikhs go there to do obeisance, and offer oblations. After this the Gurú, wandering about, came to Anandpur; one day, when a large assembly had collected, then the Gurú said : " The Turks, i.e., the Musalmáns, have given much trouble to the world, and have afflicted our race for many generations, and have also robbed us of much of our property and treasure, and have killed our children ; now let all the Khálsa assemble, and destroy them for me ! for this very reason, I have given you arms and raised this sect." The assembly, joining their hands, said : " O true Gurú ! we are at your service with our lives and property : but it behoves us to consider one thing, that the armies of the Turks are uncountable, and their power is beyond bounds, how can we, helpless, poor Sikhs, conquer them ? Therefore, it is best that you should first write a letter to King Aurangzeb, and send and give him advice, that he should no longer afflict your good, pious, and poor followers. If he shall pay regard to this and desist from his depravity, all well ; if not, we will fight with him." The Gurú, regarding this advice as good, wrote a letter in verse in the Persian language, and sent it to the king. That letter they have styled and called the Jafarnáma (letter of victory). Although there is no necessity for writing the whole of that letter here, still those parts of it, which are fraught with good advice, I will write here, for, from reading them, the wisdom and bravery of Govind Singh will be manifested.

The Jafarnáma (or letter of victory).

" O King ! as God has seated you on the throne, would it not be better, if you did not commit injustice towards people ? Behold ! what injustice you have done me, who lived on a mountain peak, and had never molested any of your villages or towns ; you without fault, first imprisoned my father, Gurú Teg Bahádur, and killed him, and then, joining with other rulers, you sent armies against me ; then you killed my young children, and thousands of my disciples ; you have slain my wives, and robbed my treasury ; but remember that these injustices, which are committed in your threshold, are not allowed at the threshold of God ; there, justice is most truly meted out ; there, kings and worms, (i.e., poor) are held equal. But if you have this wrong idea, that although you are a king, you eat barley bread with the labour of your own

---

[51] i.e., they do not mention the name of Sarand until after they have taken their morning meal. Sikhs never mention it by the name Sarand, but call it "Gurúmúri."

hands,[52] then look at the horse; for it does a great deal of work and always eats barley. But if you say that you read the Kurán, then what is the good? for until one purifies one's heart with good deeds, the reading the Kurán with one's lips does no good, but the fire of hell is made still hotter for one. If you have this thought, that, from doing service to God, you will escape from the pains of hell, then listen; reading four verses with your mouth is not called true service, but subduing your appetites is real worship; you, on the contrary, with the intoxication of royalty, foster your lusts. Behold! you, for the pleasure of your heart, killed your own father and brothers; what service do you call this? But if you hold this wrong idea, that the prophet will deliver you from the fire of hell, then listen; all the prophets have said that they will deliver those who shall obey their commands, and, leaving their bad ways, shall take to good actions; if you do not obey their orders, why will the prophets deliver you? wherefore know well, that punishment is ready for you in the presence of God. Again if you wrongly suppose that you hold fast the law of the prophets, because you demolish Hindú temples and the temples of Shiva, and thus uproot idolatry, then listen; you have not done away with it, rather you have increased idolatry; for formerly, when temples existed, the Hindús knew for certain that, when they wished, they could come to them and do worship; but now, that you have destroyed the temples, on this account every Hindú has placed an idol in his home, for until they do worship, they cannot take their food.[53] Again, if you wrongly suppose that people praise you, then listen; the flatterers[54] used to praise King Pharaoh, but, in the end, he did not escape from the fire of hell. And if you have this hope, that as God is merciful, He will have mercy on you and deliver you, then listen; as you do not show mercy to people, but are intent on giving them pain, then why should God show mercy to you? This can never be, for a man does not sow sprouts of akh[55] and reap mangoes; rather it thus happens, that whatever seed one sows, its fruit one reaps."

Having written these words of advice, then he also wrote some words about the ways of government, viz., "Beware! as you have oppressed people much, so also will the Khálsa tor-

---

[52] It is usual for true worshippers only to eat barley-bread; Aurungzeb is said never to have tasted food purchased with money from the royal coffers, but from what he obtained from the proceeds of his own handiwork. He used to employ himself in making cups, &c. This then is as much as to say; "Don't imagine, that although you eat barley-bread, you are a true worshipper.
[53] *Lit.* "Bread and water."
[54] *Lit.* "Men with an object (gharaj.)"
[55] Also called madar; it is a bitter plant, which grows wild, and, from the leaf of which, a thick milky substance exudes.

ment you. Now the day of your retribution has come; God is very angry with you. Behold now: I will, with the help of God, take my revenge from you, for the Khálsa has only been raised to kill you."

HISTORY OF GOVIND SINGH—(continued).

Gurú Govind Singh, having written that letter, gave it into the hand of a Bháí, named Dayá Singh, a Sikh, and said "Do thou go to Dillí, and give this letter into the hands of king Aurangzeb himself. When Dayá Singh departed from Anandpur and reached Dillí, then he went and gave that letter to the king. The king, on reading it, was much ashamed, and, although, after reading it, the king, in his heart determined to go and see him, he however (did not fulfil his intention, for he) died a few days after its perusal. In short, the king, having read that letter, said "The Khálsa, which has now been formed, has been formed forty years before its proper time: hence it is well, for it will suffer much affliction." The Gurú, hearing of the death of the king, was greatly pleased, and said to his disciples. "Behold! God has given much ease, otherwise many people in the world would have been killed." When, after Aurangzeb, his son Bahádur Sháh obtained the throne, and his brother tried to take away the kingship from him, then Bahádur Sháh commenced a contest with his brothers. Moreover, in that war, Gurú Govind Singh also sent his army and somewhat helped Bahádur Sháh; rather, it was chiefly owing to the Sikh army, that Bahádur Sháh obtained the victory over his brothers, and again sat on the throne. From that day Bahádur Sháh became very friendly with Gurú Govind Singh, and often sent trays of rarities and fruits to Anandpur to the Gurú. Once, the Gurú wished to go and travel in the eastern countries, and, having determined thus, he departed from Anandpur with those five disciples: after wandering about, he arrived in the city of Agra, and there heard that King Bahádur Sháh had also come there. The Gurú, for the sake of meeting him, went and stood at the gate of his fort: now the Gurú always rode on horseback, and carried a hawk (bird) on his hand, and wore a crown with a plume on his head, and always had with him those five armed Sikhs. When the gatekeepers saw his state, they said "Leave your arms here, otherwise you will not be allowed to go into the fort." The Gurú gave reply "We will not take off our arms; do you go and give the king news of me." The gatekeeper, having gone inside, petitioned, saying: "A Sikh, named Govind Singh, has come to see you, and is standing at the gate, and says: 'I will go inside with my arms on: therefore, according as you may order, so we will go and tell him.'" The king, immediately on hearing his

D

name, said " You have acted very wrongly, in that you have hindered him from coming inside ; therefore go quickly and bring him in just as he pleases." The Gurú went in, with the gate-keeper and his five Sikhs, into the presence of the king, and greeted him with much joy ; and, after asking him all his news regarding his pleasure and health, they conversed together a good deal about travelling and sport ; when some time had thus passed, one of the king's ministers, a Musalmán began also to discourse on religious matters with the Gurú ; afterwards a Kází who was seated in the Durbár, asked this question " O Gurú! the Gurú has commanded that the creature has been sent into the world to do service ; so will you please point out what service the creature should do?" He gave reply "The creature should do this service, viz., that he should remain free from sin, but at the same time regard himself as a sinner." The Kází, on hearing this, was satisfied and said " Yes, it is true, that the creature can never say before his God, that he is free from sin." The Gurú remained there some days, and the king gave him much wealth and presents. After this, the Gurú, wandering about, came to Anandpur; and when several of the hill kings again began quarrelling with him, the Gurú, taking an army of his Sikhs with him, attacked them. In short, at a city called Bhiána, which is in the hills, a very great fight took place. Then all the kings, who had not very much power, being afraid of the Gurú, at last fled away. Afterwards Govind Singh built a large handsome building at that place, and, having placed in it a copy of the Granth, called the name of that place Dehra. After this, as the Gurú, after having conquered the Rájas, was returning to Anandpur, then in one place on the road his pánnta, or foot ornament, fell off, and the Gurú, dismounting from his horse, picked it up. On this, the residents of that place thought, " If we build a temple here, people will come and worship, and make offerings " ; they therefore made a temple there, and called, and made known its name as Páuntá Sáhib, and, now-a-days, a very large fair is held there. After this, the Gurú came to Anandpur and rested for some days. Large assemblies used to collect, and this is what occurred one day ; as the Gurú was seated in Anandpur, some actors came there to act. The Sikhs, who were greatly harassed by the masandas, or priests of the Gurú, said to those actors " Do you act the doings of some masandas; " the object of the Sikhs was this, that the Gurú might hear of the depravity of his masandas, and give them punishment.

The actors at once commenced to act the part of a masanda, and, from thence, set forth for the house of a Sikh ; the masanda, taking a prostitute along with him, and, having drunk a bottle of wine, mounted a horse: and, in company with four or five men, came to the house of that Sikh. When the Sikh saw that a masanda of the Gurú had come to his house, then, joining his hands, he stood up and said "O great king! fortunate is my fate, that you have visited me. Come, sir! and sit down here; you are welcome." When the masanda had sat down, then the Sikh, having sold some of his pots, brought gram and grass for the horse, and prepared bread and dál for the masanda. The masanda, seeing the dál and bread, became very angry; moreover, casting away that bread on to a dung heap, he threw the dal into the fire-place and said, " Why, O wretched Sikh! have you set before me dry bread as an offering, which my dog even would not eat? Go, quickly depart, and get ready some Karáh Parsád and some Mahá Parsád."[56] That Sikh, who was very poor, having sold his wife's rings, prepared every thing. The masanda, having eaten and drunk, began to say "Now bring your offerings before me." The Sikh, having pledged his counterpane with some difficulty, brought him a rupee, and said "O Gurú! I am a poor Sikh; have mercy upon me, and accept this offering." The Gurú, first having touched the rupee, flung it to the prostitute, and, himself throwing down that Sikh, began to kick him; while the Sikh was on the ground being kicked, he, joining his hands, began to say "O Gurú! I am a poor creature (like a cow), forgive me." Then Gurú Govind Singh, becoming very angry, asked his Sikhs, "O my disciples! do my masandas go to 'your houses, and act in this way?" The disciples gave reply, "O true king! they give us even greater pains than this:" and those actors also petitioned, saying, "O Gurú! as, at this time, the masandas are seated before you, from fear of them, we cannot act the part in full; but do you know for true, that your masandas give your disciples a hundred times more pains." When the Gurú had heard these things about the masandas, then he issued an order by beat of drum to his disciples, saying: " Do you proclaim to all the assembled multitude and tell them, not to let the masandas get away." The assembled multitude, hearing the proclamation, immediately stopped all the masandas. The Gurú, having shut up many of them in rooms, put them to death, and others, he killed by hunger and thirst; and others were tied up and slain, and others were beaten to death: whilst others were seized and fried in frying pans, filled with hot oil. After this, the Gurú said: "Let whoever is my disciple never associate with the masandas; for they are great sinners and the stricken of God, and the cursed of the Gurú." From that very day, people have kept aloof from the masandas; after this, on another

---

[56] Meat.

occasion, the Gurú, taking a large concourse with him, went to wander about; and, after roaming about, he arrived at the banks of a river and amused himself with hunting tigers in several places; and then, proceeding on, put up at a village, called Chamkaur situated in Ropar. When he had stopped there some days, he then built a large temple there, and the name of that village is now known as Chamkaur Sáhib. Once, the Gurú was seated in his court, when one of his disciples brought his son before him, and said "O Gurú! this my son, from hearing your words, has become disgusted with the habits of the world, and will not marry; do you have mercy and explain to him, that he should marry and enjoy pleasure in the world." The Gurú asked that lad, "Why have you become an ascetic from hearing my words?" He replied, "O Gurú! from hearing the following words which are in the Anandjí (song of joy), I have become disgusted with the world; and these are those words:

This family, which you see, will not go with you;

It will not go with you, therefore do not fix your thoughts on it;

Undertake not such a business, of which you may, afterwards, altogether repent;

Listen thou to the advice of the Gurú, who will always be with you;

Bába Nának has said, 'Hear, O dear one! always hold fast the Truth (God).'

As you, O true King! have left off living with your family, then how can I devote myself to my family?" The Gurú embraced him and said "O child! praised be thou, that, regarding the words of the Gurú as true, thou remainest indifferent towards thy family; but listen! those who are the beloved of God, they, although they may live with their family, do not cut themselves off from the love of God; moreover, those people who live in the married state, they can perform the service of the hungry and thirsty; listen! I will tell you a story, as to how those who are married, should live, and how those who are fakírs, should live. In a forest, a bird and its mate lived on a tree, and, suddenly, a traveller arrived there; the bird said to its mate 'O dear one! we are married, and the religion of the married state is this, that if any hungry or thirsty one should come to one's house, one should do service to him.' Having thus said, the bird brought some half-burnt, ignited goat-dung, and placed it before the traveller, and then, knocking down its nest, threw it on the ignited dung. The female then threw herself into the fire, and was roasted. After this, when the traveller, having eaten her up, was not satisfied, then the male bird also threw himself into the fire; and then the hunger of the traveller was somewhat abated. This, O child! is the advantage of being a married man, that, like that bird and its mate, you can show mercy; and those people, who only marry for the sake of filling their stomachs, and do not help others, it is with them that God is displeased. He is a true married man who regulates his own food, and brings it into use, to relieve the hunger and affliction of others. Therefore, if you will be such a married man, then undoubtedly marry; there will be no (cause of) fear in your doing so. Now I will tell you a story of a fakír. A fakír lived in the jungles and never asked anything from any one; once on a time, the will of God was this, that, for eight days, he got no food from anywhere; then the fakír thought to himself, 'As God has given me hands and feet, I will go into the city and beg.' When he went into the city, then he saw a wedding taking place at a house, and went and sat down at the door; although many good and holy men were being fed by the master of that house, none of them asked the state of the fakír; in the evening, becoming hopeless, he went away from that door, and setting out for his own hut, met two men coming along with lighted grass torches. They said to him 'As that marriage throng kept you seated all day, and sent you away without giving you any thing to eat, if you will give us the order, we will set fire to their house with these grass torches.' He said, 'Very well; but give me a torch, so that I may also do some thing (take part).' When they had given that torch into his hand, then he began to set them on fire. They said 'What conduct is this that, instead (of the house), you are setting fire to us?' He replied 'You are great sinners and very unjust; for you have given me very bad advice; behold! their not giving me anything to eat was the Will of God; and if God had wished them to give any thing to me, no one could have stopped them; then it does not become me to be displeased with the Will of God, rather it becomes me, to regard nakedness, hunger, grief and joy as the Will of God, and always to return thanks to His Will.' On hearing this, those people said 'You are a perfect saint; may God always give firmness to your faith.'"

The Gurú then said to that lad: "If any man shall become a fakír in the road of God, then it behoves him, like that fakír, to keep his heart filled with mercy, religion, forbearance and patience; otherwise it would be better for him to be a *thug* than a fakír." In this same way, the Gurú continued giving advice to many people. Gurú Rám Rái was still living in the time of this

Gurú, and the two, for many reasons, were at variance with each other, and the assemblies of the two parties often wished to fight with each other, but were restrained. Gurú Govind Singh also always bore enmity towards[57] the Sodhís of Kartárpur in his inmost heart, because of their refusing to give him the Granth; moreover, on this very account, he wrote in his code that his disciples should not hold intercourse with the Dhirmallíyas, which is the name of the Kartárpurís. After this, the Gurú continued wandering about and visiting various countries and regions. In short, in his life-time, 125,000 Sikhs embraced his sect; although this Gurú continued to be styled the representative of Nának, it, however, appears from many of his words, that he differed from him. His religion was not confined to any one book or prophet or incarnation; but it would appear that he picked out various customs and habits of the old prophets and incarnations (i.e., Muhammadan and Hindú), which were good for giving strength to his sect, and bringing him other advantages, and these he made current among his followers.

Gurú Govind Singh's whole life was passed in wandering about, and in reflection and thought; the particulars of his death are thus related; one day, Govind Singh went to the east country to travel, and on the road, at some place, he met with a Pathán. That Pathán was the grandson of that Paindc Khán, who had a fight with the sixth Gurú, Har Govind, in Kartárpur. The Gurú showed much affection towards that Pathán, and moreover kept him as a servant with himself, and said, "Come with me and visit the east country." He began to live with the Gurú, and the Gurú never even mentioned the former enmity to him; rather, when he used to come to him, he used to talk most affectionately to him. One day, the Gurú, after behaving to him in his usual manner, began to joke and chaff with that Pathán; when the Gurú saw that he took his chaff as chaff, then he began to tease him further, and said to him; "O such and such a Khán! if a certain person's father killed a certain person's grandfather, and his son, or grandson, came and obtained his bread and water from him; then say, would he not be very shameless?" He gave answer "If any one, having remained with the enemy of his father and grandfather, should thus get his living from him, then that man would be very shameless and a rogue.[58]" Again, the Gurú said, "O such and such a Khán! if a certain Pathán should become the servant of the enemy of his father, then what would you think of him?" He said, "I should not

---

[57] *Lit.* "He never forgave."
[58] *Lit.* "Nose cut" it being the custom in the East to punish offenders by cutting off their noses.

consider him a Pathán, but a weaver."[59] Again, the Gurú said: "If the enemy of your father and grandfather were to meet you any where, and you were at that time armed with your weapons, say, what would you then do?" He gave reply "I would never allow him to escape alive." Afterwards, that Pathán began to think to himself, "Why does the Gurú continually question me in this way?" Then, having thought, he remembered that Gurú Govind Singh was of the offspring of that Gurú Har Govind, who had fought with his grandfather in Kartárpur. Having thus thought, he became very ashamed in his heart; moreover, from that day, he determined for certain to himself, that if, at any time, he should get the opportunity, then he would, most assuredly, take his grandfather's revenge. This is the event of one day; a certain Sikh brought a very beautiful dagger from some foreign country for the Gurú; the Gurú, seeing its lustre and splendour and fine edge, was greatly pleased, and always kept that dagger by himself. One day, the Gurú asked that Pathán "O such and such a Khán! from how many blows of this dagger would a man die?" He replied, "One blow even of it would be ample." Again, the Gurú said: "Well, if he, who killed your father and grandfather, were to come before you, and this dagger were in your hand, then say, what would you do to him?" He, from hearing this speech, became very angry in his heart, and could make no reply. After a short time, the Gurú fell asleep, and all the attendants retired to their respective homes. Then that Pathán, who had remained seated near the Gurú, having looked around him, slowly took that dagger out of the Gurú's hand, and said to himself, "To-day I will take the revenge of my grandfather from this infidel," then, having drawn the dagger from its sheath, he said the Bismillah, and plunged the dagger into the Gurú's stomach. Then, thinking he was quite dead, he got up from there and ran away; but, as the Gurú was not then dead, on seeing the wound of the dagger, he called out "O Bhái Sikhs! I am dying": all the disciples collected, and, having scoured the country in all direction, they caught and brought that Pathán to the Gurú. To be brief, the Gurú, having praised the bravery of that Pathán, let him go, and said to all those other people, who, from seeing the Gurú's wound, had become very sad and thoughtful, "O Bhái Sikhs! why are you so thoughtful? this affair has been brought to pass by God. Behold! that Pathán did not kill me; but I, making him ashamed, myself roused him to kill me; do not you be sorrowful, rather be pleased with the Will of God." Afterwards,

---

[59] i.e., a coward, for Patháns are brave but weavers are regarded as cowards.

hearing this news, that the grandson of Painde Khán, Pathán, had stabbed the Gurú, to take the revenge of his grandfather, King Nádir Sháh of Dillí became greatly distressed: moreover, sending some of the royal physcians, he gave them strict injunctions "You must do your very best to cure Govind Singh." When the surgeons arrived near the Gurú, then they sewed up all the wounds, and began to apply plaster and ointment. In a few days, all the wound healed up, and he obtained ease; one day the Gurú fired an arrow at some game, and, as he pulled the bow with force, all the threads of that wound again broke, and the blood began to flow forth; the physicians, on seeing this his state, were much perplexed; they again applied many remedies, but he obtained no ease. The hakims, being helpless, returned to Dillí, and the Gurú, seated in a pálkí, wandering about, went to the Dakkan. When he arrived at a city called Nader, in the Dakkan, then the Gurú became very helpless from the pain of that wound; moreover, he said to his assembly " O Bháí Sikhs! now I have no hope of my body remaining to me; it is therefore well, that we should now remain in this city. If my life shall leave me here, then it will be well, for, by reason of their being a city here, after my death, a wooden coffin and a shroud will be able to be obtained." The Sikhs remained there and found it difficult to leave him for any time. After they had stopped there some days, and no alleviation of the pain was obtained, then the Gurú said to his disciples " Do you now give some alms; there is no profit from medicines." On hearing this, the Sikhs made a very huge feast, and, having prepared various kinds of food and edibles, fed the Bráhmans and the good and holy; and they presented, in the way of alms, much ornaments and clothing. Then the Gurú said to his Sikhs: " Now my body will quickly leave me; do you have the bier and coffin ready." The Sikhs, agreeably to the Gurú's orders, got every thing ready; and then they all, joining their hands, asked " O True Gurú! now that you adopted this way of proceeding, whom will you place on the seat of Gurúship for our guidance?" The Gurú said, "I shall not do as the former nine Gurús who preceeded me, and who, at the time of dying, appointed some other Gurú to sit on the throne. I have made you and all my followers over to the embrace of the Immortal one; after my death, do all you people regard the book of the Granth Sáhib, as your Gurú; whatever you will ask, it will point out to you. If any of my disciples, be he shorn, or grow long hair, let him regard the Granth Sáhib as the form of his Gurú: and whatever disciple of mine has a desire to see me, let him offer up Karáh Parsád to the value of a rupee and a quarter, or as much as he desire, and let him open the book of the Granth Sáhib, and do obeisance, and he will obtain as much profit as if he had seen me." After this, the Gurú gave various other kinds of counsels; as, for example: "O Bháí Sikhs; people of various kinds live in the world; but whoever is my disciple will take care not to mix with them. If any one, showing forth wonders and miracles, should wish to break up the religion of my disciples, then he must not be believed; and although any one might extract oil out of sand, and cause walls to gallop as horses, and show them to you, still this is your religion, that you should regard them as the play of Indrajál (juggling), and not believe them; for people will show you many curious sights to try and make a flaw in (break up) the Sikh religion: but do you always read and remember this verse with affection:

> 'O Lord! having given me Thy hand, do Thou keep me from roving.'"

After uttering these words, the Gurú became much distressed; then the Sikhs made a funeral pyre of sandal wood, and, bringing all the requisites, placed them by him, and then they all began to worship the Wáh-Gurú. When a little while only was left to the Gurú's death, then he said to his disciples: "Do you, having bathed me, put on a clean suit of clothes, and do you at this time fasten on all my arms," and he added this also: "When my life leaves me, then do not take off these arms and clothes, but burn me with all my clothes and arms." Having said these words, he went and sat on the funeral pyre; at that time, placing his thoughts on God, he gave utterance to this quatrain with his mouth, with much affection:

QUATRAIN.

> Since I seized Thy feet, I have brought nothing else under (my) eye:
> O merciful Rám! the Puráns and the Kurán teach various systems, but I did not regard one (of them);
> The Simriti, Sástras and Vedas, all teach many modifications, but I did not heed any one (of them):
> O Dispenser of Happiness! bestow mercy (on me);
> I have not ever said 'I': I recognized all as Thee.—
> (Trumpp's Adi Granth.).

Having said these words, he closed his eyes, and in the year 1765 B.B. *i.e.*, the year 1708 A.D., he departed this life. They say that, for many generations, there was a mark of leprosy on the feet of the Gurús. At that time, from all quarters, the sound of blowing of shells arose, and flowers began to rain down.

All the disciples and holy men, who had collected from all parts having uttered the words : "Jai Jai Kár (victory victory)," began to sing beautiful songs : and many, filling their eyes with tears, began to weep and lament at separation from the Gurú. In all quarters, all players on the rubab (a kind of harp) began to sound their instruments, and hundreds began to read the Granth Sáhib. At that time, it appeared as if there was the rejoicing of heaven : many holy and good men, becoming ascetics, withdrew at that time from worldly affairs : and many, regarding the pleasures of this world as vain and false, gave their lives along with the Gurú. Many people became martyrs there ; and many houses for fakírs were erected in that place. Amidst them all, they erected a shrine over the Gurú, and, near his burying place, they made many other mausoleums and dharmsálas, and deposited Granth sáhibs in them. The name of that city, which was called Nader, was changed to Abchalnagar. In the present day, many Sikhs go there, and offer their oblations with much devotion. In that tomb, thousands of swords, shields, spears, and quoits, are to be found at all times ; moreover the Sikhs, who go there, all worship those arms. The Sikhs believe this, that all those arms were formerly the property of Gurú Govind Singh himself. All Sikhs eat whatever oblations are offered there in worship : moreover this also is a custom there, that if any one shall be put to great expense in going there, then the Sikhs there write to the Sikhs of other countries in the Gurumukhí character, and send a command to them to help them ; and religious people, on seeing such a written command, offer whatever offerings they can to them. They have called the name of this written command, the Hukmnáma (or letter of command) ; and the seal, which is attached to it, was, they say, the very seal of the hand of Gurú Govind Singh himself ; and in that seal there is written in the Gurumukhí character " God is one ; may there always be victory to my cauldron (offerings) and sword, and may the victory be without delay ;[60] but victory to Nának and Gurú Govind Singh is only from the Help of the Immortal One." And if any serious quarrel break out among the Sikhs, it is also settled amongst them by a Hukmnáma (issued) from there (Nader). Those, who are good and true Sikhs, never disobey what is written in a Hukmnáma. Now this is a matter for reflection. Behold, what plays are performed in the world, and how many warriors good, honourable, charitable, obstinate, and wealthy men have been born, and, in the end, all have been mixed in the dust. Is this world not a spectacle of a dream ? whoever here, forgetting

---

[60] i.e., may neither the religious devotion, nor the martial spirit of my followers ever decrease, but ever be crowned with success, and be on the increase.

CHAP. X.—ACCOUNT OF GURÚ GOVIND SINGH.

his death, for an instant stretches out his feet,[61] is a great fool. From this effacing and making of the world, which God has settled, man gets this warning, that he should not fix his thoughts too highly on it, and should not, all his life long, be filled with anxiety and thought about it; for if any one, even after much thought, collects together a little in the world, still he himself will not always remain here.

---

[61] i.e., lives in a state of carelessness and regards not God and the day of his death.

PART II.

RELATING THE EVENTS FROM THE TIME OF MAHÁRÁJA RANJÍT SINGH TO THE ARRIVAL OF THE ENGLISH.

CHAPTER I.

The names of the twelve Misals.

IT was quite necessary, that I should, in this place, write the circumstances of Mahárája Ranjít Singh : but I will not do so (at once) as I must (first) briefly relate how the Sikhs flourished after Gurú Govind Singh, and who obtained the chiefship among them; accordingly I will first write about the twelve Misals or divisions [62] of the Sikhs. When Gurú Govind Singh's body left him, then for some days, several of his special disciples kept the assemblies under their hands, but after some time, when the assemblies had become unmanageable, then, for some reason or other, a certain Bairágí saint took the Sikh baptism. He was exceedingly clever and wise, so that, by his wisdom, he collected together all the old Sikhs and made them into one body ; moreover it so happened, that, as the Sikhs had collected with him in many thousands, for this reason, they created much disturbance ; the name of that Bairágí was formerly something else, but afterwards in the Sikh Khálsa, his name, for some reason or other, became known as Bandá. On one occasion, that Sikh, named Bandá, committing violence and robbery, arrived in the district of Siálkot ; when they reached that district, the Sikhs began to rob the goods of the Musalmáns, and then again a great quarrel arose between them ; at last, after some fighting, that Bandá, taking many Sikhs with him, went to the hills, and the hill kings also, as they did not behave well to him, suffered much distress at his hands ; but at last, one hill chief, by some stratagem or device, having caught him with several hundred Sikhs, sent him to the Governor of Dillí. As the occupants of the throne of Dillí at that time were of very hard disposition, and were especially angry with the sect of the Sikhs, they were much pleased at the capture of Bandá. At that time, a king, named Farukh Síar, was seated on the throne of Dillí ; he caused

---

[62] Misal really signifies "dependency to a chief, or petty ruler, who is under the authority of a Rájá."

CHAP. 1.—NAMES OF THE TWELVE MISALS.

Bandá, with all those Sikhs, who were with him at that time, to be put to death, and further gave orders, that wherever any of their sect was found, he was to be caught, and brought to him, for he wished to efface their seed from off the earth. When the Sikhs heard that their chief, named Bandá, had been killed, and an order had been issued by the —ng to seize all Sikhs and take them to him, then, leaving their houses and families, some began to wander about in the jungles; and others, taking their households with them, went and hid in the mountains; and others, finding huts in the deserts, went and took up their abode in them. In the meanwhile, Farukh Síar, having reigned but two, or two and a half, years, died, and after him, his son, Jahándár Sháh, obtained the throne. The Sikhs, after this, for some years continued wandering about begging, and in wretched circumstances; for this reason, in those days, their sect greatly diminished; and wherever the Sikhs, even thus despised, lived, there they supported themselves secretly with much difficulty. One day, a Birak Jatt named Kapúrá, who had a quarrel with his own brothers, came from a village named Singhpurá, which is in the district of Tarantáran, and put up in the hut of a certain Sikh; that Sikh, taking pity on his poverty, kept him with himself for some time. When some days had passed, then the Sikh said to him: "It would be a very good thing if you were to be baptized." Kapúrá, on hearing this speech, was baptized as a Sikh, and from that day, his name was called Kapúr Singh. When that Kapúr Singh had remained there for some time, many Sikhs, seeing his religious habits, collected around him, (and this) in such numbers that all, who lived in the neighbouring villages and jungles, regarding Kapúr Singh as their lord, joined him. When 2,000 or 3,000 Sikhs had assembled, then Kapúr Singh thought it advisable to rob the neighbouring villages and bring them under his power, as there was no one to prevent him; for in those days, after the death of King Farukh Síar, a great dispute had arisen about the kingship, and no one had as yet been permanently seated on the throne, and Kapúr Singh perceived that, by reason of the dispute, no one would pay any attention to him. Having thus thought, he first came and attacked the village of his birthplace, which was then known as Fajullápur. Having killed the Lambardár (land steward) of that place, he brought it into his own possession. The name of that village was formerly known as Fajullápur from the name of Nawáb Fajullá Beg; when Kapúr Singh took it, then he called the name of that village Singhpurá, and, from the name of that village, the chiefs of one of the twelve misals, of which I shall afterwards make mention, were called Singhpurás. When the renown of Kapúr Singh had somewhat increased, then many people came and were baptized by him as Sikhs; moreover, Sardár Jasá Singh, who was the ancestor of the Ahlúwáliyás, was also baptized by him. Afterwards, when Kapúr Singh had baptized several people, and gained the affection of vast numbers, and had collected many with himself, then, in other places also, other Sikhs set themselves up as Sardárs (chiefs) ; their names will, in due course, be found in the misals. In short, whenever any one wished, then, having collected a small throng, they set themselves up as chiefs.

When Kapúr Singh's renown increased more and more[63] every day, then, from seeing it, others also set themselves up as chiefs ; accordingly, there arose twelve misals, called after those chiefs ; although I might trace the origin of these all from Kapúr Singh, still, as they got their names from some other (chiefs), I shall therefore write about them hereafter.

The names of the twelve misals :—

1st the misal of the Bhangís.	7th the misal of the Sahíds.
2nd ,, ,, ,, ,, Ramgarís.	8th ,, ,, ,, ,, Phúlkías.
3rd ,, ,, ,, ,, Ghanís.	9th ,, ,, ,, ,, Nagrías.
4th ,, ,, ,, ,, Ahlúwálías.	10th ,, ,, ,, ,, Dálálías.
5th ,, ,, ,, ,, Sukar Chakkías.	11th ,, ,, ,, ,, Karorías.
6th ,, ,, ,, ,, Fajullápurías.	12st ,, ,, ,, ,, Nisánwálís.

[63] *Lit.* Had become one and a quarter.

CHAPTER II.

An account of the Misals, or Clans.

1. This is the account of the Bhangís; amongst them there were three noted chiefs, Harí Singh, Jhandá Singh, and Gandá Singh. The three were Jatts by caste, and inhabitants of a village named Panjbar; 10,000 or 12,000 troopers always remained with them, and Laháur and Amritsar and Gujrát were in their possession. As the chiefs of this misal took much Bhang, therefore they were called Bhangís; and whatever they did was said to be done by the Bhangís. Another reason of their being called Bhangís was this; that, being very abject, they performed service to the sect, and therefore the rest gave them the name of Bhangís.

2. They relate the circumstances of the Rámgarís as follows; their ancestor was named Jassá Singh, and was by caste a carpenter, and his old home was in a village named Rámgar, in the district of Amritsar. He, by some means or other, collected two, or two and a half, thousand troopers with him, and always committed inroads, and inflicted oppression on the neighbouring villages: moreover, he, by his wisdom, brought into his power the country of Sirí Har Govindpur and Kádi, which is in the district of Watála, and always had the hope (desire) of increasing his possessions. As this chief was formerly the resident of Rámgar, therefore the name of the misal was called Ramgarí.

3. This is the true account of the Ghanís; their ancestor was by caste a Jatt, named Jai Singh: as this chief was a resident of a village named Káhna, therefore the name of his misal was called Kahniyá; some also say this, that their name was called Ghaní for this reason, that Sardár Jai Singh was of a pleasing appearance, and was one day seated with a number of Sikhs, when a Sikh asked him " Bháí! where is your home"? He replied " In a village named Káhna." Then that Sikh said " Yes Bháí, it is correct; as you are an inhabitant of Káhna, therefore your appearance is pleasing like Kán, *i.e.*, like Krisn :" he further said " Kánjí is also called Ghaniáji: therefore your name also is Ghaniá"; and, from that day every body began to call his misal the Ghanías. Seven or eight thousand troopers used also to remain with him, and the cities of Watálá, Dínánagar, Káhnuwán, Sujánpur, Loháán and Fategar, Kalánaur, &c., were in his possession. Amongst these Ghanís, the most celebrated chiefs were the following, *viz.* :—

Jai Singh, Khaján Singh, Fate Singh, Chainan Singh, Gurbakhs Singh, Hakikat Singh; all these chiefs were called Gḥanís.

4. The account of the Ahlúwális is given as follows: their ancestor was called Jassá Singh, and was by caste a Kalál (distiller); and as this chief was of old an inhabitant of a village named Ahlúwála, therefore the name of his misal was called Ahlúwáli. About four thousand troopers always remained with him, and Jagrámán, Ísrú, Phagwára, Kapúrthalá, Fatiábád, Tarantáran, Wairowál, &c., were subject to him. As this chief was very firm in the Sikh religion, many Sikhs and chiefs were baptized by him.

5. The account of the Sukkarchakkis is reported as follows; the name of their ancestor was Sardár Charat Singh. The Sardár was by caste a Jatt, and by family a Sáhansí; and, from his offspring, Mahárájah Ranjít Singh, whose account will be afterwards written at full length, was born. As that Sardár Charat Singh was an inhabitant of a village named Sukkarchakk, therefore the name of his misal was called Sukkarchakkí. Ten or eleven thousand troopers always remained with that Charat Singh, and the whole of the district of Sakkarchakk was subservient to him.

6. The account of the Fajullápurís is as follows: the name of their ancestor was Nawáb Kapúr Singh, and this was that same Kapúr Singh, who, after the death of Bandá, revived afresh the Sikh religion, which had greatly waned, and, himself, having been baptized, baptized thousands of Sikhs, and, having brought the neighbouring villages under his power, set up the standard of royalty. This chief by caste was a Jatt, and an inhabitant of the village Fajullápur; and, as he was an inhabitant of Fajullápur, his misal was therefore called the Fajullapúrís; about three thousand troops always remained with him.

7. The account of the Sahíds is as follows: their ancestors were Sardár Gurbakhs Singh, and Karam Singh; about seven or eight thousand troopers always remained with them, and the country to the east of the Satluj was under their control. As amongst their ancestors, several persons became martyrs for the sake of their religion, for this reason, the name of their misal was called Sahíds (martyrs); and some people also say this, that their two chiefs, on one occasion for the sake of their religion, were prepared to give their heads, and for this reason the Khálsaji called them Sahíds; for this reason, this rank was bestowed on them, and the name of their misal also was known as the misal of the Sahíds (or martyrs).

8. The account of the Phúlkías is thus given: their ancestor was Álá Singh, by caste a Jatt. This chief was an inhabitant of

CHAP. II.—ACCOUNT OF THE MISALS.   65

Patiála, and he kept up an army of about six or seven thousand strong always with him. As the name of some ancestor of this Alá Singh was Phúl (Singh), therefore the name of the misal was called the Phúlkíwálá.

9. They thus relate the circumstances of the Nagarís; the name of their ancestor is not known, but the misal was called Nagarís for this reason, that their chief lived in a village named Nagarí, which is in a district of Multán, and therefore the name of the misal is known as the Nagarís. A body of about two, or two and a half, thousand troopers used always to remain with him, but there is nothing known of his caste or place of residence.

10. The account of the Dáliálías is given as follows: their ancestor was known as Sardár Tárá Singh, and this Sardár was by caste a Kanjh Jatt, and an army of about seven thousand troops always remained with him. As this chief was an inhabitant of the village Dallí, which is on the banks of the river Ráví, therefore the name of the misal is known as the Daliálís.

11. The circumstances of the Karorís are narrated as follows; their ancestors were Sardár Godar Singh and Baghel Singh, who, by caste, were Jatts, and they always kept up an army of about eleven thousand men. Although they were originally inhabitants of another place, still, afterwards, they took up their abode in the cities of Nakodar and Talwan. If you wish to have the particulars of this misal in full, you must read the book called Gulsan Panjáb.

12. The account of the Nisánwálís is this: their ancestors were Sangat Singh and Mohar Singh, who, by caste were Jatts, and they were, of old, inhabitants of a place Sáháwád. A body of about ten thousand troops always remained with them; Ambálá, Thanesur, Karnál, and the other neighbouring districts, were subservient to them.

In this way, these twelve misals of the Sikhs, which were respectively known in this land by the names of their chiefs, remained bearing enmity to, and fighting with, each other. Often one misal, having fought with another, conquered it, and took their country into its possession; and, afterwards, it also lost its country, and restored it to the former owner. In short, until the renown of Mahárája Ranjít Singh was spread, till then they remained fighting with each other.

F

CHAPTER III.

An account of the Rise of Mahárája Ranjít Singh.

When Sardár Mahá Singh conquered the fort of Rasúlnagar, then, two years afterwards, on the 2nd of the month of November A.D. 1780, a son was born in his house. Mahá Singh, with much joy, having summoned the Pandats and priests, called the name of that child Ranjít Singh. When Ranjít Singh had grown up a little, then small-pox broke out on him so severely, that no one scarcely had any hope of his living. Although God preserved his life from the small-pox itself, still he lost one of his eyes from it. Sardár Mahá Singh, at the time of that illness, gave much of his goods and chattels and wealth to Bráhmans and poor people, and sent various kinds of clothes and jewels to the goddess of Jwálá Mukhí and Kot Kángrá. When Ranjít Singh had grown up a little more, then a widow, named Sadá Kor, who was the wife of a chief, gave her daughter, named Partáp Kor, in marriage to Ranjít Singh. After a time, in the year 1792 A.D., Mahá Singh became ill and died, aged 27 years, at a city named Gujránwála. When Ranjít Singh had obtained leisure from his funeral obsequies, then, during the month Chet, he succeeded to the seat of his father. As, at that time, he was only twelve years of age, for this reason, he was not fit for the business of government; and although he was at that time seated on the throne of the kingdom, still his mother did not approve of his conducting the affairs of the kingdom. When he reached seventeen years of age, then, by the mercy of God, every one, of their own accord, became subservient to him. Accordingly, in the year 1796, a king, named Sháh Zamán, who ascended the throne after the death of Taimúr Sháh, setting forth from Khurásán, came to the Panjáb. As no chief opposed him, he entered Láhaur through open gates. Having come to Láhaur, and seeing that the Panjáb could not, for many reasons, be controlled by him, he returned back. Afterwards he said to the Chief of his Ordnance, named Sahanchí : "Do you efface the name and trace of the Sikhs." On this, he, taking some artillery with him, attacked Rámnagar, but the Khálsa fought well with them ; from that day moreover, the dread of the Patháns was entirely removed from the hearts of the Sikhs. As, at that time, the renown of Mahárája Ranjít Singh was daily on the increase, many people, from seeing it, became very jealous at heart.

CHAP. III.—RISE OF MAHÁRÁJA RANJÍT SINGH.

Ranjít Singh fought with a tribe of people, named Chatt*h*as, who had set themselves up as rulers on the banks of the river Jhanái; their chief was Hasmat Khán. This chief was, from the first, the enemy of Ranjít Singh, and he had this idea always in his heart, that if, by any means, Ranjít Singh should fall into his hands, he would kill him. Once, Ranjít Singh, with a small army, alighted in his country. That Pat*h*án, having caught Ranjít Singh out shooting, struck at him with his sword, but Ranjít Singh, with much dexterity, warded off the blow of the sword; and then Ranjít Singh, becoming very angry, struck at him with a sword, and his body was cut in two. After his death, all that country which was in the possession of Hasmat Khán, came into the hands of Ranjít Singh.

His second fight was at Miání. The circumstances of it are as follows: Ranjít Singh's mother-in-law, Sadá Kor, reported that the chiefs of the Rámgarís gave her much trouble; and, as she had not the power to fight with them, she wished him to help her. Ranjít Singh, on hearing this, went to the fort of Miání, which was the place of abode of Jassá Singh, the Rámgarí; but as, at that time, Ranjít Singh had not the proper means of conquering a strong fort, therefore the fight lasted for a long time. In the meantime, a great flood of the river Jhanái (the Chínáb) took place, and the water filled that fort; as the Sikhs were unable to cross it, they were obliged to go back. Sadá Kor got up this war for this reason, that Jassá Singh, Rámgarí, had killed her husband, Gurbakhs Singh, in a fight.

In the year 1855 B. B. in the month Poh, Sháh Zamán again came to Láhaur, and as no Sikh chief opposed him, he entered Láhaur without any fighting. At that time Ranjít Singh was at Rámnagar; although Sháh Zamán remained four months at Láhaur, Ranjít Singh used often to attack the fort, and, under cover of the bastions, killed many of the Mughals. At last, Sháh Zamán returned to his own country; on the way, as he was crossing the river Jhanái (Chínáb), twelve of his guns were lost in the river. The king sent word to Ranjít Singh: "If you will get out my guns and send them to me, then, in return for it, I will give you Láhaur." Ranjít Singh, after great efforts, got out eight of the guns, and sent them to the king. The king, agreeably to his promise, gave Láhaur to Ranjít Singh, and he immediately took possession of it.

VERSES.

When the days of any one are good,
Wealth wanders around him;
When evil days begin to come, brother!
All happiness even becomes pain-giving.

Listen to the story of Mahá Singh [64];
He was a man of no reputation;
Wherever he showed his face [65],
He took the country, but suffered trouble (in doing so).
But when Ranjít Singh was born,
Then God Himself made him great ;
Without trouble, he obtained the kingship,
And, without effort, he got greatness ;
Whomever God Himself exalts,
That man, day by day, increases ;
No one will be able to do him harm,
If God is his protection.

Afterwards when all the chiefs of Láhaur, and many Rájás and Ránás of the neighbouring countries, had become subservient to Ranjít Singh, then, after a few days, in the year 1802 A. D., a son was born in the house of Ranjít Singh, of his Queen Ráj Kor; and, agreeably to the command of the Pandats, his name was called Kharak Singh.

As at that time quarrels were going on between Hamáyun, Mahmúd, Sháh Zamán, Sáhsujánl and the other kings of Kábul, Ranjít Singh, in the year 1804 A.D., invaded the districts on the banks of the river Atak, and when he had beaten all the chiefs of those parts, and had taken tribute from the ruler of Multán, named Mujaffar Khán, he returned to Láhaur. Afterwards, in the year 1805, A.D., he went to bathe in the holy Ganges, and, after having bathed, again returned to Láhaur.

Afterwards Ranjít Singh began to harass those chiefs, whose countries lay between the rivers Satluj and Jamná, and, having come to Ambálá, gave some of this country to the chiefs of Kaithal and Nabhá, and then, having levied a tax on Thanesur, again came to Anmritsar.

Sir Charles Metcalfe, who had come on the part of the English to Ranjít Síngh, said to him,—" This is the desire of the English Government, that you should fix the Satluj as the boundary of your country." Ranjít Singh at first did not agree to this, but afterwards, having seen somewhat of the power of the English, he agreed; and the English agreed to this also, that they would also not interfere with the villages, which were north of the Satluj. On one occasion, when Ranjít Singh, at Anmritsar, saw a parade of the English army, then he was greatly pleased; moreover, from that very day, he began to drill his own army also after the English fashion.

---

[64] The father of Ranjít Singh.
[65] *Lit.* " Forehead."

CHAP. III.—RISE OF MAHÁRÁJA RANJÍT SINGH.

Again, in the year 1809 A.D., in the month of May, the army of Ranjít Singh set out for the fort of Kángrá, for a Gorkhíya, named Amar Singh, had, at that time, surrounded the fort at that place; and for this reason, the king of that place had asked help of Ranjít Singh; when the army of the Sikhs reached Kángrá, then the Rája Sansár Chand would not allow them to come into the fort. The Sikhs, on hearing this, with much bravery, broke into the gate of the fort, and, entering, took possession of the fortress. On hearing this, Amar Singh retreated to his own country.

Again, when in the year 1810 A.D., King Sujául, having been turned out by his brother Muhammad Sháh, fled from the country of Kábul, and came to Láhaur, then Mahárája Ranjít Singh received him in a very kind way, on the 3rd of January, and met him in a very friendly manner. Afterwards the king departed to Rául Pindí, to meet his brother Sháh Zamán, and Mahárája Ranjít Singh went to Multán to settle something with Mujaffar Khán. Ranjít Singh demanded three lakhs of rupees from him, and he, being helpless, wrote an agreement to give one lakh and eighty thousand. Ranjít Singh then returned to Láhaur, and, day by day, having conquered the kings and chiefs of the neighbouring countries, confiscated their territories, and whoever opposed him, he took prisoner and sent to Láhaur.

Afterwards, in the middle of the year 1818 A.D., Mahárája Ranjít Singh married his son, Kharak Singh, to the daughter of Jaimul Singh, the Ghaniya, at Láhaur. That wedding was performed with much pomp and grandeur, and the renown thereof was spread through all the neighbouring countries.

After this, when the state of the Patháns of Kábul had become somewhat upset, then Ranjít Singh, having collected a very large army, went and invaded the country on the other side of the Atak. Having gone there and subdued Khairábád and other forts, he entered the city of Pasaur. Yár Muhammad Khán, who was the governor of that place, was not able to oppose the army of the Sikhs; moreover, quietly leaving Pasaur empty, he fled away. Mahárája Ranjít Singh, having stopped there a short time, made Jahándád Khán the ruler of it, and himself marched to Láhaur. After Ranjít Singh had returned from there, that same Yár Muhammad Khán, getting assistance from his people, again attacked Pasaur; as, at that time, Jahándád Khán had no army or materials of war ready, he was unable to oppose Yár Muhammad Khán, who, having driven Jahándád Khán from Pasaur, himself again took possession of it.

VERSES.

The story of this world is very curious;
Do you all give your hearts, and listen, O men!
God has made a play,
At seeing which, all are astonished, O brothers!
Behold the wonderful play of the world!
A *tolá* is turned into a *mása*,
Again, sometimes, that which was a *mása*,
It becomes turned into a *tolá*; [66]
Sometimes, the afflicted become happy,
And, sometimes, the happy become afflicted;
He can turn a grain of mustard seed into a mountain,
And can place an umbrella on the head of a worm; [67]
All the grief and happiness, which are in it,
They never remain the same;
Kings sometimes become poor,
And the poor often become rulers of the world.

DISTICH.

Behold! Muhammad Yár Khán was the ruler of Pasaur,
And Jahándád Khán turned him off his throne.

VERSES.

Again when it pleased God,
Jahándád Khán was turned off:
And that same Yár Muhammad Khán,
He again became ruler.
Now those persons, who are wise,
Never weep at undergoing trouble,
But show firmness in their hearts,
So that should trouble come, it may be removed.
One's days will not remain the same,
And excessive trouble will not always continue;
If God shows you trouble,
He will, of Himself, again bring you joy.
O people! place your hopes on Him;
He will order all your affairs aright;
Whoever does not place reliance on Him,
That person is a fool, devoid of understanding.

---

[66] *i.e.*, sometimes the rich become poor, and again he, who was poor, becomes rich.
A *mása* is the twelfth part of a *tolá*.

[67] An umbrella was formerly a sign of royalty, and a worm being a very insignificant thing, the meaning is, God can, if He will, place a crown on the meanest of His creatures.

CHAP. III.—RISE OF MAHÁRÁJA RANJÍT SINGH. 71

When Muhammad Yár Khán had driven Jahándád Khán from Pasaur, than the latter again came to Láhaur to Mahárája Ranjít Singh; and when Muhammad Yár Khán also saw that perfect tranquillity was not to be had there, departing from Pasaur, he went to Barát.

Afterwards, in the year 1819 A.D. in the month of April, Mahárája Ranjít Singh took counsel how he might conquer Kasmír. Having thus thought, he sent an army with Missar Diwán Chand and despatched him to the hills; and having placed another army under the command of his son, Kharak Singh to help the former, he sent him after Missar Diwán Chand. Those armies went to the mountains to conquer Kasmír, but Mahárája Ranjít Singh remained in the Panjáb, to arrange about sending them supplies, and to watch over the Panjáb. When the army of the Sikhs arrived in the hills, then a very great fight ensued with the Patháns, and, in the fight, about a thousand Sikhs, and five or six chiefs also, were killed, and of the other side, a large number also were slain. When the news of this fight reached Ajím Khán, that many Patháns had been killed, then he, departing from Kasmír, went and resided at Jaláláwád.

Afterwards, Ranjít Singh went to Pasaur, and there Muhammad Yár Khán, presenting himself before him, petitioned: "If you will give Pasaur to me, then I will continue paying tribute to you; moreover, whatever revenue shall come in, I will send it to you to Láhaur in full." Ranjít Singh, having accepted his request, made over Pasaur to him, and, having taken a written agreement signed by his hand, returned to Láhaur.

Shortly afterwards, Ajím Khán died, and the Patháns again created great tumult. Mahárája Ranjít Singh himself went, and settled that dispute, and then returned to Láhaur.

In the year 1826 A.D., the Nawáb Sádik Muhammad Khán, who was the ruler of Bahánlpur, died, and his son, Bahául Khán, ascended the throne, and ratified whatever his father and grandfather had promised to Mahárája Ranjít Singh.

Afterwards, a person, named Saíad Mahamdi, set up a Muhammadan flag in the hills, and incited the Musalmán by these words; "It behoves us to slay these infidel Sikhs agreeably to the orders of our prophets." When the Musalmáns began making a tumult, then the Mahárája, having sent an army across the Atak, severely punished Saíad Mahamdi.

When Mahárája Ranjít Singh had conquered all the hills, then he gave the fort of Jammú to Guláb Singh and Suchet Singh. At that time Dhián Singh, the brother of the ruler of Jammú, was superintendent of the threshold of Ranjít Singh, and as Ranjít Singh loved his son, Hira Singh, very much, he therefore gave him the rank of Rája, and Ranjít Singh always wished this in his heart, that he might marry Hira Singh to some girl of high caste. On one occasion, Anrudh Chand, the son of Rája Sansár Chand, was going to a marriage of the Ahlúwális at Kapúrthala; on the road he had occasion to stop at Láhaur, and Mahárája Ranjít Singh sent for him, and, by some means or other, got him to write that he would marry his two sisters agreeably to the commands of Mahárája Ranjít Singh. When his grandmother heard this, then she, taking those two girls with her, went and lived in those hills, which were in the possession of the English. Again, after a short time Rája Anrudh Chand also fled, and Mahárája Ranjít Singh took all his country into his own possession, and drove his brother Fate Chand out of it

On one occasion, the Mahárája Ranjít Singh, having had made a very large tent of pusmína (wool of goats' hair), sent it as an offering to England for the king; then the king of the English on seeing it, was greatly pleased; moreover, in return for it, he sent four very beautiful mares and a horse to be given to Mahárája Ranjít Singh. The Mahárája received the agent, who brought them, with much courtesy; after having remained some days in Láhaur, that gentleman, who had brought the horses from England, went to the Hill of Simla to meet Mr. (Lord) William Bentinck, who was the Governor-General of India, and told the circumstances of his arrival to the Governor-General. On this, the Governor-General wished that, by some means or other, he also might meet Mahárája Ranjít Singh. The Governor-General wrote to Captain Wade to, by some means, bring Ranjít Singh to Ludihána, for him to have an interview with him. The Mahárája, having sent his minister, Motí Rám and Sardár Harí Singh and Fakír Ajíj Dín to the Governor-General, stated that he would meet him at Ropar, which is on the banks of the river Satluj. The Governor-General, on the 22nd October 1831, came to Ropar, and the Mahárája also arrived at Ropar on the 25th of that month. At that time, there were with the Mahárája about 10,000 troopers, and 6,000 footmen. The Governor-General, having heard of the arrival of the Mahárája, sent his Agent and Secretary to pay his respects to Mahárája Ranjít Singh; and then, Ranjít Singh, having sent his son Kharak Singh, and six or seven chiefs of very high position to the Governor-General, said that he would assuredly come in the morning and see him. Next day, when the Mahárája was ready for the interview, then, before his own departure, he despatched 3,000 regular troopers, and also sent 800 irregular cavalry; and after them, he despatched his chiefs seated on elephants, and then himself set forth after them

CHAPT. III.—RISE OF MAHÁRÁJA RANJÍT SINGH.

all. When he had arrived very near the tents, then they both met; moreover both of them, seated on their elephants, proceeded to the tents. The Governor-General gave many curiosities, and various kinds of presents, to the Mahárája and his son, and the other chiefs; and then the Mahárája returned to his own tent. Next day, the Governor-General went to the Mahárája's tent to visit him. All the chiefs presented offerings to the Governor-General, and the Mahárája also gave many valuable horses, with gold and silver trappings, and other curiosities to the Governor-General. Then there was a review of the Mahárája's, and the English, armies. Ranjít Singh, seeing the smartness and dexterity of the English army, was much pleased. That same evening, they met for the last time (*i.e.*, to say good bye), and, that very day, the Governor-General gave the Mahárája a present of an iron bridge. Next day, both rulers departed to their own countries.

Afterwards, when in the year 1838, A.D., the English invaded Kábul, the Mahárája Ranjít Singh sent 6,000 of his army to help them. When the army arrived in Kábul, but before the expedition had accomplished (its object), Mahárája Ranjít Singh, who before had been very ill, accomplished (his years of life) in the year 1839.

COUPLET.

The great, who, in this world, sit with their legs stretched out.
In the end, death seizes them, and kills them in a short while.

VERSES.

Those, who come into the inn of the world,
Are not allowed to stop in it for ever;
The very great, kings, and the proud,
The wise, the skilful, and the powerful,
All live but four days,
And then the tents of all are (got ready for) the march;
The drum of marching is always sounding,
And none can manage to stop here;
Now this is becoming to every one,
That they should regard the pleasures of the world as false;
For its wealth, riches, joys and pleasures are all delusive;
Its possessions, lands, and titles, are all vain;
Those, who live here sorrowful,
Do not hope to remain here always,
And therefore do not get dried up with grief;
For they only are grieved, who are in love with it (the world).

Who can make himself great?
Verily I am happy, for grief burns me not[68];
And, if for sometime I am happy,
(I know) in the end death will take away all my pleasure.

CO**UPLET**.

Accomplish the journey through this world well;
It is not good for one to remain fearless in it, therefore
draw near to God.

After the death of Ranjít Singh, many Ránís performed satti and great grief arose in the Panjáb, and the walls, as it were, appeared to be weeping. After him Rajá Dhíán, by his sagacity, kept the kingdom so well in control, that one should really regard him as the master of the kingdom. Ranjít Singh, whilst he was alive, allowed him such immense power, that sometimes he prevented the princes Kharak Singh and Sher Singh, who were the sons of the Mahárája Ranjít Singh, from coming into the palace; he also implanted the idea in the king's mind, that, as Kharak Singh was a great fool, and mad, for this reason, he was not fit for the kingdom; and regarding Sher Singh, he raised this doubt in the Mahárája's mind, that he was not his own son. As there was no hindrance (offered to it), Dhíán Singh used to go into the female apartments, and, for this reason all the queens used to be much afraid of him; and as Hírá Singh, the son of this Dhíán Singh always remained with the king, from this fear, the queens were not able to tell their griefs to the Mahárája. Up to the time of the death of Mahárája Ranjít Singh, he had such great power in the management of the affairs of the kingdom, that he could do what he pleased.

When Mahárája Ranjít Singh was dying, then, having called his son Kharak Singh, he made him over to the care of his minister, Dhíán Singh, saying "Dhíán Singh; you are my true minister and the protector of the Ráj; so, in return for the kindness and obligations I have conferred on you during my whole life, do you keep this my son, Kharak Singh, happy. Never commit perfidy, nor be false to your salt, nor deal badly with him, and always regard him as in my place."

---

[68] *Lit.*—"Is just like mustard to me."

CHAPTER IV.

Description of the character of Ranjít Singh.

Ranjít Singh was not at all literate, yet nevertheless, he used to sit and himself listen to the business pertaining to the government, and whatever he perfectly understood, on that, after reflection and thought, he passed his written orders ; when the order had been written, then he used to hear it a second time, and reflect on it; so that he might see that the scribe had not at all changed his order in writing it. In his very childhood even, he was very generous, and used to give many presents to his attendants and others. Whatever urgent matters came into his mind in the night time, he used at once to have them written down, so that he might not forget them, and when he went to sleep at night, he used to think over all important affairs, so that his kingdom might flourish; he, by the quickness of his understanding, and the goodness of his memory, had this wonderful power, that, by looking at the face of a person, he used to be able to tell his sagacity, ability and goodness; he was a man of very medium size, and was blind of one eye, and, as the marks of small-pox were on his face, for this reason, his countenance was somewhat spoilt: but owing to his long beard, which reached to his navel, it did not show so much, and his face looked filled up and handsome. He used to laugh a great deal with people, and talk openly to them, so that people used to get drowned in their affection for him, and, seated in his society, used to tell him the secrets of their hearts. He was very fond of riding on horseback, and, in his old age even, he used to ride on horseback, after being helped on his horse by others. He knew many stratagems and manœuvres of warfare and used to beat his enemies principally by these stratagems and manœuvres. Although, in his youth he was very athletic and strong, in his old age he became very feeble. He was of a very plain simple disposition, and, for the sake of setting off his durbárs, he ordered his attendants, that they were all to come to his durbárs dressed in diamonds, pearls, and jewels. Some people say that he aged, and became old and feeble, owing to his drinking so much wine. He had a great desire to advance his religion, and was himself most firm in the Sikh doctrines, and used for a long time together to listen to the Granth. He himself carried on a traffic in shawls and salt, and used never to do any thing without first consulting his (Bráhman) astronomers and (Hindú) astrologers. At an early period of his life, when he was thirteen years old, on his ascending the throne, this base deed was done by him, namely, that he turned out of office the minister named Lakhá, who had been the minister of his father, and sent him on an expedition to Katás, where the unfortunate creature died. People had informed Ranjít Singh that this minister had an intrigue with his mother, and he therefore, had poison administered to his mother, and had her killed also.

CHAPTER V.

The Circumstances of Mahárája Kharak Singh.

After Mahárája Ranjit Singh, Kharak Singh ascended the throne ; as he knew well the disposition of his minister Dhián Singh, he, first of all, for the sake of diminishing his power, said to him that he was not to go into the royal female apartments ; and he moreover said, " Do not be angry with me for this, for I will not allow your power and authority to be decreased any further." Dhián Singh, on hearing this, took great offence at it at heart ; moreover such a difference sprung up between those two from that very day, that very great enmity arose between them.

Some days after a man, named Chet Singh, who was a favourite of Kharak Singh's, said to Kharak Singh, that the minister Dhián Singh gives out that, until he obtains the full powers he formerly had, he will not conduct the duties of minister properly ; and, with many other such like reports, he turned Kharak Singh against the minister.

When Dhián Singh saw that Kharak Singh would give him much trouble, then he devised this plan for his own safety ; he gave it out everywhere, that Kharak Singh and Chet Singh had made an agreement with the English, and that, from fear of them, they had agreed to pay six-sixteenths of the revenue to them, and, therefore, he would soon dismiss the army and all the officers and chiefs. This report was spread throughout Láhaur, and the Khálsa began to treat Kharak Singh with indifference. After this, Dhián Singh called the Prince Nau Nihál Singh from Pasaur, and Rájá Guláb Singh also entered Láhaur in company with him.

The minister, and his brother Guláb Singh, misled Nau Nihál Singh and his mother and Kharak Singh, and obtained an order to put Chet Singh to death. Prince Nau Nihál, and his mother, further said, " Seize Mahárája Kharak Singh, and, by some other means, depose him from the government."

They caused many spurious letters, sealed with the seal of Kharak Singh to be written, and shewed them to Nau Nihál Singh and his mother, saying, " Behold, he is writing these letters, and making terms with the English." The mother of Nau Nihál Singh, on hearing the name of the English, was greatly terrified, and deemed it advisable to imprison her husband (Kharak Singh).

When this had been fully determined on, then the minister, Dhián Singh, and his brother, two watches before the break of day, entered the fort and got into that room, where Mahárája Kharak Singh used to sleep, and, having killed Chet Singh, made Kharak Singh prisoner. When the day broke, having imprisoned Kharak Singh in the fort, they seated his son Nau Nihál Singh on the throne.

CHAPTER VI.

The Circumstances of Nau Nihál Singh.

After a few days, Dhíán Singh sent some holy men, Bráhmans and astrologers to Nau Nihál Singh to gladden his heart, and, they said thus to him, "O Mahárája; in a short time, all from Láhaur to Dillí and Banáras will be your kingdom"; and, in this way, Dhíán Singh attached the spirit of the prince (to himself), and raised suspicions in his mind regarding Kharak Singh; and, through his instigation, he became so irate against Kharak Singh that, if any one mentioned his name in Durbár, then he would begin to abuse him.

Again after a few days Dhíán Singh gave out that the Mahárája Kharak Singh was very ill, and himself appointed some wonderful physicians for him, who right well cured that helpless creature; that is to say, agreeably to the bidding of Dhíán Singh, they gave him a powder of a very deadly poison, from which he died in the month of November A.D. 1840.

At that time, Nau Nihál Singh, for some reason or other, was not in Láhaur. Mahárája Kharak Singh remembered him and said "Bring Nau Nihál Singh to me, that I may forgive him my blood"; from this, it appears that he believed that his son Nau Nihál Singh had imprisoned and killed him. When Nau Nihál Singh arrived in Láhaur after the death of his father, then he asked, "Did my father remember me at the time of his death or not?" Dhíán Singh replied, "As he was mad at the time of his death, therefore what issued from his mouth is not fit to be told, for he abused you badly." Alas! alas! that that sinner Dhíán Singh not only created such enmity between Kharak Singh and Nau Nihál Singh, that, whilst he (Kharak Singh) was alive, they kept aloof one from the other, but he also turned him (Nau Nihál Singh) against his father even after his death. Nau Nihál Singh himself came and burned his father, and performed all the funeral obsequies (laid down) by his religion. Having finished all the obsequies, he came to the city; and many Sikh chiefs were with him, the most distinguished of whom was Udham Singh, the eldest son of Rája Guláb Singh. These were coming along with Nau Nihál Singh and, when they arrived at the gate of the city, the lintel of the gateway suddenly gave way, and Udham Singh was, by its fall, killed on the spot, and Nau Nihál Singh was placed in a pálkí and brought to Dhíán Singh in the fort. It is not known why that pálkí had been placed there[69]; when he had been taken inside the fort, then the gate of the fort was closed, and an order given that no one was to be allowed to enter. Although Lahiná Singh, Majíthíyá, and other chiefs, wished greatly to go in with the pálkí, Dhíán Singh would not let any one in. Moreover, leaving the chiefs out of the question, his mother and brother even, when they came to enquire after him, were stopped at the gate. At that time, much lamentation and crying and weeping arose at the gate, but that sinner Dhíán Singh, although he heard all their grief, would not let any one in. After a little while, all the chiefs, being helpless, returned to their own homes; then, when Nau Nihál Singh had died, Dhíán Singh furtively came to his mother, and said; "Your son is now dead, but if you make this known at once, then the Sikhs will create great havoc in the kingdom; this, therefore, is my advice, that, at present, you should keep this matter secret, and that you yourself should sit on the throne, and I will make all the people obey your orders." In short, having thus advised her, he went to his own house, and, having called all the principal officers, told them the whole circumstances, and gave them very strict instructions that, at present, no one was to allow this news to be known.

Then, after this, Dhíán Singh wrote a letter and sent it to Mahárája Sher Singh to call him from the city Watálá; and in it, he wrote thus: "If you wish to be king of Láhaur, you must come to Láhaur within twenty-four hours." On Sher Singh's arrival in Láhaur, the news of the death of Nau Nihál Singh was made known throughout the city: but, before Sher Singh arrived in Láhaur, they had caused this report to be spread regarding Nau Nihál Singh, that he was very ill from a blow (received at the gateway).

After the death of Nau Nihál Singh, when discord found its way into the kingdom, then Dhíán Singh thought thus; "If Chand Kor sit on the throne, then the Sandhewálía family will degrade me and my brothers from our rank;" he therefore called all the chiefs and began to devise another plan[70] and said "O Sikhs! this does not appear good, that the sect of the Khálsa should obey a woman; therefore this appears proper that you should seat Mahárája Sher Singh, who is the son of our lord Mahárája Ranjít Singh, on the throne of the kingdom." Having thus said, he took a small part of the army with him and began to devise for placing Sher Singh on the throne. On hearing this, the Sandhewálía family, and Rája Guláb Singh, prepared to help the mother,

---

[69] By this it is meant to imply, that the whole affair was pre-arranged, and the falling in of the gateway was not an accident.
[70] *Lit.* "He began to write something else on the wooden slate."

CHAP. VI.—ACCOUNT OF NAU NIHÁL SINGH.

Chand Kor; Dhián Singh, seeing that he had given rise to a general quarrel, said to Sher Singh: "Whereas, at this time, a very great and serious tumult is about to take place, it will be a difficult matter to give the throne to you; therefore do you now go back to Watálá; I will make proper arrangements for giving you the throne, and will then send for you." On hearing this, Sher Singh went to Watálá, and he (Dhián Singh) having left his agents and spies at Láhaur, himself proceeded thence to Jammú; and he also sent this message to his kinsmen: "Do you get ready armies for the assistance of Sher Singh, and send me intelligence (when they are ready)."

After a month, Dhián Singh's people sent him information in Jammú, that they had got ready an army for his assistance, and that he should bring Sher Singh along with himself and come to Láhaur. On hearing this, Dhián Singh wrote and sent to Watálá to Sher Singh: "Do you come to the Sálábágh-wála Gate at Láhaur and remain ready. I, bringing an army, will join you." Then, Sher Singh, taking about 300 horsemen with him, arrived at the Sálábágh Gate, Láhaur; but not seeing Dhián Singh, he became very sad. One of his aides-de-camp, by name Juálá Singh, said to him: "Do not you be sad; I will bring the whole of the army from Mián Mír to your assistance." At first, the army would not agree to help Sher Singh without Dhián Singh's order: but, at last, having been brought to reason by Juálá Singh, it turned out to assist Sher Singh. Accordingly, next day, at daybreak, the officers of the army, having come to the brick kiln of Buddhú, saluted the Mahárája Sher Singh, and said to him; "O Mahárája! We are all for you." Having said this, they commenced to fire a salute of guns, and all the people, having called Sher Singh king of Lahaur, began to offer him their congratulations.

F

CHAPTER VII.

The Láhaur Campaign.

When the news of Sher Singh's arrival became known, Guláb Singh consulted with Chand Kor and Khusál Singh, Jamádár and Sardár Tejá Singh, as to how it behoved them then to act; and, having got together a small portion of the army of his brother Dhián Singh, sent them off to oppose the enemy. As the army was going off to fight, he himself went after it and brought it back from near the Hazúrí Bágh, and, with the assistance of that army, came and took possession of the fort. He then sent word to the Rání (Queen) that the 60,000 troops, which were in Mián Mír, had all joined Sher Singh, and there were only about 2,000 men with him, and that, with these, it would be difficult to get the better of Sher Singh. Guláb Singh hoped, that Sher Singh would not enter the fort, till Dhián Singh, came, but Sher Singh, contrary to his expectation, without waiting for Dhián Singh's arrival, came with the army and commenced to attack the fort. Guláb Singh determined to resolutely hold the fort as long as he was able till Dhián Singh's arrival; so that Sher Singh might think that he had conquered the fort with Dhián Singh's assistance. After this, in the evening, Guláb Singh mounted an elephant, and went to the different gates of the city, and, having given much money to the watchmen, said to them, that, should Sher Singh try to enter, they were, as long as possible, to prevent his doing so. Then, having come into the fort, and having sent for the officers of the army, he took oaths and vows from them, that they would not let Sher Singh take possession of the fort as long as any life was left in them; and further, having given all the army four months' pay on the behalf of Chand Kor, said to them that, after the war, they should obtain very great rewards.

Next morning, when two watches remained to dawn, Sher Singh, having come by the Dillí Gate and the Tak Sálí Gate, entered the city along with the army ; and the whole army shouting, " Satt Sirí Akál (true is the Immortal One); O Sect of the Wáh Gurú! victory be to the Wáh Gurú," went straight to the fort. At that time, there were with them so many guns, that, even if they had been mounted close together on all sides around the fort, there would not have been enough room for them to stand.

Then the guns began to be fired from all four quarters, and a great fear arose in the fort; but, after a short while, the cannon

CHAP. VII.—THE LÁHAUR CAMPAIGN.

balls ceased to be fired, and the noise, which had at first been made, all subsided. Then those twelve guns, which were mounted at the Hazúrí Gate, began to be fired; when, the gate of the fort had been forced in by their fire, then two or three hundred Akális,[71] having made a charge, proceeded to enter the fort; but the guns from inside were fired so well, that a hundred Akális were killed by their fire; hearing the sound of those guns from inside, the enemy fled, and many of their guns were damaged. Seeing this state, a small portion of the army from the fort, without orders from Guláb Singh, raising a hurrah, charged down on the enemy, and drove them out from the Hazúrí Bágh; and, in that fight, three hundred Sikhs were killed. When Sher Singh heard of this disturbance there, then, taking six guns with him, he charged the Mastí Gate, but the volleys, fired by the artillerymen in the fort, caused them to retire. On this, Sher Singh began to fire all his guns, but the people from inside fired their guns with such precision that a great many of the artillerymen of Sher Singh were killed, and many, leaving their guns, fled. Then the army of Sher Singh, having made embrasures in the walls of the streets, and in the houses, for their guns, began to fire them. As there were no holes in the fort, there were no places for embrasures; the people inside therefore made holes in the breastworks and wished to construct embrasures in them; but, as the lime and brick failed, they were helpless and obliged to desist from doing so, but made bastions, inside the fort, of earth and wood, and threw down the walls in front. At that time, there were 1,200 Sikhs in the fort; they formed a resolve to create a disturbance in the fort, and to go and join their brothers. In this way, after much fighting and after having suffered many hardships, Mahárája Sher Singh, at last with the assistance of Dhián Singh, obtained the throne.

When Guláb Singh, having vacated the fort, was going to Sáhdara, then the minister of Sher Singh incited the army to pursue and kill him; but, at the command of Dhián Singh and Sher Singh, the armies desisted from it. As Dhián Singh always regarded Juálá Singh as the enemy of his life, for this reason, with much dexterity, he turned the heart of Sher Singh against him; and on one occasion, when Juálá Singh was taking about six thousand troops towards Sáhdara, then Dhián Singh, having said something to Sher Singh, made him (Sher Singh) fight with Juálá Singh. In that fight, Sher Singh took Juálá Singh prisoner, and he afterwards died in confinement. This was that Juálá Singh, whom Mahárája Sher Singh, from his great affection for him, wished to

---

[71] Akális are Sikhs, who dress in blue, and wear the quoit round their turban.

make his minister, but that wretch, Dhián Singh, from fear of losing the ministership, himself turned the Mahárája so greatly against him, that even after his death, in speaking of him, he (Sher Singh) used to abuse him much.

The Ráni Chand Kor had obtained a grant of land (jágír), worth nine lakhs of rupees, in the territory of Jammú, for her subsistence, and Guláb Singh was her manager; but, out of this jágír, he used to give her only enough for her actual expenses. Again, on one occasion when Mahárája Sher Singh wished to marry[72] Queen Chand Kor and make her his own wife, then Guláb Singh did not approve of this; but, having instilled many kinds of suspicions into the Queen's mind, he made her the enemy of Sher Singh; for he thought, should she become the wife of Sher Singh, then all her property, goods, and jágír, would go out of his own hands into the hands of Sher Singh. Although Sher Singh once or twice again sent and asked Chand Kor to marry him, still she did not agree, but sent some ambiguous reply that she thought the Mahárája wanted to kill her. At last it thus happened that Sher Singh, having promised her four female servants some estates, got them to kill Chand Kor. The Mahárája Sher Singh, on hearing of her death, was greatly pleased; and Guláb Singh also obtained much profit from her death, for he became possessor of all her wealth and property.

Again after a short time, inward enmity arose between Mahárája Sher Singh and the minister Dhián Singh; and the minister, Dhián Singh, having, through (the instrumentality) of Bháí Rám Singh, invited the Sandhewális, who had been turned out of their estates and imprisoned, formed friendship with them, and used often to address them thus: "Although Sher Singh outwardly shows friendship to you, inwardly he is the enemy of your life; and, if it were not for me being between you, he is prepared to act very cruelly towards you."

When in this way, he had turned their hearts, then they thought there must have been some quarrel between the Mahárája and him. After Guláb Singh had gone to Jammú, Dhián Singh found out that there was another son of Mahárája Ranjít Singh, named Dalíp Singh, about 5 or 6 years old, and thought it advisable for him by all means to turn Sher Singh off the throne, and make Dalíp Singh the king of Láhaur. From that day, Dhián Singh, having called Dalíp Singh, began to show him much affection, and, seating him in his lap, used to make

---

[72] *Lit.* "To throw a sheet over"; this is the expression used for marrying a widow.

saláms and pay respect to him ; Sher Singh, on hearing this, determined that he would, by some means, turn out that minister, (for he knew that) otherwise he would give him great trouble.

On the one side, this plan had formed itself in the mind of Sher Singh, and, on the other, in the minds of the Sandhewális, from hearing the words of Dhián Singh, it had become firmly established that the Mahárája Sher Singh, on account of former differences, still bore inward enmity against them. Afterwards it came into their minds that as Dhián Singh bore some animosity to the Mahárája, he therefore wished to kill him by their hands. Having reflected in their minds over all these different motives, the Sandhewális went to Sher Singh and, joining their hands, said to him : "O true king! as for a long time we have eaten your salt, therefore, as you have been dishonoured before us, behold, we cannot bear it any longer ; therefore we now relate to you the conduct of your minister Dhián Singh, whom you regard as your own body and life ; it is this, that Dhián Singh has sent us to you at this time to kill you, and, in return for this, he has promised to give us a jágír of 60,000 rupees. His intention is, after having killed you, to place Dalíp Singh on the throne, and thus himself continue in his ministership." Having heard this speech, Sher Singh believed their words to be correct and true, for he had, before this, heard of the giving of the throne to Dalíp Singh ; Sher Singh, at that time, with much decision and promptitude, drawing his sword from its sheath, gave it into the hands of Sardárs Lahiná Singh and Ajít Singh, Sandhewális, and said. " Take this, brothers ! if this is your intention, then cut off my head with my own sword ; but remember this, that he, whom you now regard as your friend, will afterwards show great hatred towards you, for he will never let you go alive." From hearing this, a great effect was produced on the minds of the Sandhewális, so that they, joining their hands, said : " O true king! do you yourself consider : if this had been our intention, why should we have come and told you the secret ? do you know for certain, that we, regarding you as a brother of the Sikh religion, and openly acknowledging you as our master, have come and given you this information. We have not come to kill, rather to save, you. But do you also remember, that this base minister is not, from to-day only, desirous to take your life, but has been so for some time past. We, acknowledging the obligations of our salt (i.e., our oaths), have told you this secret : but if that sinner had sent any one else, you would not have escaped alive. We, therefore, purpose to kill that vile and treacherous minister ; if he shall remain alive, he will certainly devise some means for killing you." Sher Singh, on hearing this speech, at first said nothing openly, but afterwards spoke out plainly " Well you know best ; to kill that wretch would perhaps be well. " The Sandhewális, having considered this, that, afterwards, they might be punished for the crime of the murder of the minister, therefore caused Sher Singh to write in his own hand to them : " Do you kill Dhián Singh." Then they said thus : " We are now going to Rájesánhsíya, which is near Anmritsar, and, having gone there, we will collect an army for the purpose. It therefore behoves you one day to take a muster of your army, and do you also call and send for us to be mustered ; we will immediately come to be mustered, and, when you give us the sign, we will at once surround Dhián Singh and his son Hírá Singh, and kill them. " Then they said this also : " From our coming, you must have no anxiety on our account, for we are amongst those subjects who are truly loyal to you."

When the Sandhewális had thus thoroughly arranged every thing, they departed ; but those base traitors, instead of going to Rajesánhsíya, went straight to the house of Dhián Singh ; having gone there, and taken many oaths from Dhián Singh, they said, " If you will not tell any one, then we will tell you something of advantage to yourself." He said "I will not tell any one." Those base Sandhewális then placed before him that paper, on which was attached the seal of Sher Singh, with orders to kill Dhián Singh. On seeing the paper, Dhián Singh became comforted, and said to them : " Brothers ! you have shown great kindness to me, in that you have told me of this ; but now do you point out what plan I should adopt ?" They gave reply " Do not you fear, for we will kill him ; for he is hostilely inclined towards you." Dhián Singh, on hearing this, became delighted, and said " Do you do this, and I will give you as much reward as I can."

They then proposed that same plan to him for killing Sher Singh, which they had fixed with Sher Singh for killing Dhián Singh ; saying : " On the day of the muster, we will accomplish and complete this." Then they said this also, " Do you, on that day, send such part of the army to the king's palace as will not spoil your business."[73] Having determined this, those knaves and wretches went to Rajesánhsíya ; as long as they remained at Rájesánhsíya, the Rája Dhián Singh did not go to Durbár ; for he, from this fear lest Sher Singh should kill him, had sent this message to the Durbár that he was somewhat out of sorts.

Again, after a few days, the Sandhewális, bringing about five or six thousand very good picked horsemen with them, came to

[73] *i.e.* Men on whom you can rely.

Láhaur. At that time, Mahárája Sher Singh was at a place called Sáhbalaur, at a distance of about three kos from Láhaur, and the Sandhewálí chiefs also proceeded there, and, leaving the rest of the army outside, went in with only about fifty horsemen. At that time Sher Singh was seated on a chair with a head pillow behind him; Ajít Singh, Sandhewálí, taking a double-barrel gun in his hand, came to the Mahárája, and, laughing, said: "Look Mahárája! I have bought this gun for 1,400 rupees; if any one now were to give me 3,000 for it, I would not take it." On hearing this, the Mahárája put out his hand to take the gun. That artful Sandhewálí at once pulled the trigger of the gun, and the two bullets, which were charged in each of the barrels, went into Sher Singh's breast, and he then, staggering from the chair, fell on the ground, and died. That wretched Sandhewálí immediately cut off his head, and carried it off in his hand; and no one, who at that time opposed any of the Sandhewális, escaped alive. After this, the Sandhewális went to that garden where Sher Singh's oldest son was reading. That boy's age at that time was 13 or 14 years. When the lad saw Lahiná Singh coming towards him with a naked sword, getting up, he fell at his feet, and weeping, said: "O my lord! spare my life." That sinner, Lahiná Singh, shewed no mercy, but cut off the head of that guiltless child. Then, having settled the business of the father and son, they returned to the city. At that time, there were with Ajít Singh 300 horse and 200 footmen, and about 200 horse with Lahiná Singh; as these two were going along, one behind the other, after a while, they met with Rája Dhián Singh. Ajít Singh said to Dhián Singh. "Come! why are you now going out? we have fulfilled the promise we gave you to kill Sher Singh." Dhián Singh, at that time, was greatly afraid in his mind, lest they might kill him also. But seeing that his army was small, he joined Ajít Singh. When they entered the fort, then the Sandhewális stopped Dhián Singh's troops at the second gate. Seeing this, Dhián Singh became greatly alarmed in his heart. Having gone on a little, Ajít Singh gave a nod to one of his soldiers, who, coming behind Dhián Singh with a loaded carbine, shot him; and then a second soldier came up and put another bullet into him, and he died there; a Musalmán soldier, who was the servant of Dhián Singh, when he saw his master being killed, opposed them a little, but they, having killed him also, threw his corpse, together with that of Dhián Singh, into the ditch of the fort.

Distich.

The world is a play of four days; no one remains always in it. Cursed is their life who make quarrels.

Verses.

This Dhián Singh Sardár,
(Who) was a wretch and a sinner and a worker of vile deeds,
He committed many wickednesses,
And many people were killed by him;
No one has seen a deceiver like him,
For he passed all his life in great craftiness;
Behold how many he killed!
But with what stratagem and fraud he kept himself aloof;
He killed Nihál Singh,
And then created bad feeling against the mother.[71]
Then, becoming the friend of Sher Singh,
He cut off the head of Chet Singh;
He, after this, for Sher Singh,
Laid many stratagems and traps;
And all the Sandhewális
Were turned against him by this sinner;
And when they killed Sher Singh,
It was all done through his advice;
He committed many sins,
And he murdered many people;
At last his turn came,
And he forgot all his cleverness:
None can escape from God,
He destroys the root of every sinner,
When his time of death came,
Then he was not able to say any thing;
His heart's thought remained in his heart, and the words of his mouth in his mouth.
When death came and seized him by the arm:
Alas! Alas! that, in the world, man
Commits whatever violence his mind wills,
And does not fear God,
And does not keep this thought in his mind,
'No one always in this world remains stretching out his feet,
Then why should I cause many quarrels?
And why should I keep the pleasure of the world in my heart?
For a life of four days,
Why should I distress many people?
There is a meeting for two days of all pleasure.

---

[71] This refers to his telling the people, that it was not good for them to have a woman to reign over them.

And then all the play will become confused;
Now do you all listen to this!
This world does not belong to any one;
As one acts, so one obtains (his reward);
And one's father and mother cannot save one;
The fruit of one's deeds will necessarily come,
And no one can remove it;
Therefore do every thing that is good:
Eschew evil and fear God.

They then went and sat down in the fort, and reflected that if Dhián Singh's son, Hírá Singh, and his brother, Suchet Singh, should hear of his death, then they would charge down on them and kill them; and it was therefore necessary to devise some plan (to save themselves). Those sinners then wrote a letter from Dhián Singh to Hírá Singh and Suchet Singh to this effect, "I am seated in the fort with the Sandhewális, and am taking counsel with them; do you also, immediately on reading this letter, come to the fort:" for it was the intention of the Sandhewális, that when those two came into the fort, then they, finding them alone, should kill them. When this letter reached them at the brick kiln of Buddhú, then their advisers, seeing something curious in it, wrote this reply: "We have not the slightest objection to come, but we will only come, if a letter shall reach us written by the hand of Dhián Singh himself." When they saw that they had understood their letter, then they sent 500 horsemen to seize and bring Hírá Singh and Suchet Singh; but those troopers were not able to catch them; and, one hour after this, the news had spread everywhere, that the Sandhewális had killed Mahárájá Sher Singh and the minister Dhián Singh. On hearing this news, Hírá Singh lost his senses, and, uttering exclamations of regret, began to roll on the ground. Seeing his childish crying and sobbing, Rái Kesrí Singh said: "What means this, that you are behaving like a child? what has happened, has happened; it behoves you to devise for the future, for there is no knowing what other calamities those Sandhewális may create." On hearing this his speech, he came to his senses, and, taking all those chiefs with him, went to the army, so that, by its means, he might take his revenge on the Sandhewális. Hírá Singh, accompanied by all the chiefs, placed his sword before the whole army, and said: "O Khálsájí! behold Mahárájá Ranjít Singh, from my childhood even, honoured me more than his own sons; and my whole life-time I have enjoyed great happiness, for I have never seen any suffering; but now the Sandhewális have done away with all my joy; behold! they have killed our king Sher Singh, and my father: if you will help me to take my revenge for this, then I shall be your debtor my whole life long; they have done this deed for this reason, that they might bring the English into this country, and destroy the sect of the Khálsa; for, when they lived in Hindustán, they then promised the English that they would call them to the Panjáb. They have now written and sent several letters to Ludehána and Parojpur saying 'We have now made the throne of Láhaur empty : let the English come and take it under their sway' : therefore behold O Khálsají! your religious sect is now in danger, and the English will come and take away your arms, and, having taken your honour from you, will make you take to agriculture. If you do not exert yourselves and do something now, then, no trace of the Khálsají will be left any where. Fifty thousand British troops will soon cross the Satluj, and come and kill you, and then you will be able to do nothing; the English will give you great distress, for, besides destroying your religion, they will do away with your name and trace. Well, even if you do not regard the arrival of the English as any harm, still look at my father, with what stratagem the Sandhewális have killed him. Hark! I will say one other thing to you; you know how much wealth my father had, and how much treasure belonged to the Mahárája; so that if I were to spend for a hundred years even, I should not be bankrupt; but now this is my resolution, that I will forsake every thing else, and foster the army. Behold! from to-day I will give twelve rupees a month to a foot soldier, and thirty a month to a horseman. If you do not believe me, then I swear, and promise you, that I will sacrifice all my uncle's and my father's wealth on you; I have no other design, but I only wish this, that I may kill the Sandhewális and, stopping the English at the Satluj, keep my country in peace and quiet. If we shall not do this, then our whole life long, there will be disgrace to me and to you; remember this, that the Sandhewális are the enemies of your country, and of the Hindú religion and the Sikh faith : and if we shall not kill them, then there is no knowing what will become of our religion."

The army, on hearing this speech, became inflamed with rage, and, there and then, leaving their food and drink, and pots and pans, prepared to fight. The army then said to Hírá Singh, "Do you go with ease of heart to your camp at the brick kiln of Buddhú; we will come with you and take revenge on those sinners in right good style." Hírá Singh, in this way by his sagacity, got 40,000 of the army on his side; when they were thus preparing to assault the city, then the Sandhewális, having given some money to the few troops of the army, who were in the fort and city, won them over to help them. Although, for the sake of keeping secret the death of Dhián Singh, they gave out in the city that

Mahárája Dalíp Singh had become king, and Dhíán Singh his minister, still the death of the latter did not remain secret in the town. At evening time Hírá Singh, taking the army of the Khálsa with him, set out for the city.

On hearing this, the Sandhewális, for the sake of abating the wrath of the Sikhs, having covered the corpse of Dhíán Singh with a shawl, and sprinkled it with rose-water, sent it to the army, along with the corpse of that Musalmán soldier, who had died with him, and said, "Alas! alas! this Musalmán soldier has, without our order, killed the minister, and we are greatly grieved; and we, there and then, killed this base traitor." However the wrath of the Khálsa was not assuaged by these words; rather, with a loud voice shouting "Victory to the Wáh Gurú" they entered the city, and came and surrounded the fort. Hírá Singh, having called the gunners, said "Do you fire and make a breach in the fort, so that the whole army may be able to enter the fort." He moreover said to them: "I will give you much money for these your services, for it is the intention of my heart, that I will not take my food and drink, until I see the heads of the Sandhewális cut off." Afterwards he said to the army, which was looting the city, "If you will cut off and bring to me the heads of my enemies, then I will give you an order to loot the fort also." On hearing this, the army, for the sake of entering the fort, cajoled the artillerymen much, that they, with their guns, should make a road into the fort; the gunners, having fired the guns, at break of day made a breach in the fort, and the army, by that road, made an attempt to enter the fort. When the army, with much fury, charged and attacked the fort, then the inner army did not oppose them in the least; and those Sikhs of the inner army, who did oppose Hírá Singh, being powerless, were not able to offer much resistance. When they saw the great violence and impetuosity of Hírá Singh's army, then Ajít Singh, Sandhewálí, for the sake of saving his life, jumped out over the wall of the fort. The army, recognising him, seized him, and, immediately cutting off his head, brought it to Hírá Singh. Hírá Singh pleased them by bestowing on them money, jágírs and much wealth, and said, "I, in my life-time, am determined to efface the seed of the Sandhewális, and I will sacrifice my life to effect it."

Then Hírá Singh lifted the head, and brought and placed it at the feet of his mother. His mother, on seeing it, was greatly pleased and said: "I am now pleased, and I will pray for blessings on you at the threshold of God, for you have right well taken the revenge of your father." Having said the above, she prepared for satti, and, having seated herself on the pile, said: "Do you do much charity after my death, and always keep your thoughts on the rights of the deserving." Then she said to the other Sardárs "Place on the head of Hírá Singh the crown of the kingdom." When the chiefs had placed the crown on his head, then his mother said "Enough! I am now satisfied; set fire to my funeral pile." The people then set fire to it and, at that time, thirteen other women also did sattí with her.

The following circumstance is worthy to be narrated: that, of those thirteen women, one, a servant who used to do service to the mother of Hírá Singh, was only ten years old. When she wished to burn herself along with the Queen, then the Queen, seeing her youth, said "Do not you do sattí with me, for I have made you over to Hírá Singh, and he will always keep you happy in every way." On hearing this, that girl began to cry, and said, "I have no desire for any thing else; take me also with you, where you are going;" then she said this also "If you will not let me do sattí, then I will die in some other way." When the Queen and other people saw her firm resolve (to die), then they thought it right to let her do sattí also. Then she, along with them all, being burnt, was turned into ashes.

When the fight was finished, then Hírá Singh gave orders that no more looting was to be allowed in the fort: then the search for Lahiná Singh commenced. He was not found amongst the wounded or in any other place, but they obtained a clue of him in a cellar. He had broken his leg, and, there was with him at that time a servant, who although fifty years old, was still very powerful. He, at that time, very nobly showed his loyalty; for, to deliver Lahiná Singh, he went and stood ready for opposition at the entrance of the cellar. When the Sikhs saw him, then they said "Do you go away from here; we have got nothing to do with you." but he would not listen to what they said, rather he replied "I will give my head in place of my master." On hearing this speech, the Sikhs became very angry. When the Sikhs wished to shoot him, then he said "To shoot me is nothing, but I will regard him as brave, who will draw his sword and fight with me." The Sikhs, on hearing this, desisted from shooting, but a number of them,[5] drawing their swords, rushed on and attacked that single man: but bravo to his bravery! for he died after having with his own hand killed thirteen men. At the time of dying, he said "O Sikhs! my master is already wounded; you must not cut him up and kill him now." They did not listen to what he said, but a Sikh, from behind him, fired a gun so well, that Lahiná Singh was killed by its shot.

---

[5] *Lit.* "Ten or twelve men."

CHAP. VII.—THE LÁHAUR CAMPAIGN.

Then the army agreed to this, that, if Hírá Singh would agree to these their terms, then they would obey him, otherwise what God willed, that should happen.

Those terms were as follows:—

1*st.*—That no annoyance was to be given to Pasaurá Singh and Kasmírá Singh, and they were to be called to Láhaur and the army was to be called back from Siálkoṭ.

2*nd.*—Pandat Jalá was to be turned out of the Durbár, or to be made over to their hands.

3*rd.*—Missar Belí Rám, who was the old treasurer, was again to be restored to his post.

4*th.*—Bhái Gurmukh Singh was to be recalled.

5*th.*—That Sardár Juáhar Singh, who was the uncle of Dalíp Singh, was to be released from confinement.

Agreeing to the first term, Hírá Singh sent a letter to Siálkoṭ, directing that the army was to come back from there. Regarding the second term, he said "Pandat Jalá is my servant, and, if he shall commit any fault, I will punish him; but do you forgive him his former offences" and he added this also, "Well henceforth, he shall not again come to the Durbár, nor shall he give any advice about state affairs." Regarding the third term, he said "Missar Belí Rám and Bhái Gurmukh Singh were deposed by the advice of the army for misbehaviour; therefore you know best about this."[76]

Regarding the fifth, at that time it was agreed that Juáhar Singh should be released from confinement, and that two thousand rupees should be given him, and 10,000 to the army, for expenses.

As the army were very determined on Hírá Singh accepting these terms, and Suchet Singh saw that there was some difference between the army and Hírá Singh, he therefore determined at once to come to Láhaur. When Suchet Singh arrived in Láhaur, then he saw another state of affairs. On this, he wrote the circumstance of his coming to that army, which had given him the news of their difference, and called him from Jammú. The army replied "Hírá Singh has now agreed to all our terms; we therefore will not now break our word with him; it is therefore best for you, that you should quickly return to Jammú; for if you shall remain here, you will suffer great loss." On hearing this, he was greatly ashamed, and, being filled with rage, he determined to give his life. Although Hírá Singh himself also sent and told Suchet Singh, that if he did not return to Jammú, it would be very serious

---

[76] i.e., You can do as you like.

(to himself), still even he did not listen to any thing, but said "I will not retrace my steps without dying and fighting."

Then Hírá Singh, taking 15,000 troops, pursued Suchet Singh At that time Suchet Singh had alighted in a Muhammadan Masjid, and all his attendants were then listening to the Granth Sáhib. Hírá Singh's army began at once to fire ball, but Suchet Singh would not give up listening to the Granth: when all the walls of the Masjid had been knocked down by the guns, then Suchet Singh, taking his sword in his hand, fought very bravely. At that time, there were with Suchet Singh about 200 men only. On this occasion, Suchet Singh's small army showed great spirit and fought very bravely, for they were all killed fighting for their master; and one hundred and sixty of them were killed in this fight. After the fight, when Hírá Singh came to the place of the fight, and saw that Rái Kesrí Singh was wounded, then he laughed at him greatly, and afterwards that Kesri Singh died from thirst. But when Hírá Singh saw his uncle's body among the slain, then he began to cry very much at seeing the corpse of his uncle. He then had him placed in a pálkí, and brought him to that place, where was the tomb of Guláb Singh's eldest son, Udham Singh, and, on arrival there, he burned him.

Whilst he was absent from Láhaur, Pasaurá Singh and Kasmírá Singh wandered about, lurking and prowling ; and, having despaired of saving themselves, went and took refuge with Bháí Bír Singh. This Bháí Bír Singh, by wandering about in the Manjhá country, and taking offerings and gifts and presents, had become so powerful, that 1,200 footmen and about 300 horse and two guns always remained with him. All the chiefs, that were turned out of the darbár at Láhaur, used to go and live with him. Hírá Singh felt certain of this also, that, as Bháí Bír Singh kept such a large army, his intention was to take the throne of Láhaur, but Hírá Singh, by reason of fear, could never even mention the name of fighting with Bháí Bír Singh, for the Sikhs placed so much confidence in him, that if, through forgetfulness even, Hírá Singh had mentioned the idea of killing him, then they would have killed him himself that very moment. In the cook-house of Bháí Bír Singh, food was always prepared for 1,500 men.

Hírá Singh and his friend Pandat Jalá formed this resolve that, by some means, they should kill him without the army obtaining information of it; and they devised this also, that the disgrace of killing him should also not be attached to them ; thus determining, it came into their thoughts that they should first write a friendly letter to him, and then see what was to be done. These two wrote and sent to Bír Singh saying "O Maháráj ! do you offer up some good prayer for us "; and having sent it (the letter) with many fine things (as a present), added this also " If you wish it, ask (me) and I will appoint a jágir for you, for the expenses of your cook-house are very great." The object of all this was this, that Bháí Bír Singh might have no suspicion of him. Then Hírá Singh made Mutáb Singh, Majíthiyá his counsellor, and began to show him much kindness and gave him much money also; after this, he said to Mutáb Singh "News has come to me from India, that Sardár Atar Singh, Sandhewálí, has made some agreement with the English to fight with the Sikhs; moreover, it is also reported that he has enlisted the chiefs on the other side of the Satluj on his side; I therefore now regarding you as (of) one mind with myself,[77] consult you as to what should be done; and I have hopes, that if you will help me in this matter, then all this business shall be accomplished satisfactorily. Mutáb Singh, being entangled in his friendship, replied " I am at your service in every way." Hírá Singh, regarding him as his helper, said " Do you take your regiment, and go to Anmritsar: and, from there, write and send a letter to this purport to Atar Singh; 'All the army and officers are your friends'; and then use your endeavours also to get him to come without fail to Bháí Bír Singh's house, after reading that letter, so that I may obtain an interview with him through the above Bháí." On hearing this, General Mutáb Singh was pleased, and at once went to Anmritsar. As he was leaving, he (Hírá Singh), said this also to him " I have sent for you not only for this business, but my intention is, that if the English shall be defeated in the fight with Guáliár, then I will take my whole army, and, crossing the river Satluj, make a raid on the British frontier." When Mutáb Singh, agreeably to the saying of Hírá Singh, had written to Atar Singh, then he came and put up at the house of Bháí Bír Singh; Hírá Singh, on hearing this, sent and said to Bháí Bír Singh " It is not proper for you to go collecting all these Sikhs with you; however I say nothing about the other chiefs, but you must turn out one Atar Singh from your house." Bír Singh sent and said " I am a fakír, and can put no restraints on any one coming to, or leaving, my house." Hírá Singh, on hearing this, became filled with rage, and, having sent a large army, surrounded the house of Bír Singh, and all the Sardárs in it; having gone there, the Sikhs fired off their cartridges, and one ball struck the leg of Bír Singh, who died from the wound, and they threw his corpse into the river.

After this, Hírá Singh began to reign in comfort and ease in Láhaur. Again, after some time, on one occasion Hírá Singh wished to go for some reason to his own country; but this sus-

---

[77] i.e., my friend.

picion arose (in peoples' minds), that he wished to take away the treasure of Láhaur and carry it off to Jammú. The Sikhs, taking a large army with them, crossed the river and went and surrounded him; and after a severe fight, Juáhar Singh, who was the uncle of Dalíp Singh, killed Hírá Singh, and the Pandat Jalá; and, after that, Juáhar Singh began to carry on the duties of minister. This man was very wicked and debauched, and the Sikhs regarded him in a bad light. One day, on the plain of Miáu Mír, they suddenly killed him, and, after that, Rája Lál Singh became minister. During his administration and rule, the army became very uncontrollable, and began to plunder greatly in Láhaur. At that time such calamities arose in Láhaur, that no one could go to sleep in peace. Afterwards, as there was no one to control the army, and they became unmanageable, then the whole army, collecting, set out to fight with the English; and, without any quarrel or action (on the part of the English), they set fire to the station of Ludeháua. After this, the English came with great force, and drove back the Sikhs; then, after a great many battles, when the Sikhs had been defeated, Guláb Singh went and got what he could (out of them and made terms with the English.)

Whilst Guláb Singh was still there, the Queen Jinda thought that, as the Sikhs had now become outrageous and unruly and uncontrollable, there was no knowing but that they might go over perhaps to the English and give her trouble: and as there was no one over them, it therefore would not be surprising, if this company of demons were to make differences between Dalíp Singh and herself. Having thought over every thing well, she determined that, for keeping the throne of Láhaur and helping Dalíp Singh, she would call the English to Láhaur; for, besides them, there was now no one to oppose these violent ruffians; for, although, from their coming outwardly there might be harm, still, in reality, they would give her much ease. Having thus thought, she said to her female servant, named Manglán "Do you, taking Dalíp Singh, go to the English, and tell them from me, that since Maháraja Sher Singh died, and went to heaven, from that time, much disturbance has taken place in Láhaur, for there is no master of the Sikh army, and whatever chief gives them any wealth or goods, they go with him, and begin to kill other people; and, behold! they have killed various chiefs, who were ready to give their lives to save the throne of Láhaur, and then, after that, they killed my brother most unjustly, and then fought with you. I am greatly afraid of them, and there is no knowing what else they may do." These two went to the English, and said all (they were told to say), agreeably to the command of Jinda Kor, and added: "The Queen

Jinda Kor has asked you to come to Láhaur to help her." On hearing this, the English thought "Is there any other design in this or not?" Then, when they had fully ascertained that the Maháráni was certainly much afflicted by the Sikhs, and her calling them was really in earnest, after a little thought and reflection, they prepared to go to Láhaur. There is no advantage in writing all the circumstances of that matter, for there is much written about it in other books; but this much should be known, that, agreeably to the calling of the mother, Jinda Kor, in the year 1902 in the month of Phagan (February-March), the English people came to Láhaur. Afterwards, their power gradually increased to such a degree, that the entire government and revenue of Láhaur, rather of the whole Panjáb, became theirs. God, day by day, has caused their grandeur and greatness to increase, and that of the Sikhs to diminish in power daily. Then, after some time Jinda Kor made this mistake, that she tried to create discord among the British troops, and win some of them over to herself;[78] and as the Mahárája Dalíp Singh and Jinda Kor appeared to be the cause of many troubles and intrigues in the administration of the kingdom, the English Government therefore seized the persons of both of them, and had them sent to their own country (*i.e.*, England) with much care.

COUPLET.

No one comes into, and always remains in, this world.
But whoever comes into it, only remains at ease two days.

VERSES.

Behold the play of this world :
People meet each other for four days :
Kings, subjects, rich, and poor,
Trees, stones, ants, and men,
Whoever has come into this world,
Has never always been allowed to stop in it ;
This is like the road of a highway ;
All people pass over it (but never stop) :
Whatever is to-day, that
Will not be seen again always[79]
Those, who had numerous armies,
And those, who were wise, good, and holy,

---

[78] The story is that a soldier was attacked by a bull, which butted him with its horns, on which the soldier, who had a gun in his hand, shot it; this was reported to the sepoys, and Jinda Kor tried to intrigue with them, and work on their feelings, and win them over to herself.

[79] *Lit.* "Morning and evening."

G

He enforced his orders most resolutely;
They all have gone, their names have not been remembered ;
Saints and prophets all have been destroyed ;
Those persons, who here remain sad,
They will enjoy happiness, and put an end to grief (hereafter).

COUPLET.

He, who is small, becomes great, and he, who is great, becomes small ;
The rich become poor, and again the poor become rich.

VERSES.

Those persons, who were formerly poor,
They afterwards have become filled with wealth,
And then again, they have become deprived of wealth ;
(For) diminishing and increase are in the power of God.
Those, who have given many orders,
And were renowned in all quarters,
Behold ! they too have become beggars ;
The power of God is wonderful ;
Whom that Creator approves of,
Him no one can kill,
And, whom He wishes to kill,
How much (people) may try to save him, he cannot be saved.
Behold Sardár Mahá Singh[50]
Was small in power,
But when Ranjít Singh was born,
He (Ranjít Singh) became mighty in a few days.

COUPLET.

Much territory and wealth came into his power,
And, in a short time, God showed him many sorts of pleasures.

VERSES.

All the Panjáb became subservient to him ;
Whoever obeyed him not, was destroyed ;
Various kinds of things were done by him,
And he got the kingdom into his hands.
No one saw his back.[51]
His agents went to all countries ;

---

[50] The father of Ranjít Singh.
[51] *Lit.* " He was never defeated."

But at last he also died;
After him, many chiefs
Became very arrogant and proud.
But, like him, no other
Could rule the kingdom;
This is a true saying, O Brother!
To whom God gives greatness,
No one will be like him,
And if any one become (proud), God will destroy him.

COUPLET.

The state of God can never be known,
But, in an instant, He can destroy what has been preserved for ages.[82]

VERSES.

All thought this for certain,
That the Sikh dynasty would never be overthrown;
As the greatness of Ranjit Singh,
Was such, that it increased day by day,
They thought it would never be removed,
And it would certainly remain thus;
But, when it pleased God,
He effaced it altogether in an instant[83]
So, O reader of this book!
Well ponder over this matter in thy heart;
To increase and decrease is the way of the world;
Therefore place your eyes (hopes) on God (alone).

---

[82] *Lit.* "For a hundred thousand years."
[83] *Lit.* "In a single watch."

PART III.

REGARDING THE RITES AND CUSTOMS, AND SONGS AND PROVERBS OF THE VARIOUS CASTES IN THE PANJÁB.

CHAPTER I.

Rites and Customs.

According to the saying of the Sástrás, eight kinds of classes are known in India; of these four, *viz.*—Bráhmans, Chhattrís, Vaisas, Súdras, are called baran or castes; and four, namely Girists, Brahmachárs, Bánprastas, and Sanniásas, are called Ásram or religious orders; from these eight have arisen the various castes and sects, which are multifarious in the Panjáb.

Now the account of the Bráhmans is as follows: they are the offspring of Brahmá, and altogether there are ten kinds of Bráhmans; amongst them, the Sársuts, Kánkubajas, Gaurs, Utkals and Maithals, are called Panjgaurs; and five, the Drábars, Tailangs, Mahárástars, Gurjars, and Kárnátaks, are called the Panjdrábars; of these ten kinds, those who live in the Panjáb are chiefly Sársut Bráhmans. Although the Sársut Bráhmans are all one, still, on account of their different families, they do not intermarry with each other. To write about all the families here would be very difficult; but it is necessary to write about one or two, for if this should not be written, then their ways of marrying and betrothal could not be known. Amongst Bráhmans, those who are called Báhrís (*i.e.*, the twelve), marry and give in marriage to twelve houses only; and those, who are called Bunjáhís (*i.e.*, fifty-two), give and take the daughters of fifty-two houses, that is to say, families; and they do not give them to, or take them from, any other houses, except these. It would take a good deal of space to write of the twelve houses of the Báhrís and the fifty-two of the Bunjáhís; but of one kind of Sársut Bráhmans, who are called the A*th*wáns (eight families), there are these eight families; Josís, Kurals, Sands, Pátaks, Bhárduájís, Soris, Tibárís; these eight families give their daughters to, and take them from, each other, and will have nothing to do with any other families. The Josís are of two kinds; one, Marúrs, and the other, Mullammás; they are therefore called the Á*th*wáns. A náí (barber) or parohit (priest) goes and arranges the betrothal of the daughters of other Bráhmans, but on account of the fewness of the families (of the A*th*wáns) they know all the A*th*wáns of the Panjáb, and make the necessary enquiries, and betroth (their children), among themselves.

The ceremony of betrothal in the Panjáb is as follows: the father sends by the hand of his nái (or barber) seven dates and one rupee to the house of the boy to be asked for; when the nái arrives at the house of the bridegroom elect, then the head of the house, having sprinkled oil on both sides of the door, takes the nái inside, and, after making enquiries after his health, the panch (or council) of the village, and the brotherhood, assemble and cause a chaunk of átá [84], to be made by the Pándhá, (family Bráhman). When, agreeably to the rites of the Vedas, the Pándhá has caused the boy to do worship in the chaunk, the nái, having placed those seven dates and that rupee in the lap of the boy, presents the *t*ikká, and puts it on the boy's forehead and with his mouth addresses this speech to the father of the boy "Congratulations, O great king!" Then the father of the boy, according to his means, gives rupees and money to the Bráhman and nái, and sweetmeats to his brotherhood. Then all the people, having congratulated the father of the boy, go away to their houses; they call the name of this custom the sagan (or betrothal). Again, when the day of marriage comes near, then the family of the bride send a letter by the hand of their nái, and give their news to the bridegroom-elect's people; they call the name of that letter, the sáh, or (appointing the day), letter. And the brotherhood and panch assemble in the same way and place the letter on the boy's lap. From this letter, it becomes known how many carriages, and how many persons, the girl's family have asked to accompany the wedding party, and what day the wedding will be. When seven days remain to the wedding, then the mother and father of the boy and girl give va*t*ná[85] (which they also call máíá) to the boy and girl. Again, when the bridegroom arrives at the house of his father-in-law's family, then they dress him in his best jewels and clothes, and place a crown of silver and gold on his head, and a fringe of gold thread round his forehead. Afterwards, when the time of the wedding has been fixed by the Pan*d*ats according to the rites of the Vedas, they make a fire, and having done service to it, cause

---

[84] A chaunk is a square place prepared on the ground over which flour is spread. The square is divided into divisions by a Bráhman or barber, and the names of the planets are then inserted in them, to obtain favourable omens. These marks are worshipped by the bride and bridegroom.

[85] A mixture of meal, oil and some fragrant material, which is used as a substitute for soap, having the property of making the skin soft and delicate.

the boy and girl to walk round it four times.[86] People call these circumambulations lámán[87]; when once they have made a girl go round the fire, then after that no one can marry her a second time.[88] Then next day, the bride's people entertain the wedding party and feed them with various kinds of sweetmeats, and sing songs; the name of the hospitality of this day is called mith́ábhatt, and the name of that which takes place the day after this, khattá-bhatt. The Athwáns, mentioned above, perform all the business of the marriage like other Bráhmans, except that on the day of mith́ábhatt, they do not give sweets to be eaten but merely spread various kinds of fruits on a sheet, and give people bowls of milk to drink; then, according to their means, having bestowed clothes, jewels, and money, on the bridegroom's people, on the fourth day they dismiss the wedding party. Again, two or three years after this kind of wedding, the bridegroom-elect goes to the house of his father-in-law to bring his bride home; the name of that custom is called mukláwa (or bringing home a wife). At the mukláwa also, they call a l'ándhá in that same manner, and cause him to make a channk (covered with átá), and, at the time of departing, it is the custom to give jewelry and clothes and money to the bride according to their means. The clothes and jewels, which are given to the bridegroom's people, at the time of the marriage and the mukláwa, they call these (khatt) the dowry. When the bride's people send the betrothal to any one's house, then four questions are first asked about the boy; and if there is any deficiency in replying to any of these questions, then the betrothal does not take place; those four questions are as follows: of what got (family) is the boy? of what got are the relations of the boy's father's mother? of what got are the family of the boy's mother? and of what got are the family of the boy's mother's mother. If, in the reply to any of these four questions, there should be any deficiency, or if any of the gots correspond with the got of the girl, then they cannot form affinity. But, as the Athwáns Bráhmans are very few, they form affinity in spite of the correspondence of the gots of the boy and girl. Afterwards, when a child is born, that same day the father consults the Pandats and causes his horoscope to be written. The Bráhmans regard themselves as unclean for eleven days, commencing from the birth. Sutak is the name given to this state of ceremonial uncleanness; and in whosoever's house there is sutak, for eleven days no one can eat or drink with them. Again, after forty days, the mother performs ablution, and

---

[86] The ends of the sheets worn by the bride and bridegroom are tied together in a knot, and they then walk round the fire, either four, or seven, times.

[87] This is the plural of láun, the title for one circuit of this ceremony.

[88] She can be married, but not according to these rites.

the people of the brotherhood call the priest, and give the child its name; the name of this custom is known as nám karan (naming). Then, for five years (and sometimes for three years) they do not allow the infant's hair to be shaved, and when the day fixed by his ancestor arrives, then, having gone to some place of pilgrimage, as a holy spot like Jnálá Mukhí, they shave the hair of the child, and the name of that custom they call bhaddan (first shaving). Afterwards, when the child reaches the age of eight years, then they shave his head, and, according to the rites of the Sástras, having called an assembly of Brahmachárís, they have the Brahminical thread put on his neck by the Gurú.

Again, when any Bráhman dies, then his son, or grandson, according to their means, having made a very beautiful bier, and having placed the dead body on it, cover it with a shawl or some other silken cloth; and although all the males of the family shave their heads, still the eldest son, for the sake of performing the funeral rites according to the rites of the Sastras, shaves his head, and, having put on his hand a ring of kusa,[89] which they make agreeably to the rites of the Vedas, takes three other men with him, and they lift the corpse. The other people of the house throw flowers, sweetmeats, pice and rupees on the corpse, and, uttering this speech "Srí Rám Rám Satt hai" (the name of Srí Rám is true) go to the place of burning, and, having placed the corpse a little this side of the burning ground, make an offering of rice balls[90] and, having made a stream of water flow around[91] on all four sides of the corpse, they then break the earthen pot; then, when they arrive at the burning place, they place the corpse on the burning pile, sometimes with the shawl on, and sometimes having taken it off.[92] Then, on the fourth day, having collected his usts *i.e.*, his bones, they send them to the Ganges. The Bráhman, who, at this time, for eleven days, according to the rites of the Vedas, performs the funeral obsequies and takes alms, him they call acháraj (an instructor, in matters of religion) or the Mahá Bráhman (chief Bráhman); and no one eats, drinks, or associates with that acháraj, and they all (*i.e.*, the Acháraj), have their own separate castes. In whosesoever's house, the dead man dies, he for eleven days purifies, *i.e.*, cleanses himself,

---

[89] Or dabbh, a species of spear grass, used in certain social ceremonies.
[90] Used by Hindus at the srádh of deceased relations.
[91] The water is made to flow from the head and return there again; if any water is left in the pot, it is emptied; the pot is then dashed on the ground and broken to pieces. It is said that, on hearing the sound of the breaking of the pot, the deceased becomes aware that he is dead. The pot is called adhmárg, *i.e.*, half way, because broken on the way.
[92] If taken off, it is given to the Bráhman.

and other people do not eat and drink with him. On the eleventh day, after having given much jewels, clothes and money to the acháraj, they perform the funeral obsequies; and afterwards, when four years have elapsed from the deceased's death, every year they perform srádh[93] in his memory, and feed Bráhmans with various kinds of food.

The account of the Chhattrís is as follows: those people who are called Chhattrís in the Sástras, that is really the name of the Khattrís. In the Sástras they call one who carries an umbrella (i.e. a king), a Chhattrí; but as all the world cannot be kings, for this reason, persons, for the sake of getting a living, began to follow mercantile occupations, which originally was the occupation of Vaisas, i.e., bániyás. In the Panjáb, for the sake of easy pronunciation, Chhattrís began to be called Khattrís. The rites and customs at birth, death, betrothal, bhaddan, &c., and marriage amongst these Khattrís, is like that of all Bráhmans, with this difference, that they observe the purification at birth and death for thirteen days. Amongst them also there are Bahrís and Bujáhís, and they form affinity also only amongst their (several families). As amongst the Bráhmans there are Athwánsas, so amongst the Khattrís, there the Dháiyas; and they only marry into Dháiya families, but they do not regard it wrong to marry girls related to them on the mother's side.

The Vaisas; such they call bániyás; but now, contrary to the Sástras, the Káits, Súdras, and Bhábras, and other castes, also style themselves Vaisas; but if one reflects properly, they all belong to the Súdras. The families (gots) of the bániyás are many, but they all have but two kinds of religion; one springing from Vaisno, and the other from Saráugí; those who are Vaisno bániyás, they observe the same rites at birth, death, putting on the Brahminical thread, and marriage, as all other Khattrís, and Bráhmans, but they differ somewhat in the custom of mithábhatt at their marriages, and in (their ceremonies) at eating and feasts.

The Saráugí bániyás do not regard the Vedas and Sástras, or the gods or goddesses, and forms and ordinances, set forth in them; and the funeral obsequies which ought to be performed at the time of death, these they do not perform at all. For this reason, Vaisno bániyás used not to intermarry with them, but in the present day, for sometime back, some have even begun to intermarry with them. In the same way as the Khattrís regard

---

[93] A Hindú ceremony in which they worship and feed Bráhmans, on some day during the month Assu, in commemoration of their deceased ancestors and for their special benefit.

CHAP. I.—RITES AND CUSTOMS.

the Sársut Bráhmans as their family priests and give them alms; so also do these bániyás reverence the Gaur Bráhmans as their family priests. Some of the Khattrís eat meat and drink wine; but bániyás regard mentioning the name even of these things as sin. There is one caste of bániyás, who are known as *Dhúsars*, and although they are like the bániyás in their ordinances and rites, still other bániyás will not intermarry with them. These *Dhúsars* principally live in Hindustán; up to the present time, there is not a single family of them in the Panjáb.

The Súdras; such they call barbers, washermen, wine distillers, potters, carpenters, and other low castes. The customs, at birth, death, and marriage, of all these people are all like those of the three, which have been above mentioned; but there is a vast difference in their rites at eating and feasts, and at sútak[94] and pátak.[95] Amongst them, the sútak and pátak last a month and a quarter; these people do not wear the Brahminical thread; for this reason Khattrís and Bráhmans refrain from eating bread at their houses, in fact they will not even drink water, or the like, from them. Although the *Jatts* are also among the Súdras, still all Khattrís and Bráhmans will drink water at their hands; and although a jhíúr (Hindú water-carrier) is also a Súdra, still every one will drink water at his hands. The Súdras do not regard as wrong, in the same way as Khattrís, Bráhmans, and other high-bred people hold as highly improper, the buying and selling of their daughters, and the marrying them to relatives already connected by marriage, and the remarriage of widows, rather they shamelessly and openly do these things; and if they desire to marry a married woman, then, contrary to the rites of the Vedas, having thrown the sheet (of marriage) over them,[96] they marry her. Amongst Súdras, barbers, washermen, and many other castes do not worship any one but their ancestors, who have died beloved of the Supreme Being. Accordingly the náís (barbers) worship Sain Bhagat, the washermen worship Bábá Nám Deo, and do not regard any but these as good. Although the Rájpúts of the Panjáb in the present time pursue agriculture like the *Jatts*, still they are not Súdras by origin; but, on the contrary, they are pure Khattrís, for their descent is from the Khattrís, who are descended from the sun, and who are called the offspring of Sri Rám Chand. Their customs at birth, death, and marriage, &c., are according to the

---

[94] Purification at births.
[95] Purification at deaths.
[96] That is, they do not marry her according to proper rites, for widow remarriage is forbidden. The expression "throw the sheet over" is applied to marrying a widow.

rites laid down in the Vedas ; these people wear the Brahminical thread, and perform sandhiá[97] and Gátrí.[98]

Now the account of the four Ásrams is as follows :

1st, Girisatí is the name of all family people, who, according to the rites of their religion, live in the world ; in the Vedas, they are called grisatí.

2nd, Bráhmachárí was the name of a sect ; formerly, all people in their youth, at the time of receiving instruction, used to be received into the sect of Brahmáchár ; and then, on marriage, used to cohabit with their wives[99] ; but now Brahmachárí is the name of a kind of religious mendicantship. These people, having shaved their heads and faces, become medicants, and wear the Brahminical thread and tuft of hair. The Brahmachárís are of four kinds ; at the end of their names, titles, such as Nand, Pargás, &c., are added, as Rámá Nand, Siámá Nand, Sukh Pargás. After death, all their funeral obsequies are performed according to the rites of the Vedas ; and they burn the corpse on a fire, and build a Samádh (mausoleum) over it ; and after the death of one of their Gurús, the chief disciple sits on the throne.

3rd. Bánparast also is the name of a kind of mendicantship ; these people, leaving their families, go to the woods, and perform penance, and undergo various kinds of fastings and afflictions.

4th. Sanniása is also the name of a kind of mendicantship, which has principally spread from Suámí Sankarácharj and Dattátreya. The Sanniásís are of ten kinds, namely, Bans, Bhártís, Aranns, Girís, Purís, Parbats, Sarassutís, Tíraths, Ságars, Ásrams ; and these ten kinds are known as the Dasnáms (ten names.)

All the above titles are affixed at the end of the names of the Sanniásís ; e.g., Rám Ban, Gopál Bhártí, Sib Áránn, Deo Giri, &c., are well known (names) ; and of whatever sect a Sanniásí may be, that title is affixed to his name. These people formerly used to reverence all the Vedas and Vedántas ; but now, except the Paramhansas, all the other Sanniásís, who are called Gusáins, have begun to acknowledge the religion of a goddess named Bálá Sundarí. There is not much difference between this creed and the Bámmárg, which they also call the Sákat Dharm ; (in fact) there is only this much difference, that the Sákatakas,

---

[97] Repeating mantras, i.e., prayers or charms, and sipping water at sunrise, midday, and sunset.

[98] The name of a mantra, repeated by Bráhmans, whilst turning their rosaries.

[99] Their only desire is offspring, and if the cohabitation results in a child being conceived, they leave their wives and go off.

CHAP. I.—RITES AND CUSTOMS. 107

agreeably to the rites laid down in the Sástras, read charms and couplets, and perform worship and penance, whilst the former read the songs and prayers composed in the dialect of this country, and worship the goddess with them; those five things flesh, wine, falsehood, adultery, and mudras,[100] which the Sákatakas eschew, these also eschew them, and make no difference therein. Many other people from associating with Gusáins have also entered this sect, and they call the name of this sect the Kundápanth. The customs of the Gusáins are as follows: they do not wear the Brahminical thread or tuft of hair, and, like the Girisatís, do not perform any funeral rites or obsequies; their distinguishing marks are wearing rosaries, made of seeds of the rudráchh tree, and reddish yellow clothes, and besmearing themselves with ashes. They do not burn their dead bodies, but rather, having filled a large pot with salt, they bury the corpse in it, and then, erecting a mansoleum over it, continually do worship to it; many of them adopt a naked state; others marry, and others, having received instruction, become Paramhansas, but they are all called Sanniásís.

In the same way as the Sanniásís are known by ten names, so also are there twelve orders of the Jogís: all these orders are known by the title of Náth. The customs of the Jogís, as laid down in the Pitanjal Sástra, are not now observed by any of them, but the Jogís of the present time principally follow the rules of the Kundápanth, which have become prevalent amongst the Gusáins. These people greatly reverence Bhaíron and Kálí also. This is their custom that they make a hole in their ears, and wear earrings, and carry a small musical pipe, attached to a thread, round their neck; when any Jogi dies, they bury him like the Gusáins. These people do not read the Vedas or Sástras at all, but obtain pleasure from reading the verses composed in the time of Gorakhnáth. Amongst them, those, who pierce their ears and wear earrings, are called darsanís (prudent), and those, who do not pierce their ears, are called nughars (indiscreet). As Gorakhnáth, who was the founder of this sect, in his commands, forbade them to marry and settle, they, therefore, merely take the children of some Girisatí for their disciples, and thus continue their lineage, and, at last, having given the throne to that disciple, they die.

The account of the Bairágís, who live in this country, is as follows: Rámá Nand, who is known as Rámá Nuj in the Sástras, founded their sect. These people wear the Brahminical thread and tuft of hair, and observe the funeral rites and obsequies and all

---

[100] A kind of worship with the hands joined together, the fingers being intertwisted.

the other religious rites laid down in the Vedas. If any Bairágí should die, then like the Girisatís, they throw him into a fire, and, on the fourth day, collecting his bones, send them to the Ganges. This is their custom, that they believe in Vísnu Bhagwán and Rám Kisan, with his other incarnations; and, besides him, they do not place the slightest faith in any other god or goddess. Their distinguishing marks are to wear a necklace of basil round their throats, to make a high-reaching mark on their foreheads, and to wear white clothes. Until a Bairágí has been to Duárká and had the mark made on his shoulder with the shell and heated quoit, till then the other Bairágís will not let him come into their eating square. These people do not eat bread cooked by the hands of any one else, and are very firm in their abstinence and purity, and regard it as wrong even to touch any one else. These people used formerly not to marry, but now many of them become heads of a house (*i.e.*, marry). They also take many disciples from amongst the Girisatís, and fix their religious thoughts on Visnu. As the Bairágís worship Visnu, and believe in no one else but him, for this reason, the name of their sect has been called Vaisno Dharm. These people so greatly detest meat, wine, and other unlawful edibles, that they do not utter the names of these things in their dreams even.

Now the account of the Udásís is as follows: they regard themselves as disciples of Nának, and follow his rights and customs. Bába Sirí Chand, who was the eldest son of Bába Nának, founded their sect, and began to practise customs different from former Jogís and Sanniásís. Although they are divided into four orders still all of them collectively are called Udásís. This is the custom of these people; when they leave the Girisat state and become saints, then they do not marry. Some of them wear long hair on their heads, and some short hair; and some have a custom of twisting the hair round the head like long ropes, and some regard it as proper to shave their heads and faces. These people regard all the customs at birth, death, and burial, according to the rites of the Vedas, but they do not wear a Brahminical thread or tuft of hair. Their distinguishing marks are to wear clothes dyed in red brick dust, and to have a high mark on their forehead, and to read the Granth Sáhib. Although they burn their dead bodies, still they always erect mausoleums over them like the Jogís and Sanniásís. Although formerly these people used to remain much absorbed in the worship of God only, now certain of them have become great men of the world, and pursue agriculture, and have thrones and houses, and quarrel about small pieces of land; certainly, in some places there are some very good saints of their sect, but they do not live in houses, and, being without avarice, beg for bread, and

CHAP. 1.—RITES AND CUSTOMS.

thus gain their subsistence. After the death of an Udási also, the seat goes to the eldest disciple, and no other disciple can lay any claim to it. Some of them also are very severe on themselves, and make a hole in their person, and put on a lock of very heavy iron or steel, in the hope that they may escape from the evil practices of the world. These people address one another as Bháijí, and, morning and evening, playing on cymbals and harps, sing the worship and praises of their God.

There are many sects among the Nának Panthís; of them one sect is called Suthrá. These people formerly might have been good, but now it consists of those men, who drink wine and eat meat, and gamble, and becoming debauched, live extravagantly in their homes, and then, leaving their families, go and join the sect of the Suthrá. The followers of this sect of mendicants know no worship or service, but they are great hands at taking charas and bhang, and in committing sin. Formerly, some good fakír, who was their chief man, caused it to be written by one of the latter kings, that if any of these fakírs went to a market, the market folks were to give him a pice each as a present; accordingly, these people always beat their sticks together in the bazaar, and beg for pice in every market, and fill up their sins to the full. They wear round their head and neck a thread of black wool, and, on their foreheads, a black mark; and they carry two little (castinet) sticks in their hands. Although these people perform the customs at births, deaths and marriages according to the rites of the Sástras, still they do no other worship or devotion. When a Suthrá dies, then, having burnt him according to the rites of the Sástras, they build a mausoleum over him, and, having collected his bones, throw them into the Ganges. These people are all called Sáh, and they accordingly always affix the title Sáh after their names; as for instance, Ráwel Sáh, Chabelí Sáh, Sirní Sáh, and Paurí Sáh. These people read nothing but the verses of Nának and the praises of the goddess (of Jnála Mukhí): and wherever there are places of worship or mausoleums of the ten Gurús, commencing from Nának, there they go and offer oblations, and worship and do homage. These people regard the uttering of every bad or good word in a shameless way as truth and sincerity; and whoever associates with them, becomes quite an adept in shamelessness and debauchery. In the Panjáb, there is no city where there is not a house of the Suthrás, and, owing to their kindness, the children of the cities become quite depraved. Although, amongst them there is the rank of Gurú and disciple, still there is no idea of respect and disrespect amongst them; the Gurú, seated before his disciples, laughs with dancing girls, and the disciple, seated before his Gurú, drinks wine. In short, in the Panjábí tongue, Suthrá signifies good, but these people, contrary to this, body and soul, are bad; there is no knowing what goodness the last king (before mentioned) saw in them, that he made every one pay tribute to them; in my opinion, if the market-folk were to leave off giving them money, and they were to work, or beg for flour and bread, like other fakírs, and get their living in this way, then the sons of great men would not adopt this kind of mendicancy.

In this country, that sect, who are the Diwáná saints, they also are called the disciples of Nának. Some amongst them are good fakírs, and do worship to God. These people, like other Sikhs, wear long hair and carry a necklace of shells round their necks. Jatts and Chumárs principally become followers of this sect; on their heads, they have a very long peacock feather, and they are always repeating to themselves "Sattnám." Of them, many are married, and some unmarried; all their customs are like those of the Sikhs and Udásís, and they reverence the Granth Sáhib.

Among the followers of Nának, one sect is called the Nirmala Sádhú; originally these people were of the sect of the Gurú Gobind Singh, but, on account of their ancient origin, they are also called the disciples of Nának; these people are very perfect Sikhs, and, with heart and soul, firmly believe in the Granth of the Gurú. Formerly, agreeably to the orders of Gobind Singh, they acknowledged none but the Sikh religion, but now, many of them, having read the Vedántas and Sástras, have become Paramhansas. Formerly, it was their custom to wear no clothes, except of a white colour, but now, agreeably to the orders of the Vedántás, they have begun to adopt clothes of a reddish yellow colour. These people formerly, agreeably to the orders of Gobind Singh, lived principally at Anmritsar and Mukatsar and other places of pilgrimage, but now, copying the Sanniásís and Paramhansas, they have begun to live a good deal on the banks of the Ganges and Jamna, and at Banáras and other places. These people regard the customs at birth and death agreeably to the rites of the Sástras, and burn the dead body in the fire, but at marriages, they erect a wooden canopy under which they get married;[101] they do not regard it as right to perform their marriages, according to the decrees of the Vedas.

In this country, amongst the disciples of Nának, there has arisen, from a short time back, a sect called the Gulábdásís, and

---

[101] A ved is a wooden canopy or pavilion, under which Hindú marriages are performed.

CHAP. I.—RITES AND CUSTOMS.

their circumstances are as follows: they do not regard God as the Creator of the world; these people are atheists and very wicked; they say that all this world was formed of itself from the effects of the five elements, and that the account, which is given in the Sástras, of hell and heaven, and punishment and salvation, is false; for when a man dies, then his body remains here, and, afterwards having fallen into pieces, joins with its own elements, and no one goes to heaven or hell. Although these people give themselves out as Vedántas, still there is a great difference between them and the Vedántas; for the Vedántas hold that the soul is separate from the body, whilst these think that there is nothing but the body; rather they say this, that, from the influence of the five elements, something or other has become the impeller of the body, and there is no soul. Although these people, from fear of the world, have customs like other Hindús, and regard caste also, still, in their inward hearts, they have no respect for caste. These people do not acknowledge the Vedas, Puráns or other books, and fearlessly commit every evil deed, and do exactly as suits their pleasure. This is their custom, that they regard the pleasure derived from eating food and dressing as the very highest profit (in life); and, although they are very wicked and abominable, still they call themselves saints. Bába Gulábdás, who was formerly an Udásí fakír, founded their sect, and he himself was a very depraved man and an atheist, and had no fear of this world or the next, and lived in a village called Chattha in the district of Kasúr. From associating with him, the minds of thousands of men have been perverted, and they have become atheists; he too, for the sake of teaching his disciples, composed many Granths of his own faith. Their customs at births and deaths are not fixed according to any book, but at those times, they perform whatever ceremony may suit the occasion.[102] In short, these people, by their counsels, have made the inhabitants of this country very depraved; and the other Sikhs of this country, if they know that any one belongs to this sect, will not allow him to enter their line[103] for eating and drinking; and all other people also are very loath to associate with them, and do not care to drink water from them. In the Sástras their sect is called the Chárbák.

Now, in this country, there are people called Saráugís; their account is as follows: they are called Jainís, that is to say, they follow the religion of a most holy man called Jin. These people pull out all the hair of their head every six months, and

---

[102] That is, the custom is that a body should be burnt in the day and not at night, but these people burn their dead at all hours both of the day and night, as necessity requires.
[103] Hindús do not sit round in a circle to eat their food, but in a line.

always fasten a strip of white cloth over their mouths.[104] They carry with them a broom of white wool, which they, in their language, call rajohaná; and whenever they wish to sit down, they first clean the spot with the broom, so that no insect may come under them, and be killed. These people do not possess much goods, clothes, vessels, or money; but are very great hermits and ascetics. They keep very severe fasts, for often they do not bring food to their mouths for a month at a time; when these people go to beg, then, taking into consideration matters which are very difficult to understand,[105] they take food; and, although other people do not indulge in the custom of giving them bread and water (food), still the tradespeople, who are their disciples, and know all their customs, do service to them with very great affection. These people regard the slaying of an insect as a very serious crime, and, from fear of killing an insect, they will not drink uncooked water, but if, by begging, they can anywhere get water that has been heated, or the water left over in vessels, in which people have cooked their food, they clear it and drink it, and satisfy themselves; and they will not drink it, if they have to draw it themselves from a well or river. From fear of killing an insect, they do not wear shoes on their feet or any cloth on their head; and, as they have found out that animals die in water, for this reason they bathe very little, rather, on account of having to use water, they always keep their clothes soiled and their bodies dirty. What a wonderful thing is this, that, although these people perform such severe acts and hardships, still they do not believe in God! Their belief is this, that all this world, from time everlasting, has gone on making and destroying itself, and there was no creator of it; and what a wonderful thing is this also, that they regard no creator of this world or any giver of happiness and pain. Still according to their religion, they do service to, and worship, the twenty-four incarnations; and amongst these twenty-four, one who is called Párasunáth, and his worship they regard as very profitable. These people, in their dialect, call these twenty-four incarnations, the Tithankar. Amongst them, some make images of those Tithankars, and worship them in their homes; and some regard the worshipping of images as wrong. There are two kinds of these Saráugís; one, those who wear a strip of cloth over their

---

[104] This is done to prevent their killing any animal or insect with their breath even, as they hold it, as the greatest sin, to kill any living thing.

[105] That is to say, they ask if a person's family has already eaten, and if the reply is that they have, the Jainís will partake of their food: if not, they will not, lest one loaf should run short, and another cooking be therefore necessary, in which water, &c., would have to be used, and the lives of some insects be sacrificed, the sin of which, they consider, would attach to them.

months, and pull out the hair of their heads, and these are called *Dhúndíyas*, and the other are those who do not wear the strip of cloth, and do not pull out the hair of their head ; and they are called Jatís. Those, who are called *Dhúndíyas*, they do not possess any houses or goods or money; but the Jatís possess thousands of rupees and property and land, besides many other things. Although there is much difference between the conduct and habits and customs of the two, still their faith is one. These people do not believe in the Vedas or Puráns, nor do they reverence the places of pilgrimage. or fasts, laid down in any of the Sastrás : the religious works of these people also are not written in Sanskrit, but in Prakrit, which is a very old language. Although the language is Prakrit, still the letters are not so, but they write all their religions books in the letters used in the Sástras. They do not marry, but their customs at death, in burning the dead body, are like those of other Hindús ; and if any married disciple becomes the follower of these people, he is called a Saráugí. Although Bráhmans and Khattrís, from associating with them, have begun somewhat to believe in the Sarñug religion, still Bhábrás and bániyás[106] chiefly follow this persuasion. Those Bhábrás and bániyás, who belong to this denomination, although they wear the tuft of hair on their heads, at the same time do not wear the Brahminical thread round their throat. These people do not hold funeral or marriage feasts, and do not perform any funeral obsequies, according to the rites of the Vedas or Puráns. This is the custom of those Saráugís, that they may not undertake any business or traffic, in which there can be loss of life to any animal; hence, when they undertake any traffic or sale, then they only sell such precious, or dry, things in which no insect nor any animal can come ; accordingly, some of them are cloth merchants, and bankers, and some are pedlars, and many become braziers, and get their living in this way ; and they none of them sell any wet, greasy, or sweet things. There is also another caste of Saráugís, who are known by the name of Oswárs, but none of them are to be met with in the Panjáb: they principally live in the land of Márwár, that is to say in the neighbourhood of Bíkáner, Jaipur, and Jodhpur. Although all their written codes of the Saráugís, regarding religion, mercy, patience, and continence are very good, still, as they do not regard God as the Creator, for this reason, people regard them as infidels and unbelievers.

Those people, who live in this country, and who are called the Dádúpanthíyas, their religion was founded by a cotton

---

[106] The Bhábrás are of a Jain caste, chiefly engaged in traffic and the bániyás are a Hindú caste, generally merchants.

corder, called Dádú Rám. These people are very very good and religious and beloved of God, and they, thoroughly believing in the Vedás, Sástrás and Puráns acknowledge all its other customs, but they will not agree to wear the Brahminical thread or tuft of hair. It appears that formerly Dádú Rám used to give them advice about religion, but, now, several of them, having studied Sanskrit, have become Vedántás. Several amongst them get their living by asking alms, and others, by taking service in the army, gain a means of livelihood. None of them marry, but, by simply adopting a disciple, thus continue their line. These people are very good in their love and affection, and, as much as possible, remain attached, to their Creator.

Now the account of all the Hindús, who live in this land, is as follows : that there is very little reliance to be placed on any single word they say ; some worship gods and goddesses and the shrines and burying places of the dead, and others, forsaking the religion of the Vedas and Sástras, which was the primeval religion of the Hindús, have begun to do service to Sarwar Sultán, and demons and evil spirits ; and there are very few, who worship God, the Creator, as their Maker and Destroyer according to the religion which was handed down to them from the beginning. Behold the people of other religions, how firm they are, for they never forsake their own religion and adopt that of the Hindús ; but the Hindús are so unstable that, if they even hear the praise of a brick anywhere, they begin to rub their noses against it for the sake of obtaining food or offspring.[107] Many Bráhmans also may be seen of such a nature, that they do not at all know the value of their own religion ; but wherever they hear of the shrine of any saint or of any old tomb, there they will begin to burn lamps and offer flowers ; and they do not understand this, that no one can give them happiness but God. In this way, many Khattrís also, for the sake of pleasing Visnu, fast all day long, on the 11th day of the light and dark half of every month, and if that day should be a Thursday, then, for the sake of pleasing Sarwar Sultán, who was a Musalmán of the Multán district, at night they sleep on the ground and keep vigils [108] ; and they do not see

---

[107] That is to say, they offer up their prayers and make their vows at the shrines, made of brick, of deceased saints, and rub their noses against the bricks, saying, that if they shall obtain a good cow, which shall give plenty of milk, they will make an offering of such and such an amount, and that if they shall be blessed with offspring, they will offer certain thank-offerings.

[108] They sleep on the ground, instead of on a bed, from religious motives that is to say, in order to fulfil a pilgrimage without sleeping on a bedstead and this is called, keeping vigils. The custom is that whenever a company of pilgrims stop at any place on their journey, those who intend to join them from the surrounding villages, come there, and bring many of their friends with them. They all keep watch through the night and do not sleep, and in the morning, the friends of the pilgrims bid them farewell and return home.

that, according to the ordinances of the Sástras it is proper to worship Visnu, and that Sarwar Sultán, who was a Musalmán, is not mentioned in their books; therefore why should they worship him? In this way, the creeds of the people of this country are innumerable; not one in a thousand of them believes in his religion, and, although they are outwardly called Hindús, still, inwardly they profess various kinds of religion, and do not place their faith in any one single thing.

CHAPTER II.

Music and Songs of the Panjáb.

Now this is the account of the songs of this country; that those six rágs, or musical modes, which are known in all countries according to the rites of the Sástras, these they also use in the Panjáb. The six modes, according to the ordinances of the Sástras, are these; the first Bhairon, the second Málkauns, the third Hindol, the fourth Dípak, the fifth Sirí, and the sixth is known as the Megh mode; and there are five female modes, and eight infant modes, (modifications), of each of these modes, and these are sung with various variations, and they all have different embellishments. They do not sing these six modes at all times, but some they sing in the morning, and some in the evening; accordingly, they sing the Bhairon about the morning watch (3 A.M.) and the second Málkauns at midnight; and the Hindol, when one watch of the day has gone (10 A.M.); and the Dípak exactly at midday; and the fifth which is the Sirí mode, that they sing at evening; and the Megh mode, whenever it rains. All these kinds are written fully about in the book called the Rágmálá, and if any one wants to know more about them, let him look in that book. All these six modes are sung in the seven notes, and he who does not understand the seven notes, he cannot properly tell the forms of the male and female modes. The names of the seven notes are as follows: the first Kharj, the second Rikhabh, the third Gandhár, the fourth Maddham; the name of the fifth is Pancham, the sixth is called Dhaiwat, and the seventh Nikhád. All of these notes occur in some of the modes; and, in some modes, six, five, or four only come in. Those modes, which are known in the world by the names of Rág and Rágní (male and female modes), are made up of no other notes but these seven; a note is only the name of a sound; and from the difference in their length and shortness, and sharpness and flatness, they are of seven kinds; and whatever songs are sung in other countries, besides the Panjáb, they also have no other notes but these seven. Again, whatever male or female mode may be sung, if its time should not be correct, then wise people do not regard it as pleasing. According to the rites of the Sástras, time is of twelve kinds, but all these kinds of times are not used in the present day in this country; those amongst them which are well known, those singers use at the time of singing; accordingly, the three bar, and four time, and the Yakká thaththá and the times called the Súlphákatá and Dháiá are now mostly used. Time is the name given to the beats (or length) of sound, and when singers begin to sing with their mouths, then others beat the time, either with their hands or some instrument, according to the measure of the mode; and if one does not know the time and notes, then one cannot enjoy pleasure from the singing of the modes. The musicians have divided all the musical instruments in the world into three-and-a-half kinds. The first kind consists of wire instruments, amongst which are included three-stringed guitars, guitars, fiddles, bins,[109] &c.; the second are wind instruments, amongst which are included flutes, trumpets, and all other such; the third kind are skin instruments, amongst which come tambourines, kettle drums, drums, small drums, and timbrels, &c. The half kind of musical instruments are those played only by the hand, or some other means, or by a cracking of the fingers, by which the measure of the mode is completed; and these are called half instruments for this reason, that they only give a rumbling sound, and no note is distinguished in them, but in all the other instruments some of the seven notes can be distinguished. In short when musicians sing, they sing their songs according to some of these six modes.

Although Rág and Rágní are only names of the variations of singing and the adjustment of the notes, still those measures, which are sung in the Rágs and Rágnís, are of several kinds; as for example; Dhurpad, Kabitt, Chhand, Sargam, Khiál, Tappa, Tarána, &c., and all these measures are used in the Rágs. All these measures, according as they are sung in different Rágs and Rágnís, (manifest) different pleasures and different forms. The Dhurpad and other measures, which are mentioned above, are not only used with songs in the Panjábí language, but when the people of the Panjáb sing, they also sing them to Brijbhásá and Hindí words, which correspond to the Sanscrit.

Dhurpad is the name of measures of the following kind :—

Khahío he udho, tum nai jo bíjá bíyog, man kino maddham, birwá lagá rádhá ke man.

Drig tálan kúp kino asuán jal bhar bhar palakán sinch sinch tántere bhaye birhá sakal ban.

---

[109] An instrument something like a Jews' harp.

Dhúán wiráǵ hirde jár pándhí rom ros pánch bán rach hiyen Kach kuch ris bhar líyen.

Láj bharo nainá.

Ras ke prabhú prítam phal phúl nag aur beg daras díjo jí dhan man.

The meaning,[110] of the above is this, that once on a time, the cowherdesses sent and told Krisan, by the mouth of a devotee called Udho, of the affliction (they suffered) in their separation, saying "O Udho ! do you go to him and say thus ; 'The separation which you have sown (in our hearts), it has become a tree in the mind of Rádhá, and her heart has become languid' and then they said this, "Our eyes, from crying, have filled the tanks and wells with the water of our tears ; and the eyelids of all our eyes, having irrigated (the ground) with the water of crying, have caused trees to spring up from the pain of separation." Then they said "The smoke (of the fire) of separation from you has entirely burnt up our hearts, and all the hairs of our wicked bodies, having become distressed, have created great uproar, and Kám Deo (Cupid) has struck the five arrows into our hearts. Say that our (kach, that is the) hair of our heads, and our (kuch) breasts are filled with anger, for they are filled with ris, i.e., passion ; and as our eyes are filled with shame, we cannot tell our state to any one." The composer of this Dhurpad, a poet named Ras, said this on the part of the cowherdesses. "O Lord of Ras, Krisan jí ! quickly send and give us a sight of yourself ; for you are our wealth and desire ; and you are our flower and fruit, and you are our green shoot, and you only are our (prítam) beloved one."

Kabitt is the name of a measure of the following kind :—

Jab te padháre prán piáre sukhdenwáre akkhíán panáre bah rahín hái híyará.

---

[110] The following is the translation of the above :—

O Udho ! go and tell (Krisn) that since he sowed the seed of separation our hearts have become listless, and (separation) has become planted like a tree on the heart of Rádha.

The water of the tears of our eyes have filled the ponds and wells ; our eyelids, from the flow of tears (caused) by separation from him, have indeed all become like a forest full of trees.

The smoke of his separation has burnt our hearts, the hairs of our wicked bodies have all become angry, and have struck the five arrows into our hearts.

The hairs of our heads, and our breasts, are filled with rage.

Our eyes are filled with shame.

O Lord of Ras ! thou art our beloved, our fruit, our flowers, our young shoots ; do thou quickly show thyself to us, our wealth and desire.

The five arrows referred to in the third line are lust, anger, covetousness love, and pride.

CHAP. II.—MUSIC AND SONGS OF THE PANJÁB. 119

Ká so manpír dhar dhír ko sunáún álí birahon jaráí haun na hoí tan síyará.

Jo pai sudh pátí to na akkhián lagátí bhúl ab jo uklátí haun na bujho prít díyará.

Ábe ghan sayám mito birahon withá kí ghiám biná hari áe sukh páwe nánhi jíyará.[111]

The meaning of this is as follows : that, once on a time, Rádhá, being distressed by the absence of Srí Krisn, began to say " O my companions! from the day that my heart's love and giver of pleasure, Srí Krisn, has departed, my eyes have begun to flow like torrents; alas! alas! O my soul! what shall I do now?" Then she said " O companion! now having comforted my heart, how can I tell its grief to any one ? alas! alas! I, from separation, am being burnt, but my body does not become cool. If I had known that there was so much pain in love, then, from forgetfulness even, I would not have joined my eyes in love, and now, that I am distressed and agitated, the light of love cannot be extinguished in my heart; if Ghan Siyám, i.e., Srí Krisn shall come, the sunshine of the pain of separation will not be hidden, and if he shall not come, then, without him my life will not obtain pleasure." In this stanza, the poet has shown this cleverness, viz., he has said that when a black cloud comes before the sunshine, it becomes shade ; now Ghan Siyám is the name of a black cloud, so when Srí Krisnjí, who is called the black cloud, shall come, then the sunshine of the pain of her separation would be removed (i.e., thrown into shade).

Chhand is the name of a stanza of this kind, viz. :—

Janam ját hai brithá piá bin kánso kahún pukár
Dibas rain kal parat na moko nain bahit jaldhár ;
Sukh ko rukh kát dukh boyo ab hú lehu sanbhár
Kai dukh haro miratmukh dáro he púran kartár.[112]

[111] Since you left, O beloved of my life ! O giver of joy ! my eyes have become water spouts, and (my tears) have flowed in streams ; alas, O my heart ! (what shall I do ?)
O companion ! to whom shall I, fortifying my heart, tell my sorrow ? separation has so burnt me up, that my body will not cool down ;
If I had known the pains of love, I would not even forgetfully have fixed my eyes on thee ; but now I am distressed, the flicker of my love will not extinguish.
If Ghan Siám (Krisn) shall come, then the cloud of separation and absence will be removed ; without Hari's coming, my heart cannot obtain joy.
[112] My life has passed uselessly without my husband ; to whom shall I cry out and tell my state ?
Day and night I obtain no rest, my eyes rain streams (of tears) ;
The tree of joy has been cut down, that of pain has been sown ; now even I pray thee, take notice of my condition ;
Either remove my pain or kill me, O Thou Perfect Creator !

The meaning of this is, that a certain wife, in the absence of her husband, is saying "My life (lit. birth) is being wasted without my beloved; to whom shall I call out, and tell this my grief? Behold! I do not obtain rest by day or night; the water of my weeping eyes flows forth like a stream." Then, placing her thoughts on her husband, she begins to say "O Beloved! thou hast uprooted the tree of my pleasure, and hast sown grief in my heart; for this reason I have become very helpless; if thou wilt remember me now, it will be well, otherwise thou will not again see me alive!"; then, turning her soul to God, she says "O Perfect Creator! by some means let me meet my husband, and remove my grief; otherwise grant me death, for life with so much grief is not agreeable to me."

Sargam is the name of a stanza of this kind, viz. :—

Nis gamá papá dhámá pamá gaggá mamá dhadhá, níní dhamá pamá gá;

Dháni sásá sare níní dhadhá mamá dhadhá níní dhamá pamá gá.

Dháni dhamak dhamak dháni sásá níní sá sáni sirig sar níní dhadhá mamá dhadhá níní dhamá pamá gá.

This stanza has no meaning; sargam is merely the name for adjusting the notes; by taking the first letter of each the seven notes, kharj, rikhabh, gandhár, maddham, pancham, dhaiwat, nikhád, which were mentioned before, the seven letters, s r g m p dh ní, are obtained. In short, if one wishes to take the name of any of these seven notes, then from saying that one letter, the whole name is understood; thus from saying *kh*, kharj, from saying *r*, rikhabh, from saying *g*, gandhár, from saying *m*, maddham, from saying *p*, pancham, from saying *dh*, dhaiwat, from saying *ní*, nikhad, are understood; in this way there are seven letters for the seven notes. In the gamut of any mode, one can tell from the letter which comes first, that note is the first note of that rág; so, in this last verse, the letters in the gamut come in the order ní s g m, &c.; therefore it is known that in this rág, nikhad comes first, then kharj, then gandhar, and then maddham; and in whatever rág or rágní, these letters occur first, it is called Kámsch Rágní; and thus one can tell them all. In the Sástrí language, in place of *kh*, they say *s*; for this reason the first letter of kharj, is written as *s*.

Khiál is the name of a verse of this kind, viz.—

Umad ghamand ghan áiorí mái
Barkhá rut apní garaj garaj chahún or baras búndán jhar lagáí,

CHAP. II.—MUSIC AND SONGS OF THE PUNJAB. 121

Paban parwáin badaríá chamakat bhíg bhíg gai hamar;
chunríá,
Kaíse kar áún rí main piá ko samajháún.[113]

The meaning of this is ; that a wife, at a time, when it was raining, in the absence of her husband, writes and sends this to her mother-in-law; "O mother! how can I come to your house, for the clouds have come rolling from all four quarters, and the rainy season, according to its will, is thundering around, and the rain is dropping continually on all four sides, and as at this time the east wind is blowing, and the clouds are gathering, my sheet has been wetted in it, then, how can I come at this time, and, O mother-in-law! then how shall I draw my husband out of his anger, and conciliate him?" It must be understood, that her husband was angry in the house, and her mother-in-law wrote to the wife and said "Do you come and conciliate your husband," and the wife wrote and sent back this stanza in reply to her mother-in-law.

Tappa is the name of a stanza of this kind, viz. :—

Re jánewále sáín dí kasam pher áu nainááwále,
Áunde jánde tusín dil lai jánde áu sajan gal lagg
sáhansáh matwále.[114]

In short, the stanza, called tappa, does not occur in any language but Panjábi, and Mánjhá, and Sindhí : there are also a few very curious tappás, which people sing in the language of the Suketmandi hills. The meaning of the above (stanza) is this, that a poet, named Sáhansáh, says to some woman "O passing-by friend! Do thou, for God's sake, come back again ;" and then he says "O beautiful-eyed one! thou, coming and going, hast robbed my heart, and hast taken it away; therefore now come O drunken friend! and embrace me."

Taráná is the name of a verse of this kind, viz. :—

Taradím tánádím nádání re tádaní,
Udedáná diraná tannú diraná tánnú diraná táná diraná,
Tá magar hamchun sabá báj bajnla phetn rasam.
Hásalam dosat bajuj nál he sabarigír na búd.

---

[113] O mother! the clouds have come with great violence; it is the rainy season; of its own will it thunders around, and the rain drops are streaming down;
The wind is from the east, the lightning shines; my sheets have become wet;
How shall I come and tell my husband (my state?).

[114] O departer! I swear by God, I pray thee come back, O beautiful-eyed one!
Coming and going away, you have carried off my heart; come, friend, and embrace me, O drunken one! (thus writes Sáhansáh) the composer.
Sáhansáh has no meaning; it is merely brought in to point out the composer, as it is usual to insert his name, at the end of all verses.

In this stanza, called taráná, there is no meaning; like sargam, taráná is only the name of the order of the notes; but the singing of sargam and taráná is very difficult; and none but very good singers can sing them. In this, there are two lines "tánádím tánádím;" and after them, some Persian verse, like that given above, is added and mixed up along with it; and then the tánádím tánádím is again repeated. On hearing the taráná, the musicians, who beat the drums and little drums, and give the time for this rág, become very confused, as giving the proper time for a sargam or taráná rág is very difficult, and none but a firstrate musician can give the proper time; many people sing the sargam and taráná in such a wonderful way (!) that the musicians' hands cease playing the instruments, and the melody is interrupted.

Visanpada is the name of a verse of this kind, viz.:—
    Govind, nám sudháras píje,
    Álas tayág jág kar mánas janam suphal kar lije.
(Chorus) Govind, &c.
    Chhin chhin hokar andh siráni jatha ámghat páni,
    Bálúbhít samán dehsukh tá maun man nahin dije.
(Chorus) Govind, &c.
    Bikhayan maun bahu janam biháne nahín rám sudh liní;
    Án achának jam nai pakaro dekhat hí sukh chhíje.
(Chorus) Govind, &c.
    Mát pitá sut banatá bándhaw nehún bandhe dukh páwe.
    Sardhá sánt na páwe koí biná rám ras bhíje.[115]

The meaning of this is that a poet, named Sardhá Rám, according to the custom of this country, gives advice to all

---

[115] The name of God is like nectar, drink it;
Leave off sloth, awake, and make profitable the life of (thy) manhood; *Chorus.* The name of God, &c.
Thy life will gradually pass away as water leaks through unburnt pots,
Thy body enjoys pleasure (which is) like a wall of sand (and easily totters away); therefore do not fix thy mind on it!
Chorus. The name of God, &c.
When (thy) life has been passed in folly, and thou hast had no thought of God,
The angel of death will come suddenly and seize thee, and in an instant thy joy will depart.
Chorus. The name of God, &c.
If mother, father, son, wife, relations or any worldly love have won thy heart, thou wilt suffer grief.
Sardhá (the composer says) "no one will obtain true life, until he becomes absorbed in the name of God."

people, saying "O people! drink the water of immortality of the name of God; eschew negligence and, waking from the sleep of thoughtlessness, make your life fruitful. Behold the life of man passes away and, drop by drop, leaks like water through an unbaked vessel, and can be seen passing away; so also is your life passing away day by day. Regard the pleasure of the body as a wall of sand, which perishes quickly, and give not your soul to them!" Again he says "O people! much of your life has passed in sloth, and you have not taken thought of your God; but reflect, when death shall suddenly come and seize you, then all your pleasures will be gone; the soul, which is bound up in the love for father, mother, wife, son, or other relations suffers pain." The poet named Sardhá Ram says "so long as a person does not enjoy the pleasure of God, he never obtains contentment."

Visanpadás are of various kinds; some are about the greatness of God, and man's servitude, and some about the sports of Krisanjí and Rámjí; and others are about separation. Although every Visanpadá should be either of eight, or of four, lines, still if any are of less or more lines than this, they do not consider it any fault; and the opening bar, which is at the opening of every Visanpadá, is, at the time of singing, brought in and sung (as chorus) after each couplet; some people also look on the Visanpadás as songs (sawad); accordingly, in the Granth of Nának, all those Visanpadás, that are inserted therein, are called songs. In the East, those people, who sing the Visanpadás, are known as Bhajans.

All the songs that are current in the Panjáb and Hindustán are generally about love making; some, on the part of wives, sing about the pain of absence from their husbands, and some, on the part of husbands, extol their wives.

In short the Tappá, Khiál, Dhurpad, and the other tunes which are used, are all full of love; but when a Visanpadá is sung, to whatever kind of words it be sung, still the worship of God is necessarily related in it; and, from hearing it, the love of people is, in a more or less degree, drawn to God.

All the respectable folk of this land use all the above kinds of rágs and rágnís, but the common people, who do not understand the science of music, their song and metres are very coarse and quite distinct. Although all the songs, which are sung by the common people of this country, on account of their being full of great immodesty, cannot be written here, I will, however, just mention a few kinds, which are not outwardly so bad. All the songs, current in this land, are full of love-making matters. Most of the people of this country sing, in the Panjabí tongue, those songs, which were originally written in the Persian letters from alif down to ye. In these verses, which are called chhand, there are four lines thus :—

> Alaf[115] Án piáre dekhí hál mera main tán kúnj wángú kur-
> láundí hán ;
> Mere nain tarsan tere dekhne nún dino rát main kág
> udáundí hán ;
> Tere ráh di wal main kharí dekhán atthe pahir main
> ausián páundí hán,
> Kadí án jání gal lagg mere tere nám nún sadá dhiáundí
> hán.[116]

The meaning of this is evident, that a wife, in the absence of her husband, is uttering forth her grief.

Although their verses are of many kinds, still a verse called *dúdhí* is now chiefly sung in the Panjáb, *e.g.* :—

> Alaf[28] Asá nún á mil jánín kinu main mano bhulái sudh
> bisaráí ;
> Os gharí nún main pachhtáwán jad main prít lagáí hoi sudáí ;
> Meri ján dukhán nai gherí jad te baní judáí at dukhdáí ;
> Main balihár áu ghar mere hun ná karín paráí je lar láí.[117]

The meaning of this is evident, that a wife sends a message to her engaged, saying, " Do you come and join me quickly ?"

In this country there is a song called *dholá*, thus—

> Merí kattaní de wichch chaunk hai :
> Mai nún piá de milan dá saunk hai :
> Jind paí taras di *dholá*.[118]

---

[116]Come, beloved, and see my state, how I am bemoaning like the crows;
My eyes are longing to see you; day and night, I am flying crows;
I am anxiously watching the road for your return, and am, all day long, drawing lines ;
Come at least, friend, and embrace me ; I am always repeating your name.

In the second line, there is an allusion to taking an omen from crows. If an astrologer sees some crows, and any one wishes to know if a certain person will return, he questions the crows : if they fly away, he will return; otherwise, he will not.

In the third line, another way of taking an omen is alluded to, which is thus done ; a horizontal long line is drawn, and under it, a number of small vertical lines are quickly drawn ; they are then counted up: if the total number of these vertical lines is an odd number, the person will return, if even, he will not.

[117](Alaf). O friend! come and join me ; why have you forgotten me, and why do you take no thought of me ?
I repent that hour when I gave you my love, and became mad ;
Sorrow has enshrouded my life ; since I have been separated from you, I have been greatly distressed ;
I sacrifice myself to you, come to my home; regard me not as a stranger, since you have taken me as a friend.

[118]My head ornament is in my spinning basket ;
I have a desire to meet my husband ;
Dholá (says) " My soul longs for thee."

Some *dholás* are of such a description that their meaning cannot at all be understood, but they sound pleasing, owing to their being sung with a long accompaniment to the singing.

Again, in this country, a song, called Sadd is well known; the sons of jímíndárs chiefly sing it. These songs are principally sung regarding the state of Sassí and Punnún, and Mirjá and Sáhabán, who, in that neighbourhood, were renowned as great lovers, and gave their lives in that cause.

They call the following kind of songs Sadds, *e.g.* :—

Sun punnún de dukkh nún sassí ní main ape maut kabúlí;
Pí saráb main kecham pahunchá merí sudh budh sabho bhúlí;
Doh didár hun jhahde mai nún isak anherí jhúlí;
Main anján na bolan jáná mai nún isak jharáiá súlí.[119]

The meaning of this is as follows; that a Baloch, named Punnún, of a city called Kecham, who was a friend of Sassí, came and stopped with the princess called Sassí. His (the Baloch's) brothers, having made him senseless by intoxicating him with drink, were taking him to the city Kecham; when he recovered his senses, then, weeping, he turned his thoughts to Sassí, and began to sing the song mentioned above. At last, having come to a place where the tomb of Sassí had been erected, he died.

The sadds about Mirjá and Sáhabán are of this description, *e.g.* :—

Bas be bháío kamalío mere Mirje nún ná máro,
Mirjá merá hatth *t*unde dá is dá marná man nádháro;
Je Mirje nún máran laggon tán pahilán mai nún koho;
Main sáín wal te bar páiá merá dilí suhág ná khoho.[120]

The meaning of this is as follows: that a certain man called Mirjá, leaving his house, ran away with his female companion, named Sáhabán; as he went along the road, he slept under a jan*d* tree, and Sáhabán was seated near him; the brothers of Sáhabán, coming up after them, wished to kill Mirjá;

---

[119] Punnún accepted death, on hearing of the grief of Sassí (who had died), saying :—
Having drunk wine, Punnún went to Kecham, and forgot me altogether;
Show thyself to me quickly, for the storm of love has fallen on me;
I am ignorant and can say nothing; love has pierced me through, and killed me.

[120] O mad brothers! do not kill my Mirjá; my Mirjá is as a hand to me, who am handless; do not think of killing him;
If you wish to kill my Mirjá, first kill me;
I have obtained him as a husband from God; do not kill the husband of my heart.

at that time, Sáhabán began to address these words (which people sing as written in the above sadd) to her brother.

In this country, many people sing songs about Hír and Ránjhá, thus :—

Ní máo ikk naukur rahindá tán ákhen tán rakkh la-iye;
Ná kanmchor ná sagat jubáno jo kahiye so kahiye;
Manjhín cháre jái kináre uh dí minnat múl ná kariye;
Lákh taká kurbán máhí pur sir saddak kar dhariye.[121]

The meaning of this is as follows : that a Jatt, named Ránjhá, was the friend of a Jattí, named Hír, and those two wished to always live together in one place. One day, Hír said to her mother, "O mother! a certain man wishes to live in my house as my servant : if you will say (yes), then I will take him on;" then she began to praise him, saying, "That servant is not lazy, nor does he ever give a sharp reply to any one, rather he is so gentle, that whatever you might wish to say, you might say, and he would not take it amiss." Again she said, "He will go ever so far, and feed our buffaloes, and it will not be necessary to entreat him like other servants; he is a very good servant, so that if you should sacrifice a great deal to keep him, it would be well, for there will be no deficiency in him, and he is one, who performs service with all his body and soul."

Most of the people of this country, whether Hindús or Musalmáns, sing various kinds of songs also in praise of a king, who is called Lakhdátá, e.g. :—

Hatth katora tel dá; merá pír pírán wichch kheldá; main wárípírá hai.[122]

The meaning of this is as follows; that the people, who sing them, compose songs by joining together metres, containing words like "Hatth katorá tel, &c., with some agreeable metres with no meaning to them, but which from the long prolongation of the voice, are pleasing to listen to; but there is no actual meaning in it.

---

[121] O mother! a servant wishes to take service; if you will give the word,
I will take him on;
He is not lazy, nor given to using hard words; you can say what you like
to him (without fear of retort);
He will go of himself and graze the buffaloes; there will be no need to
beg of him, or to cajole him (to do so);
Although you may vow a lakh of takás on that herdsman, you may do so
(for he is so good, that it will not matter).
[122] There is no meaning in these lines; the words are simply put together
for the rhythm.

CHAP. II.—MUSIC AND SONGS OF THE PANJÁB. 127

In the same way, they go to those places, where there are graves of saints and holy men, and compose pleasing elegies, as follows :—

Pír tere raujo pur ajab bahár hai ;
Jó koí tere mele áwe uh dá berá pár hai ;
Pír tere rauje pur ghuggián dá jorá ;
Jo koí tere mele áwe tis nun káhdá torá,
Pír tere raujo pur.[123]

In this country, people go to pay their respects to Juálá Mukhí and other goddesses, and the songs, which they sing in praise of the goddess, these they call offerings (bhet) to the goddess, e.g. :—

Main áwán charanán pás hatth jorke karán bentí sun merí
  ardás ;
Wichch pahárán ásan terá sant bolan jai jai káro ;
Sabh dí karen bháuní púrí bhare rahin bhandáre ;
Main áwán charanán pás garí chhuáre dhajá lalerá pahilí
  bhet charáwán,
Ád kuárí durge hain tún tai nún sís nimáwán,
Main áwán charanán pás nangín pairín tere akbar áiá tis dá
  mán ghatáiá
Hatth jorke charanín laggá sone chhatar charáiá,
(*Chorus*). Main áwán charanán pas,[124]

The meaning of this is plain ; in all those which are sung as songs to the goddess, their opening bar is repeated at the end

---

[123] Although these words really have no meaning, they may be translated as follows :—
O saint ! around thy grave is a wonderful elegance ;
Whoever shall come to thy grave, his boat will reach the opposite shore ;
At thy shrine there are a pair of doves ;
Whoever comes to thy grave, will suffer no loss.
[124] I have come (a petitioner) at thy feet, with joined hands; listen to my request ;
Thy temple is in the hills ; the pilgrims, who come to it cry "Victory Victory, (to the goddess) ;
Fulfil thou the desires of (us) all, and may thy treasuries always remain full ;
I have come (a petitioner) at thy feet ; I will first offer thee some garí, (white of cocoanut), dates, flags, and a whole cocoanut ;
O Durga ! thou art the first origin ; I will bend my head to thee ;
I have come (a petitioner) at thy feet ; with bare feet, Akbar came to thee, when thou hadst lowered his pride ;
With joined hands, he then paid his respects, and gave thee a golden umbrella ;
I have come (a petitioner) at thy foot.
The allusion to Akbar is as follows : he is said to have disbelieved that the fire came forth by itself, out of Juálá Mukhí, and not understanding its volcanic nature, he first had a large iron plate put over its mouth to prevent the flames issuing, and then tried to extinguish them with water ; the last line means that he afterwards acknowledged his mistake and regarded it as a miracle, and presented a golden umbrella to the goddess.

of every couplet, as in a Visanpadá, *e.g.*, " Main áwán charanán pás," which is repeated over and over again. Those songs, which Hindús sing with much musical accompaniment before their gods, when doing worship to them, are known by the name of **árti** (hymns); and these people sing different hymns for every god. For example, the hymn of Gangaji is as follows :—

Jai Gangá mái ;
Jo jan terá darsan páwe páp ná rahisí rái
Jai Gangá mái
Tan man dhan te simarán tai nún tún jag wichch sukhdái
Jo jan terá dhián karat hai mite páp kí chhái
Jai Gangá mái
Brihamá visan manáve tai nún sankar sís tikái
Sarab jagat de páp haran nún tún dhartí pur ái
Jai Gangá mái
Hor páp sabh dukkh niwáro man dí haro burái
Din din tere charan kamal wichch bhagatí wadhí suái
Jai Gangá mái.[125]

The meaning of this is plain; but women generally sing the best hymns.

Now those songs which the *Jatts* sing to their flutes are as follows ;—

Terí bharí juání be ranjhetiá jinú ganne dí ponrí
Hoí terí merí be ranjhetiá híre lálán di jorí
Main paí udikán be ranjhetiá paí prít dí *d*orí
Tere balbaljáwe be ranjhetiá palpal rádhán gori.[126]

---

[125] Victory to thee, O mother Ganges!
Whatever man obtains a sight of thee, his sins will be entirely effaced (and will not appear even) as a mustard seed;
Victory to thee, O mother Ganges!
Whoever remembers thee with all his body, soul, and wealth, thou wilt give him happiness in the world;
Whatever man meditates on thee, the shadow of his sins will be removed
Victory to thee, O mother Ganges!
Bráhma and Vishan reverence thee; Shivá (Sankar) has bowed his head to thee,
For the sake of removing all the sins of the world, thou didst come on the earth;
Victory to thee, O mother Ganges!
Do away with all my sins and all my sorrows, and destroy the badness of my heart;
Every day, (lying) at thy lotus feet, may my faith ever be increased.
Victory to thee, O mother Ganges!

[126] O Ranjhetia! thy youth is full of the juice (of pleasure) like the joints of the sugar-cane.
O Ranjhetia! may the union between thee and me be like that of the ruby and diamond;
O Ranjhetia! I am longing for thee; thy love has bound me as with a rope;
O Ranjhetia! the beautiful Rádhán offers herself every moment as a sacrifice to thee.

CHAP. II.—MUSIC AND SONGS OF THE PANJÁB.

In short, some say that this song is addressed by Hír to Ranjheta, *i.e.*, Ránjha, whilst others say, that it is addressed by Rádhá to Srí Krisanjí.

Another of the rágs of the Jatts is as follows :—

Kachche taláu dián pakkián paurián gadawá bharliá pání Dá

Jándo pakhír nai kuchh ná dekhiá joban lutt liá niání dá[127]

Another rág of the Jatts, which boys sing, is as follows :—

Chhaddín chhaddín be mahiramán lar merá

Main ta kadí ná dithrá dar terá

Ná main jandí ná main puchhándí tain kitthon ánke páiá jherá

Chhaddín chhaddín be mahiramán lar merá.[128]

Another rág of the Jatts is this—

Wagdí wagdí ráwí wichch ghuggián dú jorá

Ikk ghuggí nd gaí pai giá bichhorá.[129]

Another rág, which the Jatts sing at fairs, is this—

Main ramaján terián samajhán dardí ná kundá kholdí

Gharí gharí áwen tún pherián páwen tai nún dar nahín ráí

Je main ákhán ápne kaunt nún sabh bhull jáwe chataráí

Main ramaján terián samajhán dardí ná kundá kholdí.[130]

The meaning of this is, that some bad man, having gone to a woman, began to say "Open the door"; that good woman, understanding his signs that he wished to have union with her, said : "I understand your signs, and therefore will not open the

---

[127] He filled his waterpot at (had union with) a kachchá taláu with pakká steps ;
On entering, the fakír (*membrum virile*) met with no opposition, and robbed the young thing of its youth.
By a kachchá taláu with pakka steps is meant a young virgin well up in the arts of love ; the last sentence means, he deflowered her.

[128] O friend ! let go, let go my clothes ;
I have never seen thy house ;
I do not know or recognize thee ; why are you teasing me ?
O friend ! let go, let go my clothes.

[129] On the flowing Ráví there was a pair of doves ;
One dove flew away, and they were separated.

[130] I understand your signs, and therefore will not undo the bolt ;
Why are you continually coming and going ? have you not as much fear as a grain of mustard ;
If I should tell my husband, you would soon forget all your clever dodges;
I understand your signs, and therefore will not undo the bolt.

door; why are you incessantly coming and wandering about here; what, have you no fear of anyone? Look, to yourself if I were to tell my husband of your goings on, then he would beat you severely, and you would forget all your clever ways."

Another song, which women sing, is as follows :—

Pippal diá pattá be kehí kharkhar láí
Merá kaunt pardesín be kuchh khabar ná áí
Main paí udíkán be un khabar ná ghallí
Main bahut samajháiá be par wáh ná challí
Túa ghar áwín kauntá be main kharí udíkán
Meriän dusmanán naí main nún láián líkán
Be main balbal jándí tere lamán sadakke
Ghar á jáh sajjaná tere raste takke
Be main chhej bichhámán kadí áwo júní
Be main már guáí tere nainán dí kání
Be main dukhkhín gherí main nún sudh ná káí
Pippal diá pattá be kehí kharkhar láí [131]

The meaning of this is plain, but, in order that its sense may be somewhat understood, I will write it. A woman was seated in the absence of her husband, and the leaves of a peepul tree were rustled by the wind; on this she began to say to the leaves; "My heart is already in a state of inflammation like a boil, from separation from my husband, therefore why, O leaves of the peepul, do you rustle and harass my heart more?" Again, she says "As my husband is in a strange land, and no news has come of him, I am always looking out for him, but I can obtain no news of him;" then she continues, "At the time of his going away, I expostulated with him much, but he would not listen to me. I am always saying 'Come home,' and he, your friend, who will not let you come home, has become my enemy, and causes me distress; I am watching for your return, and am crying and longing to give you a kiss, do you quickly come home; I am pierced with the glance of your eyes, therefore, spreading my bed, and

---

[131] O peepal leaves; what a noise you are making;
My husband has gone abroad, and I have obtained no news of him;
I am looking out continually for him, but he has sent me no news of himself;
I tried to dissuade him (from going), but he would not listen to me;
O husband! return home, for I am continually looking out for thee;
My enemies are troubling me much;
Oh! I sacrifice myself, to thee, and long to give thee a kiss;
Come home, beloved! I am watching for thee;
I will spread the bed; come soon, O beloved!
The glance of thine eyes has entirely overcome and dazzled me;
Affliction has surrounded me, I have no sense left in me;
O peepul leaves! what a noise you are making.

CHAP. II.—MUSIC AND SONGS OF THE PANJÁB. 131

seated thereon, I say to you, 'O beloved! come quickly';" and then she says, "O leaves of the peepul! I already am overcome with grief, why therefore do you increase it with your rustling."

That song, which the women sing in the rains during the month Sáun, is as follows:—

Chari ghatá ghanghor sáman áiá
Paun sarake ghatá barase chamak bijli áí
Kaunt biná dar pámán sajaní nain nínd ná páí
Sáman áiá
Pingháu khán huláre mere barasan nain phuáre,
Piá biná sabh sukh dukhiáre ro ro samá bitáiá
Sáman áiá.
Hornán sakhián dhari gudáí manlí mainhdí bindí laí
Mai nún phariá birahun kasáí prem baddal char páiá
Sáman áiá.[132]

The meaning is this; that a woman, in the absence of her husband, looking at the clouds, began to say "Alas, O my lord! although the month Sáun also has come, in which, by reason of the rain, all are made happy, still my husband has not yet come home, so that, seeing his face, the rainy season might be pleasing to me. Behold! clouds are overhead, the wind is blowing, and the lightning flashing, then how can I be happy without my husband? and, therefore, I do not get a wink of sleep; the swings are swinging, and my eyes, by reason of my tears, are raining like fountains, and all my happiness appears as grief; all my other companions have done up their dhari, (the back hair of the head), and have fastened it with the manlí, and dyed their hands with henna, and made the bindí mark on their foreheads,

---

[132] The clouds have gathered with great force; Sáman has come;
The wind is blowing, the clouds are pouring, and the lightning shines;
Without my husband I am sad, O my companions, and my eyes obtain no sleep;
Sáman has come;
The swings are swinging, my eyes are jetting out torrents like fountains;
Without my husband, all joys are to me sorrows; I pass my time in weeping;
Sáman has come;
All my companions have plaited their hair, and have tied it with the maulí, and have dyed their hands with henna, and made the mark of adornment on their foreheads;
Separation has seized me, like a butcher: my love has become a cloud (hiding all joy from n.c);
Sáman has come.
N.B.—Sáman is the month Sáwan, or the rainy month of July-August. A maulí is a variegated ribbon with which women tie their hair.

and have adorned themselves, but as for unfortunate me, the butcher, called absence, is slaying me, and the clouds of my love are continually drizzling their tears of grief; alas! alas! how can I live in this grief."

Those songs, which women sing at marriages, are of various kinds, but amongst them are three songs, which are called sitthní, ghorí, and lámán, those I will write about here. The first, called sitthní, is sung by way of jesting before the wedding guests and other people, and is of the following kind :—

> Kurme joro járaní járaní asín nahín pukární pukární
> Joro kahindi kurme táín main kítá haí jatt nun sáín
> Tún ná sáde behre áín kehí páí bagár ní bigár ní
> Kurme joro járaní járaní.[133]

The meaning is this, that the women say to the betrothed man's father, "The wife is an adulteress, but we should not tell it; she is thus saying to herself, 'I have taken a Jatt for my husband; if you now incessantly come to my house, listen, you will be only as a bigár.'"

Those sitthnís, which are sung by common people, are as follows :—

> Phuláne joro chhinár sá nún chhale kará dih,
> Ki damrí de chár sá nún chhalen kará dih,
> Chhale kará dih chhápán kará dih nál kará dih
> Hár sá nún chhale kará dih[134]

In short, this is only sung in joke among the common people, but there is no special meaning in it.

Ghorís are as under, thus :

> Barasan lagará rúp abehá
> Kihdá tún bháí mallá kihdá juáí kis goří dá tún kanta he,
> Nháí dho-i-ke ghorí chariá kadí ná dithará darsan ajehá[135]

---

[133] "O father! the wife-elect is an adulteress, but we will not publish it; She is thus saying to you, 'I have taken a Jatt for my husband; Do you not come to my house; you will only be a bigár;'
O father! the wife-elect is an adulteress, but we will not publish it."
N.B.—A bigár is a labourer, who is not paid for his work.
[134] These verses may be translated as follows : -
"Such a woman is a whore, make us a ring;
Four can be got for a damrí; make us a ring;
Make us a ring, make us a ring, make us a necklace with it, make us a ring."
[135] "Thy beauty appears like the rain;
O Sir! whose brother art thou? whose son-in-law art thou? and of what beautiful woman art thou the husband?
Washed and bathed, mounted on horseback (as thou art), I have never seen any one as handsome as thee."

CHAP. II.—MUSIC AND SONGS OF THE PANJÁB. 133

The meaning is this, that when at the time of marriage, the boy, having been washed and bathed, is mounted on a horse, then the women sing "Your face has assumed such a wonderful form, that we cannot sufficiently praise it. O my lord! whoso brother art thou? and whose son-in-law art thou? and tell us this also, of what beautiful woman art thou the husband? for that beauty, which is on thy face now that thou hast washed and bathed, is such that we have never seen the like thereto; in short, the being seated on horseback becomes thee exceedingly."

Lámáns are sung according to this manner, viz.:—

Pahilarí láun sirí rám manáiye
Jis de manunne sabh dukhkh ján ate phal páiye,
Dújrí láun harí biáhan áiá
Tan man dhan sukh cháu surúp suáiá.[136]

In this way, seven Lámáns are sung, for the Hindús make the bride and bridegroom go, either four or seven times, round a fire, and those songs, which are sung at those times, are called Lámáns.

In this country, many people sing couplets, which they call dohrás, e.g.—

Ao mere sajjano bai*tho* man chit lái
Sanjh paí ghar jámná ápo apne dáí.[137]

The meaning is this, that some good person is saying "O my companions! giving your hearts, do you come and sit by me and listen to me; for, when it becomes evening time, (that is, at the time of death), we must all go to our home (that is the other world) our own ways."

Again, many people in this country sing jhanjho*tí*s. Jhanjho*tí* is the name of a kind of song, which they sing in the hills; although, originally, it was only sung in the hills adjoining the Panjáb, but now, on account of their liking its strain and melody, many Panjábís also have begun to sing it, e.g.

Kaulán de chi*tthú* main kín deí jáh be máhanúṅ
Kaulán de chhi*tthú* main kín deí jáh be
Tikkalú binddalú main tusán kín deni hán hor gálá dí hassí
Chi*tthú* de pajjú main kín milí jáh be sajjaná túsádí súrat
asán man bassí.

---

[136] In the first circumambulation say, " Lo worship to Sri Rám;
For, from worshipping him, all sorrow departs, and joy is obtained;"
In the second circumambulation say " Harí has come to be married;
Our body and soul, wealth, joy, pleasure and beauty, all are increased (thereby)."
[137] "Come, O friends! and sit by me, and give heed to me;
At evening time, all go home of themselves."

(*Refrain*) Kaulán de chitthú main kín, &c.

Tusán jo asádre dilán jo tarsándo ho súrat dá mán ghanerá

Mate chhailá mijo chhátíá jo láí lai jiá tarassada merá.
(*Refrain*) Kaulán de chitthú, &c.[138]

The meaning is this; that a woman is saying to a man "Do you give me a basket of lotus-flower fruit, and I will give you, in exchange for them, the *tikka* on my forehead, which is made of gold, and my forehead-ornament, and my silver throat-ornament.

The purport is this, that as she was fascinated with his form, she wanted him to come to her, under pretence of bringing the basket, and says. "O youth (*i.e.*, man) and friend; your form has taken up its abode in my heart, and now, whilst I am longing for you in my mind, you are proud of your form; therefore, O beautiful lord, *i.e.*, very handsome one! embrace me, for my heart greatly desires you."

Another jhanjhoti people sing is as follows:—

Hírá Singhá Sardárá be rátín dere ná áiá,
Dero ná áiá kuthún man parcháiá láṛiá kín kihán bhuláiá.

(*Refrain*) Hírá Singhá Sardárá be, &c.

Asán kin tusádí súrat na wissare dine rátín base man main,
Tusán jo asádrá milná ná bháwe marasán main terí lagan main.

(*Refrain*) Hírá Singhá Sardárá be, &c.[139]

The meaning is plain, that the bride, *i. e.*, wife of a chief, named Hírá Singh, is reproaching him, saying "Why did you not come home at night?"

---

[138] "Give me a basket of kauls O man! Give me a basket of kauls; Then I will give you my *tikkalú* and bindlú and my hassí (to wear) round your neck.
Under pretence of (bringing) that basket, come and be one with me.
O friend! for your beauty has taken up its abode in my heart;
Give me a basket of kauls;
Although you have no desire for me, O you proud of your form!
Still, O very handsome one! come and embrace me, for my soul longs for you.
Give me a basket of kauls."
N.B.—The kaul is the fruit of the lotus flower; *tikkalú* and bindlú are head ornaments made of gold or silver.
A hassí is a silver necklace with a mirror in the centre of it, in front.
[139] "O Hírá Singh, Sardár, why have you not returned home at night?
Why have you not come home? Where are you engaged? Why have you, forgotten your wife?
O Hírá Singh, Sardár, why have you not returned home at night?
I cannot forget your form, day and night it lives in my heart;
If you do not wish to live with me, still I greatly desire you.
O Hírá Singh, Sardár, why have you not returned home at night?"

CHAP. II.—MUSIC AND SONGS OF THE PANJÁB.

The songs, which the common village people of this country sing are such, that one cannot see any meaning and metre in most of them; and although the metre in a few can be distinguished, still the metre of one does not blend with that of another, nor can one see any meaning in them; but one of their intelligible songs is as follows:—

O beliá meriá mahiramá oe
Koí din máṇ laí *thandíán* chhámán *jattá* oe
Ákhar challana thir nahín rahináhú.[140]

The meaning of it is plain.

Another song, of which the meaning is not to be understood, and the metre does not blend, is as follows:—

Nainán de wichch kajjalá ní aríe tere *jatt* bakainá láwe.
Tukke wánjhú binh giá mai núṇ terá makhkhan kalejá najarí áwe.
L*utt* lai oe mahiramá mítará oe.[141]

What shall I write as to the meaning of this, for I believe the poet, who composed it, did not, himself even, understand it.

Another rustic song is as follows:—

Terí merí yárí hai natthá sinhán
Jagg wichch khuárí hai natthá sinhán
Challu mere ghar nún dekh mere dar nún
Amín be tún sajjaná.
Tai núu laike bhajjaná natthá sinhán.[142]

The meaning of this is plain; many songs like this are sung in this country.

---

[140] "O my friend and acquaintance!
Come and enjoy yourself for some days,
O *Jatt*! At last you must die, you cannot always remain here."
[141] "Put antimony on thine eyes, O sister! a *Jatt* has sown a bakain tree in my house;
Like an arrow, he has pierced me; to me my lover appears like butter;
My friend and acquaintance has robbed me (of my heart)."
[142] "O Natthá Singh! there is a friendship between me and thee;
It is well known in the world, O Natthá Singh;
Come to my house, and look in at my door,
O friend, do you come;
(If not) I will catch you and run away with you, O Nattha Singh!"

CHAPTER III.

Proverbs.

Now it is necessary that I should explain a few of the proverbs, which are in vogue in various places in this country; as for instance,

(1). "Come, bullock, and strike me."

The meaning of it is this; that a certain fool said to a respectable man: "Do you retain me with you (as a servant)." He replied "Brother! he will retain you, who would say thus, come bullock and strike me."

---

(2). "(With) a hundred wise men (there will be but) one opinion;
(With) fools, each will have his own."

The meaning of it is this, that although a hundred wise men might be collected, still their opinion would be one; but if you were to collect a hundred fools, then the opinion of each of the hundred would be different, for fools, when they do any thing, undertake it without thought or reflection.

---

(3). "Every one's business becomes himself, and, if another do it, it will be spoiled (*lit.* it will be struck with the washerman's stick)."

A thief entered the house of a washerman, on which one of his asses brayed; as the washerman did not understand the cause of his braying, becoming angry, he struck it a blow with a stick. In the same way, if a fool forsakes his own business, and begins to do that of another, no profit will accrue to him from it, but he will obtain loss; so, as it was the business of the dog to make a noise on the coming of the thief, and the ass undertook his business for him, he got no profit.

---

(4). "A pair of combs on the head of a bald woman."

Just as when a bald girl wears combs, it does not appear well, so also, when a poor man assumes the status of a rich man, he becomes the place (object) of ridicule.

(5). "A bald man standing on his head among thorns."

That is, as when a bald man plays at turning head over heels among thorns, he thereby suffers pain, so also, if a poor man undertakes any business beyond his means, he suffers pain.

———

(6). "An inexperienced calf, the guide of a herd of calves."

If an inexperienced calf should set out as the guide of a herd of calves, then, as he himself does not know the right road, he will not be able to show the herd of calves the right road. In the same way, there will be no advantage to others, from following those who are themselves ignorant.

———

(7). "A bad dog gets its master abused."

If any one keeps a bad dog, then that bad dog, by interfering with other people, gets its master abused; so also, if a man keeps an useless person with him, he is himself looked on by men, as an useless man.

———

(8). "He has no house or home, but is the chief of a mahalla."

A certain Muhammadan had no home, but, one day, having gone to another town, he began to extol himself, saying "I am the master of a mahalla in such and such a place." Afterwards some people came, and enquired from the people of that place; "Where is the house of such an one?" On this, the people of that place taking his name (in derision), ridiculed him much. In the same way, if any one is not fit for any business, and, himself extols his own greatness, then, at last, he becomes a laughing stock.

———

(9). "If a blind man go for your betrothal, will he look out for himself or his brother?"

If you send a blind man for the betrothal of a brother, then he first looks out for a wife for himself, and does not think about the brother. In the same way, if one sends a poor person on any business, then he will only spoil your business, and accomplish his own; hence has arisen the above proverb "If you send a blind man for your betrothal, will he look out for himself or his brother?"

(10). "To beg from the poor is the business of the accursed."

A certain man himself got his living by begging, and another man went to him begging and asked alms. The beggar, whose house he came to, cursing him, said, "Your state is like that which a certain wise man has described : 'To beg from beggars is the business of the accursed'" So also, if any one shall go to a person without means, and ask him for anything, he will get nothing from him but abuse.

(11). "She called out without being asked, 'I am the (father's sister) aunt of the bridegroom.'"

A certain woman went to a house, where a wedding was taking place, and began to say, "Ask some counsel from me also, for I am the aunt of the bridegroom." The people seized her, and turned her out of the house, and said, "This is she, about whom that proverb has been used 'She called out, without being asked, I am the aunt of the bridegroom'" In this same way, if any one interferes in any way, or gives advice in the affairs of other people, without being asked, he, at last, is put to shame.

(12). "From sleeping on a dung-heap, he dreamt of a glass palace."

A certain man went to sleep on a dung-heap; when he arose, he began to say "Last night, I rested in a glass palace." The hearers turned him into ridicule, saying : "Yes, it is true, brother." In the same way when they, who are base by birth, undertake lofty deeds, people turn them into ridicule and say, "From sleeping on a dung-heap, he dreamt of a glass palace."

(13). "From being a seller of coal, one's face becomes black."

If any one deal in coal, at last his face becomes black ; so also, if any respectable man undertake any base deed, he will obtain no advantage in the world, but only blackening of the face (shame), and the above proverb will be applied to him.

(14). "The cat, having eaten nine hundred mice, has gone on pilgrimage."

A certain cat, which had eaten mice all its life long, determined to give up its evil ways, and, accordingly began to admonish other cats. Hence people say "The cat, having eaten nine hundred mice, has gone on pilgrimage." In like manner, if any one be a thief or adulterer, and admonish others, people will not listen to him, and if he be a bad man and should even do a good act, for the sake of getting a name, still people will say of him, "The cat, having eaten nine hundred mice, has gone on pilgrimage."

(15). "The old woman was singing with great difficulty and people came to look on the spectacle."

A certain old woman, for the sake of amusing her child was, with great trouble and difficulty, trying to sing something; the people (about), on hearing it, came to look on at the spectacle. She said, "I am, with great difficulty, amusing my child; have you come to see the spectacle?" In the same way, those people, who indulge their own fancies, and trouble their neighbours, the above proverb, "The old woman was singing with great difficulty, and people came to look on at the spectacle" is applied to them.

(16). "The poor rich man revolves in his mind many trips (which he will undertake for the purpose of traffic.')"

As an indigent person or a poor rich man, ponders over in his mind the trips he will undertake for gain, so also, if a poor man does nothing, but builds great castles in his heart, the above proverb "The poor rich man revolves in his mind many trips" is applied to him.

(17). "The washerman's dog gets food neither at home, nor at the washing place."

When a washerman's dog goes from home to the washing place, the washerman, as he eats his food, thinks to himself "It has been fed at home; I will not give it anything to eat;" again, when it returns home, the washerman's wife says to herself "It must have been fed at the washing place;" in this way, it (the dog) remains hungry at both places; so also, if any one does not keep firm to one thing, and one place, he will remain disappointed everywhere, like the washerman's dog.

(18). "The country ass speaks Kuresání."

A certain man, after having stayed a short while in a foreign land, on coming home, when he talked about anything in his native country, always used the language of that other country; the people therefore became very angry with him, and invented the above proverb about him. In the same way, those people, who, to show off their learning, talk to the people of their own country in the language of another country, are like the above (donkey).

(19). "Let the gold, which, eats away one's ear, be put into the fire."

A certain poor man found a gold earring, but when he put it in his ear, owing to its weight, it began to rend his ear; when he had become much distressed, then a certain wise man said to him "You will suffer pain, until you take it out of your ear." He replied "Why should I take such a valuable thing out of my ear?" Then the wise man addressed the above proverb to him, and took the earring from him. So likewise, those fools, who for a little pleasure, undergo much hardship, and will not free themselves therefrom, the above proverb is applied to them "Let the gold, which eats away one's ears, be put into the fire."

(20). "A brocaded canopy on the tomb of a prostitute."

A certain wise man, on seeing a brocaded canopy on the tomb of a prostitute, said to himself "This is a take in;" so, all people, who are inwardly bad, but outwardly try to appear respectable, wise people, on seeing them, say "A brocaded canopy on the tomb of a prostitute."

(21). "A *Domni*, on forgetting the tune, looked up above for it."

When a *Domni* begins to sing and forgets the tune, she begins looking up above for it, but nevertheless, it does not come to her. In like manner, those, who set about their affairs without due reflection, afterwards become perplexed and greatly ashamed; that is to say, those people, who understand a thing thoroughly, but do not do it at the right time, miss their opportunity and are put to great shame.

(22). "You have not a house, and yet have brought five holy men with you (as guests)."

A houseless man was taking five holy men with him to his own house, to entertain them; the people, on seeing what he was doing, began to laugh at him in their hearts; so likewise, if a poor man try to assume the condition of the great, he will be put to great shame.

(23). "A grass hut with an ivory water-spout."

If one should put an ivory water-spout on a grass hut, then every one would laugh at him; so also, if any worthless person be dying of hunger, but, nevertheless, has valuable jewels made and wear them, people will apply this proverb to him "A grass hut with an ivory water-spout."

(24). "When the headman destroys the village, who will populate it?"

If the headman himself begins to destroy a village, then no one will live in it. Likewise, when good people, who give advice, do base deeds themselves, then who will be able to act properly?

(25). "She was to blame herself, but put the fault on the courtyard (people)."

A certain woman was very quarrelsome and sharp-tempered, and, when she did anything wrong, used to throw the blame on the people of the courtyard, and make herself out in the right. So also, those people who throw the blame on others, and make themselves out in the right, to them is applied this proverb, "She was to blame herself, but put the fault on the courtyard (people)."

(26). "The decision of the panch (or arbitrators) is accepted, but let this drain remain here."

The panchait (or committee of arbitrators) of a village said to a certain man, "You must not have this water-spout here, for it causes much damage to other people." To be brief, he agreed to what they said, and added: "True, Maháráj (sirs);" but, in the end, did exactly what they had forbidden. So likewise, those fools, who obtain instruction, but after hearing advice from the wise, cannot bring their hearts to follow it, to them will be applied the above proverb "The decision of the panch is accepted, but let this drain remain here."

PART IV.

THE JANAM SÁKHÍS, OR TWENTY DISCOURSES, REGARDING THE LIFE OF NÁNAK.

CHAPTER I.

Discourse with Gupál, the Teacher.

When the holy Nának reached the age of seven, then Kálú took Nának to the teacher, and went and said to him, "O teacher! as (the astronomers) look (on this) as an auspicious moment, I am leaving Nának with you; do you instruct Nának." Then Gupál, the teacher, said: "Very well, sir! I will instruct him. Now is a favourable time for engaging therein." Afterwards, having had the *tikka*,[143] rice, betul-nut and usual fees, brought from his house, he presented them to the teacher. After this, the teacher wrote a copy on a wooden slate,[144] and said, "Nának, read it." He read for one day, and, after that, retired into silence. Then the teacher said "Nának why will you not read?" Then Bába Nának replied, "O teacher! do you know anything at all yourself!" Then the teacher replied, "O Nának! I know every thing; the alphabet, spelling, mensuration, and accounts, all these I have learnt, and I know all the business of a *patwárí*." Then the Srí Gurú Bába Nának gave vent to this verse and sang it in the Sirí Rág, in the Saríat measure.

"Having burnt the love (of the world), rub it and make it ink; make understanding the best paper.

Make love, the pen; make the mind, the writer; having asked the Gurú, write the decision.

Write the name, write (its) praise, write that which has no end nor limit.

---

[143] The *tikka* is the mark on the forehead.
[144] In the Panjáb, children use small wooden slates, painted black or red, on which they write with a mixture made from white chalk, and the writing is easily obliterated.

CHAP. I.—DISCOURSE WITH GUPÁL, THE TEACHER.

PAUSE.

O father! know to write this account! Where account will be asked, there will be made the true sign (or signature)."[145] (Trumpp's Ádi Granth, page 24).

. The meaning is, that Sri Bába Nának said, "Listen, O teacher! the praise of that Person, Who is boundless, is boundless; well if you understand this, do you read it, and teach me also to read. Listen sir! what I said above is true learning, and if you do not understand it, then listen, and learn and practise it from me; cut the noose of your birth, and learn His praise, Who is boundless;[146] but if you understand it, then write it, read it, and teach it; so that, from reading it, you may escape from the (hereafter) account, and then, at that place where account will be taken from you, you will have in your hand, a token of having remembered the True God, and, after that, no further account will be asked from you. The remembering of God is a token of the true threshold[147]; so if you wish to escape at the true threshold, then read this writing. Listen saint! in whose fate, this decree (of obtaining God) is written, he will obtain profit from (remembering) His name. Listen, teacher! God cannot be obtained by words only, for that which is said is nothing but words, and words are often false, and words are of no avail; and he only will obtain this (profit), who loves God, and he only will get (profit from remembering) God's name." Then again the Srí Gurú said, " Listen, O Pandat (wise man)! to read any thing else, but the name of God, is all wind." Then the Pandat Gupál said, "O Nának! point me out something more to read, from the reading of which I may obtain freedom, Sir." Then the Srí Gurú said, "Listen, O saint! the reading, which is of the world, may be compared, as follows: the ink is made from the wick of lamps; its paper, of hemp: and its pen, of the reed; the mind is the writer, and, if one write with these, what will he write? The troubles of the love of the world will be written, from writing which arise all kinds of troubles; whereas the true reading is after this fashion; having burnt the false love for the world, from it one must make one's ink: of devotion, must be prepared one's paper, and whatever love there is in one's heart, of that one must make one's pen; and one's heart must be the writer, and what sort of writing will one then write? One will write the name of the Divine God, and one will write (His) beautiful praise, from which writing all disorders will be removed, and one's body will

---

[145] i.e., At the day of accounts, all other accounts or writings, will be of no avail.
[146] i.e., Learn this, and then you will obtain salvation, and you will not require to be born or die again.
[147] i.e., Heaven.

be made happy:[148] but His end can nowhere be discovered, O Pan*d*at! If you can understand this writing of truth, then do you yourself read it and teach me also to read it; and if you cannot understand the writing of Truth, then do not read yourself, nor teach me to read. Listen, O Pan*d*at! when your life leaves you, then this reading of Truth will be to you a token of Truth, and death will never come near you." Then the Pan*d*at asked, " O Nának! where have you found out these things? but listen, Nának! (tell me), those who now keep the name of God (in remembrance), what advantage will they obtain?" Then Srí Bába Nának gave utterance to the second verse.

" Where greatness will be obtained, always pleasure and delight;

(There) from their face, marks will issue, in whose heart the true name is.

If it does accrue by destiny, then it is obtained, not by prattle of words." (Trumpp's Ádi Granth, page 24.)

" The meaning of it is this, " Listen, O Pan*d*at! where your soul goes, there you will be blessed, from having remembered God; there, there will always be pleasures, and you will be incessantly blessed with abodes of happiness and joy; and those only, who have remembered Him with all their hearts, will obtain great honour at the True Threshold. He, for whom it is designed, will obtain this. God is not to be won by words." The Pan*d*at, on hearing this, became greatly frightened. Again, after this, the Pan*d*at enquired " O Nának! those who take the name of God, no one even knows them, and they do not get a sufficiency of bread either; whilst those, who are kings, live in great ease and are not in the least afraid of the Great God; then tell (me), what will be their state at the True Threshold?" Then the Gurú Bába gave utterance to the third verse—

" Some come, some rise and go,[149] to whom the name of chieftain is given,

Some are born as beggars, some have great courts.

Having gone onwards (to the other world), it will be known that without the name, there is change of form."[150] (Trumpp's Ádi Granth, page 24.)

---

[148] *i.e.*, He will obtain rest.
[149] *i.e.*, Some are born, and some die.
[150] Dr. Trumpp says, change of form here implies transmigration, and he who is not imbued in the name, will be subject to a course of transmigration.

I believe, however, that the following is a simpler and better translation of the last sentence; "that. except the Name of God, all else is useless."

CHAP. L.—DISCOURSE WITH GUPÁL, THE TEACHER.

The meaning of it is, "Listen, Pandat! some are comers, some are goers;[151] some are called commanders of armies, and some poor people get their food by begging; some are kings, and hold great courts, but those, who do not remember God, they will obtain the same punishment, as the washerman gives clothes, or the mill gives the grain, or the oil-presser gives the oilseed; and those who remember God here, they will obtain greatness at the Threshold of God." On hearing this, the Pandat was frightened and alarmed; then again the Pandat began to say "This is some very holy person." Again, the Pandat asked. "O Nának! why do you utter words of this kind? you are at present a child: try a little the joy of having a father and mother, a wife and family; behold (your age is) yet (on the increase),[152] where then will be the end of your words?" Then the Srí Gurú Bábá read the fourth verse—

"Out of thy fear, dread is very great: being consumed, the body becomes tattered.

Those who had the name of Sultán and Khán have been seen becoming ashes.[153]

Nának! when one has risen and departed, all false love breaks down." (Trumpp's Ádi Granth, page, 24.)

The meaning of it is this, the Srí Gurú said, "Listen, O Pandat! I have such fear of that Lord, that, from fear of Him, my body is greatly filled with fear; those, who were called kings and kháns here, they have died and been turned into dust; those, from dread of whom the earth remained frightened, and those, whose commands used to be obeyed, they also have departed from here. Listen, O Pandat! for what, Sir, should I show such false love? I also must put off these clothes;[154] (then) these miserable clothes (of existence) shall all be turned into a heap of dust. I will do service to Him, who can save my soul; why should I show any affection for this fickle world?" Then the Pandat made an obeisance, and departed, saying, "This is some very holy man."

---

[151] *i.e.*, Some are born, some die.
[152] *i.e.*, You are yet but a growing lad.
[153] "Dust" would be better than "ashes," for Muhammadans are not burnt; "dust," moreover, is the proper meaning of "Khehi."
[154] *i.e.*, I too must die.

K

CHAPTER II.

Discourse regarding the Brahminical Thread.

When the Srí Bába reached nine years of age, then they wished to invest him with the Brahminical thread, and the Bráhmans set to work to teach him channká,[155] sandhiá, gáitrí[156] and tarpan;[157] and, having put on him a sikhá,[158] sút,[159] waistcloth, Brahminical thread, rosary, and tilak,[160] they began to instruct him regarding (the use of) these six articles. After this again, they bathed the Srí Bába, and, then, they seated him in the place of devotion. When the Bráhmans began to put on him the Brahminical thread, then the Srí Gurú Bába said "Listen, O family priest! from investing me with this Brahminical thread, which you are putting on, what religion is taught me?" Then the family priest said: "Listen, O Nának! the purport of being invested with this Brahminical thread is this, that it is laid down in our religion (to be worn) by Khattrís and Bráhmans; and until one obtains the Brahminical thread, one is impure; and after that,[161] one cannot approach any thing that is impure; and one, who has obtained the Brahminical thread, is no longer impure; and without washing, it is not good to go into one's cooking place; and when one obtains this Brahminical thread, then he becomes of the religion of Khattrís and Bráhmans, and can perform gáitrí, sandhiá, tarpan and (use) the six articles above mentioned, and becomes respectable; Khattrís and Bráhmans obtain the Brahminical thread for this reason; and without the Brahminical thread, the religion of Khattrís and Bráhmans would not remain." On this, Bába Nának said, "Listen, O Pandat! does the religion of Khattrís and Bráhmans consist only in wearing the Brahminical thread? or does it rest on good works? Listen, Pandat! if a man gets the Brahminical thread, and does evil deeds, will he remain a Khattrí or Bráhman or will he become an outcast?" When the Sri Gúru

---

[155] Channká is the making ready a square for worship, and plastering it.
[156] Sandhiá and gáitrí are forms of Brahminical prayers.
[157] Tarpan is the making an oblation with water, which is taken up in both hands, and poured forth, to the memory of one's ancestors.
[158] Sikha is the tuft of hair, worn on the top of the head.
[159] Sút is a handkerchief, which is thrown over the left shoulder, during the performances of worship.
[160] Tilak is the mark worn by Bráhmans on the forehead.
[161] i.e., Before putting it on, eating unclean things is not regarded as a sin, but, afterwards, it is.

CHAP. II.—BRAHMINICAL THREAD.

Bába had said this, then all the people who were seated there, were astonished and began to say, "O holy God! he is, at present, but a lad, but what good words does he give utterance to!" Then the Bráhman asked, "O Holy Sir! what Brahminical thread is that, in the obtaining of which religion consists?" Then the Srí Bába gave utterance to this stanza:—

> "Mercy is the cotton ; patience, the thread ; chastity is the knot, and truth is the twisting ;
> And such is the Brahminical thread of the soul ; if you have such a thread, put it on me ;
> It will neither break nor soil, nor burn, nor be lost.
> 'Those persons' (says) Nának, 'are blessed, who wear a thread like this.'"[162]

The meaning is this, that the Srí Gurú Bába Nának said, "Listen, O Holy Pan*d*at! the religion of one, who wears such a Brahminical thread, will continue, *i.e.*, he who shall make mercy the cotton, patience, the thread, truth, the twist, and chastity, its knot ; and he, who inwardly has a Brahminical thread of mercy and patience, he will become cleansed and purified. O Pandat ! a Brahminical thread of this cotton (you offer me) is of no use to me, then why have you wasted the cotton by twisting it (into the thread) ? A thread of this cotton, if it falls into the fire, is burnt, and, if a little mud attaches to it, it becomes soiled, and becomes old, and then breaks ; but that Brahminical thread, which consists of mercy, patience, chastity and truth, it never becomes soiled or old, nor does it break nor burn. Listen, O Pan*d*at! happy are those persons, who have obtained a Brahminical thread of mercy, patience, chastity and truth. Listen, Pandat! all other Brahminical threads are false ; if you have this Brahminical thread, then put it on me, otherwise do not put it on me ; the Brahminical thread, made of cotton, is of no value." Then the Bráhman said, " O Nának ! I did not to-day institute the putting on of this Brahminical thread ; what! do you think, I have done so ? If the wearing of this Brahminical thread has been settled by me, then forbid me ; but it was established long ago." Then the Srí Bába said, "O Pan*d*at ! this is a raw Brahminical thread ; it will remain here, and will not go afterwards with you." Then the teacher said, "O Nának ! this

---

[162] Dr. Trumpp gives the following translation of these lines in his Ádi Granth, Page 646.

"(If) kindness (be) the cotton, contentment, the thread, continence the knot, truth the twist.

(If) this be the sacred cord of the creatures, then, O Pan*d*at put it on. This does not break, nor does filth stick to it nor is it burnt nor does it go off.

Blessed is that man, O Nának, who departs having put on (this) on his neck."

Brahminical thread, of which I am speaking, all people, from the beginning of the world to the present time, have worn it; then O Nának! why do you forbid it (being put on you?)" Then the Srí Bába gave utterance to another stanza:—

    "For four damrís (=one paisá) it (the janeu) was bought and sitting in a chaunká it was put on.

    Instruction was delivered into the ears (of the receiver of the cord), a Bráhman had become the Gurú.

    This one died and that one fell off; he went off without a cord.

    Lakhs of thefts, lakhs of fornications, lakhs of falsehoods, lakhs of abuses.

    Lakhs of deceits (and) frauds are day and night (current) with the creatures." (Trumpp's Translation, Ádi Granth, page 646).

The meaning is, Gurú Nának said, "Listen, O holy Pandat! the matter is thus; men have settled all this matter; the Brahminical thread, made of cotton, can be bought; men themselves bring the cowdung, and make the chaunká; then, afterwards, that man himself goes and sits in that chaunká, and a Bráhman comes and sits down and admonishes him, and puts the Brahminical thread round the neck of the disciple, and that Bráhman is regarded as a Gurú; tell me, can such an one be my Gurú, who, after having been given instruction, obtains the Brahminical thread? Listen, teacher! when that man dies, that Brahminical thread is left behind him, and his soul goes away without that thread; all the things, which have been settled by the world, will all be left here; their praise will continue in this world only, but, above in the Threshold of God, they have no praise; and those things, which God has settled, they are not pleasing to the world, but if any one shall acquire the things of God, he will obtain praise at the Threshold of God. O saint! our business is with God, and we have nothing to do with the world; these worldly things, that you teach me, they are of no use to me." All those who heard these words, got up and said, "Bravo! bravo! O Divine God! what mercy hast thou not shown to this lad." Then that Bráhman said, "O Nának! Kálú has expended all this wealth for you to obtain this Brahminical thread, and many people have assembled to invest you with the Brahminical thread; if you will not now put on the Brahminical thread, then all (this sum) that has been expended on this great feast, and all the people who have collected, will be for nothing; but now, do you put on this thread, and afterwards you may do as it pleases your heart." Then the Srí Bába read another stanza:—

"The (sacred) thread is spun from cotton, the Bráhman comes and twists it.

A goat is killed, cooked and eaten, every one says, put it on.

When it becomes old, it is thrown away, and another is put on again.

Nának (says) the thread does not break, if there be strength in the thread."

(Trumpp's Ádi Granth, page 646).

The meaning of it is, that the Srí Gurú Bába said, "O saint! the world says, if this thread is broken, one becomes impure; O saint! then give me that Brahminical thread to wear, which will never break; having spun the cotton, they make a thread, and then they make a string, and if the string should break, it must not be worn any more; what virtue is there in getting such a thread, which a Bráhman can again make, and which one can obtain afresh? If there is any strength in this thread, then why does it break? That string, which has strength, that string the Great God has given me; you may put on as many other strings as you like, (but they will profit nothing)." Then they forcibly put the Brahminical thread on the Srí Bába, and afterwards the Bráhman said, "O Bába, this your Brahminical thread is a token for the world; but what you say is quite true. But, sir, that kind of thread, which is strong, and never gets dirty, and never breaks, and in the end goes to heaven, tell me about that thread." Then the Srí Gurú Bába recited another stanza."

"He, who reverences God's name, his honour increases; the praise of God is the true thread;

It is found in the Threshold of God, that thread never breaks, and is always pure."[163]

The meaning of it is, that, from the reverencing of the name of the Divine Being, the honour of man increases; and the doing of service to God is the true thread; and this is the true Brahminical thread, at the Threshold of God; and the string of this pure Brahminical thread never breaks. Then the Pandat made an obeisance, and departed.

---

[163] Dr. Trumpp gives the following translation of these lines (Ádi Granth, page 647):—
By minding the name, honour springs up, praising (God) is the true thread;
The thread, that is obtained within the threshold (of God), does not break (it is) pure.

CHAPTER III.

Discourse with the physician.

Gurú Nának, having got into a state of religious enthusiasm, laid down as one helpless; on this, the whole family of Vediyas, being distressed, began to lament and to say "This is a great matter of regret, that Nának, the son of Kálú, should have become mad." Then the Srí Bába remained quiet, and, for three months, lay prostrate inside (the house), eating and drinking nothing. Then all the family of the Vediyas became very anxious, and they all began to say to Kálú "Why do you now remain seated, when your son is lying prostrate? call some physician to cure him; then perhaps God, by your spending a straw, may give much profit,[164] otherwise the world will say of you, that Kálú does not cure his son, (as he has greater) love for his money; listen Kálú! you will have plenty of money, when your son shall be cured." Then Kálú rose and got up, and called a physician. The physician came and stood, and began to seize the arm of the Bába; then the Bába withdrew his arm, and rose and sat up, and said, "O physician! what are you doing?" The physician replied; "I am seeing what inward disease you have." Then the Srí Bába recited the following verse in reply to the physician:—

"The physician was called to cure, he seized my arm and began to feel (for my pulse);

O simple physician! do you not know, that the pain is in my heart;

O physician! go to your home, and do not receive a curse from me;

I am in love with my husband (*i.e.* God); to whom will you give medicine!

O physician! you are a very wise physician, but you should find out the disease;

Find (it) out, and bring that medicine by which all diseases are cured;

If there is sickness, then there is plenty of physic, and many physicians will come and stand around;

---

[164] This is a proverb, signifying that if one only spend a little on the doctor the will obtain much profit, from getting cured.

The body weeps, and the soul cries out, 'Physician, give me not medicine,
Go, physician, to your own home, for few know (what is wrong with me);
'He who has created this disease, He,' (says) Nának 'will cure me.'"

Then he recited another verse in the Malár Rág;

"O simple physician, give me not physic;
This heart is obtaining the punishment of its own deeds;
I am in pain, and my body tormented;
This physic is of no use, O brother!
Pain is a poison; the name of Harí is its antidote;
Patience is the grinding stone; the hand for grinding it is alms;
Continually take (the medicine of) His name, and then your body will suffer no pain;
In the end, the angel of death will destroy you;
O thou rustic! take such a medicine;
From taking which all your diseases may depart.

PAUSE.

Kingship, wealth and youth are all like a shadow, [165]
The track of the car, as it moves on, is left, but does not always remain;
When one dies, neither a man's body remains, nor his name nor his caste;
There (in the future world) it is all day, but, here, it is all night;
Regard worldly joys as fuel, and its desires as ghí and oil (to burn thereon).
Burn lust and anger in the fire.
But oblations, sacrifices and religious books.
Which are pleasing to God, these only are acceptable (to Him);
Make devotion your paper, and on it write your name and signature;
They, who have written thus, (on the paper).
They will appear wealthy, when they go to His portal;
Nának (says)! 'Blessed is the mother of that one, who is born and remembers his God.'"

When the physician had heard this stanza, then he withdrew, and said "O brother! he has no disease; do not you be at all anxious for him."

---

[165] i.e., They do not last, but come and go, like a shadow.

CHAPTER IV.

Discourse about the Store.

There were given him a thousand rupees in cash; then Bálá Sandhú said, "O Bába Nának! you have now taken over the store, therefore now give me leave to go." Then Gurú Nának said, "O brother Bálá! you have formed an imperfect affection for me; what! will you leave me whilst I am still alive?" Then Bálá said, "Thou art the son of a Khattrí and doest thine own business; why should I also not do mine?" Then Gurú Nának said, "O brother Bálá! let things continue for some time as they are; this business must be done by us, who else will do that which is our business; do you behold the show (play) of the Creator, and see how the Creator acts! stay then and live with me." Then I (Bálá) said "Yes, sir! your pleasure shall be accomplished, and what you shall say, that will I do." Then I also began to live with the Gurú, and we began to carry on the business. When two years had passed in this way, carrying on the business, then Mahitá Kálú came to get information about it, and met with Gurú Nának. Then Gurú Nának getting up fell at the feet of Kálú; and Mahitá Kálú kissed his forehead, and pressed him to his neck, and began to ask, "O son Nának! it is two years since I sent you here; what have you made, and what have you spent?" Then Gurú Nának replied, "O father! I have made a good deal; and I have spent a good deal; but I have not accumulated anything." Then Mahitá Kálú began to quarrel with me (Bálá), and to use hard words (to me). On this Gurú Nának made a sign to (me) Bálá, intimating, "Brother Bálá, you must say nothing to Kálú;" on this I remained silent. Then Kálú began to say, "I thought, that Nának was now employed in the business, and that which he had (formerly) spent of mine, he would (now) give back to me;" then Kálú began to talk in the same (angry) way, as he was wont to do.

Then he (Kálú) went to see Nánakí and Jairám, and, on meeting them, began to ask; "What have you done? have you ever looked after him at all? you have neither looked after what he was doing, nor have you done anything about his betrothal; why have you not done so?" Then Bíbí Nánakí said, "O father! since he has been here, he has wasted nothing of yours; are you not thankful that he is employed, and engaged in his work? Some day, he will make some profit; and arrangements are being made also for his betrothal, and, in a day or two, they will be completed; he causes no loss to us; but, O father! if it (the betrothal) is being arranged by you any where, then do you arrange it; although it is a matter of anxiety to us, it will be doubly so to you."

(*Reply of Kálú*).—" Child, daughter Nánakí if it could be arranged by me, then why should I ask you (to arrange it)? and, daughter, if you do arrange it, then you must arrange it in a proper family, and see that it is a good Khattrí, but it must not be in an indifferent (family).''

(*Reply of Nánakí*).—" We do not wish to put you to any expense: there is one, Múlá Choná, who is the land steward of the village, Pakhoke Randháwián; he will betroth his daughter without taking anything :[166] I hope to make arrangements for his betrothal there: and what is pleasing to the Lord, that will take place. O Mahítá, do you remain easy in your mind, God will arrange everything well." Then Kálú said, " O son-in-law Jairám! (in such matters) one's sons-in-law truly feel as much shame as one's sons. I was saying in my heart, that as I have seen the happiness of Bíbí Nánakí, and my eyes were rejoiced thereat, so now I wished, whilst I lived, to see the joy and desire of Nának fulfilled, and then my soul would be made happy." Then Jairám said, " O Mahítá! do you remain here and, I will call (your wife), the mother (of Nának)." Then Kálú said, " O my son Jairám! stopping here is irksome to me, and I cannot manage to stay here, as I have lots to do there (at home)." Then Jairám said, " O Mahítá! you are to me as Parmánand (my father), and you are my father." Kálú said, " Behold Jairám! immediately Nának is betrothed, you must instantly give me information, and you must keep my son Nának in sight, and see that he does not waste any money or cash." Then Bíbí Nánakí said, " O father! are you not thankful that he is now happy; you used (formerly) daily (to trouble us by saying) that to-day he had caused this loss, and he had wasted that. O father! when he feeds the poor, then our hearts are troubled, lest the master's money should be diminished, for then we would be disgraced before the master. But father, whenever he renders the accounts to his master, then, there is always some profit over. This is some manifestation of the Creator." Then Jairám said, " O Mahítá! this is why we cannot say anything to him." Then again Kálú said, " O my son Jairám! if, when you shall again take the account,

---

[166] *i.e.*, Without taking any money for her. Betrothals are of two kinds; by payment of money, and without.

any profit shall have accrued, you must take it yourself, and then you will do well; for, in his sight, a lakh (of rupees) and a straw are of equal value; and do you also send for Bálá and admonish him; let you and I both speak fully to him (on the subject)." Then Jairám, having sent a man, called Bálá, and Bálá came; then Jairám said, "O Bháí Bálá! you are the special, ever present, companion of Nának, and we look on you in the same light as we look on Nának; therefore do you keep a look-out on Nának, and see that he does not waste the money." Then again Kálú added,[167] "O son Bálá! remember there will be shame (attached to you), on account of your living with him, (if anything should go wrong)." (Bálá said) "Jairám's speech did not appear disagreeable to me, but the speech of Kálú hurt me." Then I said to Kálú. "O Mahitá! do you think any evil (of me, Bálá) in your heart, and that because, I, Bálá, live with Nának, I also indulge in extravagance; for, Mahitá, in my sight, ghí is even a forbidden thing, and I look on any other covetous desire as wicked; and in that I live with Nának, I live with him for my own (future) advantage, for I look on Nának as God. Listen, Mahitá Kálú! you have a longing for money, and I have only this desire, viz., whatever he does, let him do it, it will be well, and I will make no objection thereto. Do you take and collect whatever you can lay your hands on; I cannot do such a thing as to say any thing to him; but if you can do any thing, then come and do it." Then Jairám said, "O Mahitá jí! Bháí Bálá speaks the truth. Nának is not a man; he appears to me to be something else; but be happy, Mahitá jí, and set off home, and the instant Nának is betrothed, I will act at once; then perhaps, he may form affection for his family, and he will then be admonished." Then Kálú went to his home. When one month had passed, then a certain good man came to Jairám, and told tales about Nának, saying, "Listen, Jairám! your brother-in-law is the steward of this shop, then why do you not admonish him? do you not know of what description is the temper of the Patháns?" Then Jairám, on hearing it, became distressed, and, in that state of distress, came home; when he reached home, he took Nánakí aside, and began to say to her, "Listen, O handmaid of God! to-day a certain person has come and said to me. 'Jairám, your brother-in-law, who is the steward, is wasting the money; why do you not admonish him? Do you know the temper of the Patháns or not?' Therefore, wife, what shall I do? Whatever you shall say, that I will do." Then Nánakí said, "Sir, whatever comes into your heart, that do; what shall I say? It behoves me to act according to your

[167] *Lit.* "Said in an off-hand manner."

CHAP. IV.—DISCOURSE ABOUT THE STORE. 155

directions." Then Jairám said. "Wife, do you give me some counsel, and then I will act thereon." Nánakí said, "Sir, have you not yet any faith in him? You seem to think that I take the part of my brother, and that whatever wealth and treasure of the world is in his charge, Nának is letting it slip through his fingers; but Sir, if you have any doubt in your mind, then do you thus act; do you now at once take the accounts from him, and if the accounts be correct, and if there be no loss or damage, then for the future, you must not be misled by the sayings or talk of any one." Then Jairám said. "Dear one! I will not take the accounts: as you have faith (in him), what occasion is there for me to do so?" Nánakí said! "Sir! now you cannot retract; I will call my brother, Nának". Then Bíbí Nánakí sent her maid, Tulsán, to call Nának, with this message; ("Your sister says) 'O brother; do you have compassion and shew yourself to us?'" Then the girl Tulsán went and made her obeisance to him. Thereupon he said, "What is it, Tulsán? Why have you come to-day?" Tulsán said, "O my lord! your sister said, 'Do you go to my brother, and tell him to come and show himself to me;' this is why I have come." Then Gurú Nának said: "Depart, Tulsán, I am coming." Then Tulsán went home, and when she arrived, said, "O my mistress, he says 'I am coming.'" Afterwards, Gurú Nának said "Bháí Bálá! Why has my sister called me?" Then I said, "Sir! she must have called you, because she wants something." Then Nának said, "Bháí Bálá! my heart tells me, that some one has told tales there about me." Then I said. "Sir! what tales can any one have told there about you? What (evil) have you done?" Gurú Nának said, "Bháí Bálá! bring a pot of patásas."[168] Then I brought the pot of patásas, and Gurú Nának emptied the contents into his lap,[169] and whatever patásas were in the pot, he carried them all away; there were about two and a half sirs of patásas in the pot; these he carried all away, and, taking them, Gurú Nának came to Bíbí Nánakí. Immediately, (on his arrival), Bíbí Nánakí arose, and got up and said, "Come, brother," and then gave him a seat, and Nának sat down on the seat. I, Bálá, also came with him, and the Bíbí also gave me a small chair. Then Gurú Nának asked "Bíbí! why, have you called me?" (She replied) "Brother! many days have passed since we have seen your face, and we had a desire to see you, therefore I have called you, and I said to Tulsán, 'Go and call my brother.'" Then Gurú Nának said, "Bíbí! I have my suspicions, as to why you called me; do you tell me what it is?" Then the Bíbí said,

---

[168] A kind of sweetmeat.
[169] *i.e.*, Taking up the skirt of his coat.

"O brother, you know everything: there is no occasion to tell you." Then Gurú Nának said, " Bíbí, I know in my heart, that some one has told tales about me here: I, also, therefore, say, 'Take the accounts from me.'" Then Bíbí Nánakí began to soothe him; on which Gurú Nának began to say, " No, Bíbí! it has come to a matter of accounts: here you must not allow your shame or regard for any one to interfere." Then Bíbí Nánakí said: " Very well, brother."

In the year 1543 on the fifth of the bright half of the month Maughar, he gave the accounts, and settled up his books for three months; one hundred and thirty-five rupees remained over, after paying all expenses.

Nának said to his brother-in-law, Jairám: " Behold brother-in-law! has your face now not been disgraced? How is it now? Now you must make this store over to some one else. God is my (Preserver)". Then Jairám fell at his feet, and Bíbí Nánakí began to weep and to say, " Sir! first kill me, and then go wherever you like." Then Gurú Nának said, " Now has my account been delivered in full; but even if there had been any deficiency, what misfortune would it have been to you?" Then Jairám said, " Brother Nának! I only partly understood you before, and I partly did not understand you; but now confidence has come to me in every way: do you forgive me this my fault; forgetting myself, I listened to tales, and did not heed what my wife said." Then again the Bíbí said, " Brother! hereafter, whatever shall be short, I will give account of that, whatever it be." Then, I, Bálá, said, " O Nának! you are evidently a true prophet, for how else could you know about things beforehand? Well, Nának! your sister and your brother-in-law both entreat of you, so do you look to God (and forgive them); and O Gurú, do you show love to me in this matter." Then, Gurú Nának said, " Very well, Bháí Bálá! as you have said so, I cannot turn away from it." Then, I, (Bálá) made my obeisance. Then Bíbí Nánakí and Bháyá Jairám began to say to me, " Bháí Bálá! you have to-day given Nának to us afresh." Then they counted over to Nának one hundred and thirty-five rupees, the profit, and also gave over to him seventeen hundred rupees besides; and Nának, taking them, went and sat in the store; and all the people of the establishment came, and began to congratulate and praise Nának, and Hindús and Musalmáns both were pleased.

CHAPTER V.

Conversation regarding the betrothal of Nának.

In the year 1544, on the 5th of the bright half of the month Maughar, Nának was betrothed in the house of Múlá Choná of Pakhoke Randháwa. Then Jairám and Bíbí Nánakí sent the news and congratulations to Mahitá Kálú and his (Nának's) mother, and sent and called them, saying, "If you will come, then the expenses for the marriage preparations will be paid." Then Kálú, on hearing it, was greatly pleased, and the mother was also greatly pleased: and they filled the mouth of her who had taken the news with sugar with their own hands; and having filled it, began to say, "We sacrifice ourselves to your mouth,[170] as you have brought us this news of the welfare of Nának." At night, all the hangers-on and relations of the Vedís came and sat down and began to sing, and to say, "In our family, one Nának has been born with a good spirit, for he has been betrothed according to religious rites (and not for money), and he has dignified our family thereby." Then his (Nának's) mother sent congratulations to her parents in the Mánjhá[171] Rámá (of the) Jhangar (family) was that lady's father, and there were also the maternal grandfather and grandmother of Nának, and the mother-in-law and father-in-law of Kálú; then the mother sent news to them also and said, "If you will come, then come to Sultánpur, and the money for the marriage preparations will be paid." Then the grandmother Bhiraí came there, and the grandfather Rámá and the maternal uncle, Kisna, also; for the three of them, on hearing of it, were greatly pleased. Then they came to Talwandí and met Kálú; then the people of Talwandí, assembling together, set forth: Kálú, Lálá Vedí, Ammán Bíbí (Nának's mother) and Rámá and Kisna, Jhangars, and the grandmother Bhiráí, these six people, got ready, and, with the two servants of Rámá, there were twelve persons in all: now Rámá, Jhangar, had much goods with him; when they were about to set forth, then they went to Rái Bulár to wish him farewell: and Kálú, going before the Rái, stood before him; then the Rái said "What is it, Kálú?" Then

---

[170] *i.e.*, We feel ourselves deeply indebted to you.
[171] The central part of the Bári Doáb.

Kálú replied, " Your slave Nának has been betrothed; the marriage party are going to Pakhoke Randháwa to pay the money for the marriage preparations; will you please give us your permssion to go." Then the Rái said " Kálú, remember what Nának was before! take care (not to quarrel with him)." Then Kálú said, "O Rái! do not raise doubts in my heart." Then the Rái said, " No. Kálú, that is not it; I meant something else; he is nothing more than a holy man; (take care not to quarrel, for) perhaps he may say something unpleasing to you." Then Kálú said, " No Rái! he is the desire of my heart, (*i.e.*, my son); and O Rái! God has made you the master here, therefore, have kindness on us and give us (your blessing and your permission to go)." Then the Rái said, " Go Kálú! may God fulfil your desire; this is also my hope; but Kálú, it behoves me also to kiss the forehead of Nának, do you touch his feet with (your) hands for me, and make my apologies to Jairám; go, may God protect you." Then Kálú got into the cart, and, on the fifth day, arrived at Sultánpur. He arrived on Thursday, and entered the house of Parmánand, and began to utter his congratulations. Then Nának received intimation that his father and mother had come; and that his paternal uncle, and paternal grandmother and grandfather, and maternal uncle had come, and also Mardáná, the *Dúm*. Then Nának, immediately on hearing it, got up and came running, and forthwith fell at the feet of Kálú. Kálú kissed his forehead; then Nának said, "O father! was the Rái well?" Then Kálú said, " Son, he remembered you most kindly; the Rái told me to kiss your forehead, but I had forgotten it." Then Gurú Nának fell at the feet of his mother, and then fell at the feet of his uncle Lálú. Lálú pressed him to his neck, and said, " Son! you have dignified our family; God knows what will happen hereafter; but in this world, you have dignified it." Then Nának fell at the feet of his maternal grandfather Rámá; then his maternal grandfather, Rámá, pressed him to his neck, and would not leave off embracing him. Then Rámá looked around to see if there were any beggars near; [172] then his maternal grandmother Bhirái said, " Let him go from thy neck." Then Rámá said to Bhirái, " When my desire shall be fulfilled, then I will let him go; and when I shall have sacrificed twenty rupees on the head of Nának, then my desire will be fulfilled." Bhirái said, " Make the sacrifice then." Rámá said, " How? there is no one here to take it." Then Nánakí said, " Go Tulsán, and if you see any beggars, call them here." Tulsán went and called (some). Then Nánakí said "O grandfather!

---

[172] *i.e.*, He was so pleased that he wished to give some alms; but he did not see any one on whom to bestow them, although, usually on such occasions, there are a number of hangers-on ready to receive such.

CHAP. V.—BETROTHAL OF NÁNAK. 159

will you have the twenty rupees in silver or coppers?" Then Rámá said, "O daughter! I will do as you shall say." Nánakí said, "Send for coppers." Then Rámá called his son Kisna, and said, "Take these twenty rupees and bring coppers." Bhirái said, "Bring ten rupees worth for me also." Kisna also gave five rupees, and in all they sent for thirty-five rupees of coppers. Rámá offered as sacrifice twenty rupees for himself, ten rupees for the maternal grandmother, and five rupees for the maternal uncle, Kisna.

In the year 1544, on the full moon of the month Maughar, on a Thursday, having carefully selected the time, they set forth from Sultánpur: who went? Kálú, Lálú, Rámá, Kisna, Parmánand, (by family a) Paltá, Jairám, and besides them, the servants; Nidhá Bráhman had been sent on to Pakhoke Randháwa, of which village Múla Choná was the land steward; when Nidhá Bráhman gave the information to Múlá Choná, he said, "O Mahitá Múlá! be happy;" then the Mahitá Múlá said, "Congratulations to thee, O Pándhá! come Sir! whence have you come?" Then Nidhá said, "I have come from Sultánpur." Then Múlá said, "Pándhá, why have you come?" Then Nidhá said, "Bhái Jairám and Kálú Vedi, the father-in-law of Jairám, have both come to give the money for the preparations for the wedding; and Jairám has said, 'Go and give intimation to Múlá,' and therefore have I come, Sir." Then Múlá said, "Come, you are welcome."[173] He came on Sunday, the 10th, when about a watch (three hours of the day) had passed; then Múlá got ready the requisites, and Parmánand, Paltá, himself undertook the wedding preparations; and the receiving of congratulations and other regular rites and customs were performed on both sides. Then Kálú Vedi said to Parmánand, "Bháiyá! do you ask for the marriage-day to be fixed." Then Parmánand took Múlá aside, and seated him; and, having seated him, told him all the circumstances in a friendly manner, saying, "Behold, Mahitá ji! the lad is of age, and the girl also is of age; do you therefore fix the day, for all the people of Talwandí have come, and all the Jhangars, the relations of the mother of the youth Nának, have also come from the Mánjhá." Then Múlá thus gave answer, "Bháiyá! do you remain easy in mind; give me a little time, and then I will, after due thought and reflection, fix you a good day, and let you know of it," and then, being dismissed with honour and much respect, they came and entered Sultánpur. Then the congratulations began to be made, and Bibí Nánakí, calling her companions, made them sit down and sing. On the fourth day, when they

---

[173] *Lit.* " With all my heart and forehead."

were taking leave, Mardáná the *Dúm* said, " Nának, do you yourself now give me some marriage gift." Then Guru Nának said, " Mardáná, what will you take? Have I any business with you?" Then Mardáná said, " Sir! give me some good thing." Then Gurú Nának said, " Mardáná, do you want some good thing? but (take care, for) you will be affected with grief (from taking) that good thing." Mardáná said, " Sir! if you shall give me some good thing, then why should I suffer pain from it?" Then Gurú Nának said, " Mardáná, you are a Mirásí, and do not know anything about the future world." Then Mardáná said, " Nának, if you have any good thing, then give me it." Then Gurú Nának said, " Mardáná! I will give you skill on the strings, for it will be useful to me also." Then Mardáná rose and stood up, and made an obeisance. Then Gurú Nának said, " Mardáná, listen to one thing I have to say." Then Mardáná said, " Sir, command." (He said) "O Mardáná! you are the family bard of the Vedís; therefore you must not beg from any one else." Then Mardáná said, " Sir, I have agreed to this matter; but Sir! do you have a care for me." Then Gurú Nának said, "Listen, Mardáná! the Creator takes care of all." Then again, they all departed for their homes, after meeting each other, with happiness and joy. Then the old state again came over Gurú Nának, and whoever came, he never sent him away empty (handed). Then people began to give rise to various reports, saying, " Nának is now about to go away; (therefore), come and let us tell Nánakí and Jairám." Then Nánakí said to Jairám, " See to it and do not be made doubtful by what people say." Although Jairám was inwardly reflecting over the matter, he did not outwardly give vent to (his thoughts). One day, Nának himself said, " Sir, do you take all the accounts of the governor; for it is a long time since you have done so." Then Jairám petitioned the Nawáb, saying, " Nawáb! peace to you: Nának, the storekeeper says, 'It will be well, if the Nawáb takes the accounts.'" The Nawáb replied, " Jairám, call the storekeeper." Then Jairám, sending Nidhá, the Bráhman, called Nának. Nának, taking his account book, set forth with joy; but the people were saying in the ears of the Nawáb, "O Nawáb, peace be to thee! the storekeeper is stealing your money." When Nának, bringing his account, came before the Nawáb and made his obeisance, then the Nawáb said, "O storekeeper! what is your name?" Gurú Nának said, " My name is Nának Nirankárí."[174] Then the Nawáb said, " O Jairám! I do not at all understand what the storekeeper has

---

[174] He received this name, because he was heard to be continually saying Nirankár, Nirankár."

CHAP. V.—BETROTHAL OF NÁNAK. 161

said." Then Jairám translated it for the Nawáb into Persian. "He says, 'I am the servant of Him, Whose epithets are the Incomparable, the Unsimilar, the Undoubtable, the Unparalleled.'" Then the Nawáb laughed, and said, "O Jairám! has the storekeeper been married (yet)?" Jairám said, "No, he is not yet married." The Nawáb said, "Now, I understand that he is married (to God), inasmuch as he gives vent to such words." Then the Nawáb said, "Listen Nának! I have heard that you are stealing my money; do you know that I am Daulat Khán, the Lodí?" Then Gurú Nának said, "Nawáb, peace be to you! do you take your accounts, and whatever may come out, as the portion of this poor one, then, if it pleases you, give it, if not, do not give it." Then the Nawáb said, "O Jairám! what is the storekeeper saying?" Jairám said, "Peace be to you! the storekeeper is truthful, the storekeeper is not at fault." Then the Nawab said, "Call Jádo Rái, the writer." Then Jádo Rái, the writer, came, and made his obeisance. The Nawáb said, "O Jádo Rái, take the account from Nának." Then they began to settle the accounts. The accounts took five days and five nights (settling). Jádo Rái, the writer, made many enquiries, but found that he had not acted in any way, against God and the truth. Three hundred and twenty-one rupees came out as surplus for Nának; then Jairám was pleased, and made his salaam to the Nawáb. The Nawáb said, "What Jairám! are the accounts done?" Jairám said, "Nawáb, peace be to you! call Jádo Rái." Then Jádo Rái was called. When Jádo Rái came, he made his salaam to the Nawáb. The Nawáb said, "O Jádo Rái! have you taken the accounts?" Jádo Rái said, "O Nawáb, peace be to you! the account has been taken, and three hundred and twenty-one rupees remain over to Nának." The Nawáb said, "To me or to him?" Jádo Rái said, "O Nawáb, peace be to you! they are due from you to Nának." The Nawáb said, "Then why did people say, that Nának was robbing my money?" Then Jairám petitioned, "O Nawáb, peace be to you! people show much enmity to him." The Nawáb said, "Call Bhawání Dás." The treasurer came and made his obeisance. Then the Nawáb said, "O Bhawání Dás, make over to Nának whatever is due to him, and also give him three thousand rupees besides." On this, Bhawání Dás paid up the three hundred and twenty-one rupees due, and gave three thousand rupees besides. Then Nának, taking the bags, came home; some he took to the store, and the rest he placed with Bíbí (Nánakí). Then Jairám was greatly pleased and returned home, much rejoiced. Then Nánakí asked, "How have the accounts turned out, Sir?" Then Jairám said, "Listen, O beloved of God! I was greatly surprised, for Nának is always throwing away the money, but whenever the account is taken, a

L

balance comes out to his credit." Again Nánakí said, "Sir! what balance did there remain to-day?" Then Jairám said, "Three hundred and twenty-one rupees surplus remained after paying all expenses, and (accounting for monies) given away." Then Nánakí said "Sir, no one has gained so much profit, as Rái Bulár has in this." Then Jairám said, "Listen, O beloved of God! not only has the Rái made profit in this, but many people will obtain profit from him." On this Nánakí was highly delighted.

CHAPTER VI.

The Discourse regarding the Marriage of Nának.

In the year 1544, on the ninth of the bright half of the month Hár, the marriage of Gurú Nának was fixed to take place. Then Bíbí Nánakí made great rejoicings in her home, and having written a letter, sent it by the hand of Nidhá Bráhman, after having sprinkled it with kungú ;[175] she also sent sweetmeats and cardamoms and five rupees in cash to Talwandí to the house of Kálú. Then joy and pleasure arose in the house of Kálú. Kálú sent a man to the Mánjhá to his father-in-law, and then rejoicings were made there also, and bhájís[176] were sent out. Then Kálú went to Rái Bulár, (who was the headman) in his own village, and having gone there, said, " O Rái! may you be blessed!" Then the Rái said, " What is it, Kálú? " Kálú said, " The marriage day of your slave Nának has been fixed." Then the Rái said, " Do not again call Nának my slave ; if you do, then I shall be very angry." Then Kálú said, " Sir, to be respectful is incumbent on me." (The Rái asked) "What Kálú! are other forms of respect too few?" (Kálú said) " Well, Sir! forgive me this fault ; I forgot myself." Then the Rái said, " Go, Kálú, God will forgive you ; go, may your desire be fulfilled, and give my respects to Nának." Who went on the day fixed for the marriage? Kálú, Lálú, Parasrám, Indrasain, Phirandá, Jagat Mall, Lál Chand, Jagat Rái, Ja*tt* Mall, and all the Vedís that came ; these all got ready to go ; when the first of the month Bháddon came, and seven days had passed, then they set forth from Talwandí and from the Mánjhá ; the maternal grandfather, Rámá, also came ; the maternal uncle, Kisna, also came ; and when they came, they stopped at Sultánpur ; they began the festivities in the house of Parmánand, Paltá, and Jairám. When five days remained to the marriage day, then, having had the fortunate moment for departing settled, they set forth from Sultánpur, and, departing thence, they arrived on the marriage day. Parmánand, Paltá, the father of Jairám sent Nidhá Bráhman to the house of Múlá, saying " Go, Nidhá and give information to Múlá, saying, ' Do you know that the wedding party of the Vedís has come ?'"

---

[175] The name of a very fine pure composition of a red colour, made from the aunlá, a medicinal plant, and used by women to anoint their foreheads.

[176] A present of fruits, sweetmeats, &c., sent by the parents of a bride and bridegroom to their friends, when inviting them to the wedding.

Then Nidhá Bráhman went and gave information to Mulá Choná and, on arriving gave him a blessing and said, "O my client!"[177] may you be happy!" Then Mulá quickly replied, 'O Pándhá (accept) my salutations." Then Nidhá said, "O my client! the wedding party has arrived and put up in the garden, and they have sent me to give you intimation. Bháiyá Parmánand said to me, 'Go and give intimation to Mahitá Kálú.'" Then Mulá collected his brotherhood and went to Hittá Randháwá, and, standing before him, began to say, "O Master! the marriage party of the Vedís has come, and alighted in the garden." Then Hittá Randháwá said, "O my son Ajita! do you go with Mulá, and whatever Mulá may ask, supply him with, and do you also remain with them. Listen Mulá! my body has become old, otherwise, I myself would go with you." (Mulá said), "O my master! whatever are your orders, they are (received as coming) from yourself." (Hittá said), "Listen, Mulá! respectable people have come to your house, and you must show them proper respect, and keep your tongue silent; this is my command. I have heard that Kálú Vedí, the land steward of Bha*tt*íán, uses hard words and you also have a sharp tongue; but Parmánand is looked on as a man who shows respect; you must also, on your part, show respect." Then Mulá said, "Very well my lord! you are my protector: my hope is from you and from God." (Hittá said) "Well Mulá, go and receive them with respect and bring them here." Then Mulá, having assembled the village committee, sent a choice batehrí;[178] Ajitá Randháwá remained present with them, and treated them with honour. Afterwards, at night, the wedding party set forth and, with much singing and music, entered the village. On the 20th of Bháddon, the marriage commenced, and, in the early morning, when five gharís of the night were left, the four circumambulations round the marriage fire took place, with the following song in the Súhí Rág :—

The first circumambulation (is made) in the name of God, to give firmness in worldly works; I sacrifice myself to Thee, O God.

From the words of Bráhma, *i.e.*, the Vedas, religion obtains strength, and sin is forgiven: I sacrifice myself to Thee, O God.

---

[177] Jajmán is a person, on whose custom Bráhmans, barbers, &c., have a legal claim. The hereditary Bráhman, barber, &c., of a village must be paid his fees, whether his services be employed or not.

[178] The food, which, according to a custom among the higher classes of Hindus, is sent by the family of a bride to the lodging of the bridegroom and his family on the first day of the wedding ceremonies, as it is contrary to rule to receive the bridegroom and his family under the bride's roof on the first day.

CHAP. VI.—MARRIAGE OF NÁNAK.

Make your religion firm, and meditate on the name of God;
the name of God is also remembered in the Simrits;
Look on the True Gurú as a perfect Gurú, for He will efface
all impurity and anger and sin;
The blessed obtain joy with ease, for the name of God
sounds sweet to their heart:
At the first circumambulation, Nának (says). "The business (of remembering God) is commenced."

The second circumambulation (is made) in the name of God, and the True Gurú is obtained by man; I sacrifice myself to Thee, O God!

Then the fear in one's mind becomes fearlessness, and one's pride is washed away; I sacrifice myself to Thee, O God!
One obtains the pure fear from singing the praises of God;
God, Himself, lives in all hearts;
God is in the spirit of man, and God fills everything;
Within and without, there is one God; the worshippers of
God assemble and laud His name.

At the second circumambulation, Nának (says), "Innumerable musical instruments began to be sounded."

The third circumambulation (is made) in the name of God; the minds of the Bhairágís are filled with joy; I sacrifice myself to thee, O God!

The holy have union with God, and he, who obtains God, great is his fortune; I sacrifice myself to Thee, O God!

He, who obtains the Pure God, and sings God's praises, his
mouth always utters His words:
The holy are very fortunate, for they, who obtain God, tell
forth the untellable tale of God;
In the hearts of all, the thought of God arises; that soul
only can take his name, in whose fate it is so written.
In the third circumambulation, Nának (says). "The (love of the name) of God arises in the heart of the worshippers."

The fourth circumambulation (is made) in the Name of God; the heart is comforted when God is obtained; I sacrifice myself to Thee, O God;

I found God through the saying of the Gurú, and God, then with ease, appeared sweet to[179] my body and soul: I sacrifice myself to Thee, O God!

---

[179] i.e. Was believed in by.

He, to whom the Name of God is sweet, is pleasing to my Lord, and his hopes are continually fixed on Him;

What his heart wished, of it he obtained the fruit; O saint! the name of God gives great joy;

When God, the Creator and Lord, directs one's affairs, then thanks to His name appears as wealth to the heart of His worshippers.

In the fourth circumambulation Nának (says) " God, the Lord, the Everlasting One, is obtained."

The wedding took place and was performed with much joy; then, I, Bálá, said, "O Gurú this is what I have to say; I say it, after having seen with my own eyes, and I do not say what I have only heard." Gurú Angad, from hearing certain things, was pleased, and from hearing others, began to long for separation (from the world). Now Gurú Nának, at the time of the circumambulations, had said, (to me) " O Bálá, do thou remain with me," for whatever secret expenses Nának had, were paid by me. I replied, " Very well, Sir! I will remain with you! O Gurú! it has been performed with much joy." For three days, the wedding party continued, and the fourth day, they departed; and having brought (the bride) in a dolí, they came to Sultánpur. Then Kálú, Lálú, and Jairám said, " Let the bridegroom and bride remain here, for if not, then, afterwards, who will carry on the business of the store?" Then Kálú said, " O son Nának! your mother is seated here, waiting for you; her desire is for you to have happiness." This contention was going on, when afterwards Múlá came in. Then Múlá Choná said, " If the bride and bridegroom remain here, and are not sent to Talwandí, then the dispute will not be continued." Then Parmánand said, " O Múlchand, this is the first time (they have come) since their wedding; and this is also the pleasure and desire of the boy's mother, that they should go to their house, and then come back and remain here. The business of the store is certainly here; then how can they arrange to live there?"[180] It must be done in this way; let them take (the bride in) the dolí to their house." Then they took the dolís with Nának and Mátá Choní seated in them, to Talwandí. When Nának was setting out for Talwandí, then he said to me. " Bhái Bálá; do you carry on the business till my return." I replied, " O Gurú! I am a Jati, how can this business be carried on by me?" Then again the Gurú answered, " Bhái Bálá! God will carry on the business; do you remain as my medium.[181] I will, certainly return in a month; do you till then carry on the business." Then

---

[180] *i.e.*, Let them go, but they must not stay, but return quickly.
[181] *i.e.*, Representative.

CHAP. VI.—MARRIAGE OF NÁNAK. 167

I said, " Very well, Gurú jí ! whatever you shall tell me to do, that I will do." Then they all went to Talwandí. The Gurú gave me no information of what took place there ; I do not know what joys the Gurú experienced in Talwandí, or how he passed his time. Then the Gurú, having come from Talwandí, settled in Sultánpur ; and when he came, he went and visited his sister Nánakí, and Jairám also. Then Mátá Choní also came and fell at the feet of her sister-in-law ; on this, Bíbí Nánakí, said " Be happy," and kissed the forehead of Mátá Choní, and, having pressed her to her neck, seated her by herself. Then next day, Gurú Nának came and sat in the store, and Mátá Choní went to her parents' house ; Múlá came and fetched her ; then Gurú Nának came and began to carry on the business of the store. As Kálú had said, so Múlá found to be the case, and Nának went on behaving just as he used to do, and used to show little love for his wife ; on this, Mátá Choní became annoyed and vexed, for the Gurú showed no care to please her ; and the Gurú never spoke to her, and two months passed without his going to his house. When Múlá came to see his daughter, then the daughter said to Múlá, "O father ! where have you given me (in marriage) ? This man only feeds (poor) people, and has no care for his family." Then Múlá went to Jairám, and entering into words with him, said, " You have drowned me and my daughter," and he said to Nának, "O you ! where were you born ? you were written in my fate, therefore I have got you (as a son-in-law)." Then the Gurú Nának said nothing in reply, and being greatly vexed, he (Múlá) got up and went away. Then he sent for Mátá Choní, and she came to the house of the Gurú ; and they (the parents of Mátá Choní) came and quarrelled with him, and always made it a habit (to do so). Chandoráni was the name of the mother-in-law of Gurú Nának ; and the daughter used to weep much, when with her ; and she (the mother-in-law) became greatly enraged ; and being angry, began to fight with Nánakí and to say, " What wonderful commands are these you have begun to issue ? Have you no fear of God ? Why do you not bring your brother to order ? Will you not look after your sister-in-law ? and will not the sister's husband (Jairám) explain to the sister's brother (Nának) ? What has come into your hearts ? " Then Bíbí Nánakí said, " Listen, O aunt ! if I admonish my brother, what shall I say to him ? My brother is not a thief, nor an adulterer, nor a gambler, nor does he commit evil acts, and whatever he earns, he can do as he likes with it. You may complain if your daughter should remain naked or hungry ; but if, when she is well and happy, with plenty to eat and drink, you abuse us, then you can (do so) ; you know (best). I will not disgrace my mouth by saying any thing to you. As regards jewels, she has jewels, as much as are required, and with regard to clothes, she has clothes sufficient, and as regards food, she suffers no hunger; and I always receive her with welcome, and I never speak to her without using the respectful title of 'Bhábbí' (sister-in-law); but if you shall, unjustly and unprovoked, blame me and the son of a Khattrí, then what can we do? Do as you please, we will say nothing to you. You talk nonsense." Then Chandoráni became silent, and departed, and could say nothing; and, being ashamed, went away. Then she went to her daughter and said, "Listen, O daughter. Sulakhní! (the name she was called by in her mother's house was Sulakhní) your sister-in-law has shamed me, and I could give her no answer. Behold, daughter! do you also soften a little, and be quiet." Then Sulakhní replied, "Mother, I do not remain hungry or in want of clothes; as to jewels, clothes, food and drink, I have all I want." (Then the mother said) "Daughter, if you have all, then why do you blame and abuse the son of a Khattrí?" Then Mátá Choní said, "Mother, what shall I do? he does not love me at all, and he does not speak kindly to me; what shall I do? To whom shall I tell my tale?" Then Chandoráni again came to Bíbí Nánakí, and, on arrival, began to say, "O Nánakí! I spoke again to your brother's wife, Sulakhní; on which she began to say, 'O mother, I do not remain hungry or in want of clothes; I have lots of jewels and clothes, but he never speaks kindly to me, and he never loves me, what shall I do?'" Then Bíbí Nánakí replied, "O my aunt, Chandoráni! do you listen; my sister-in-law's manner is very hard and exacting; and if I send for her, sometimes she comes, and sometimes she does not come; and how does she come? She comes on fire as a red hot iron; but then even, I do not let it come into my mind that she is younger than I, but I say, 'May you be happy.' Well! as she was betrothed through my instrumentality and is the daughter of a respectable Khattrí, perhaps she will gain experience; I will not put her under any obligations;[182] there has been no quarrel[183] between us." Then Chandoráni said, "True, daughter Nánakí; there is no want of anything, but you yourself must know, that the desire of women should be fulfilled." Then Bíbí Nánakí said, "True, my aunt: you speak truly, and she also speaks truly; perhaps God may make things turn out right; do you comfort your daughter, and explain (the matter) to her. O my aunt! you must well know whether I am taking my brother's part. Well aunt! do you now go home; if God will, then I will give

---

[182] i.e. By giving her advice.
[183] Lit. "Joining together." The signification of this sentence is, that if two pieces of cloth are joined together, there still is some very small division left between them; but Bíbí Nánakí says, there has been no joining together between us, for we are, and always have been, one.

CHAP. VI.—MARRIAGE OF NÁNAK.   169

my sister-in-law much comfort." Then Chandoráni went home. One day Gurú Nának came to see Jairám, and he also saw Bíbí Nánakí. Then Bíbí Nánakí said, "God has been very merciful to us to-day, in that you have given us a sight of yourself." Gurú Nának replied, "O Bíbí, I am your slave, you are my elder." Then the Bíbí said, "O brother! in age I am greater, but not in actions; brother, he is the greater, who is greater in actions." The Gurú replied, "O Bíbí, God has revealed this to you; God has been kind to you." Then the Bíbí said "O brother! I shall regard God as being kind to me, when you will do as I say." Then Gurú Nának, being pleased, said, "Speak, Bíbí, I will do what you say, you are my elder sister ; speak then, and whatever you shall say with your mouth, I will do." Then Bíbí Nánakí said, "O brother ! I am made greatly ashamed, because you never give any pleasure to my sister-in-law, and Sir, when we bring into our own family the daughter of our respectable brotherhood, then if they are not made happy, one suffers great shame therefrom. You are a holy man, do you reflect in your mind, and do as I have said." Then Bába Nának said, "O Bíbí! is she in want of anything?" She said, "Brother, why should she be in want, when, by God's gift, she has every thing ; but the comfort received from words is greater than every thing else ; and even if one has nothing else, still one must receive the comfort of kind words, and this the nature of women most certainly demands." Then the Bába said, "O Bíbí! do you take comfort in your mind in this matter; I will do what you say ; and now do you leave off the mention of this, and speak of something else." Then Bíbí Nánakí said, "O brother! this is the matter that is in my mind, that I may behold your offspring and carry them about in my lap." Then Gurú Nának said, "Very well, Bíbí! that which you desire, it will certainly be done." Then having said this, he set off, and did as Nánakí had asked, and began to show affection to his wife.

CHAPTER VII.

The Discourse with Pandat Sámá.

Sámá Pandat said, "Come Múlá, let us see where Nának is?" Múlá said, "Sir! he lives much in the graveyards." Múlá and Sámá both came to Nának. Nának was then seated in a graveyard. Sámá Pandat said, "O Nának, what disguise is this which you have assumed? and what foolish[184] deeds are these you are doing? Come! and set yourself to some work." It was then the spring season (basant), and there came into Gurú Nának's mind a verse in the Basant Rág.

"The king is a child, the city is half built and is in love with the five wicked ones.
There are two mothers, and two fathers, who are saying, Pandat, consider this.
O holy saints, give me such an understanding, by which I may obtain my God (soul's lord)."

The meaning is; the body is a half built city, the mind is the young king; lust, anger, avarice, love, and pride are the five evil things; the two mothers are the eyes; the two fathers are the ears, and they even, in seeing and hearing, are longing for worldly things."

Then again Múlá, the father-in-law, said, "If this fire (of the love of God) has been set alight in you, then why have you given birth to children, and then, being distressed, forsaken them?" Then Gurú Nának recited another verse;

"Within there is a fire, and the forest is putting forth its fresh leaves; the sea is the body;
The sun and moon are both within the body; but you have not obtained this knowledge."

The meaning of it is; the fire within one is desire, and the forest (for keeping up the fire) are one's sons, daughters, wives, wealth and means of subsistence. You, O Sámá Pandat, are the kurm and jawái.[185] The light of the moon is the heart, but the moonshine will only cast its light abroad, when a perfect Gurú is found.

---

[184] *Lit.* "Raw."
[185] Kurm is a daughter's father, and Jawái a son-in-law.

CHAP. VII.—DISCOURSE WITH PANDAT SÁMÁ.

Sámá Pandat said, "O Nának! do you live in your house, but at the same time, both remember God and employ yourself in (the duties of) your own vocation, for God takes care of all." Then Nának recited a third verse—

"Look on him as a worshipper of God, who regards all (friends and foes) as one;

Regard this, as His custom, that He possesses the power of forgiveness."

The meaning of it is, that Rám takes care of all, but His kindness is especially shown on those, who show love and patience, and he, to whom He has given these qualities, His kindness is particularly shown to him. Múlá said, "To-day, he has become mad, and will not listen to the saying of any one." Then Pandat Sámá asked, "Will you listen to what any one will say?" Then Gurú Nának recited the final verse—

"(Alas that) he, who is my companion, will not listen to me, and only desires something to eat;

Nának, the slave of slaves says, "Sometimes it is pleased, sometimes angry."

The meaning of it is this, that the tongue obeys the saying of no one; it utters both praise and reproach; it (desires but) knows not what is fit to eat and what is not; it speaks both bitterly and sweetly, and with it, one has continually to remain; (Nának continued) "Listen, O Sámá Pandat! If God be merciful, then this evil tongue, evil deeds, and evil pleasures will all be removed." On hearing this, the Pandat Sámá was comforted.

CHAPTER VIII.
The discourse with Nawáb Daulat Khán.

Then Múlá Chouá, the father-in law of Gurú Nának, went to the Nawáb and complained. Nawáb Daulat Khán, Lódí, said, "O Yár Khán! who is this? and of whom does he complain?" Yár Khán asked "Múlá! who are you? and of whom do you complain?" Múlá replied, "I am the father-in-law of Nának, the storekeeper, and I complain against Nának." Yár Khán said to the Nawáb, "Nawáb! peace be to you! this is the father-in-law of Nának, and he has a complaint against Nának." The Nawáb said, "Yár Khán, bring him before me." " Yár Khán brought Múlá before him, and the Nawáb asked Múlá, "Well! what complaint have you against Nának?" "Múlá petitioned, "Nawáb, peace be to you! the seven hundred and sixty rupees, which remained over surplus to Nának, I pray that they may be given to Nának's family."[186] The Nawáb said, "O Múlá! but Nának says, give them to beggars." Again Múlá said, "Nawáb, peace be to you! Nának is somewhat mad." Then the Nawáb said, "They certainly have a right to them; let Nának be made over to a Mullá." Then a Mullá went and began to use his charms on the Gurú Nának, but Gurú Nának sat before him quite absorbed in thought, and when he began to put the burnt roll of candle-wick to the nose of Nának, then the Gurú said;—

STANZA.

"He, whose field is spoilt, there is no occasion for (his having) a threshing floor;

Alas for their lives, who write the name of God (on paper), and sell it (as a charm)!"

Then the Múlá began to say, "Who are you? tell me your name." Then the Gurú uttered these verses in the Márú Rág;

"Some call me an evil spirit, some say I am a devil;

Some say, I am a man; but I am simple Nának;

But Nának, the insane, has become mad (only in love for) his God.

And now he knows no one but God.

---

[186] By family, wife is meant.

CHAP. VIII.—DISCOURSE WITH NAWÁB DAULAT KHÁN.

PAUSE.

They look on me as mad, because I am mad in fear (of Him);

There is only one Lord; I do not know any other but Him.

They look on me as mad, because I am always doing the work of That One;

I recognize the command of my Lord, and look on none other but Him as wise;

They look on me as mad, because my Lord has become dear to me;

They look on me as wicked, and all the rest of the world as good."

The Múlá was comforted, and began to praise him, saying, "Nawáb, peace be to you! Nának is not mad; he has met with some saint; he is in his senses." The Nawáb said, "Call Jairám." Jairám came and paid his respects. (The Nawáb asked) "O Jairám! what shall I do? we cannot keep Nának's money, and Nának says, 'give it to beggars;' his father-in-law has complained against him, and the Múlá has said, 'Nának is in his senses;' therefore as you shall say, so I shall act." Jairám was greatly afraid of Nának, and therefore remained silent. The Nawáb asked, "O Jairám! why do you not give an answer?" He gave reply, "O Nawáb, peace be to you! you know everything; what shall I say in reply?" Then the Nawáb said, "O Jairám! his family certainly has a just right to it." Jairám said, "O Nawáb, peace be to you! Nának himself is also present, and has not gone any distance off." The Nawáb said, "Send for Nának." Some one went to call Nának, but Nának would not come. The man returned, and when he came back, said "He will not come." The Nawáb Daulat Khán, becoming angry, said, "Go, seize, and bring him." Then some persons went and told him, "O Nának! the Nawáb is very angry." Nának then rose and got up, and came and paid his respects to the Nawáb. The Nawáb, being very angry, asked "O Nának! why would you not come?" Nának said, "Listen, Nawáb! when I was your servant, then I used to come; now I am not your servant; I am now the servant of God." Then the Nawáb said, "If such be your mind, then come along with me, and say your prayers, for it is Friday to-day." Then Nának said, "Come along, Sir, what you say is very proper." Then the Nawáb, in company with Nának and the Kází and many[187] other respectable people,

---

[187] *Lit.* "How can they be counted?"

went and came and stood in the Juma Masjít;[188] then all the people, who were in the Juma Masjít, began to say, " Behold! to-day Nának has joined this sect." This was noised abroad among all the Hindús; and Jairám, being greatly grieved, returned home. When Nánakí saw that her husband was very sad that day, she rose and got up and said to him, " Sir! what is the reason that you are so sad to-day?" Jairam said, " Hear, O beloved of God! what thy brother Nának has done to-day; he went with the Nawáb to the Juma Masjít to say his prayers, and it has been noised abroad among all the Hindus and Muhammadans of this city, that Nának has, to-day, become a Musalman; then, why should not I be sad?" Then Nánakí said, "Just you get up and eat your food, and do not have any anxiety on account of Nának, but remain happy at heart; O my husband! Nának is my brother and God is his keeper, and no one can look on him with an evil eye; therefore, do you just get up and eat your food." They were thus conversing when a noise was heard. Now Jairám had left Nidhá Bráhman as a spy. Nidhá Bráhman also arrived soon after, and came and blessed Jairám, saying, "O my client,[189] all is well; you need have no anxieties." Then Jairám and Nánakí both began to ask, " Say, O Nidhá Bráhman! how did it end?" Nidhá said, " Sir! I was not inside, but I heard from the mouth of the Musalmáns, that, when the Nawáb said his prayers, Nának stood up; then the Nawáb said to Nának ' O Nának, you came to say prayers; then why do you not say your prayers?' Then Nának said, ' With whom was I to say my prayers?' Then the Nawáb said, ' You could say your prayers with me.' Gurú Nának said, ' You had gone to Kandahár to buy horses; with whom could I say my prayers?' Then Daulat Khán said, ' O Nának, why do you say such false things, when I am standing here?' Nának said, ' Listen, O Khán! your body was standing here, but that, which says the prayers, had gone to Kandahár to buy horses.' Then the Kájí said, ' See, Nawáb, peace be to you! what lies this Hindu tells!' The Nawáb said, ' Kájí! Nának spoke true; at the time, I was bending my head in prayer, my mind had gone to Kandahár to buy horses.' Then the Kájí began to whisper, saying, ' Listen, Khán! I had not gone any where; why could he not say his prayers with me?' The Nawáb said, ' Nának, you could have said your prayers with the Kájí?' Nának said, ' O Nawáb! the Kájí had gone to his home to look after his colt, lest the colt should have fallen into a pit.' On this, they both were satisfied. Bháí, I have just heard this

---

[188] *i.e.* Mosque or Juma Masjít.
[189] Jijmán (feminine jijmání) is the client of a Bráhman, barber, &c., *i.e.* person on whose custom they have a legal right and who must pay them a fee, whether he employ them or any one else.

CHAP. VIII.—DISCOURSE WITH NÁWÁB DAULAT KHÁN.

and come here." Then Bíbí Nánakí said, "Bráhman? where have you left my brother, Nának?" Nidhá said, "O my (female) client! I left him there." Then Jairám began to quarrel with Nidhá, saying, "If you had remained there, Nának would have come out, and you would have met with him." Then Nidha said, "Sir! he was in the Masjít; but all the people had departed and gone to their homes; I did not see him, nor do I know where he went to." Then Nánakí comforted Jairám and began to say "Sir! do you not have any anxiety about him! Nának will come immediately." Just then, Nának came and entered the house of Jairám, and Tulsán, the maid, called out from below. "Your brother has come, O mistress!" Then Bíbí Nánakí was greatly delighted[190] and said, "Sir! did I not say that God was Nának's Helper, and that no one was able to look at Nának with an evil eye?" Jairám was greatly pleased and began to say, "Wife! you indeed have great faith in him;" he then began to ask Nának, saying, "Say brother Nának! what are the circumstances of the occurrence? we were greatly alarmed; do you tell us your own story." Then Nának said, "O brother-in-law! let it be! let the past be past." Then, again, Jairám said, "Brother Nának! if any one shall ask me about this, what shall I say? there is no reliance to be placed on what one hears from people, but what I shall hear from you, that (I know) will be a correct account." Then Gurú Nának said, "Brother-in-law! Daulat Khán began to say his prayers and the Kájí also to say his; but I remained standing on one side. When the Nawáb had finished his prayers, then he began to say to me, 'O Nának! why (this)! I thought you came to say your prayers; then why did you not say your prayers?' I replied.

'The forehead, he knocked on the ground; the heart he raised to heaven;

(But the soul of) Daulat Khán, Pa*th*án, (had gone) to Kandahár to buy horses.'

The Nawáb said, 'I do not understand at all (what you mean, when) you say, I had gone to Kandahár to buy horses; and with whom should you say your prayers.' Then the Kájí said, 'See O Khán! what lies this Hindú tells.' Then the Khán said, 'Kájí, the Hindú speaks truth; at that time when I bent my head, my heart had gone to Kandahár after horses.' Then again the Kájí said, 'Sir, you had, perhaps, gone after the horses, but I had not gone anywhere: could he not have prayed with me?' Then I said to the Kájí. 'Kájí, thou wast in the Masjít; in (thy) courtyard a pit was dug; while bowing down on the ground, (thy) spirit

---

[190] *Lit.* "From one became four."

was with (thy) colt.' Then the Nawáb said : 'Nának, what is this you have said ?' I said 'O Khán! the Káji's horse had brought forth a colt, and in his courtyard is a pit; when the Káji was making his bow, his spirit was dwelling on the colt, (thinking that) perhaps the colt might fall into the pit and be killed; this is what I said, O Khán!' Then Daulat Khán laughing began to say, ' Why Káji! what is Nának saying ? Speak truly!' The Káji replied, 'O Khán, it is indeed so.' The Nawáb said 'Káji! Nának is a perfect devotee, now we can say nothing to him.' Then the Nawáb said, ' Nának, we do not wish to keep your money, but as your father-in-law has complained, and requested that we should not give it to beggars, say now, to whom shall we give the money?' Then I said to the Nawáb, 'I have already told you (my wishes); the rest you can decide.' Then the Nawáb said, ' Listen, Nának! I will give half the money to your family, and half I will give into your own hands to give to beggars.' Then I said, ' I know nothing about it, but you know best.' I have now come, after having said these words. Now, brother-in-law, your heart may either take it well or bad." Then Jairám said, "O brother! whatever you may have done, was good." Then again Nánakí said, "Sir! do you not yet believe? get up and eat your food." Then Jairám said, "O wife! you are Nának's sister, and therefore, you are somewhat partial to him. I was suspicious without cause; Praised be God! Praised be Gurú Nának, and praised be you also, who are his sister, and praised a little be I also, that I am married to you." Then Jairám, Nának, and I (Bálá) ate some food. We were seated eating, when Múlá arrived, and Chandoráni, who was the mother-in-law of Nának, also came with him. Before (this), Múlá and Sámá Pandat, had been quarrelling about Nának, but when Chandoráni, the mother-in-law of Nának, came and saw Nának, she flashed as the lightning flashes, and began to say, "Listen, O Nának! did you marry for this reason that you should have a family and leave them ?" On this, Nának recited a verse in the Márú Rág.—

"When the father and mother join together, the body is formed;

But God decrees what is to happen to that (body):

He decrees its wealth, its glory, and greatness;

But it (the body), being taken up with the love of the world, destroys that form;

O foolish heart! why are you so filled with pride?

(Know) that you will have to depart, when it is your Lord's Will.

PAUSE.

Eschew the world's joys, and then you will easily obtain
   true joys;
We must all leave this house, for none can stay here.
(It would be right) to spend part, and to save part,
If (we knew that) we should return again to the world.
Whilst in the world, we adorn our bodies, and wear silk,
And issue many commands;
We have handsome beds and sleep peacefully;
But why do we weep, when about to die?
This house (of the world) is a whirlpool, O Brother!
Our sins are as stones, which cannot swim therein;
But make a boat of the fear (of God), and seat your soul
   thereon.
Nának says ' (God) reveals (this matter) to a few only.' "

Then Chandoráni went on chatting. Múlá did not again give up his daughter. Lakhmí Dás was at that time a baby in arms, and Sirí Chand was about four years and three-quarters old.

CHAPTER IX.

The discourse with Rái Bulhár.

Then Gurú Nának and we two (Mardáná and Bálú), setting out from Emnábád, arrived in seven days at Talwandí. Then the Rái was informed that Bálá and Mardáná had brought Gurú Nának : Kálú and Lálú and the Ammán Bíbí were all three seated together. They heard that their son Nának had come, but (did not know) where he was. (They said) " He will be at the well of Chandrabhán, Sandhú." Chandrabhán was the name of the father of Bálá ; the three went there together. They went to see, but when they looked, they were surprised at[191] the appearance of Gurú Nának : it was as follows : he had a cloth, about a yard or two long, over his head and shoulders, and a sheet over him, and he also had another cloth round his waist. Kálú, on seeing this his appearance, was greatly enraged. Now Lálú, Vedí, was cleverer than Kálú, although he was his junior in years. Then Lálú said, " Brother Kálú ! we are the sons of Siv Rám, Vedí, and we are the offspring of one and the same Banársí (mother) ; therefore your shame and mine are one ; do you therefore take him to the Rái." Then Kálú became silent. On this, Lálú said, " O boy Nának ! I am your uncle, and there is very little difference in years between your (father) and me ; if you will not mind my brother Kálú, at least mind your (mother), Ammán Bíbí, and me : there is no difference between a father and uncle ; do you go home." Then Gurú Nának said, " To-day I have chosen one abode (that of God) ; and have left the many houses (of the world);" on this his mother fell at his feet. Then Lálú said, " O son Nának ! you are a holy man, and mercy becomes the holy ; well, this is your mother, and I am your uncle, and my brother, Kálú, is your father ; see, my brother is my companion (in asking you) ; you cannot therefore now make any excuse ; moreover as he is older than I, he is as my father." Then Gurú Nának gave utterance to these verses in the Rám Kálí Rág.—

> "Call patient endurance my mother, and contentment my father ;
> Call truth my uncle, for with these my heart has conquered its passions.

---

[191] *Lit.* " What was."

CHAP. IX.—DISCOURSE WITH RÁI BULHÁR.

Listen, Lálú, to these good qualities; but, as all people are bound in chains,

How can they tell what are good qualities?

Affection for God is my brother, and love of the true God is my son;

Patience has become my daughter, and in such I am absorbed.

Forbearance is my companion, and prudence is my disciple;

Call these my family, who always remain with me.

The one Supreme Being is my Lord, and He it is, who created me.

If Nának left Him, and became attached to some one else, he would be put to pain."

Then again Lálú said, "Brother Kálú! he will not mind me; do you try and take him once to the Rái, and then you also will have no further doubts." Kálú said, "Well, son Nának, do you come to the Rái." Then Gurú Nának said, "Very well, Sir, come along." At that time, the Rái was seated on a bedstead; although his body had become old, still as soon as the Rái saw Nának, he commenced to rise: but Nának immediately went and held him down to the bed, and placed his hands on the feet of the Rái; then the Rái said, "Alas, O holy devotee! you have committed a great tyranny. I had called thee to do worship at thy feet; thou hast made me a great sinner." Then Gurú Nának said, "O Rái! you are my elder; I am your servant." Then again the Rái said, "O holy devotee; do you forgive me, and ask God to forgive me." Then Gurú Nának said, "Rái! you were at once forgiven." Then the Rái said, "O holy devotee! do you show some of your kindness to me." Then Gurú Nának said, "Where I go, there you (will go) also."[192] Then the Rái said, "O holy devotee! my desire will then be fulfilled, when you shall have placed your feet on my head." When the Rái had much implored (him), then Gurú Nának came and sat on the bed, and the Rái placed his head at his feet, and was satisfied. Then again the Rái said, "Go, Umaidá, and call Sudhá Bráhman." Then Umaidá called Sudhá Bráhman. Sudhá Bráhman came, and, blessing him, said, "Rái! may you remain happy." Then the Rái said, "Sudhá! bring some cooking vessels from your house, and make a feast, and feed the holy devotee before me." Then the Rái asked, "O holy devotee! what food will you eat?" Then Gurú Nának said, "Rái, what God sends, that I eat." (The Rái said)

---

[192] I.e. We are as one.

"No! holy saint! I asked for some other reason; and if you will command, then I will have a goat killed." Then Gurú Nának said, "This is not the place for commanding; whatever you shall send, that will be well." Then the Rái said, "Come Umaidá, kill a goat and prepare it; be quick!" Then Sudhá Bráhman brought the vessels, and said, "I have brought the vessels." Then the Rái said, "Very well, Sudhá, do you first make something sweet, and then we will have something salted." Then Gurú Nának uttered these verses in the Márú Rág :—

"The sweets are His secrets, the salted things, the hope of gaining Him, and the sour food, the perfect contemplation of Him,

And he, who eats such food, that man is holy.

PAUSE.

O Rái! food of this kind is necessary, and let everything else go;

Give me the fruits of enjoying true gladness, from eating which I may be satisfied.

The tree of the True Gurú, root and branches, has brought forth fruit, do you collect that food, and eat it;

The Name of God is as nectar, and the tongue is as sweet honey, and he will drink of it, to whom God gives it;

The sight of the everlasting Form is the most perfect (form), and he who obtains that, God remains in his heart.

Nának says, 'He who enjoys the taste of the Incorporeal One, will taste much joy;

All other tastes will appear insipid to him, who is taken up with the True Name.'"

Then again the Rái asked, "Well Kálú, how is it?" Then Lálú said to Kálú, "Brother, it is not your business to speak." Then (his mother) Ammán Bíbí, pulling her sheet over her face, seized the Rái's feet, and said, "Rái, I have no other place of complaint but to you; O Rái! if you think it best, keep Nának with you." Then the Rái said, "O holy devotee! your mother is very sorrowful; I cannot however say anything to you." Then Gurú Nának said, "Rái, whatever you have got to say, that say fearlessly." Then the Rái said, "Do you remain here, and pursue agriculture; I will give you some servants (to help you) and you shall have no land-tax to pay." Then Gurú Nának spoke this verse in the Sora*th* Rág;

"The mind is the ploughman, one's deeds are the husbandry; shame is the water, and the body is the field;

The taking of God's Name is the seed, contentment is the drag for levelling, humility is the watchman;

My faith is like the soil, necessary to make the seed grow, and those people,[193] who act thus, are very fortunate;

O foolish man! be not fascinated with the love of this world;

This love for the world has fascinated the world; a few only understand its (falseness)."

Then Lálú said, "Perhaps he wishes to keep a shop; if so, let him set up a shop." Then again, Gurú Nának recited this stanza—

"Make your passing life your shop, and make the True Name your merchandise;

Make the reciting and the thinking of the Name of God your row of pots,[194] and put it in them;

Traffic with the holy, take profit (from their advice), and be easy at heart."

Then again Lálú said to the Rái, "O Rái! if his mind is set on travelling, then let him traffic in horses." Then again Gurú Nának recited a third stanza—

"Listen to the Sástras and make them your merchandise, and take about for sale the horses of Truth;

Make good words your cash, and do not put this off till to-morrow;

Go to God's country (with your horses), for there you will get an abode of joy."

Then again Kálú said, "Take service with some one." Then again Gurú Nának recited the last stanza—

"Placing my mind on God is my service; regarding His Name, my good works;

Eschew evil deeds quickly, and then you will be praised,

O Nának! do you ever remember God's Name, and your joy will be increased four-fold."

Then again the Rái said, "O holy devotee! do you command something, which we may agree to." Then Gurú Nának recited a verse in the Sárang Rág;

"I will command something, which may God grant!

---

[193] *Lit.* "houses, families."

[194] *I.e.* The vessels, in which merchandise is displayed, and which are arranged in rows.

Let me join my hands (in supplication) to Him, over Whom none has any power ;

O Rái! He is such a Master, that the obtaining the like of Him is not to be had ;

We should do those things, which are pleasing to Him ;

Wisdom and command avail nothing (before Him); let him, who wishes to prove this, try it.

Saikhs, Mashâiks, the holy, the saints, of all the fate is written (by God) ;

Ten incarnations have taken place, and they have ruled (in this world) ;

In the end, they all were laid in the dust, but obtained nothing,

Though they were very mighty men, warriors, and brave.

Nának says, 'Do you behold them all, how they have become mixed with the dust?'"

Then again the Rái said, "O holy Saint! do you become a distributer of food ; I will make over to you (the land round) three wells (for the expenses thereof); you shall have no taxes to pay, and you shall remain seated, feeding holy beggars." Then Gurú Nának recited this verse in the Asá Rág —

"There is but one kitchen, that of God, and there is none other ;

No other kitchen will last, or remain for ever in the world.

PAUSE.

O Rái Bulhár! listen to my request, I have a petition to make ;

There is one True Creator, who has formed all created things ;

He is the Pitiful and Bountiful, and He gives order to all things;

He is wealthy enough to give to all, and He takes care of all ;

He has given us life, soul, body, wealth, pleasures and joys :

Of one's self, one can get nothing, all is decreed by God ;

The head of all is The One (God), and the holy and saints are but helpless creatures ;

Nának says ' (From Him), all beg, and God is He who gives to all.'"

Then the Rái said, "O holy devotee! do whatever you wish." When some days had passed, then Gurú Nának said, " O Bhái Bálá and Mardáná! let us go from here." Then we said, "O Gurú, your pleasure is law to us." In the year 1553, on the ninth of the dark half of the month Poh on a Thursday, Gurú Nának prepared to depart from Talwandí. Then the Rái received information, that Nának, the devotee, was again about to depart, and Kálú and Lálú went weeping to the Rái. Then the Rái sent Umaidá to go and give his respects to Nának, the devotee, and to say, "Sir, give me a sight of yourself." As Umaidá was the servant of the Rái, he went and said to Nának. "O holy devotee! The Rái begs and earnestly beseeches you to give a sight of yourself to him." Then, on hearing the words of Umaidá, Gurú Nának rose and got up, and came and blessed the Rái. Then the Rái said, "O holy devotee! forgive my presumption." Then Gurú Nának said, "O Rái! you are forgiven in God's Threshold." Then the Rái said, "O holy devotee! do you do nothing, but remain seated here." Gurú Nának said, "O Rái! it is not in my power to stop here; wherever the Creator places me, there I must stop." Then the Rái began to make much entreaty, but Gurú Nának departed from there; as the Rái saw he was not going to stop, he again said, "O holy devotee! do you command me something." Now Gurú Nának said, "O Rái! I have only one, who will listen to my command: do you now give me your leave to go." Then the Rái said, "To please you is incumbent on me." Now Gurú Nának, when only the last watch of the night remained, and it was towards dawn, went forth to bathe; as he began to look around, he found[195] no well at work; then this speech issued from the mouth of the Gurú: "Alas! there is no tank here either (for me to bathe in)." When the Rái heard of this speech, and the mention of the tank issued from the mouth of the holy devotee, (he, the Rái said) "I am made happy, I will make a tank here, and call it after the name of the holy devotee." Then Gurú Nának and I, (Bálá,) and Mardáná, the musician, also, we three Bháís again went to the house of Lálú; then Bháí Lálú was greatly pleased and said, "Sons! I am greatly pleased, in that you have shown yourselves to me."

[195] *Lit.*—"Behold! what should he see."

CHAPTER X.

The Discourse regarding (the idol) Sálig Rám.

Then the Srí Gurú, after having wandered about, came to Rámtírth; many people had come there for the bathing fair of the 14th of Chet. Then the Sri Gurú saw that a Bráhman, having bathed, was standing before an image of Sálig Rám, and had made a mark of honour on its forehead, and was doing obeisance to it; he had on a dhotí, and his hair was tied in a knot on his head; and he had on his body the twelve marks[196], and was worshipping it (the idol,) and was making much ado before the people in his worship. When he began to turn his rosary, and, shutting his eyes, to reflect on the god, then the Srí Gurú said, "O holy saint and deity! thus shutting your eyes, of whom are you thinking?" He said, " Sir, I am doing service to Sálig Rám." He (Nának) again said " O saint, this image is placed right before you, but when you shut your eyes and reflect, of whom are you thinking?" The Bráhman said, "O holy devotee! in my meditation, all three worlds[197] are seen by me." He (Nának) asked,, " Is everything, that is taking place in the three worlds, seen by you?" Then the Bráhman said, " Yes, Sir! I see everything." When the Bráhman uttered this, the Srí Gurú said quietly to a Sikh, " Go and lift all the images of Sálig Rám from before him." Then the Sikh quietly lifted all the images of Sálig Rám from before him. When the Bráhman opened his eyes, then he beheld that his god was not before him, and he began to weep. Then Nának asked, " What is it, O holy saint and deity? What is this that has happened? Why are you weeping?" He said, " Sir! some one has taken my god from before me." (Nának said) " Listen, saint! when you were meditating, you saw all three worlds; look and see where it is." Then the Bráhman told him his real true (state), and said, " Sir! I, for the sake of my stomach, tell lies, and, using deception, thereby get a few morsels to eat; O holy devotee! by means of this image, I get my subsistence; therefore, for the sake of Sri Gobind, make whoever has taken it restore it to me." When the Bráhman became very humble, and began to beseech imploringly,

---

[196] *I.e.* On the forehead, tips of both ears, on the temple above both ears, throat, on the arms below the elbow, on the wrists, on the breast, and on the back, below the nape of the neck.

[197] *I.e.* The world, the world above, and the world below.

CHAP. X.—DISCOURSE REGARDING THE IDOL SÁLIG RÁM.

then the Srí Gurú took compassion on him, and said to that Bráhman, "O holy deity and saint! do you leave off telling lies, and give up this habit of telling lies for the sake of getting a livelihood; God will somehow give you food, therefore do not tell lies; but meditate on the name of Rám with a pure heart." Then the Bráhman said; "If you will have compassion on me, then I will not tell lies; but Sir, I cannot get my food without telling lies." Then the Srí Gurú Nának said, "O saint! why do you tell lies? You say that when you shut your eyes and meditate, the three worlds appear manifest to you; but have you any information at all of the wealth and goods, which are buried behind your back, just where you are seated?" Then the Bráhman said, "Sir, how can I know it?" Then the Srí Gurú said, "O saint! do you get up and dig the earth." Then the Bráhman dug the earth, and beheld and found much wealth. Then the Bráhman, on seeing the wealth, was much astonished, and came and fell in obeisance at the feet of the Srí Gurú. Then the Srí Gurú, laughing at him, spoke and gave utterance to this verse in the Dhanásrí Rag;

"It (the idol) has no power over death, or any power over time, nor has it any true power;

The place (of faith) is destroyed by it, and the world is ruined by it, and people are by it made miserable.

In this Kali age, the name of Rám is the only good thing.

But you, who shut your eyes and hold your nose, do it to deceive the world."

The meaning of this is, that Bába Nának said, "O saint! this image of stone, which you worship, has no power over death, or to keep you from dying; nor, if you do not worship it, to kill you. Is there any profit in worshipping it? but, O saint, this, that you shut your eyes and hold your nose for the sake of deceiving the world, is a snare and delusion, and will, one day, seize your own throat;[198] true salvation and pardon is that which is obtained from remembering the name of Rám; and in this, the Kali age, the name of Rám is the one good thing, therefore remember him. Listen, saint! whatever holy man shall meditate on the name of Rám with pure heart, he will obtain salvation; unless we remember the Name of God, all other service and worship, visiting the holy places on the Ganges, and pilgrimages, they are worthless acts, for they are only made to the temples themselves, and are all as wind. In the Kali age, whoever wishes for salvation must meditate on the True Gurú with perfect heart, and he will then be saved. Listen, O holy saint and deity! that

---

[198] *I.e.*, Will bring its own punishment on you.

which you worship is all falsehood and deceit; leave it off."
Then the Bráhman again petitioned, " O great king ! This wealth,
which you pointed out to me behind my back, did you put it
there, or did you get any one else to put it there ? How did you
know about it ? Tell me exactly about it." Then the Srí Gurú
said, " Listen, saint.

VERSE.

' You seize your nose with your hand, and see the three
worlds !

But you cannot see anything that is behind you ; this is
a wonderful thing.' "

The meaning is, that the lord (Nának) said, " O saint! you
said that when you shut your eyes and meditated, you saw the
three worlds, but you had no information of this wealth, which
was behind your back ? Why did you tell such lies ?" Then
the Bráhman said, " Sir ! if I had been truthful, then I would
have seen it ; but I am false, and my deeds are also false ; therefore how could I see it ?" Then the Srí Gurú said, " O saint! everything is seen by true hearts, but nothing is seen by the false ;
listen, O holy saint and deity ! all the wealth, there is in the
world, is all buried in the earth ; no one has consumed it, nor has
any one used it up to clothe himself ; the wealth of the four ages is
all collected and buried in it. We eat food, we drink water and
we wear clothes ; no one eats gold, nor does any one eat silver, nor
does any one eat copper ; this custom is prevalent in the world, and
is its regular usage ; listen, O holy saint and deity ! All who are
the servants of God, they show kindness to others, and care not
for wealth ; and their sight is like that of God, (they can see
everything) they do not see like men ; true saints can see everything ; listen saint ! why do you tell a lie, and say, that when you
shut your eyes, you see the three worlds, yet cannot see the
wealth, which is placed behind you ? those who are the true
saints of God, they can see every thing.

CHAPTER XI.

Conversation about the Árti Sohilá.[199]

Now one day, the Srí Gurú saw that the world had no information as to what things were being done in it, or that, at the Threshold of the Great God, there is consideration paid to the acts one does, and that a register is kept of good and evil deeds in God's Threshold, and that for sin, punishment is allotted, and reward to virtue. (Then he said). "Bháí Bálá! the world is entirely engaged in sin." Then Srí Bába Nának said, "O great God! according as Thou hast given me understanding, so I speak; beyond that is in Thy power." Then the Srí Gurú, Bába Nának, did obeisance, and, having done his obeisance, stood before the Creator, and began to recite this Árti song in the Dhanásrí Rág.[200]

"The earth and sky are Thy plate; the sun and moon are Thy lamps; the circle of the stars are as Thy pearls.

Sandal is Thine incense;. the wind is Thy chaúri;[201] and all the forests are Thy flowers, O God!

O fear-removing God! What sort of hymn shall I sing? Thy hymn (what is it like?)

The unending sounds of Heaven are Thy musical instruments;

Thousand are Thine eyes, but yet Thou hast no eye;

Thousand are thy forms, but yet Thou hast none;

---

[199] Árti is a ceremony performed in adoration of the gods, by moving burning lamps circularly round the head of the image, or before it, accompanied with boisterous music and ringing of bells.

Sohilá is singing practised by exorcists in praise of the person exorcised.

[200] The circumstances, under which this hymn was uttered, must be borne in mind, to a due understanding thereof. A priest had begun to perform Árti to his god, but, as Nának had none of the requisites necessary at such a ceremony, he therefore gave utterance to these verses.

[201] Or brush made of hair, or the tail feathers of the peafowl generally, to drive off flies with. It is considered a badge of honour. The plate, lamps, pearls, placed as offerings, &c., are all necessary requisites of the ceremony. These are all placed around at the time of performance.

Thousand are Thy fine feet, but yet not one of Thy feet is devoid of fragrance.

Thousand, indeed, are Thy fragrances, and I am absorbed in Thy wonderful works;

The splendour, that is in every thing, that splendour is Thine! and from its beams, light is diffused to all.

By means of a Gurú, Thy knowledge is obtained; that is a proper hymn, which is pleasing to Thee.

My mind desires the dust of Thy lotus-like feet, O Harí! and night and day, my heart thirsts for it, (Thy Name);

Give the water of compassion to Nának, who is Thy Sárang,[202] and grant that he may obtain a longing for Thy Name."[203]

The meaning is; "The sky and the earth, these two orbs, are Thy plate, O Lord! and the stars are the pearls in Thy plate; and the sun and the moon are Thy light; the scents of the earth are Thine incense, O Lord! and the wind is Thy chaúri, and all the forests of the earth are Thy flowers; all living creatures in the world, that have mouths and eyes, the light, which is in those eyes, is Thy light, and, from Thy light only, do they obtain light; and in all the innumerable forms (in the world)

---

[202] This small bird, also called the pappíhá, is said to have a hole in its head, through which it drinks and satisfies its thirst. It is commonly believed to cry very loudly for the rains to commence, as it remains thirsty for ten months in the year, and only obtains water, to alleviate its thirst, during the rains.

[203] The following translation of these lines is given by Dr. Trumpp in his Ádi Granth, page 19, but I think he has, in his translation, missed some of the principal points. It remains with the reader to decide which is best.

"The dish is made of the sky, the sun and moon are made the lamps, the orbs of stars are, so to say, the pearls.

The wind is incense-grinding, the wind swings the fly-brush, the whole blooming wood is the flame (of the lamps).

PAUSE.

What an illumination is made! In the region of existence (world) there is no (such) illumination (made) to thee. The kettle-drum sounds an unbeaten sound.

Thousands are thy eyes, and yet thou hast no eye; thousands are thy forms and (yet) thou hast not one!

Thousands are thy pure feet, and (yet) not one foot is without odour; thousands are thy odours, thus walkest thou, O enchanting one!

In all (creatures) is light, he is the light. From his light, light is made in all.

By the testimony of the Gurú the light becomes manifest; what is pleasing to him, that becomes an Árti (illumination).

My mind is longing after the nectar of the lotus of the foot of Hari, daily I am thirsting after it.

Give water of mercy to the deer Nának, by which dwelling may be made in Thy name."

CHAP. XI.—ABOUT THE ÁRTÍ SOHILÁ.

Thy form alone is present. Thousand are Thy pure feet, and all the heavenly musicians and deities meditate only on Thy honour; and all the uncountable hosts of heavenly musicians, gods, men, saints, are all fascinated with Thy doings; none can find the end of one single act of Thine, nor can any one praise Thee; then how, Lord can I sing Thee a hymn? O Most Mighty Lord! the light, which is in all mankind, it is the (reflection of the) Face of Thee, the Great God; and the light of Thee, the great God, is diffused in every heart; by Thy light, everything obtains light; the lotus-like feet of Hari, they are the lotus flower, and the dust off them is my heart; the dust of Thy feet, which is called 'Makrand,' for it my heart greatly longs. In the same way as the bumble-bee greatly longs for the lotus flower, so does my heart eagerly desire the lotus-like feet of the great Lord; and day and night, this is my desire; but what is that (desire) like? In the same way, as the rainbird cries day and night for the clouds and rain, so my heart also, thirsting after the name of the Great Lord, cries out for Thee. O holy and Great Lord! do Thou have compassion on me, and give me to drink the water of Thy name."

CHAPTER XII.

The discourse in Sanglá with Rájá Siv Náth.

Gurú Nának went to the land of Sanglá Díp to the city of Rájá Siv Náth, the king of that place: Siv Náth had such power, that whoever asked for a son, to him he gave a son: and if any one asked for rain, then he gave rain: he was a worker of miracles, but when Gurú Nának went and seated himself there, then he lost his power of working miracles, and if any one asked any thing, they did not get it. Then the king was astonished, and said to his minister, "O Paras Rám! what is this that has happened? Has any one in my city committed some sin?" Then Paras Rám replied, "O King! no one has committed a sin, but a certain wandering devotee has arrived in your city, and he has two disciples with him, and this is what has taken place (in consequence)." The king said, "O Paras Rám, enquire about them." Then Paras Rám, having prepared some good food, took it and went and placed it before Gurú Nának. Then Gurú Nának said, "What is it, Bháí?" Then the minister, Paras Rám, replied, "O holy saint! this is some food, which the king Siv Náth has sent you." Then Gurú Nának uttered this verse in the Márú Rág;

> "The delicacies and dainties of this food are many, but its sweet taste is bitter poison.
>
> Regard him only as good, on whom God shows His compassion."

Paras Rám took back the food, and went and said to the king, "O king! he will not eat the food." Then the king said, "O Paras Rám, what thing is he a trafficker in?"[204] Then Paras Rám said, "Sir! I cannot tell, but if you shall order, then I will get some fairies, and take them to him." Then the king said, "O Paras Rám! what you have said is just the thing." Then Paras Rám got some fairies, and brought them, and came and made them stand before him, (and asked) "What do you want?" (Nának replied) "Paras Rám, listen to my words." Then again Gurú Nának recited this stanza;

> "These are leaves[205] filled with poison, but they have been placed in, and smeared with, sugar."

---

[204] *I.e.*, What does he want?

[205] Nának compares the beautiful women to leaves, and says that although they have been made to look sweet and are well clothed and of lovely form, their hearts were evil, as their purpose was to win a man's heart from the love of God, and thus to destroy his life.

They have extremely lovely forms, but they ruin a man."[206]

Then again Paras Rám went to the king and said, "He will not take the fairies also." The king said, "Paras Rám, it is the cold season, take some fine clothes to him." Then Paras Rám took some fine clothes, and came and placed them before Gurú Nának. Then Gurú Nának recited a third stanza ;

"Bodily clothes are falsehood: from seeing them, be not deceived,

For gold, silver, wealth and riches are the root of hell."

Then Paras Rám, the minister said, "Tell me your desire."

Then Gurú Nának recited a fourth stanza ;

"Carry on your rule, but (know) that your power of working miracles is a falsehood :

Obey the commands of God, and then patience will spring up in your heart."

Then Paras Rám went to the king and said, "O king ! he speaks of something quite different ; he ridicules your power of working miracles."

The king was intelligent[207], and went himself to Gurú Nának and, joining his hands, stood before Gurú Nának. Then Gurú Nának recited the last stanza ;

"Listen, O Rájá Siv Náth ! if your understanding and senses are right ;

Nának says, 'Remove the veil (of ignorance) from your heart, and then you will become the servant of servants !'"[208]

Rájá Siv Náth seized the feet of Gurú Nának, and began to say, "Sir! do you bestow salvation on me." Then Gurú Nának was greatly pleased with the king. On hearing this circumstance, Gurú Angad became overjoyed with ecstasy : and Gurú Angad remained in that same state for twenty-seven watches, and such ecstasy came over him, that no one can properly describe that state. After that, when Gurú Angad opened his eyes and came to himself, then he said, "Speak on, Bháí Bálá." Then Bálá began to repeat more (as follows) for Angád to write.—Then Rájá Siv Náth took Gurú Nának to his palace, and began to ask, "Sir! what is your name ? are you a devotee ?" Then Gurú Nának recited this verse in the Márú Rág;

"He is a Jogí, who is altogether joined to the spotless Name of God for then no speck (of evil) will cling to him.

---

[206] Lit. "The birth of a man.
[207] This is brought in, to show what the verse, recited by Nának, refers to.
[208] I.e. a devotee of God or a humble servant, who does service to all).

The Lord is his friend, and always remains with him ; he will escape from (all future), births and deaths ;
O God ! what is Thy name? and what Thy caste ?
When the mind calls (God) inside its palace, it asks clear questions (from Him)."[209]

PAUSE.

Then again the king asked, "Sir! are you a Bráhman?" Gurú Nának replied with another stanza ;

"He is a Bráhman, who meditates on the Supreme Being, and offers, (in place of flowers) praise to God ;
He has only one Name, He is the only one God, and in the three worlds He is the one Light."

Then again the Rájá asked, "Sir! are you a Khattrí?" Gurú Nának replied with a third stanza;

"This heart is the scale, the tongue is the scale beam; with them, unceasingly, weigh (utter) His name ;
The shops are all one, and over them there is one shop-keeper, and the traders are all of one kind ;
The true Gurú saves one from both heads,[210] and he will understand this, who has the one hope (of God above) ; and in his heart, there will be no doubt ;
He, who deposits His songs (in his heart), will dispel all fears, and day and night always serve Him."

Again the Rájá asked, "Sir! are you a Gaurakh?"[211] Then the Gurú Nának responded with the stanza of completion ;

"Above are the heavens, and above the heavens is Gaurakh, and His unreachable form dwells there ;
From the words of the Gurú, strangers and relatives[212] appear all as one ; but Nának is an Udásí (devotee)."

Then King Sív Náth became a disciple of Gurú Nának, and began to meditate on the Incorporeal One, and caused the people of his city also to meditate on Him. In that place, Gurú Nának composed the Parán Sanglí and in it, he wrote one hundred and thirteen chapters. Gurú Nának remained with king Sív Náth for two years and five months. When he was about to depart, then the king said, "O Gurú, do you remain here." Then Gurú Nának replied, "Bháí Sív Náth ! it is imperative for me to depart." The Rájá did obeisance to him, and Gurú Nának said, "May God take care of you." (Before departing), he (Nának) seated the king on the throne.

---

[209] This is in reference to the king having called Nának inside his palace, and asking him his name, &c.
[210] I.e. Being born and dying.
[211] I.e. A god, from gau (earth) and rakh (preserver).
[212] Lit. "Those of the house."

CHAPTER XIII.

The discourse with Mián Mitthá.

Then proceeding on, he arrived at the village of Mián Mitthá and alighted in his garden; Mián Mitthá was the disciple of Sáhi Abdul Rahmán. First of all, a meeting took place between the Srí Gurú and Abdul Rahmán. Sáhi Abdul Rahmán came and sat in the garden; Mardáná was already seated there, and they engaged in much conversation with each other. Then, Sáhi Abdul Rahmán said, "O Nának! to-day you have made me very happy, and you have shown great kindness to me, Sir! you have given me a sight of yourself, and, from the sight of you, I have been much helped." Then, after this, Sáhi Abdul Rahmán returned to his house, and, as he was going along, met Mián Mitthá, who was his disciple; he began to say "O Sáhi, you, to-day, seem highly pleased." Then Sáhi Abdul Rahmán said: "I have to-day met with one of God's beloved ones, and, from seeing him, I have been very much pleased." Then Mián Mitthá, said, "What is his name? Is he a Hindú or a Musalmán?" Sáhi Abdul Rahmán replied, "He is a Hindú, and his name is Nának, do you also go and get a sight of him; then you, also, will obtain profit (therefrom)." When Mián Mitthá came to visit him, at that time Mardáná was singing a verse in the Sirí Rág; and this is what was being uttered by the mouth of Mardáná;

> "If I should become a bird, and should fly and go to a hundred heavens,
> And, in flying, should let myself be seen by none, and should neither eat nor drink anything,
> Still I could not find out Thy worth;
> How far then shall I extol Thy name."

On hearing this, Mián Mitthá suffered loss in his stock (of faith); he had gone for profit, but he suffered loss therein.

Then the saint asked, "Mián did you see him?" He replied, "O reverend saint, peace be on thee! how could I visit him? There they talk nothing but what is profane." Then the chief said, "Speak and let me hear what profane thing they were saying there." Then the Mián said, "They were there uttering this verse:—

'If I should become a bird and should fly and go to a hundred heavens,

And, in flying, should be seen by none, and should neither eat nor drink anything,

Still, I could not find out Thy worth,

How far then shall I extol Thy name?'

Now listen O saint! in our reckoning, there are in all fourteen heavens; was it not great profanity, when he talked of a hundred heavens? Now, Sir, how can there be a hundred heavens, when there are but fourteen heavens in all, seven below and seven above?" Then the saint said "You have made a mistake: Why? (because), although we have only information of fourteen heavens, still he knows of a hundred heavens; and therefore he says, 'Still I could not find out Thy worth, and how far then shall I extol Thy name?' Now do you come with me and I will have your fault forgiven." Then Sáhi Abdul Rahmán brought Mián Mitthá to the Srí Gurú, and came and fell at his feet; and making him fold his hands together, petitioned saying, "O Bába! forgive the fault of this man, for the sake of your love for God." Then the Srí Gurú said, "O Sáhi, I have not even seen this person." Then Sáhi Abdul Rahmán said, "O Bába! he went away disappointed in his intention; for the Lord's sake, forgive him his fault, for he is greatly in error." Then he (Nának) said, "As his intention (was), so will be the accomplishment of his work; for as one does, so one obtains." Then Sáhi Abdul Rahmán said, "Sir, he is still under a curse; for God's sake forgive him his fault; he is a great sinner, but he desires to come under your protection; then cast your kind glance on him." Then he again fell at the feet of the Srí Gurú Bába, on which he (Nának) said: "O Mardáná, play the rebec." Then he recited this verse;—

> "If my years were uncountable, and I lived on wind and water;
>
> If I lived in a cave, where I could see neither sun nor moon, and I had not room to sleep even in my dreams,
>
> Still I could not find out Thy worth, how far then shall I extol Thy name?
>
> The True God lives ever fixed in His Own place;
>
> I have heard His word and tell it (to others), but He can, if He will, show kindness.

CHAP. XIII.—DISCOURSE WITH MÍÁN MITTHÁ. 195

PAUSE.

Were I to continually give my body to be sawn in pieces, and were I to give it to be ground in the mill;

And were I to burn my body in the fire; and were I to be turned into ashes;

Still I could not find out Thy worth, how far then shall I extol Thy name?

Were I to become a bird, and fly and go to a hundred heavens;

And, in flying, should be seen by none, and should neither eat nor drink any thing,

Still, I could not find out Thy worth, how far then shall I extol Thy name?

Nának says, 'Had I thousands of maunds of paper, with Thy name written thereon, and were to read it all;

And if my ink should never come to an end, and I could go on writing like the wind,

Still I could not find out Thy worth, how far then shall I extol Thy name?

The True God lives ever fixed in His own place.'"[213]

But when this verse was finished, and the wrong impressions of Mián Mitthá were still not effaced, then the Srí Gurú

---

[213] Dr. Trumpp in his Ádi Granth, page 22, gives the following translation of these lines:—

(If my) life (be) crores, crores, if wind drinking (be my) nouriture.
If (dwelling) in a cave I do not see neither moon nor sun, (if) I have no place for dreaming (and) sleeping.
Yet Thy value is not found out (by me), how great shall I call Thy name.
    PAUSE.
True is the Formless in his own place.
Having heard, heard the word (one) tells it; if it pleases (to any), he longs for it.
(If) I be killed and cut (in pieces) repeatedly, if I be ground on the grinding stone.
(If) I be burned with fire, (if) I be reduced to ashes (mixed with ashes)
Yet Thy value is not found out (by me), how great shall I call Thy name?
(If) having become a bird I roam about and go to a hundred heavens.
(If) I do not come into the sight of any one, nor do drink and eat any thing.
Yet Thy value is not found out (by me), how great shall I call Thy name?
O Nának! if having read, read a paper consisting of a hundred thousand maunds consideration, (an idea of him) be made.
(If) the ink do not run short, (if) the wind move the pen.
Yet Thy value is not found out; how great shall I call Thy name?

made it plain to his mind. At length one day, Mián Mitthá obtained light on the matter, and then he said, "Nának is a good devotee, but if I shall see him again, I will squeeze him as the juice is squeezed out of a lime." Then the Srí Gurú also said "O Mardáná, what does Sekh Mitthá say?" Then Mardáná said. "He is thy musical instrument, and as you play on him, so he sounds." Then Nának said "O Mardáná; if I shall see Mián Mitthá, then I will press him as they press sugar-cane." Then Mián Mitthá said, "Come and let us go and visit Nának." Then his disciples petitioned "Sir, you have before this commanded that, if you shall see Nának again, then you will squeeze him, as the juice is squeezed out of a lemon." Then Mián Mitthá also replied, "An answer also has come to me from there, viz., 'If I shall see Mián Mitthá again, then I will press him out, as they press out sugar-cane.'" Then Mián Mitthá came to visit him, and they met. First of all Mián Mitthá recited this stanza;

"First (in honour) is the Name of God, then that of the prophet, His messenger;
If Nának shall accept the Kalima, then he will be accepted at His Threshold."

Then the Srí Gurú Bábá Nának said,

"O Mián, is there not place for any one else at His door? Surely all, who remain there, are treated alike."

Then again Sekh Mitthá said,

"Can a lamp burn without oil?"

Then the Srí Gurú gave reply,

"Study the Kurán and all books,
And place the wick of the fear of God in this heart of yours,
And then, without oil, your lamp will burn brightly;
Get this light, and then you will obtain your Lord.
If His words take effect on this your heart.
Then (you will look on) this world as transient; [214]
If you shall do Him service in this world,
Then you will obtain an abode in His Threshold;"
Nának says; 'Such an one fearlessly[215] will go to Heaven and praise Him;'
Well, even if you have not anything, then offer what you can."

---

[214] *Lit*, Coming and going.
[215] *Lit* "Swinging about his arms."

Then the Sekh petitioned, "Why should not those, who are literate, be accepted by God? and where are that Kurán and those books, Sir, from studying which, one may become perfect? and who are those devotees who are fit for that door? And what fast is that, from practising which, one's heart can be established? And what prayers are those, by the offering of which, God will show himself, Sir?" Then the Srí Gurú said, "Mardáná, play the rebec," and he recited these verses in the Márú Rág ;[216]

"O ye servants of God! He is pure and beyond our reach;
Forego the thoughts and business of the world;
Become the dust of the feet of beggars and travellers;
For such devotees are accepted at His door.

(1). Make truth, your prayer, and faith, your carpet for praying on;
Subdue your desires, and give up your Ásá ;[217]
Look on the body as your mosque, and the mind as your priest;
And take for your creed that God is pure and holy;

(2). Do good, and make it your shara and shariat; [218]
Look on giving up the world and searching for God, as the true road (tarikat);
O Abdul! look on conquering your heart as true knowledge, (márifat);
Then you will obtain the truth (hakíkat), and you will never again die.

(3). Look upon the study of God with your heart as your Kurán and other books;
And keep the ten (female) organs from wickedness;
Control the five male (passions) by faith,
Then your alms and patience will be accepted.

(4). Let love to mankind be your Makka, and let your fasting be the humbling yourself in the dust;
Let Heaven be your spiritual guide, and act according to its commands;
Look on the service of God as your Húrís, light, and perfumes, and make the pure God, your place (of shelter).

---
[216] It must be borne in mind that, in the following verses, various Muhammadan technical religious terms are made use of, and Nának explains what each really is.
[217] A stick on which the head is placed, when praying.
[218] Muhammadan Code of Law.

(5). Regard obtaining the truth as your judge, (Kájí) and purifying your heart as your pilgrim, (Hájí);

Make leaving off evil deeds your priest (Mullá), and the praising of God your devotee (darvesh.)

(6). At all times, and at all seasons, remember your Creator in your heart, O Mullá!

Make your rosary of remembrance, the subduing of the ten female (organs);

Make humility your traditions (sunnat); this is your chief duty.

(7). Regard all these things in your heart as things of fact;

And regard a family, O brother, as altogether a source of trouble;

Saints, chiefs and nobles, all will vanish;

One place only will remain, *viz.*, the door of God.

(8). Let your first (or morning) prayer be His praise; your second, patience;

Your third, humility; your fourth, alms;

Your fifth, keeping the five (male organs) in one place;

These will be all sufficient for you at the five times (of prayer.)

(9). Make, regarding God as all in all, your religious duty (madípha or wazífa);

And make the forsaking of your evil nature, the water pot for ablution (kúga) of your hands;

Know that God is one, and make this your call to prayer;

For (those, who so do), are truly great and happy.

(10). Make what is true and lawful, your food;

Wash away the infirmities of your heart in the river (of the name of God);

He, who obeys the True saint (God), he will dwell in paradise;

And he will have no fear of either Azráil or hell.

(11). (Remember) the Creator of your body, and regard faith as your wife;

Regard belief in God as your pleasure and joy;

Remove from yourself your impurities, and be pure, and regard this as your Hadís;

And make belief in the unchangeable Form, the turban (dastár) for your head.

(12). They are true Musalmáns, who are gentle hearted,
And who wash away the impurities of their hearts;
And who do not approach the desires of the world.
Such are purer and cleaner than flowers, silk and ghí.

13. And those who profess the love of God, (they do so) from the kindness of His kind love;
And that man will be truly a brave man;
Be he a Sekh, Masáikh, or Káji,
Or be he a servant of God, His eye is on them all.

14. All power belongs to the All-powerful, and all things proceed from the All-bountiful;
His praise and love are boundless, and He is the All-compassionate;
Verily the true rule belongs to the True God;
Nának says, 'Who understands this, he will obtain release and reach Heaven.'"

Then, on hearing these verses, Mián Mitthá said, "This one Name, that you praise so, what is that one Name?" Then the Srí Gurú said, "O Mián, who is able to set forth the glory of the praise of that One Name?" Then Mián Mitthá said, "Sir! be kind and explain." Then the Srí Gurú, seizing Mián Mitthá by the arm, took him aside. Then the Srí Gurú said, "O Sir! O, Sir!" Then after his saying this, the second[219] Mián Mitthá was turned into ashes, and Sekh Mitthá beheld that it was turned into a handful of ashes. Then, again, a voice was heard, and it got up. On this, Sekh Mitthá came and kissed his (Nának's) feet. Then the Srí Gurú, having passed into the house of oblivion, (*i.e.*, trance), recited the following in the Tilang Rág;

"Thy love is shown to those, who attend on Thee;
And those who wait not on Thee, they remain without Thy love;
The faithful are Thy friends;
The disbelieving are Thine enemies;
Infidelity is a great sin;
And anger is unlawful;
Carnal desire is the devil;

---

[219] It is said that Nának, by way of exhibiting his miraculous powers, produced an exact likeness of the Mián, and showed it to him.

And pride is infidelity :
The unbelieving is impure ;
And the gentle at heart is pure ;
Wisdom is gentleness ;
And those, who are without worldly desires, are saints ;
Those, who have not faith, are dishonoured ;
The ungrateful is made ashamed ;
Truth is Heaven ;
Falsehood is Hell ;
Violence is Tyranny ;
And His praise is true ablution ;
The calling to prayer is His voice ;
Theft is avarice ;
Whoredom is impurity ;
Patience is humility ;
And impatience is forbidden ;
Those, who are on the right road, have spiritual teachers ;
And those, who are out of the road, are without a spiritual teacher ;
The honest man is the friend of God ;
And the dishonest man is of no worth ;
The sword is for brave men,
And justice is for kings ;
He, who weighs these things and understands them,
Him, Nának will call wise."

Then Pír Mitthá, on hearing this, came and seized his feet, and said, " Sir ! you are some saint of God ; before, I vainly wandered about erring ; do you forgive me." Then he was pleased with Mián Mitthá, and all the doubts of Mián Mitthá were removed.

CHAPTER XIV.

The discourse with the Sidhs, or Hindú saints.

Then the Srí Gurú Nának rose, and departed from there, and as he looked about, he saw many Sidhs seated on the road. The Srí Gurú hailed them, saying, " My respects, O Sidhs!" Then Gorakh said " Our respects to the first Being! come O Nának, thou devotee!" Then again Gorakh asked in a gentle tone, "What is the cover of this earth? and what is the key of Heaven? how many stars are there in the heavens? In the Kali Age, how many gods are there, O man? and in how many streams does the rain fall?" The Gurú replied, "The heavens[220] are about four fingers breadth, and there are two circles of stars in the heavens; in the Kali Age, the gods are very many, O man! and the rain falls in nine streams." Then, again, the Sidhs called the angel of death, and he, death, read this verse;

"I will kill thee standing; I will kill thee sitting; I will kill thee sleeping.

In the four ages, my great net has been spread, then, son, where will you remain?"

Then the Srí Gurú recited this stanza;

"If I am awake in my love to God standing, awake, sitting, and awake, sleeping,

And remain apart from the four ages, then I shall be the son of my Father, (God), and shall be safe from you."

(Then death said);

"If I shall make all the earth into a cauldron and spread myself in all directions,

And if I shall turn the four ages into fuel, then where will your body be?"

Then the Srí Gurú Bábá Nának replied;

"I will subdue my organs and be true of speech, and reach above the earth;

I will become wider and higher than the heavens;

---

[220] The heavens are compared by Nának to the mouth, the two circles of stars to the eyes, the rain to the body, the nine streams being the two ears, two eyes, two nostrils, mouth, the organ of excretion and the member of generation.

My organs and tongue shall all be with the one God;
Nának says, 'By these means, I will escape from death.'"
Then death, being distressed, said, "Sir I am under your command." The Sri Gurú then comforted death, (saying);

VERSES.

"What matters it, if this body should not die,
Or if it should live in doubt for hundreds of years;
One's age may increase, but in the end, one's body must fall into the hands of death;
When death comes, where will you go?
In the sea, earth and air, death and God have rule.
When death comes, whereto will you flee?
What world is it, to which you will go and flee?
The fourteen heavens are in the power of death,
Where then will you go and flee from death?
Rám and the Muhammadan Prophet both were subjected to death.
O Nának! death must be accepted by you.
It will of itself come, and will, of itself, carry you off.
When death comes, it will carry you off as it wishes;
If you reflect well, you will know that you must die.[221]
Nának says, 'Wherever you look, there it (death) is standing.'"

Then, on hearing this verse, death became satisfied, and, being comforted, took his departure. Then the Sidhs crossed the sea. Then these words were said (by Nának) "O Mardáná! let us cross the sea also." Then the Srí Gurú also, having crossed the sea, paid his respects to the Sidhs. Then the Sidhs said, "Our respects to the first Being." Then the Sidhs said, "Knowest thou a city which has ten doors? O True Gurú! meditate and tell us the truth of this; do you meditate on God and be happy and joyful; first lay yourself waste, then make yourself populous." Then the Srí Gurú replied "There is a city, (the body) which has ten doors. Speak O true Gurú, for this is the true explanation of this; yes, do you meditate also and be happy, and joyful; first lay yourself waste, and then be populous." Then the Sidhs said, "O man! have you also taken (to

---

[221] First conquer your evil passions, and then you will be blessed with Divine knowledge to interpret this.

CHAP. XIV.—DISCOURSE WITH THE SIDHS, OR HINDÚ SAINTS.

yourself) a Gurú?" Then the Srí Gurú replied, Do you recite some of your verses, and I will choose him as my Gurú, from whose songs I obtain confidence." Then the Sidhs said, "We will recite some verses; do you listen and whosesoever's verses give you confidence, make him your Gurú." Then the Srí Gurú said, "Sirs! recite some verses." First of all, Isur Náth said,

"He is a girhí[222] who has his members under control, and who performs adoration, devotion, abstinence and alms,

And who looks on his body as to be employed in charity and doing good;

Such a girhí is pure as the water of the Ganges;

Íshur says that the True Form,

In the first element (God), has neither marks nor form."

The second, who spoke, was Gorakh; he said,

"He is an awadhútí[223] who purifies himself from evil deeds,

And eats the food of alms and affliction,

And who begs at the doors of his own body, (by thinking on the Name of God);

Such an awadhútí will ascend to the region of Shiv (heaven).

Gorakh says, that the True Form,

In the first element (God), has neither marks nor form."

The third, who spoke was Gopí Chand; he said,

"He is an Udásí,[224] who remains really sad at heart,

And, who having withdrawn his thoughts from all, above and below, lives only (with God),

And he, who can make his sun and moon[225] one,

Of such an Udásí the body will never die.

Gopí Chand says, that the True Form,

In the first element (God), has neither marks nor form."

The fourth, who spoke (was) Charpat; he said,

"He is a Pákhandí,[226] who washes his body (in the Name of God,)

And burns the heat of his body (anger) through the Name of God,

---

[222] A kind of fakír—see glossary.
[223] A kind of devotee—see glossary.
[224] A kind of devotee—see glossary.
[225] By sun and moon, anger and patience are implied, as the sun is regarded as hot, and the moon as cold.
[226] A sect of fakírs—see glossary.

And, in his sleep even, does not give way to his lusts;
For such a Pákhaudí. there is no getting old nor death.
Charpat says, that the True Form,
In the first element (God), has neither marks nor form."

Then the Sidhs said, "O boy, have you also made any verses?" Then the Srí Gurú replied, "If you shall command, then I also will recite some verses." Then the Sidhs said, "Do you also recite some verses." Then the Srí Gurú said,

"How shall the evil (in man) die, and how shall one arrange one's life?
What (profit) does one get from piercing one's ears?
One name only is True and Imperishable.
What other name is there, from which there remains any honour?
If you wish to make sunshine and shade[227] as one,
Then Nának says, 'Take the Name of God.'
O sons! although you practise the six kinds of devotion,
You will neither[228] be a Sansárí nor an Awadhút;
Those who keep their thoughts on the Incorporeal One,
Why should they go about begging?
Nának says, that the True Form,
In the first element (God), has neither marks nor form."

Then the Sidhs said, "O boy! you understood what we said, but we do not understand what you have said." Then the Srí Gurú Nának said, "Each of you, Sidhs, has six faults, and Bharathrí has nine faults." Then Bharathrí was terrified and began to weep. On this, Machhandar Náth hit him on the head with his deer skin, and said, "O Bharathrí, why are you weeping? He says that we also have each six faults." The Sidhs said, "O boy! what six faults have we?" Then the Srí Gurú replied,

"He, who looks on poison and nectar as one,
His words are accepted at God's Threshold;
I tell you, O Sidhs! you are Epicures, but are not doers of good;
First, you go forth to get something to eat,
And, if you get food to eat, then are you grateful?

---

[227] Anger and patience.
[228] Enumerated by Nának a little lower down.

Second, when thirst afflicts you, you go forth and get water;

Third, when the cold touches you, you go forth and wish for sunshine;

Fourth, when you are much vexed by the sun's rays, you go forth and wish for shade;

Fifth, when sleep overtakes you, then you go forth and sleep;

Sixth, you are much given to meditation;

But you are Epicures, and are not lovers of God."

Then again the Sidhs asked, "O Nának, what faults has Bharáthrí?" Then this speech was uttered by Nának, "Six of the faults, common to all, you have heard, and the other three are these;

First that, at night, he plays on a guitar;

Second that, in the day, he plays at chaupar,[229] and makes useless meditation;

Third, he drinks wine and he eats roast meats,

And does not fix his thoughts on true meditation;

He, who is a true Náth,[230] is free from all these things."

Then the Sidhs, having seated themselves on chariots made of their deer skins, took their departure and crossed the sea.

---

[229] A game played with long dice.
[230] A term of respect among these fakírs.

CHAPTER XV.

The discourse with the worshippers of Govind.

The Srí Gurú Bába Nának took his departure to Ajudhiá, a country in the east, and there he met with some worshippers of Govind, who said, "O Bába, Rám, Rám." Then the Srí Gurú Bába Nának replied, "Satt Rám! come, Sirs, and seat yourselves." Then, they, having made an obeisance, sat down. After having rested awhile, they said, "O Srí Gurú! We offer ourselves as a sacrifice to you, and we have one request to make of you." He replied, "Whatever you have in your mind, that say out." Then those worshippers of Govind said, "Sir! some perform alms and charity; some offer sacrifices and oblations; some perform pilgrimages, and visit tombs on the banks of the river Ganges; some perform devotion by standing in water; others pay their homage seated in fire[231]; and others give much pain to their bodies; do these things obtain salvation, or do they not?" Then the Srí Gurú repeated this song in the Bhairon Rág;

"Although one may make great feasts, offer sacrifices, do alms, devotion, and worship, suffer bodily pain, and continually endure hardship;

Still none will obtain salvation, but by the Name of God; they obtain salvation, who learn the Name of God from the mouth of His Gurú;

Without the Name of God, the being born into the world is useless;

All else that one eats is poison; all else that one says is poison.

O man! without the Name of God, the being born and dying is altogether fruitless."

The meaning is, Bába Nának said, "Man! although one offer sacrifices, and make great feasts, and perform pilgrimages, and be a Jogí or Saniásí or a Brahmachárí, and although one go naked, and have one's head sawed, although one wander all round the world, and although one show all worship and charity, and

---

[231] The fire is placed at the four corners of the place of worship, and the devotee sits in the midst.

CHAP. XV.—DISCOURSE WITH THE WORSHIPPERS OF GOVIND.

although one offer long prayers, and although one purify one's body, still unless one remembers the Name of God, he will never be saved. He will be saved when he obtains The True Gurú, and, with purity of heart, remembers His name; then will he obtain salvation. Men are born into this world that they should remember His Name; and if one remember His name, then one's life will be fruitful, otherwise one's life is wasted; and, without the remembrance of the Name of the Great God, man lives on naught but poison, and he speaks nothing but poison; and the only advantage, obtained from this (poison), evil speaking, is that man spends his time in wandering about. Listen, O brethren of God! these things are indeed so." Then those worshippers of Govind said, "O Srí Gurú! we sacrifice ourselves to you! again we ask, some read books, some study the Puráns, some perform Sandhiá at the three times, will these obtain salvation, or will they not?" Then the Srí Gurú Bába Nának said,

"Although one read books, and study religion, and grammar, and although one do Sandhiá at the three times;

How, O man! is salvation to be got, except through the instruction of the Gurú; without the Name of God, we must be captives in the world's snares, and die."

The meaning is, "Listen O, brothers of God! if one should read the four Vedas, and study the six Sástras, and peruse the nine grammars, and perform Sandhiá at the three times, and should read the eighteen Puráns, still one cannot be saved; one will be saved, when one obtains a true Gurú, and, with purity of heart, remembers the Name of God?" Then the worshippers of Govind again asked. "O Srí Gurú! we have one more request; behold Sir! some, foregoing their state of Grihast, become Atits, and go on pilgrimages; will these obtain salvation, or will they not?" The Bába replied,

"Should one have the devotee's rod and begging dish, wear a tuft of hair, keep a handkerchief on the shoulder, and wear a dhotí, and go on pilgrimage and make the circuit of temples,

Without the Name of God, patience will not be obtained, and those only, who meditate on the name of Hari, will be landed that side."

The meaning is "Listen, O brothers, worshippers of God! although one may take the devotional staff and beggar's dish in one's hand, and wear the tuft of hair and handkerchief, and be clothed in a dhotí, and put the marks on one's forehead, and may leave one's home and go on pilgrimage, and may travel all round the world, still one cannot be saved thereby. Listen, O brothers, worshippers of God! he will be saved, who obtains a true Gurú, and, with purity of heart, remembers the Name of God." Again the worshippers of Govind enquired, "O Bábá! some let their hair grow very long in knots, some besmear themselves with ashes, others remain quite naked; will these be saved, or will they not?" The Srí Gurú replied;

"Though one wear long hair on one's head, and put ashes on one's body, and go naked and without clothes,

Still, without the Name of God, patience will not be obtained, for such an one only begs for the sake of gratifying his wishes."

The meaning is, "Listen men, brothers of God! from wearing long hair, what good is there? and if one besmear oneself with ashes, what then? and if one go naked, what has one done? if one remain without garments, and do worship, what then? As long as one does not obtain the true Gurú, and, with purity of heart, does not remember the Name of God, so long one cannot be saved. What good is there in begging for the sake of fulfilling one's desires? God is not obtained by becoming a beggar." Then those worshippers of Govind said, "We entirely sacrifice ourselves to thee! will these be saved by any means or not? and if these are to obtain union with the great God, how is it to be got? please tell us this matter." Then Gurú Nának said,

"All the animals and insects of the water and earth and sky, wherever they be, in all art Thou (O God!);

O Gurú, have mercy and do thou preserve me; Nának, having shaken well Thy nectar, wishes to drink of it."

Meaning "Listen, O men! all the animals, which live in the waters and on the earth, the Holy name of God abides with the life of them all, and He lives with each animal; and He, only, can take count of Himself, and as He lives with all animals, so He also takes care of them; so also does He give salvation, but only by means of a Gurú; and without a Gurú none can be saved. O brothers! worshippers of God! in my path (of religion) this is laid down. He Himself only can take count of Himself." Then the worshippers of Govind got up, and fell at the feet of the Gurú, and began to do silent adoration to the Gurú. Then the worshippers of Govind said, "O Gurú, we have come (to place ourselves) under thy protection." Then the Gurú Bábá Nának said, "Do you always remember the Name of the great God; and the true Gurú will prosper you."

Afterwards, a discourse took place with some other worshippers of Govind, who said, "O Bábá! Rám, Rám;" and the Srí Gurú Bábá Nának replied, "Come Sirs! Satt Rám! and seat yourselves." When they had rested awhile, then those worshippers of Govind said, "O Srí Gurú, we have a question to ask ; if you will allow us, then we will ask it." Then (the Gurú) said " Ask whatever may come into your minds." Then those worshippers of Govind said, "O Gurú : that máyá, or worldly desire, which causes one to do evil and good, and wish for wealth, does it do so of itself, or does any one cause it so to do ?" Then the Srí Gurú recited this verse in the Biláwal Rág ;

"What one's heart says, that one does ;

From the mind, issue evil and good ;

The intoxication of worldly desire never is satisfied ;

One can only be satisfied and saved, when one's mind loves the True One.

From beholding one's body, wealth and family, one becomes proud ;

But, except the Name of God, nothing will go with us."

The meaning is, "No one says to this (máyá), that it should do this evil, or that it should do that good, but, rising up, it acts after its own will. If the mind be imbued with the wine of worldly desire, it will never be satisfied therewith, and even if, in a way, one's worldly desire should be satisfied, then, day and night, after obtaining its desires, it (máyá) cries, ' Alas ! Alas !' none has ever satisfied máyá, nor has it made any one else satisfied ; but when the love of God arises in the heart, then only will one be saved. This salvation cannot be obtained except through the love of God ; when one obtains a sufficiency thereof (i.e. the love of God), then only is one saved ; except the great God, one has no other helper ; nothing ever came with us (into this world), and nothing will go with us ; and that, which will be the companion of our soul, will be the Name of God." Then those worshippers of Govind said, "O Srí Gurú ! all living creatures of the world long eagerly for máyá, that, by some means, they may obtain it ; and the world says, ' If I obtain máyá, then I will perform some good deeds and alms, but without máyá, nothing can be effected.' " Then the Srí Gurú said, " Listen, brothers ! followers of God ;

"Those who indulge in the pleasures, desires and joys of their hearts,

Other people will take their wealth, and their bodies will be turned into ashes ;

Dust they are, and to dust will they return, and be spread abroad ;

And one's impurities cannot be removed, except through the Name of God."

o

The meaning of which is; "Those who bear rule, they enjoy the pleasures of rule, and obtain joy from worldly desire (máyá); they collect wealth and fill great treasuries; but neither the joys of wealth nor worldly desire will go with them, but their body will be turned into ashes, and their wealth others will take possession of; then, of what use will the pleasures of máyá and riches and family be to him? His wealth, others will spend after him, and those sins, which he committed for the sake of riches, will then go along with him: and those sins will afterwards seize him, and cast him into hell; what use will wealth, and the pleasures of wealth, and his family be to him then? and the pleasures of sin, of what avail will they be? One has no friend but the Name of the Great God, and, except through His Name, one's impurities cannot be removed; when one acquires (the joy of) His Name, then one's impurities will depart, and then one will be saved." Again, those worshippers of Govind said, "O Srí Gurú, when this soul undergoes transmigration, then how does it undergo transmigration? and if one wish to avoid it, then how can one avoid it?" Then the Srí Gurú replied:—

"From listening to music and song, sounds and tunes, and the beating of castanets,

The three qualities[232] receive life in the body, and die and are removed from it:

Duality is folly, and the pains (of it) cannot be removed.

Those only, who receive, through the Gurú's mouth, the physic of His praises, will be saved."

The meaning is, "When one undergoes transmigration, one undergoes it from one's own doings; when one plays the tune and beats time, and plays the timbrel for the singer, then the dancer, on hearing the sound of the instrument, dances; so also in transmigration, that which takes place, it thus takes place. The soul, making anger, avarice, pride, self-affection and lust, its musical instruments, undergoes transmigration on account of those three qualities. Men are continually being born and die, and the soul of man is removed from one man and goes to another, and if once he is separated from his soul, then to obtain it again is very difficult; duality separates man from his soul; it is folly, and is a sickness that attacks man, and the only physic for this disease is God's Name; and when this body shall sing the praises of God, then it will be freed from transmigration." Then again those worshippers of Govind said, "O Gurú! some are

---

[232] Rájo, love of rule; tammo, covetousness; sato, patience.

CHAP. XV.—DISCOURSE WITH THE WORSHIPPERS OF GOVIND.

called Vaisnus, some belong to the Jains, some are Tappassis, some are Brahmachárís, some are worshippers, some are Jogís and Sanniásís; some are wise and virtuous: now amongst these, who is the best?" Then the Gurú Bába replied:

"Though one wear a clean dhotí, and the marks of honor on the forehead, and a rosary round one's neck,

If anger be within, these marks are all those of jugglers;

Such an one forgets God's Name, and drinks the wine of worldly desire,

And, except by the worshippers of God, joy cannot be obtained."

The meaning is, "Listen brothers, worshippers of Govind! These are all forms of jugglery; and as, when a juggler assumes various parts, still whatever he acts, he is still known, so also, this wearing of a dhotí, necklace, and marks of honour is a mimicry of Vaisno, resembling jugglery: and if one allows anger, avarice, pride, selfish affection, and lust, continually to remain in one's heart, then what will result from this mimicry of Vaisno? And unless one performs sincere worship to the True God, one is no worshipper." Then those worshippers of Govind said, "O Sri Gurú, in this present Kali age, many people take Gurús to themselves, and, calling themselves Sikhs (disciples), adopt a Gurú of their own; but they do not walk after the teaching and fashion of the Gurú, rather they turn away their faces from the Gurú's teachings; what will be their state?" The Sri Gurú replied,

"Listen brothers, followers of God! They are pigs, dogs, donkeys,

Cats, fleas, vile, mean and base;

They, who turn their faces from their Gurú, will be transmigrated into such forms,

And be bound with fetters, when they undergo transmigration."

The meaning is, "Listen brothers, followers of God! those who shall turn their faces from their Gurú, they will return and will be transmigrated as pigs, and base creatures, and as crows and as fleas." Then again the worshippers of Govind enquired, "O Gurú, such will indeed be the state of those who turn away from their Gurú, but those who are sincere to their Gurú, what reward will they obtain?" The Sri Gurú replied,

"From the service of the Gurú, they obtain the best of things to be desired,

For, as they always carry in their hearts the Name of God,
   they will be pure,
And at the true Door of God, there will be no questioning
   them ;
And those who obey His commands, they will be accepted
   at His Door."

The meaning of which is that the Srí Gurú said, " Listen brothers, followers of God ! they who serve their God, their living will be most profitable. The name of God is a precious stone, and our utmost desire, and it will fall into the hands of such souls as these, and those who do service to God, their hearts never remain oblivious of His Name; and inasmuch as God's kindness has been shown on them, no questions will be put to them at the True Threshold, as to who they are, and where they may be going, and such Sikhs will be received into the True Threshold with much rejoicing ; and their souls will afterwards obtain praise in the true reckoning house. Listen brothers, followers of Rám! they will be fully accepted at that Threshold, who obey the commands of their God."

Again, the worshippers of Govind enquired, " O Srí Gurú ! if one wish to know the True God, then now can one know Him ?" The Gurú Bába replied ;

" He will obtain the True Gurú and know Him,
Who is constant in His service, and obeys His commands ;
And if one obey His commands, then one will dwell in the
   True Threshold ;
And death and second death will, through His power, all be
   destroyed."

The meaning of which is that the teacher said, " Listen brothers, followers of Rám ! one will then know the True God, when one obtains the True Gurú, and one looks on pain and pleasure as one ; then, one will be fully blessed in the True Place (Heaven) and one will go and dwell in the True Threshold ; and, by singing the praises of God, he will be delivered from transmigration." Then again, those worshippers of Govind enquired, " O Srí Gurú ! those who are girhasts, if they wish to serve God in that state of girhast, then how can they do so ?" Then the Srí Gurú replied, " Listen brothers, followers of Ram !

He must be an Atít and must regard all as (done) for Him ;
He must give his body and soul to Him, Whose they are ;
Then he will not undergo transmigration !
Nának speaks truly, ' He will be absorbed in the Truth.' "

The meaning is that the teacher said, " Listen brothers, worshippers of Rám! one should live in this state of girhast in the same way as an idle Atít lives in any city; for, the first day that he comes there, he knows that he has nothing in that city, and that one thing only is his, viz., God, and the families and people of that place are strangers to him, and that, in that city, he is also a stranger, and that he has no hopes except from the one Great God, and that his hopes must all be fixed on that Great God; and if any one shall give him a morsel to eat, for God's sake, then he eats, otherwise he would rather die; and if, in the same way as that stranger Atít knows, perfectly resigning himself (to God's Will,) that he has nothing in that city, and that the Great God only is his all, we also know ourselves (to be strangers), then we shall be true worshippers in that girhast state; and when we thus know ourselves, then we shall have nothing, except God, and give up our minds, bodies, wealth, and every thing for God's sake, then shall we no longer undergo transmigration, but shall be released from that state." Then the worshippers of Govind got up and commenced to fall at his feet, and said, " Praised be thou, O holy Sir! Take us under your feet, and give us instruction, holy Sir!" Then (Nának) said, " Do you give up yourselves entirely to remembering the Name of God, and then the Great God will bless you." Afterwards the Srí Gurú recited this verse;

"The true man lives in the True Threshold of the True God.

Nának, the servant (of God) says, 'When one obtains the True Gurú, one will be relieved from undergoing transmigration.'"

Then they all became the disciples of the Bába.

CHAPTER XVI.

The discourse with the Demon Kaunda.

Having seated the Rája[233] on the throne, he departed to Asaráp Náhi, where was the house of Jhandá the carpenter, on an island in the sea. At that time, Mardáná fell into a sulky mood; but Gurú Nának wanted him much to accompany him (on the rebec). Mardáná said, "I will not now go on further, give me leave to depart." Then the Gurú Nának replied, "O Mardáná! there are many demons before you on the road, do you come along with me." But Mardáná remained firm in his refusal (to go on) Then Gurú Nának said to me, "Bháí Bálá! do you speak to him, for my speaking is of no use." Then, I (Bálá) said to Mardáná, "O Mardáná! the Gurú Nának is an incarnation of God; do you understand this?" But, as a demon had seized him, Mardáná would not listen to anything. although we spoke much to him, and left the Gurú Nának. When Mardáná had gone, then, afterwards, the Gurú asked me, "Bháí Bálá! what shall we do?" Then I said to the Gurú Nának, "Come, Sir, and do whatever pleases you." Then Gurú Nának went and stayed in a forest, and would not go on. When two watches had passed, then Gurú Nának said, "Bháí Bálá, a demon has seized Mardáná, and is frying him in a frypan." Then I said to the Srí Gurú, "Sir! let him fry him, let him eat him, for he would not listen to what you said; what can we do? Can anything said by you turn out wrong? Did you not warn him that there were demons (on the road before him), but he was determined to fall into (the hands of) those demons?" Then Gurú Nának rose and got up and said, "Bháí Bálá! I cannot but feel shame, as I brought him with me, and he was of great use to me." Then, again, I asked the Gurú, "Sir! how far off is he?" Gurú Nának replied, "Bháí Bálá, he is nine koss,[234] from here." Then I said, "Sir! he will have eaten him up, before we can get there" Then Gurú Nának seized my hand, and although the twinkling of an eye is not much, even that did not elapse, before we had gone from this spot to that; (on arrival), Gurú Nának laughed (at Mardána), and, laughing, said, "What is it, Mardáná?" Mardáná was ashamed.

---

[233] Rája Siv Náth, as related at the end of a previous discourse.
[234] A koss varies from one to two miles.

Then Gurú Nának said, "Bháí Bálá! this frying-pan, which is being heated, is being heated to fry Mardáná in, but come, let us hide ourselves, (and see the fun)." Then I said to the Gurú Nának, "Sir! then our coming will be of no more use than if we had not come: if the demon shall fry and eat him, then what profit will we get? If you are going to do anything, do it." Then again the Srí Gurú replied, "Just (wait and) behold, Bhaí Bálá! the wonders and performances of the Creator, and see what the Creator will do." At that time, Mardáná was standing up; then the demon seized him and threw him angrily into the frying-pan; the frying-pan became as cold as the frost in the month of Poh (December.) The demon was quite astonished when the fire underneath went out. Then Gurú Nanák presented and showed himself, and the demon said, "O! who are you? speak truly, for when you came, my frying-pan became quite cold and chilled; speak truly, who are you?" Then Gurú Nának, laughing, said, "O Jemon Káunda! eat away; why do you not eat him? why have you left off?" Then the demon said, "How do you know my name? and whence have you sprung? speak truly!" Then Gurú Nának recited this song in the Márú Rág;

"The egg of doubt was broken, and my mind was illuminated (with the knowledge of God);

The fetters were removed from my feet, and the Gurú unfastened my hands;

O Sir! I have become free from future birth and death;

Your heated frying-pan was cooled, because my Gurú has taught me the Name of God, and I have obtained coolness (patience);

PAUSE.

From the time that I entered the society of the holy, since then the Angel of Death has no power over me;

As He (God), who bound me, gave me release, then what can the Police Officer, (you Káunda), say?

I have left behind the load of evil actions, and they have no power over me;

I have reached the opposite shore of the Ocean,[235] and God has blessed me greatly:

My home is truth, my resting-place is truth, and I am adorned with truth;

My wealth is truth, my merchandize is truth, and I (Nának) have obtained these things."

---

[235] I have left the world.

Then the demon Kaunda fell at the feet of Gurú Nának and could not get up, and said, "Sir! I have committed very great sins; do you ask forgiveness for me, and have me forgiven by some means or other?" Then Gurú Nának said, "O demon Kaunda! Mardáná the Mírasi, is your Gurú; if you will listen to what he shall say, you will be saved." The demon Kaunda replied, "Sir, I will accept any one whom you name." Then Gurú Nának laughed and said, "How is it, Bháí Bálá?" Then I, (Bálá) joined my hands before the Gurú, and said. "It is all your kindness, and you know best what to do." Then Gurú Nának said to Kaunda, "Say, Bháí Kaunda, whatever you have to say." Then Kaunda said, "O Gurú! if you give me the order, then I will buy some food, and if you shall eat, (it), then my joy will be fulfilled." Then Gurú Nának said, "Kaunda! bring something for Mardáná to eat; Mardáná has eaten nothing for many days." The demon Kaunda set off to the forest and went and brought such lovely fruits, that we all three were pleased, and when he had brought them, he placed them before the Gurú. Then Gurú Nának said, "Come, Bháí Mardáná, and eat." Mardáná said, "I have eaten all (I want); do you show me kindness : (I regret that) I did not listen to your commands." Then Gurú Nának said, "O Mardáná! I am greatly pleased with you; do you make me happy and eat the fruit." Then Mardáná said, "O Sir! give me whatever may be my share." Then Gurú Nának said, "O Bháí Bálá, divide it into three portions." I (Bálá) divided it into three shares, and gave one to Mardáná, and took one myself, and I gave one to the Gurú. Then (Nának), said to us, "Bháí Bálá and Mardáná! eat the food; and then we began to eat; but Gurú Nának gave the share, which was before himself, to the demon Kaunda. Kaunda made no objection whatever, but immediately put it to his mouth. Immediately, on the food touching his mouth, Kaunda's brain obtained the light (of the knowledge of God), and Kaunda's form also became changed. When I and Mardáná looked on him, we saw that he had obtained victory at once, (without any labour). Then Gurú Nának said, "Bháí Bálá,! behold the wonders and performances of the Creator." After this I asked the Gurú; "Why are we so greatly astonished?" Then Gurú Nának. said, " Bháí Bálá, the Creator, in that he brought us into this world, brought us for this very purpose, that we should always watch the Creator's wonderful acts and doings." Then, I, (Bálá) said " O Gurú, yes. Sir ! whatever God brings forth, that we behold." Gurú Nának remained for seven days with the demon Kaunda. On the seventh day, on his departure, having seated Kaunda on the throne, he wished him farewell.

CHAPTER XVII.

The discourse with Sultán Hamíd Kárún.

Then the Srí Gurú said, "Bhái Bálá, come on and let us also show Sultán Hamíd Kárún the road (of religion), for he is a great tyrant." Then we went there and presented ourselves. Sultán Hamíd Kárún was the king of Rúm. There was a great Kárún, who lived formerly in the time of the great Moses, the prophet; and that Kárún and Hárún were brothers. Now this Sultán Hamíd Kárún was a great tyrant, and had devastated all the country of Rúm to its utmost bounds. Then (Nának) said "Bhái Bálá and Mardáná, let us move on, and let us visit this king." I (Bálá) said, "Sir, may it be well! perhaps, from your visit, his state may be bettered; otherwise he will be destroyed, just as the first Kárún was." Then the Srí Gurú and Mardáná and I, (Bálá) we all three went and presented ourselves at the court of Sultán Hamíd Kárún. Now the former Kárún, having robbed the whole country of Rúm, had collected forty storehouses of treasure, but this Hamíd Kárún had amassed forty-five storehouses of treasure. The Srí Gurú and Mardáná began to enquire where the court of the king was. The door-keepers replied, "This is it, Sirs; and he has collected forty-five storehouses of treasure." Then the Srí Gurú enquired, "Does he administer justice, and does he give any thing in alms?" Those door-keepers replied, "Sirs! he is a very great tyrannical king, and, along with this, is a great miser, and gives nothing in alms; he is even a greater tyrant than the first Kárún." Then the Srí Gurú said, "O, door-keeper! how has he collected all this wealth?" The door-keeper replied, "Sir! he is such a tyrant that wherever, in his kingdom, he hears of there being any silver or gold coin, he never lets it go, whether it belong to rich or poor. One day, this Hamíd Kárún said to his minister, 'Is there any silver still left anywhere?' The minister replied, 'There is none left anywhere.' Then the minister said, 'One of the king's servant girls is very pretty.' Then the king said to him, 'Take and seat her in the Kaihbá Kháná Bazaar, and if any one will give one rupee for her, let him have her.' There was a certain son of a merchant who (heard this, and) went and told his mother that the king was selling his slave girl, and that if she would give him one rupee, then he would be able to purchase her. His mother replied, 'O son! where are there any rupees left in the kingdom of Sultán Hamíd Kárún? I know but of one rupee, which is buried in the mouth of your father.' The merchant's son went and opened his father's grave, and took the rupee and went to the Káihba Khána and bought the slave-girl for one rupee. Then the foot soldier, who was in charge, said (to the minister), 'Here is a rupee, Sir.' Then the king inquired, 'Who bought her?' He replied, 'Sir! a merchant's son bought her.' Then the king said, 'Seize and bring him?' Then they went and seized and brought the merchant's son. The king said, 'Sir, where did you get this rupee from?' The merchant's son replied, 'Sir, this one rupee was placed in my father's mouth, and buried with him in his grave.' Then the king gave orders, that wherever in his kingdom there were any graves, they were all to be opened and looked into (for any money).' On this, agreeably to the king's command, all the graves were opened, but no money was found in any of them. He is a very tyrannical king." Then Nának said. "He is a great sinner; he will receive a very severe punishment at God's Threshold. Curses be on his accumulations; woe! that he should live! The earth was pleased (to swallow up) the former Kárún, but no place would ever agree (to swallow up) this one." Then again he said to the door-keepers. "Do you go and give this message from me to Sultán Kárún, and say that a devotee is standing at his gate, and requests an interview." Then the door-keepers went and gave this message, and said, "Sir! O great king! a devotee has come to your gate, and says, 'Give me an interview.'" The king, on hearing this, came out; at that time the Srí Gurú was collecting little pieces of tile. The king came and greeted him and said, "O holy devotee! what will you do with these pieces of tile?" Then Nának said, "I will take these pieces of tile to the Threshold of God." Again, the king said "Sir! you will not be able to take these pieces of tile there with you, for, when you die, they will remain here." Then (Nának) said "O Sultán Hamíd Kárún! then neither will those forty-five storehouses of treasures, which you have collected by tyranny, go with you. Listen now; there was a greater Kárún than you, who accumulated forty storehouses of treasure by tyranny, but he did not take them with him; then why, have you collected all these stores?" Then Sultán Hamíd Kárún replied, "Sir, cannot this treasure be taken along with me by some means?" Then Nának said, "O king Hamíd Kárún! this wealth will only go along with you, if you shall spend it in alms in God's Name, otherwise it will remain here, and another will become the inheritor of this treasure; he will first seize on all your wealth and your country, and will afterwards arrange for your grave and coffin. Behold, there was a greater Kárún than yourself; he collected forty storehouses of treasure through tyranny; and those storehouses were so great, that one end reached to the foundations of the earth: when his treasures and armies increased, then he became very proud at the sight of his army and wealth; he regarded neither the Lord, nor did he take heed to any one else, and began to proclaim himself as a Lord and God; he began to greatly torment the poor people, and to perpetrate such tyrannies, that, one day, a voice came from the Threshold of God to the great Moses, 'O Moses, thou prophet! go and admonish Kárún, and say, 'O Kárún, do you give away a tenth part of these forty storehouses, and, distribute them as alms in God's Name.' Kárún did not obey the order, and, three times, the admonition was repeated through Moses, saying, 'O Kárún! do you give a little at all events as alms in God's Name;' but Kárún would not obey this command either, for Kárún had become very proud, for, from seeing his vast wealth and army, he paid no heed to anyone; and three times he turned from the command of God. Then Moses petitioned at God's Threshold, saying, 'O Almightly God! I have four times commanded him in Thy name, but he will not obey.' Then the earth was ordered, from God's Threshold, to go, and seize Kárún, the disobeyer, by his feet,[236] and swallow him up with all his treasure. Then the earth seized Kárún, as he was asleep on his bed, just as he was, by his feet, and swallowed him up with his treasures. Thus that Kárún was destroyed and has departed till the judgment day. O Kárún Hamíd! the earth swallowed him up, because he was a great tyrant and a miser; and that Kárún had another brother, called Hárún, who obeyed the command of God, and belonged to the sect of Moses: and Moses afterwards, on his becoming firm in his belief, bestowed on him the title of prophet. You belong to the religion of Muhammad, the chosen, and yet you show much tyranny on the country, and devastate it too, wherever you can find the trace of a single pice even. Do you turn from this your tyranny, otherwise know that the treasure obtained by your tyranny will not go with you; do you henceforth turn from this tyranny." Then Kárún Hamíd replied; "This my mind was drowned in worldly desires; what is past is past; but do you put me on the right way for the future, Sir! and give me such advice that, from hearing it, my heart may be softened, and I may be a true (walker) on God's road." Then the Sri Bába, recited this code of advice for Sultán Kárún in the Rág Tilang:

1st Muhala (or Guru).

"If God give thee the power, then do that which shall give thee a good name:

---

[236] i.e. Drag him down.

Whatever you see in the earth will all vanish;
Wealth will not last, although one have countless (riches);
Those, who possess millions, will not remain, nor will those, who have thousands, remain;
Wealth is one's to spend and to use;
If one gives and distributes, then he will please God;
If he have it (wealth), let him not store it, or spend it on himself only;
And do you know for certain in your heart, that one, who so acts, will go to Heaven;
Show humility before God, and manifest not pride,
For neither will this earth endure, nor will its transactions last;
If one have thousands of elephants and horses and soldiers,
They will all be turned into dust, and they will last no time;
Those, who are taken up with worldly occupations say, 'This country is mine';
But when death overtakes them, they say, 'It is neither, thine nor mine:'
See how many have passed away in spite of all their glory and pomp;
But One only will remain, the one True God;
Alone we came into this world, and alone we will depart (from it);
And, at the time of our departure, none of these things will come of use:
When you shall be asked for your account, then what answer will you give?
You will cry, 'Alas! alas!' and you will be assigned punishment;
(When) you exercise tyranny and violence on the earth,
You but create an uproar against your own soul;
If you accumulate wealth and spend it (vainly),
And spend it on your dress and waste it foolishly,
In the end you will regret and say 'Alas! alas!'
And when you go to God's Threshold, you will receive a heavy punishment;

CHAP. XVII.—DISCOURSE WITH SULTÁN HAMÍD KÁRÚN.

Curses will be heaped on you and on your riches,
If through treachery, you have devastated and spoiled the world;
Those, who drink wine and eat roast meats,
Behold! O people! are they who will be ruined;
He, Whose servant you are, He has given you all,
But, from avarice for the world, you have forgotten your Lord;
You have not done Him service, nor have you kept your faith;
And the world cries out that you have not ruled (it justly):
You remain seated in your palace;
You sport with your wives and perfume yourself with scents;
You neither ask nor know what is taking place outside;
And whether the lawless are killing your poor subjects.
You depopulate populated palaces, and do not re-populate them;
And, although people cry out, none can obtain justice;
You collect your uncountable riches by millions and billions,
Whilst your poor subjects die by thousands;
They call you the ruler, but you do not rule justly;
You are mad with the world, and wander about drunk with it;
You rob the country, and clothe and feed yourself;
But the fire of hell will kill and burn you up;
Do not look on with pride, O thou mad one of the world!
This (world) will not last for ever; so do not think so.
It will not be long before you will travel from this world;
And whose then will be your wealth, and whose your family?
After a few days you must depart, therefore listen to some advice (from me);
Do not long greatly for the world, thou lover of the world;
But take care that you be not ashamed (hereafter) and, with this object (in view), make yourself a good name;
Beware lest you depart, wearing the garment of curses (of your people);
If you shall be negligent, then you will be destroyed;
And neither sons nor daughters will be of help;

Repent and be not now so tyrannical,
Otherwise, even in the grave, the fire of hell will consume you:
There have been Masáikhs, prophets, kings, and lords,
But not a trace of them is now to be seen in the world;
Some have walked under the shadow of pigeons and other animals [237];
But all of them have been turned into dust, and none now ask after their names even;
One accumulated forty store houses, but lost his faith:
Behold, O Kárún! how he was destroyed;
Do you not know that this is a transitory abode;
Behold with your own eyes and see; this world is ever moving on;
O servant! do you never forget your service;
And do not lose (your life) in playing, and drunkenness, and negligence;
You have not yet repented, although you have committed many sins;
Nának does obeisance to thee and says;
'May God deliver you from such a state.'"

When the Sri Gurú had finished this code of advice, then Sultán Hamid remained astonished, and, becoming softened in heart, said, "Sir! I have been entirely drowned in the (cares of the) world; what will be my state at the Threshold of the Lord?" (Nának) said. "Repent, repent for God's sake." He said, "O Sri Bába! from hearing your advice, I have been greatly terrified; what will be my state?" Then Nának said, "O Sultán Hamid Kárún! The love of God does not lie in words; and God is not pleased with words only; so long as you do not become sincere in your service to God, so long your escape will be very difficult; and know this, that the friendship of the world will be of no use to you. The world is a friend for the sake of eating and drinking only; as long as it can get something to eat, so long will it be your friend, and whenever it can not get (anything) to eat, then it will turn into your enemy; such is the conduct of the world; be they your own family, or be they strangers, all are friends for pleasure's sake only but none are friends in trouble: and, for this reason, the world's friendship

---

[237] The meaning of this is, that they had such power over birds and other animals, that they obeyed their commands, and spread a shadow over them.

profits one nothing; the friendship of God is far better than the friendship of the world." Then Sultán Hamíd said, "I cannot get man's friendship even, then how shall I acquire the friendship of God?" Then the Srí Gurú Bába recited these verses in the Rág Tilang;

1st Muhala (or Gurú).

"O friends! the friendship of God is such a friendship that you must love Him (above all).

And obey the commands of your Lord, and act according to His word.

Pause.

One can only know what is the friendship (of God), when one learns it at the foot of the Gurú,

And, humbling one's self, falls prostrate at the door of one's Lord:

His friendship will not be difficult to (obtain), if we humble ourselves before Him.

Nának says, 'He, who has not understood His commands, has spent his life uselessly.'"

When the Srí Gurú Bába had recited this verse, then the king came and fell at his feet, and said, "Sir! as you shall command, so verily will I act." Then Nának said "Release all the prisoners in your kingdom, and, whatever things of theirs you have taken, return them to them: then you will obtain prosperity in both worlds. In future, show compassion on the poor, and then you will obtain intelligence of the road of God." Sultán Hamíd Kárún said, "Very well, Sir! I will do so from love for you." He then released all the prisoners in his kingdom, and returned them their belongings; and, after that, he never oppressed any poor man. Sultán Hamíd then began to do service to God, and established houses for feeding the poor in all his provinces, and, as far as the kingdom of Rúm extended, all dwelt happily, on account of the Srí Gurú's (advice). The king said, "Now, through your means, I have hopes of obtaining God." And the king became his disciple. Then again, the Gurú said, "O Sultán Hamíd! those who have applied themselves to God's (work) and to do His service, God orders all their affairs well, and God's love is shown on them." Then Sultán Hamíd Kárún said, "Sir! I have obtained God through your kindness." Again (Nának) said "O Sultán Hamíd

Kárún! God's love has been very quickly manifested on you, otherwise you would have been destroyed like the great Kárún! but you have quickly learnt Him, and have turned to God." Then again Sultán Hamid said, " Sir! I have found him through your kindness," Then the king made him seven obeisances, on which (Nának) said, "May God prosper you! now I am going to depart." Then Sultán Hamid said, " Sir! when shall I see you again"? Nának said, "You can keep me ever in sight in your heart," and then the Srí Gurú departed thence.

CHAPTER XVIII.

The discourse with Pandat Chattardás, Banársi.

Then the Srí Gurú continued his wanderings, and came and sat in the market place of Banáras. There was a Pandat of Banáras, by name Chattardás, who had come there to bathe; on seeing the garb of the Srí Gurú, he sat down and said, "O worshipper, you have no Sálig Rám with you; and you have not the mark of Gopí Chandan, and you have not the necklace of basil; are you an Atít or a Bhagat? To what religion do you belong?" Then the Srí Gurú said, "Mardáná, sound the rebec." Then Mardáná sounded the rebec, and Nának recited this stanza in the Basant Rág;

1st Muhalá (or Gurú)

"O Bráhman! do worship to (God, for He is) Sálig Rám, and make good deeds your basil necklace;

Fasten the chain of repetition of the Name of God on yourself, and say, 'O, compassionate One! show me compassion.'

Why do you irrigate barren soil, and waste your life?

A mud wall will fall, why put plaster on it?"

The Pandat said, "O worshipper! do you call these things irrigating barren soil? (then say) what are those things which you call watering good soil? and by which one may obtain the great God." Then the Gurú recited the second stanza;

"Make these two, lust and anger, your hoe; and with them dig the earth (of your body) O brother!

The more you dig it, the more joy you will obtain, for this will never be useless labour."

Again the Pandat enquired, "O worshipper! how will the soul bring forth without being irrigated? and how can the gardener know that it (the joy of having God) is his own?" Then the Srí Gurú recited the third stanza.;

"Make your hand, your Persian wheel, the string of your rosary, the buckets and rope, and yoke your mind thereto;

Irrigate your body with the water of immortality, and fill its beds, and then it will become the true gardener's (God's).

Then the Pandat said, "You are a very holy man, Sir! My understanding is impure; it is in love, like a bagala,[238] with its carnal desires." Then again the Gurú recited the fourth stanza;

"A bagala can be changed into a goose if Thou willest it, O compassionate One!

Nának, the servant of servants, seeks Thy protection; do Thou show pity on him, O Thou merciful One!"

Then again the Pandat said, "You are a worshipper of the great God, Sir! therefore bestow some of (your) purity on this place, and take some benefit[239] from it, Sir!" Then (Nának) said "What benefits has it?" Then the Pandat replied, "The benefit to be derived here is the obtaining of learning; and from reading here, one is much blessed; and, after that, wherever you shall sit, there the world will respect you, and from studying (Sanskrit) here, you will become a chief of devotees." Then the Sri Gurú Bába recited another verse;

"The king is a child, the city is half built, and is in love with the five wicked ones;

There are two mothers and two fathers, who are saying, 'Pandat consider this';

O holy saints, give me such an understanding, by which I may obtain my (God) soul's lord.

Within, there is a fire, and the forest is putting forth its fresh leaves, the sea is the body;

The sun and moon are both within the body; but you have not obtained this knowledge.

Look on him as a worshipper of God, who regards all (friends and foes) as one;

Regard this, as His custom, that He possesses the power of forgiveness;

(Alas! that) he, who is my companion, will not listen to me, and only desires somthing to eat;

Nának, the slave of slaves says 'Sometimes it is pleased, sometimes angry!'"[240]

---

[238] The bagala is said to stand on one leg, so as to be ready to put down the other at once to catch a fish. What is here meant is, that as the bagala is ever on the look out for fish, so was he ever on the watch to gratify his passions.

[239] *i.e.* "Learn some Sanskrit," as Banáras is renowned as a great place for learning Sanskrit and acquiring knowledge.

[240] These verses have already occurred in the seventh discourse.

CH. XVIII.—DISCOURSE WITH PANDAT CHATTARDÁS, BANÁRSÍ.

The Pandat, on hearing these verses, made an obeisance and said, "I teach the world, I have also learnt something myself; Sir ! pray give me some blessing also in God's Name." Then the Srí Gurú said, "O saint! what have you read ? and what is the first lesson you teach your pupils ?" then the Srí Gurú uttered the following lines in the Rám Kalí Rág.

"The great God (On) be praised!

The great God created Brahma ;

The great God is He who created me ;

The great God made me to travel this world ;

The great God also formed the (four) Vedas ;

By singing the great God's praises, one obtains salvation ;

By the great God, the worshippers of God obtain deliverance;

Consider the meaning of the letters o n,

For the letters o n are the root (of happiness) in the three worlds.

Listen Pándhá! and see what useless matters you write about ;

In future, write God's Name, and learn from your Gurú about Gopála."

Then the Pandat, on hearing it, fell at his feet, asking for protection : and he received instruction, and was called a Sikh, and began to meditate on the Gurú.

CHAPTER XIX.

The discourse with Kálú.

Then the Srí Bábá, becoming distressed, departed from Sultánpur, and, after 12 years' (wanderings) returned to the land of the Panjáb. At first (on his return), he came and stopped in a desert place, about two koss from Talwandí. After they had rested awhile, Mardáná made request; "Say, O king! if I have your permission, to go and get information of the people of my family, and see whether they are alive or dead." Then the Srí Gurú laughed and said, "O Mardáná! if such be your desire, then go and visit them; and go also to Kálú's house, but return immediately; but mind you do not mention my name there." Then Mardáná fell at his feet, and, after touching his feet, went off to his own home; but Bálá and the Gurú Nának remained seated there. Then, immediately on Mardáná's arrival there, a great many people collected and came and seized his feet; and all began to say, "Mardáná, the *Dúm*, from always remaining with Nának, now appears a good man. He is far raised above (us), people of the world. Therefore let those, that are come, fall at his feet." Then Mardáná, having visited his own home, set off to return, and, having come to the house of Kálú, went and seated himself in the courtyard. Then the mother of the Srí Bábá rose and embraced him round the neck, and began to weep, and lament, saying, "O Mardáná! give us some news as to where Nának is." Many people collected in the compound; Mardáná then said to them. "Brothers! when we were at Sultánpur, then we were one; but I can give no after news of him." Then Mardáná, having sat there awhile, rose and departed; on which the mother said (to the people). "This, that Mardáná departed so quickly from the courtyard, is not devoid (of suspicion); I believe that Nának is with him." Then the mother of the Srí Bábá immediately rose and stood up, and, taking some clothes and sweetmeats, followed and caught up Mardáná on the road, and began to say, "O Mardáná! do you, by some means, cause me to see Nának again." On this, Mardáná remained silent. Then the mother and Mardáná both together went on, and, having proceeded two koss, came to where the Srí Gurú was seated. When the Srí Gurú saw that his mother was come, then he rose and fell at her feet; and on this, the mother began to weep greatly. Then the mother took the Gurú into her arms, and, kissing his forehead, said, "I give myself as a sacrifice to you, O my son! and, whatever places you have visited, to them also I sacrifice myself, O my son! you have greatly rejoiced me to-day, in that you have shown yourself to me." Then the Srí Bábá, from love for his mother, began also to weep and lament, saying, "O Mardáná! sound the rebec."

Then Mardáná sounded the rebec, and Nának recited these verses in the Wadaháns Rág;

"My state (in longing for Thee, O God) is that of the taker of intoxicating drugs, when he cannot get those intoxicating drugs, and as that of fishes when they cannot get water;

And, he, who is absorbed with his Lord, he is satisfied with everything (and says),

'I will go and sacrifice myself, and cut myself into pieces, for the sake of my Lord's Name.

PAUSE.

The Lord is that most fruitful Tree, the name of which is Immortality;

And he, who drinks thereof, becomes satisfied, and to Him will I sacrifice myself;

He cannot be seen by me, although He lives with all;

How will one's thirst be allayed, if one only put one's head on a high wall (in the middle of the tank, out of reach of the water).

Nának is Thy salesman (banián); Thou art my capitalist and all my stock;

All doubts will be removed from my mind, when I shall continually remember Thy praise."

Then, again, the mother, producing the sweetmeats and clothes, placed them before him and said, "O my child, do you eat these." (Nának said), "I am quite full." Then the mother said, "What have you eaten to satisfy you?" Then the Srí Gurú said, "Mardáná, sound the rebec." Then Mardáná sounded the rebec, and Nának recited these verses[212] in the Siri Rág:

---

[212] The following translation of these verses is given by Dr. Trumpp; see Ádi Granth, page 24;—

All juices are sweet by minding (the name), (all are) seasoned by hearing (it). The acid (juices) will go off by uttering (the name) with the mouth, by the sound they are made spices.

On whom he looks in mercy, to him the thirty-six kinds of food are one substance.

"All my delicacies and sweets are obeying God, and my salted dishes are listening to His Name;

My acids and sour relishes are uttering His Name, and the subduing my passions are my spices;

My faith in Him alone is for me the thirty-six great viands of life, and those on whom He looks with kindness (obtain them);

O Mother! all other foods, though pleasing to one's self, produce pain,

And are such that those who eat them, their bodies are troubled, and many sorrows arise in their minds."

Then again the mother said, "O son! take off this long coat, and put on these new clothes."

Then the Srí Gurú recited this second verse;

"My red clothes are the being dyed with (His love), and my white garments, truth and alms;

My blue (garment) is the washing away of the blackness (of my heart), and my coat is the always meditating on Him;

My waist-band is patience; my wealth and youth are His Name;

PAUSE.

O father! other food is a poor pleasure.
By the eating of which, the body is pained and disorder rules in the mind.
(2) Red clothing is a red heart; whiteness (of clothes), truthfulness and donation.
Blueness and blackness (of clothes), wicked actions; putting on clothes, meditation on the feet (of Hari).
The waistband is made of contentment, wealth and youth is thy name.

PAUSE.

O father! other clothing is a poor pleasure.
By the putting on of which the body is pained and disorder rules in the mind.
(3) To have a knowledge of a horse's saddle, of a golden back-strap, this is thy way.
Quiver, arrow, bow, sword-belt are the constituent parts of virtue (with thee).
A musical instrument, a spear, appearing publicly with honour, (this) is thy business, O my caste!

PAUSE.

O father! other mounting is a poor pleasure.
By which mounting, the body is pained and disorder rules in the mind.
(4) My house and mansion is the delight in (thy) name, thy (merciful) look my family.
That is (thy) order, which will please thee, (though there be) other very boundless talk.
O Nának! the true king does not ask nor deliberate.

PAUSE.

O father! other sleeping is a poor pleasure.
By which sleep, the body is pained and disorder rules in the mind.

O mother! all other clothes, though pleasing to one's self, produce pain,
And are such that those who wear them, their bodies are troubled, and great sorrow arises in their minds."

Then Kálú also received information and, mounting his horse, came there; and the Srí Gurú, on seeing him, went and fell at his father's feet, and made his obeisance to him. Then Kálú also began to weep, and said, "O Náuak! do you mount this horse and come home?" Then the Srí Gurú said, "O father! this horse is of no use to me." Then Kálú said, "O son! do you give up these deeds of simpletons." Then the Srí Gurú recited the third verse;

"My horse, saddle, and golden trappings are to learn Thy way;
My quiver, arrows, bow and spear are to run and seize Thy excellencies;
My musical instruments and lances are the being received with honour by Thee, and Thy mercy is my caste;
O my Lord! any thing else one mounts, though pleasing to one's self, produces pain,
And is such that those who mount thereon, their bodies are troubled, and great sorrow arises in their minds."

PAUSE.

Then again Kálú said, "Son! do you come home for a short while; we have now got a (detached) house, quite apart (from everyone); do you come and see (your family) at all events, for you have returned after a long while; your family are there; do you come and see them, and remain a few days, and if you wish it, then you may go away again." The Srí Gurú recited the fourth verse;

"The joys of Thy name are my house, and my family are Thy merciful looks;
Thy commands (to my family) are those things which please Thee; and to say more is useless;
Náuak says, 'Thou art the True King, there is no need for Thee to ask or seek counsel':
O my Lord, all other sleep, though pleasing to one's self, produces pain,
And is such, that those who sleep that sleep, their bodies are troubled, and great sorrow arises in their mind."

Then again the Srí Gurú Bába said, "O father! (excuse me) from coming to you just now, but I will (certainly) come and visit you; but do you now listen to my request for to-day, for my heart is sad." Then on this, the mother said, "Son! how can my mind be comforted? for twelve years, you have kept me sorrowing; now that you have returned, why will you not come to your home to-day? O, my son! how can my mind be made happy?" Then the Srí Gurú said, "O mother, when I give my promise, your mind should be satisfied." Then the mother remained silent. Afterwards she said, "Listen child! why has your heart been made sad? Do you tell me at all events; if you desire it, then I will marry you a second time with great pomp and much splendour, and with much music and singing." Then the Srí Gurú recited a verse in the Súhí Rág;

"Listen, my respected mother and parent! the Name of God only pleases me:

I wonder about sad, when the Lord God does not come into my thoughts.

If he come not into my thoughts, I wander about sad; God only satisfies my soul;

Listen my maid and companion[242] is filled with love (for God), and my young heart is full of (His) youth;

And I cannot live without my Beloved (God) for one instant or second, and sleep comes not to my eyes (without Him).

Nának says truly, 'Listen, my mother! the Name of God only pleases me.'

Listen! my mother and parent! the saints possess nothing but the Name of God;

My soul was dark; the holy men adorned it in such a way, that it always returns to the holy.

It returns ever to the holy; the holy have no wealth but the Name of God;

And the Name of God is such, that it will never diminish in worth.

Although it may rain, it becomes no greener, and, if the sunshine wax a hundred fold, it never dries up;

When one departs, one's excessive youth and great loveliness will not go with one.

Nának says truly; 'Listen, my mother and dearest parent, the saints possess nothing but the Name of God.'

Listen, my respected mother and parent! this my heart will tell thee a tale;

---

[242] My passions and desires.

My Lord God often came not into my mind, and was continually forgotten through negligence;

I have forgotten Him through negligence, O mother! because my mind was absorbed in worldliness;

Every living head will there have to give an account, whether he have done evil or good;

My wedding day is fixed, and a few days only remain (to it), but my heart is still telling its tale of God!

Nának says truly, 'Listen my respected mother and parent,

He is forgotten by me through negligence'!

O my respected mother and parent! the wedding party (*i.e.* death) has arrived;

I am the bride; the angel of death is the wedding party; and death is the bridegroom,

Death is such a bridegroom, O mother! that when one departs, one can say nothing;

The five attendants[243] go to another home, and the house remains quite empty;

And he, who is to marry me, he is taking me away, and I cannot stop him:

Nának says truly! 'Listen, my mother! death is my bridegroom!'"

After this, Kálú said; "My son, I will marry you into some good family; do you come along home?" Then in reply, the Srí Gurú said, "O father dear! that Contriver and Creator of all things is a Being who never forgets; whatever he ordains, that is right." Then, again, the mother spoke, "O my son! do you now get up and come along with us, and leave off these absurd ways: how can it be known whether we shall ever meet again or not?" Then the Srí Gurú recited another verse in the Márú Rág;

"The order for me is to take the Name of my husband (God) in the early morning;

The tents, umbrellas, canopies and ready yoked chariots are all waiting ready;

Those who meditate on Thy Name they will obtain honour;

---

[243] Lust, anger, pride, covetousness and worldly love.

Father! I am an unfortunate and deceived creature, for I have not discovered Thy Name;
This my mind is blind and filled with error.
The pleasure, I enjoyed, brought forth pain, and this was written in my fate, mother!
My joys are few, my troubles are many, and my life has been passed in sorrow;
How can there be separation for those who are already separate, and what meeting for those who have already met?
It behoves us to praise that Lord, Who has manifested all the plays (of the world).
By our good fate, we obtain (God), and these our bodies enjoy pleasure;
By our evil destiny, those who are united, separate, and yet Nának says, 'This is good fortune.'"

Then again Kálú spoke, saying, "My son! take off this beggar's coat from off thy neck, and put on these new clothes, and bathe, and put on the distinctive mark on thy forehead; leave off those ways and doings of devotees, and walk on the straight road." Then the Srí Bába said, "O father dear! do you know the meaning of praising the great God." Kálú said, "I do not know what you are talking of." Then the Srí Gurú recited this verse;[244]

---

[244] Dr. Trumpp, in his Ádi Granth, page 25, translates these verses as follows:—

"(1) A body (besmeared) with kungú, adorned with jewels, perfume of aloe-wood, the breath (kept fast) in the body.
The mark of the sixty-eight Tírthas in the face, in this there is display of little wisdom.
In that is wisdom: praising the true name, the abode of (all) excellences.

PAUSE.

O Father! other wisdom other and other. If it be practised a hundred times, it is the false effort of the false ones.
(2) He (one) may apply himself to worship, he may be called a Pír, the whole world may flock to him.
He may make his own name famous, he may be counted amongst the Sidhs,
When his (honour) does not fall into account (before God) all (his) worship is (but) a wretched thing.
(3) Those who are established by the true Gurú, nobody can efface.
Within them is the abode of the name, by the name they will become manifest,
(By whom) the name is worshipped, the name is minded, they are always unbroken and true.
(4) When dust is mingled with dust, what will become of the soul?
All clevernesses are burnt with the body; it rises and goes weeping.
O Nának, the name being forgotten, what will become (of it), when having gone to the gate (of God)."

"My body is made of Kúngú, my tongue of jewels, the breath of my body is of the perfume of Agar.

My forehead is marked with the sixty-eight places of pilgrimage, inside of which the understanding dwells;

And, after being purified, I sing the praises of Him, whose Name is true; He is an ocean of excellencies;

Sir, the understanding of others may differ from this,

And, although it may be explained to them a hundred times, the false man will cling persistently to his falsehood."

PAUSE.

On this, Kálú again said, "My son! some are Sidhs, some are Pírs, and the whole world knows such, and does worship to them; and their food-houses are always open, and they feed many people, and their standing in the world is respectable, and they live comfortably. Well: will the world obtain deliverance through them or not?" Then the Srí Gurú recited the second stanza;

"He, to whom people do service, is called a Pír, and the world all look on him as sincere.

And another publishes, and makes known to the world, that he is a Sidh;

But if their honour be not held in account by God, all their worship is useless."

On this Kálú again said, "These Sidhs and Pírs are they, whom the world looks on as such (i.e. honourable); but what is that, by which one may be delivered, and by means of which one will be held in honour, by the Great God and by the world at the same time?" Then the Srí Bábá replied;

"Those of whom the true Gurú has approved, them none can dishonour;

Inwardly, they have the treasure of His Name, and, from taking that Name, they obtain great fame;

His Name they worship, His Name they respect, for it never will fail, and is always true."

On this Kálú again said, "O Nának,! what will be the state at God's threshold of those who never remember His Name all their lives, and spend all their time in doing the world's business?" The Srí Gurú recited the fourth stanza;

"The base will be mixed with the dust, and their life will be of no profit.

All their cleverness will be burnt (with their body), and, weeping, they will depart;

Nának says, 'Those who forget His Name (here), there is no knowing what their state will be, when they go to God's threshold.

O Father dear! those who forget His Name here, how will they hereafter obtain admission there?'"

Then Kálú said, "It is true Sir, this thing is indeed so." Afterwards Kálú again said, "You are a very holy man, and we did not know it; but tell me, my son! what will be our state, for we have never remembered the Name of the great God." Then this speech slowly issued from the Srí Gurú's mouth, "O father dear! as shall be my state, so shall be your state."

CHAPTER XX.

The discourse with the Pandats of Banáras.

After this, the Bába went to Káshí (Banáras), and the Pandats of that place heard that Nának, who was talked of as a great devotee, had come there; (so they said), "Let us go and see him." Then the Pandats came, and, setting forth there, paid him a visit, and asked him this question, "O Nának! how is it, that, although we are always reading and listening to the Vedas, our pride cannot be subdued, and we cannot obtain peace of mind?" Then the Bába said, "The evil of your hearts is not removed; and for this reason it takes no effect." Then the Pandats said, "Sir! how shall we obtain peace of mind?" Then the Srí Bába recited a verse in the Sirí Rág;[245]

1st stanza.

Covetousness is the dog, falsehood is the sweeper, food obtained by cheating, the carrion;

The defaming (others) is the excrement; tale-bearing, the fire; wrath the chandál.;[246]

---

[245] The following translation of these verses is given by Dr. Trumpp, in his Ádi Granth, page 23.
(1) Covetousness is a dog, falsehood a sweeper, food obtained by cheating, carrion.
Another's defamation (is stirring up) another's dirt; tale-bearing, fire, wrath, a Candal.
Enjoyments, praising thyself, these are my works, O Creator!
PAUSE.
O Father! may (such things) be spoken by which honour is obtained.
Those, who do excellent works, are called excellent at the gate (of God), those who do low works, sit outside and weep.
(2) (There is) the enjoyment of gold, the enjoyment of silver, the enjoyment of a fascinating woman (and) of the scent of sandal-wood.
(There is) the enjoyment of a horse, the enjoyment of a bed, the enjoyment of a palace; sweet is the enjoyment of meat.
So many are the enjoyments of the body; how shall the name dwell in (this) body?
(3) That speech is acceptable, by which speech, honour is obtained.
He who speaks insipid things, comes to grief; hear, O foolish, ignorant heart!
Those, who please Him, are good, what will the others say?
(4) They have understanding, they have honour, they have wealth in their lap, in whose heart he (God) is contained.
What for praising them; is any one (else) beautiful?
O Nának! without (his) glance they are not fond of giving, nor of the name.
[246] A chandál is a low, mean person, a person of low caste, an outcast.

Enjoying myself, praising myself, these (alas) are my works, O Creator!

O Father, may that be said by you, by which His honour is increased!

Those, who do good, will be deemed good at God's threshold; those, who do evil, will sit outside and weep.

There is the enjoyment of gold, the enjoyment of silver, the enjoyment of a fascinating woman, and of the scent of sandal-wood.

There is the enjoyment of a horse, the enjoyment of a bed, the enjoyment of a palace; there is the enjoyment of sweetmeats.

But, when such are the enjoyments of the body, how can His Name remain there?

That speech is acceptable, by which His honour is increased;

He, who speaks evil, suffers pain; hear, O foolish, ignorant heart!

Those, who please Him are good; and no one else will be able to say anything to them:

They have understanding; they have honour; they have wealth in their lap; in whose heart, He (God) is obtained;

What need to praise them? other praise is worth nothing.

O Nának, (those who are) outside of His glance, they will neither give alms, nor remember His Name."

The meaning is, "Listen, O Pandats! the avarice, which is (in one's body), is as a dog; falsehood is a sweeper; and getting food by deception is like carrion, and the censuring of others is excrement, anger is a fire, and is like a mean wretch. To eat good and bad things, and to praise myself, this is written in my fate; How can God's Name then remain in my heart? and until I obtain a true companion, till then, how can my heart be pure? O Sirs! we should only speak those things, from uttering which His honour is established. Those who do good deeds, they will be called good at the Threshold of goodness of God; and those who commit base actions, they will receive punishment and will remain weeping. That which is called the mind, it is ensnared in the pleasures of the body, then how can it obtain the pleasure of God's Name? Some long for gold, some long for silver, some long for women, and others long for the smell of sandal-wood; some long for horses, some long for fine beds, some long to make palaces, some long to eat sweetmeats, some long to eat meats; when all these longings exist in the body, then how can God's

Namo dwell in that body? From speaking good, man's honour remains, but from speaking evil, man's honour departs; and we should look on the word of the True Gurú as sweet; and of such (persons), the understanding also is enlightened, and they also have great honour; and his Name, which is the true wealth, is possessed by those, in whose hearts the words of the Gurú always dwell, and they are His."

Then the Pandats said " O Nának! is this not true, that such is the excellency of this city of Káshí, that it is written in the Vedas, that whatever living things, be they sinners or saints, shall quit their bodies in this city of Káshí, they will go to the city of God, and there be blessed?" Then the Bába said, " Listen Pandats! at the time of death, if one read the incantation of Shiva, and look on it as the Name, Rám, of the True Gurú, and a voice come into the ear of that creature, then that being is saved. Listen, O Pandats! The Name of God is such, that, in whatever place, people shall take it, they will be saved. So when Kabír departed from Káshí, and went and lived in Magabar, and holy sages collected there, he obtained salvation there also; and the only giver of salvation is the Name of the great King." Then the Pandats enquired and said," O Nának! The great King has many Names, but what is that one particular Name of the great King, which gives salvation?" Then the Srí Bába replied, " Listen, O Pandats! there are various kinds of boats on rivers, to convey them to the opposite shore, but one only requires one boat by which to cross over. So also, all the Names of the great King can give salvation, but whatever Name of God, one's spiritual teacher teaches one about, that Name is sufficient to give him happiness." Then, on hearing these words, all the Pandats fell at his feet, and he gave them instruction about God's True Name.

www.ingramcontent.com/pod-product-compliance
Lightning Source LLC
Chambersburg PA
CBHW030735230426
43667CB00007B/727